Why PowerBuilder 4.0? V

MW01234161

Since its arrival in the marketplace ove
to the top of its category, controlling around 50% of all sales in this area.

Competing directly with Microsoft's Visual Basic, Borland's Delphi and Oracle's Power Objects, PowerBuilder has gone from strength to strength, building upon its reputation as a dedicated database front-end creation package with full connectivity to a wide variety of back-end databases through ODBC.

PowerBuilder also supports an OOP-based language called PowerScript, and is flexible enough to allow you to fully customize the working enviroment and to create your own class libraries.

The Revolutionary Guide to PowerBuilder 4.0 covers all these areas, beginning with a discussion of the tools that Powersoft have provided for this task. It then moves on to cover how and why they should be used together.

Supported by a full working application, which is developed throughout the book, you will soon be developing advanced front-end applications that can connect to nearly every back-end database currently on the market.

What is Wrox Press?

Wrox Press is a computer book publisher which promotes a brand new concept - clear, jargon-free programming and database titles that fulfill your real demands. We publish for everyone, from the novice through to the experienced programmer. To ensure our books meet your needs, we carry out continuous research on all our titles. Through our dialog with you we can craft the book you really need.

We welcome suggestions and take all of them to heart - your input is paramount in creating the next great Wrox title. Use the reply card inside this book or mail us at:

feedback@wrox.demon.co.uk
or
Compuserve 100063, 2152

Wrox Press Ltd.   Tel: (312) 465 3559
2710 W. Touhy   Fax: (312) 465 4063
Chicago
IL 60645
USA

The Revolutionary Guide to PowerBuilder 4.0

Prasad Bodepudi

Wrox Press Ltd.®

The Revolutionary Guide to PowerBuilder 4.0

Published by Wrox Press Ltd. Unit 16, 20 James Road, Tyseley, Birmingham, B11 2BA
Printed in the USA
Library of Congress Catalog no. 95-61106
ISBN 1-874416-60-5

Trademark Acknowledgements

Wrox has endeavored to provide trademark information about all the companies and products mentioned in this book by the appropriate use of capitals. However, Wrox cannot guarantee the accuracy of this information.

Watcom is a trademark of Watcom International Corporation. Excel, Acess and Word are registered trademarks of Microsoft Corporation.

PowerBuilder, the Powersoft logo and Powersoft are registered trademarks; Powersoft Enterprise Series and DataWindow are trademarks of Powersoft Corporation.

Credits

Author
Prasad Bodepudi

Technical Editor
Graham McLaughlin

Series Editor
Gordon Rogers

Managing Editor
John Franklin

Technical Reviewers
Jay Madore
Gordon Bell
Stephen Wynkoop

Beta Testers
Larry Roof
Basant Nanda

CD Authoring
Darren Gill
Eddie Fisher

Operations Manager
Gina Mance

Production Manager
Deb Somers

Book Layout
Eddie Fisher
Greg Powell
Lee Kelly
Neil Gallagher
Graham Butler

Indexer
Simon Gilks

Proof Readers
Pam Brand
Jenny Nuttall
Emma Duncombe
Mel Orgee

Cover Design
Third Wave

For more information on Third Wave, contact Ross Alderson on 44-121 236 6616
Cover photo supplied by The Image Bank

Dedication

To the Almighty Gods and Goddesses for their divine inspiration and to my beloved grandmother for encouraging the pursuit of excellence.

Acknowledgments

I would like to thank my Managing Editor, John Franklin, who says, 'an excellent product will find its own market'. My special thanks go to Graham McLaughlin, for his painstaking efforts at checking the multitude of facts, proof reading and producing a zero-defect product. I am also very grateful to Powersoft and Susan Donahue for their invaluable and timely assistance.

I would also like to thank the following people:

Sanjay Jain
*My long suffering roommate for tolerating
my idiosyncrasies and fits of inspiration.*

Atul Save
*For pulling the drawings, clipping and
screen shots together.*

Peter Guss
*CIO at SCA, for his constant encouragement and for
arranging focus group interviews with his staff.*

Charles Silbergleith
*Who took time from his work (and play) to provide
technical reviews, thoughtful insights
and incisive recommendations.*

Jay Menon
*For his suggestions of additional topics which made
this book more comprehensive.*

Ooria A. Abraham
*Whose refreshing comments gave me a reader's perspective and
made this book understandable, even for the beginner.*

Atul Sharma
*For his contribution to the 'Building Class Libraries'
section in the final chapter*

During my sojourn in Iowa, the Chalasani family home was the creative refuge where I spent hours plugging away at my book. Vijay helped me organize my work, while his wife, Nalini, a gourmet chef, provided sustenance with her mouthwatering dishes.

Who knows, a cookbook may be my next creative venture?

CD-ROM Credits

At Wrox, we try to give you the maximum value from our titles. In addition to the source code and text viewer on the CD-ROM, we have included some professional-level demos. Please take a look at these demos and if you have any problems obtaining the full software, feel free to contact us at Wrox Press.

We would like to thank all of our contributors for their co-operation in keeping the software flowing.

A full list of contributors is available on the CD-ROM.

SUMMARY OF CONTENTS

TABLE OF CONTENTS

Chapter 17: Object Linking and Embedding **581**

Chapter 18: Embedded SQL and Dynamic DataWindows **607**

Chapter 21: The Application Design Process 695

Appendix A: Application Development Guidelines 719

Introduction

Welcome to the Revolutionary Guide to PowerBuilder 4.0. This book has been designed to give you an all-round understanding of the PowerBuilder environment, providing you with the foundation you need to launch your systems into the Client/Server arena.

It begins by running through each of the major components that make up the development environment, covering the basic usage of each, while also incorporating some handy hints and tips for the early stages of the development of your project. It continues with a review of PowerBuilder's object-oriented programming language, PowerScript, and the advantages of using OOP in your applications.

In the final chapters, we cover some of the cutting edge areas that can push your application into the realms of a user-friendly and flexible tool, such as MDI, embedded SQL and the cross-application data transfer technologies, DDE and OLE.

Scattered throughout the book are the kind of hints and tips that will make this book into one of your most useful tools, including a look at how to implement your own maintenance-free security layer, the differences between the different back-end databases that you may encounter, how to make use of Microsoft's MAPI technology in your application and how to create your own class libraries.

Who Should Read On?

As with all technical reference books, it is important that you understand the level at which this book is pitched. After reviewing all the competition, we decided that a niche existed for a low entry book, describing the basic tools that PowerBuilder has to offer. These tools are the backbone of the PowerBuilder environment and it is here that you will spend most of your time.

However, PowerBuilder is packed with so many interesting methods, abilities and potentially complex subjects, that we also faced the problem of addressing these issues to appeal to the advanced user. Fortunately, the PowerBuilder environment lends itself to this type of structure.

PowerBuilder is an immensely flexible and customizable tool. The software allows you to alter most of the functionality that it has to offer, in order to produce the results that you require. The addition of an equally flexible programming language allows the developer to produce some quite amazing results, such as the Maintenance-Free Security Layer, and the OOP aspects of the language should put inheritance and polymorphism into the everyday vocabulary of the front-end designer for the first time.

An interesting point is that all these advanced options are directly based on a sound knowledge of the working environment that PowerBuilder has to offer. This means that, as an advanced developer, you might find the first few chapters below you, but by strafing through them, you should be able to pick up some interesting hints and tips that will both improve your design and speed your application development.

As a novice developer, you should pick up all these interesting points as you go, making the second section of the book, the section deliberately aimed at the advanced developer, much easier to follow and fully understand.

What Other Equipment Do You Need?

To successfully run PowerBuilder on your computer, a 486 with 4MB of RAM should be sufficient, although 8MB to 16MB is recommended. We would also recommend that you invest in the Enterprise edition of the current software release, v4.0, even though 90% of the applications that you will develop could be created using the Desk-Top edition.

You will need access to a wordprocessor and a spreadsheet such as Word and Excel for the DDE and OLE chapters, and access to a MSMail compliant network would be useful for the chapter on Advanced Scripting.

To gain access to the additional materials supplied by Wrox Press, you will need a CD-ROM drive and the appropriate drivers to run it.

How to Use This Book

This book uses several stylistic conventions and an overall layout that are designed to make the transfer of information from the page as easy and trouble-free as possible. Below is a listing of the styles used in the book, together with a definition of what they mean.

This is code that appears in the text: `Update()`. This might include any references to word that would generally appear in your code, any function calls that we mention or any events that you might use in your PowerScript. Text that appears on the screen looks like this: w_item_master. This includes menu items, the names of objects, the output from programs and the contents of text files, such as those with the `.INI` file extension.

```
All full listings of code look like this
and important snippets of code appear in this format.
```

All references to files, including the full path names indicating the exact location of a file will be presented like this: `C:\WROX\STOPICON.BMP`.

```
If we refer to the general syntax of a function or
command, it will look like this.
```

> **This style is for really important notes on the current topic,**

> *while this style is for general points of interest.*

If we have an **important concept** to cover in a section, the title will be highlighted, and if you should use the keyboard at any time, the *keypresses* appear like this.

Hopefully, these styles will help you to get the most out of this book.

About the Sample Code and the CD-ROM

All Wrox Press books are based around the idea of hands-on learning. To this end we try to provide you with as much source code, documentation and useful tools as possible. This should allow you to uncover the advantages and disadvantages of the PowerBuilder environment as quickly as possible.

We also realize that the format of the printed page may not be your preferred vehicle for this information, so we have endeavored to provide you with a useful, flexible and comprehensive hypertext version of the book on the CD-ROM.

You are free to use, implement and customize all source code, databases and reference materials included with this book. Please be aware of and respectful of any copyrights, trademarks or other protected materials that are included on the CD-ROM. We have tried to include as much material as possible for your reference and hope that it proves useful in your developmental efforts.

For a full listing of the contents of the CD-ROM, see **CONTENTS.TXT** on the accompanying disk and for instructions on how to install it, see the **README.TXT**.

The Sample Application

Throughout the book, we build up a sample application, adding more and more functionality as we explore new subjects in each chapter. The sample application is based around a Stock Control system and runs from a database consisting of four tables:

Table	Description
item_master	This is the main table which contains all the stock information.
measurement_units	This contains details of measuring units which are used for items in the item_master table.
item_images	This contains images of all the items in the item_master table.
transaction_table	This contains details of all transactions.

The first version of our application has a Single Document Interface, displaying just the information in item_master. This version allows you to carry out various updating procedures on the information stored in this table. We then move to a Multiple Document Interface, so that we can add all the extra functionality required for the user to interact with the other tables in the database.

As well as the application, we have also included a class library of reusable objects on the CD-ROM, which you can customize and use in your own applications. Some of these objects are also implemented in our Stock Control application.

Throughout the book we've developed little stand-alone examples to illustrate points not specific to our application. These are contained in various libraries which are referred to in the text. You can look at these in the development environment by opening the relevant library, or you can see them in action by running the revpb application in the **EXAMPLES.PBL** library.

For a full list and description of all the examples contained on the CD-ROM, refer to the **EXAMPLES.TXT** file on the accompanying disk.

The Hypertext Book

The text included in this book is also supplied in electronic format on the accompanying CD-ROM using the Microsoft Multimedia Viewer. Each of the chapters is separated into Topic Sections to break up the text even further, providing you with screen-friendly chunks of information.

If the code appearing in the topic is excessive, it has been placed into a separate window that you can open and close as you wish, and by taking advantage of Viewer's copy feature, you can move the code directly into your scripts.

One of the most useful tools that Viewer offers to the reader is its search engine. This engine allows you to search on any word, while also supporting logical expressions. This means that you can isolate the topics that might contain the information you require using multiple criteria:

window AND object

Viewer also supports the following tools:

- A full index
- A history list
- A bookmark facility
- A contents page

For a full listing of how to use the electronic version of the book, take a look at the **VIEWER.TXT** file on the CD-ROM. Microsoft provide a generic help file on how to use their software, which can be found under the Help menu when the software is running.

The Tools and Demos

As with all Revolutionary Guides, we have attempted to provide you with as much useful information in our books as possible. To this end, not only do we rigorously test and amend the book itself, we also try to provide as many tools and demos on the CD-ROM as we can.

> The only criterion that we place upon the addition of a tool or demo to our CD-ROM, is that we consider that the software will be useful to you, as a developer. If it is simply marketing hype or a useless disk space soaker, we endeavor to screen it from the CD-ROM.

We don't operate any kind of 'favorite' contributors policy - the door is open to anyone who wishes to gain exposure though our books. If you would like to contribute any software to the second edition of this book, please get in contact with us here at Wrox, and we will be pleased to accept any offers that pass our criterion.

To Conclude...

We are always interested in obtaining as much feedback as possible on what you think of the products that we provide for the marketplace. Please feel free to return the reply card at the back of the book or send your opinions to either our on-line or snail mail address - see the front pages of the book for more information on these addresses.

Reading this book may also prompt you to think about writing or reviewing other books by Wrox Press. If you think 'I could do better than that!' or 'That's not the best way to do that!', why not take a look at our offer at the back of the book, and see what you can do to improve the information that is available to computer users of all levels.

For now though, just settle down and enjoy The Revolutionary Guide to PowerBuilder!

PowerBuilder and the Outside World

When you first come across this product, whether it's while flicking through a magazine or via a conversation with a colleague, two questions will instinctively spring to mind:

- What does this product do?
- Why is it better than all the rest?

To answer these 'important' questions, this chapter will cover the niche that PowerBuilder has exploited and built into its own fortress subject, before moving onto a look at PowerBuilder's 'shopfront', the tools that are on offer to the developer to help get the job done.

In this chapter, we will cover:

- The Client/Server environment and how PowerBuilder fits the model
- The tools that PowerBuilder has to offer the developer
- The layout of the PowerBuilder environment
- The advantages of v4.0 over v3.0a

Client/Server Architecture

The Client/Server computing model is slowly emerging as what historians will call 'the dominant force that influenced computing in the 1990s'. As users are now coming to terms with the power of computer technology and have started demanding more and more from their systems, advances in chip speed and computation power can no longer keep pace by themselves.

Software companies are forever evolving newer, more powerful applications to fulfill user demands, which in turn increase these demands, prompting newer versions of the software. Clearly, this is not a solution to this problem for two reasons: minimum requirements and practical usability.

The Implications of Software Evolution

Each evolution of the software brings even more powerful, useful tools to the user, but at a price some may say is too high: minimum requirements. Each new release comes with a set of minimum requirements that the system must fulfill before it can be successfully run - a much higher spec machine is usually required to run the package within the user's tight tolerance levels. These requirements may place demands upon your:

- CPU
- Available RAM
- Monitor
- Disk Drive
- Operating System
- Input Media

As a new version of software is released, who wants to update their hardware, a potentially expensive task, to run the software?

Practical Usability

The second reason is highlighted by looking at the problem from a different angle. The normal user not only wants up-to-the-minute tools and the latest software, but also a reasonable response time for all of the software elements (loading, saving, etc.). As the software becomes more complex, offering more options and tools, with better features and more intuitive screen displays, the footprint (the demands that the software makes upon the hardware) grows ever larger and more power-hungry. A larger footprint implies slower machinery, software with less agility and more angry users. Fortunately, this is mainly due to an antiquated hardware architecture, which is where Client/Server technology comes into the picture.

Making the Most of Your Hardware

As we have seen, improvements in either (or both) your software and hardware can't lead to a long term solution to the problem of user demands, but fortunately a revolution in the organization of these two key elements can.

By moving away from general purpose, centralized systems and moving towards architectures that use a collection of specialized servers connected via advanced, high speed networks, you can achieve much higher levels of performance with more lightweight machinery, so providing a favorable, cost effective solution that is welcomed by users and developers alike.

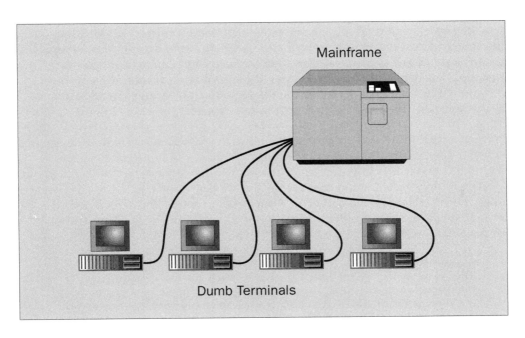

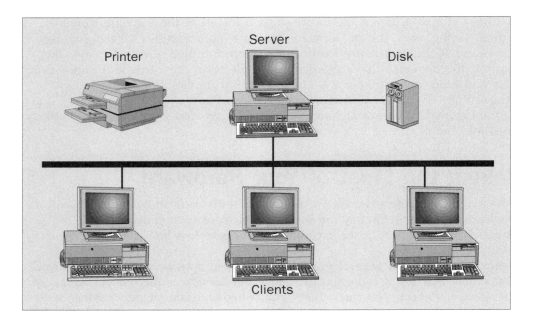

The difference between centralized systems and the Client/Server model is the area of the network that handles each part of the process. In a mainframe-based system, the workstation simply sends a request to the central core and the mainframe handles everything from there; the mainframe accepts the parameters, sorts out a solution based upon those parameters and returns it to the workstation, even handling the layout of the information on the screen. The mainframe CPU is fully occupied with the request from a given workstation until the solution has been painted on the user's screen.

When you employ the Client/Server model, each individual system is designated as either a client or a server depending on whether it is requesting or performing a service. It is the client that initiates the request for the service, but the server is only called upon to provide the service itself - it is the client that handles the results from the server in terms of formatting the screen layout, 'interpreting' the servers results and drawing its own conclusion based upon those results.

> This view of the Client/Server model is based on the first initial interpretation of the idea. However, this model can be applied to the interaction of different software applications on one system, as in the case of OLE. In the following sections, we'll see how this hardware model can also be applied to software.

Generally speaking, there are certain functions that are best left to clients, while there are others that are best performed by servers. One common example is that of the database management systems (DBMS). When this service is added to the Client/Server model, it is usually run on a server. Now let's move to a detailed look at what makes a client and a server what they are.

Server

Logically, a server provides services to a requesting client. The functions that a server should perform are determined, in a large part, by the type of requests that clients can send to the servers. Clearly, a client shouldn't send an unsupported request to a server.

Typically, a server can offer any combination of the following services:

- File sharing
- Printer sharing
- Database access
- Communication services
- Facsimile services

PowerBuilder concentrates upon the support of database access on a Client/Server-based system and therefore this is the focus of this book. To illustrate the domain of the server, consider the following example:

Your company is running its business records on a **SQL Server** database operating on a UNIX-based machine. The server is not dedicated to running the database, as the machine is also acting as a file server, thus allowing file sharing, one of the generic services that a server offers.

Focusing on the SQL Server process in the UNIX environment, you can see how the server takes care of database security, backup and recovery, transaction processing and so on. In other words, the server takes care of the data maintenance and does nothing towards the display of the data, the composition of any reports or the requests for more information from the user.

13

One other task that it does service is that of client requests. Some of the server's time is devoted to looking for requests from its clients, even when it is processing requests from other clients. SQL Server can perform this task because it is multithreaded, a talent that allows the server to allocate threads to each request for information, so dividing its time between tasks in the most efficient manner possible.

Another advantage of multithreading is that the information is controlled directly between the server and the client because the request for information doesn't appear as a process on the operating system. This effectively hides the operating system from the user/developer, illustrating one more advantage of the Client/ Server model over that of a centralized system - the Client/Server model is not restricted to one operating system; it can easily combine a Windows-based client with a UNIX-based server.

In summary, the client requests services, while it is the SQL Server that knows how to read incoming data, update the data currently held in the database, maintain the lock mechanism to preserve the integrity of the data if more than one client tries to work with the same record at the same time, transaction processing and so on.

> *Transaction processing is the ability of a DBMS to allow changes to the data, rolling back those changes if a critical condition is not met, committing the changes to the database if the condition works out to be true.*

Client

The major functions that are performed by a client system include the visual presentation of the data on screen, report generation and the application of business logic to any data input. End-user interactions with an application are performed through the presentation logic. This is the application layer that, on one hand, interacts with the business logic of the application and, on the other hand, interacts with end users. The latter includes all interactions with the physical device (terminal) and handling of actual end-user performed input/ output (screen I/O, keyboard I/O, mouse etc.).

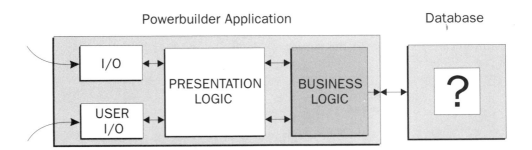

Traditional presentation functions dealt with character-based displays, where the processor sequentially displayed characters received from an application in a fixed font onto the user's screen. The continuous evolution of presentation functions has been closely linked with high-performance workstations offering more and more complex graphical display capabilities, until in today's world of user interface design you can include sound, video, drag-and-drop mouse support and a variety of other interesting effects.

When it comes to the graphical user interface, the client application should be user-friendly, reduce the burden associated with keying in commands and be capable of responding to events. Some common events that occur when using a graphical user interface are as follows:

- Keyboard events occur when a user has pressed or released a keyboard key.

- Mouse events occur when a user has moved the mouse pointer into or out of an entity, clicked on a mouse button within or without an entity or released the mouse button.

- Menu events occur when a user selects a command from the menu.

- Resize events occur when a user has changed the size of the window.

- Activation/Deactivation events are generated by the GUI to allow a user to change the current, active window.

In summary, the client system is in charge of all of the customizable features of the system. Each client can be outfitted with its own rules and logic, its own display and reporting functions, all going towards the ideal of a truly flexible company-wide business application. The only core components that each and every client should support are the requests for the same data and the ability to communicate that data to the server.

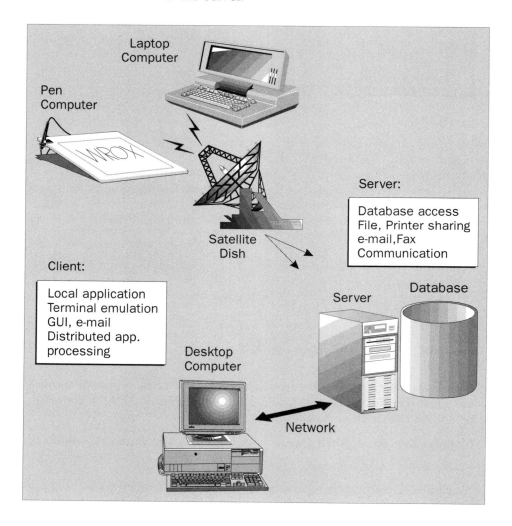

As you can see, the world of Client/Server computing is diverse and all-encompassing, generating new, interesting problems for the hardware engineer and application developer alike. Now let's take a look at how PowerBuilder fits into this model.

You should be aware that the Client/Server model can also apply to software. Some part of your system can operate as the server to another part's client. This occurs a lot when talking about OLE or DDE. This idea is discussed in detail in a later chapter.

Enter PowerBuilder

PowerBuilder is a high powered, graphical user interface for the development of Client/Server applications. Applications developed in PowerBuilder can serve as front-ends to a wide variety of data sources including Sybase, Oracle, dBase and text files, without any modification to the core of the application.

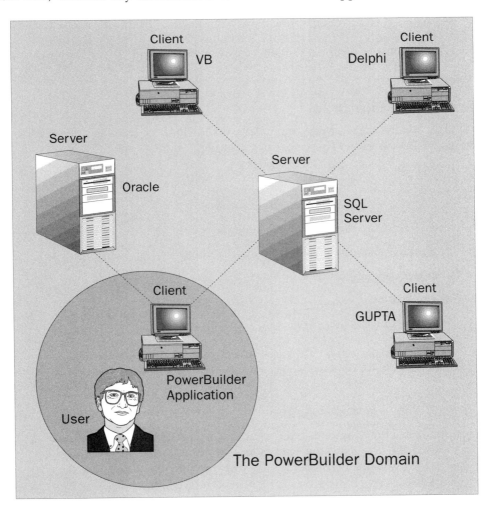

17

The PowerBuilder interface is very user-friendly, and the PowerScript fourth-generation scripting language is both easy-to-learn and master. PowerBuilder implements most object-oriented concepts, allowing you to reduce development time by building objects.

The data used by a PowerBuilder application resides on a database server, running software such as SQL Server. The server typically operates on a powerful mid-range computer and allows multiple users to work at the same time. It takes care of transaction processing, backup and recovery, and security.

In this environment, PowerBuilder helps you to develop applications for this Client/Server model. Applications developed in PowerBuilder usually act as clients, but when dealing with applications running on the same machine, they can act as servers using Dynamic Data Exchange (DDE). Most of the applications developed until now connect to the DBMS and act as the client application.

PowerBuilder Features

With this use of the software in mind, let's take a look at the basic features that PowerBuilder has to offer. These features include:

- Visual development environment
- Support for object-oriented programming
- User-friendly application development
- Integration with other Windows applications
- Extended connectivity
- Easy migration
- Transaction processing
- PowerScript
- Enterprise Client/Server development

Visual Development Environment

With simple click and drag-and-drop techniques, you can create great user and database interfaces. To create the user interface, there is no need for endless streams of code as in COBOL or C, you simply paint the screen the way you would like to see it at run-time. It provides a standard interface for logging onto several databases, removing the need to remember strings of syntax or complex commands.

Support for Object-Oriented Programming

PowerBuilder supports event-driven programming and most object-oriented programming concepts, such as Inheritance, Encapsulation and Polymorphism. It supports multiple inheritance in an efficient way, even though it doesn't use a classic, direct implementation.

Broadly speaking, a typical application consists of menu options that allow the user to select different modules in the application, as well as screens for capturing and reporting data. In third-generation language (3GL) applications, the screens, menus and reports are all part of the program you have to develop. When using PowerBuilder with its basis in object-oriented programming, all of these items are objects – screen objects, menu objects, report objects (DataWindow objects) and so on. All these objects are stored in a file called a library.

Allows Development of User-Friendly Applications

PowerBuilder ships with standard objects that support 3D effects and allows you to create your own objects. It allows you to use external objects, picture animation and user-friendly labeled toolbars. It supports Multiple Document Interfaces (MDI) and provides drawing objects to make the application more attractive.

Integration with Other Windows Applications

PowerBuilder supports Dynamic Data Exchange (DDE) with other Windows applications, Object Linking and Embedding (OLE2.0) and the Message Application Programming Interface (MAPI).

More Connectivity

PowerBuilder ships together with interfaces for:

- Popular e-mail packages such as cc:Mail
- Groupware packages such as Lotus Notes
- CASE tools such as ErWin

19

▲ Version Control packages such as PVCS

▲ Native database driver connections with popular DBMS, RDBMS

▲ Open Database Connectivity (ODBC)

Easier Migration

PowerBuilder will be available for all popular operating systems. As long as you use ANSI SQL with the bare minimum of changes to your PowerBuilder application, you can migrate from one database to another. Note that there is no need to change the presentation logic when you migrate to another database.

Allows Transaction Processing

PowerBuilder allows two types of transaction processing: auto and manual. Using the auto option PowerBuilder takes care of issuing **COMMIT** and **ROLLBACK** statements. The manual option allows you to have more control on the process, by passing domain over these statements into your hands.

PowerScript

A powerful, easy-to-learn scripting language, PowerScript allows embedded SQL statements and, in some cases, a single PowerScript command can take care of a number of ordinary commands. For example, **UPDATE()** generates the respective **INSERT**, **UPDATE** and **DELETE** statements and sends the commands to the database.

PowerScript allows you to incorporate more functionality in the client application. PowerBuilder applications can be designed to shift some processing load from the server and it can also be used to integrate database events with work-group packages such as e-mail.

Best Solution for Enterprise Client/Server Development

PowerBuilder comes with canned software routines, held in class libraries, that developers can incorporate into their programs rather than writing their own routines from scratch. Consequently, a company can cut application development time or spend more time improving rather than building a basic application. It supports a multi-programmer development environment, source control and third party optimized libraries that can be used to cut development time.

The Development Environment

Now that we have seen how PowerBuilder fits into the marketplace for Client/ Server development tools, let's take a look at the development environment that you will be using to design your PowerBuilder applications. The rest of this chapter explains how to navigate around the package and how to customize the interface to suit your needs. At the end of the chapter you will find three sections that cover:

▲ The advantages of PowerBuilder compared to other products

▲ The sequence of application development in PowerBuilder

To begin with, let's take a quick look at how to get PowerBuilder up and running, customizing the environment so that it is comfortable for you to work in. This includes the remodeling of the native and custom toolbars that PowerBuilder has on offer and a look at the different ways that PowerBuilder helps you develop Client/Server applications.

Invoking PowerBuilder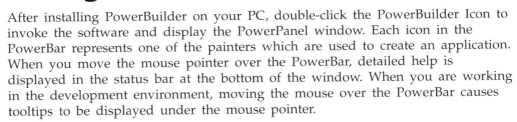

After installing PowerBuilder on your PC, double-click the PowerBuilder Icon to invoke the software and display the PowerPanel window. Each icon in the PowerBar represents one of the painters which are used to create an application. When you move the mouse pointer over the PowerBar, detailed help is displayed in the status bar at the bottom of the window. When you are working in the development environment, moving the mouse over the PowerBar causes tooltips to be displayed under the mouse pointer.

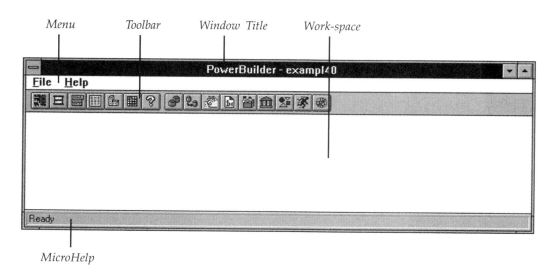

Menu   Toolbar   Window Title   Work-space

MicroHelp

Painters

The 16 icons can be broadly divided into three categories: object creation, object/ environment management and other painters. We'll look briefly at what each icon represents before going into detail in the following chapters.

Object Creation Painters

These are used to create objects which make up an application.

The Application Painter

The **Application Painter** helps you to specify application level properties and allows you to write application object level code such as error handling, script to execute when the application is idle and so on. The application level properties typically include:

▲ The application name

▲ The icon for the application

▲ The default colors, fonts and font sizes for the application's screens

▲ A list of libraries where the application will look for objects

The Window Painter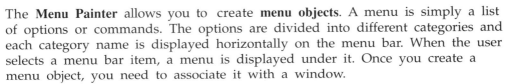

The **Window Painter** helps you to build screens (called **windows** in PowerBuilder). A window is the main interface between the user and the PowerBuilder application. You can use standard controls such as CheckBoxes, RadioButtons and EditBoxes to build windows. You can use these controls to display data as well as for data entry.

The Menu Painter

The **Menu Painter** allows you to create **menu objects**. A menu is simply a list of options or commands. The options are divided into different categories and each category name is displayed horizontally on the menu bar. When the user selects a menu bar item, a menu is displayed under it. Once you create a menu object, you need to associate it with a window.

The DataWindow Painter

The **DataWindow Painter** allows you to build **DataWindow objects**; these objects are used to retrieve, display and manipulate data. They allow you to retrieve data from a number of RDBMS/DBMS/text files and display the information in a variety of built-in report styles.

Once you build a DataWindow object, you need to associate it with a DataWindow control contained in a window.

The Data Pipeline

The **Data Pipeline** allows you to copy tables and their data from one database to another, even if they are located on different DBMSs. For example, you may want to work on a local Watcom database, but you need some SQL Server data which resides on the network. In this case, you would use a data pipeline to copy the SQL Server table to your Watcom database.

The User Object Painter

The **User Object Painter** allows you to create customized objects that are derived from PowerBuilder standard objects. You can also create customized objects from external sources such as VBX controls or Windows Dynamic Link Libraries.

> *A DLL is a special kind of executable file that can contain blocks of code, resources or data that can load and unload itself when needed. Its design enables multiple tasks to share the same code [functions] or data in a Windows environment. A VBX is a specialized DLL designed for the Visual Basic environment.*

The Query Painter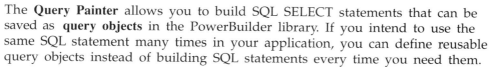

The **Query Painter** allows you to build SQL SELECT statements that can be saved as **query objects** in the PowerBuilder library. If you intend to use the same SQL statement many times in your application, you can define reusable query objects instead of building SQL statements every time you need them.

The Function Painter

The **Function Painter** allows you to build **function objects** that can be used to define a series of frequently executed commands. In PowerBuilder, a function is a collection of PowerScript commands and/or embedded or dynamic SQL statements. You can also refer to these functions in your PowerScript.

The Structure Painter

The **Structure Painter** allows you to create **structure objects**. A structure is nothing but a set of related variables (which may have different data types) grouped under a single name. It allows you to manage related variables without much fuss. You can refer to the structures in your PowerScript.

Object/Environment Management Painters

These painters help you to control the application environment and objects.

The Library Painter

The **Library Painter** allows you to create and maintain PowerBuilder libraries. Objects you create using the PowerBuilder painters (application, windows, menus, functions, queries, structures, user objects and DataWindow objects) are stored in an operating system file; this file is called a **library** in PowerBuilder parlance. The Library Painter allows you to organize the objects that were created with the other object creation painters.

The Database Painter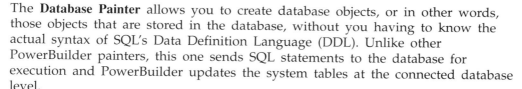

The **Database Painter** allows you to create database objects, or in other words, those objects that are stored in the database, without you having to know the actual syntax of SQL's Data Definition Language (DDL). Unlike other PowerBuilder painters, this one sends SQL statements to the database for execution and PowerBuilder updates the system tables at the connected database level.

It also has a sub-painter that allows you to perform database administration. This combination of painters is therefore mainly used by Database Administrators. In version 4.0, you can also execute the database administration painter from the PowerPanel.

Preferences

Preferences is used to set the default values for the development environment. For example, you may want to connect to SQL Server whenever you invoke the database painter, or you may want a window to have a particular default background color. These defaults are only applied in the development environment; they are not used in scripts.

The Project Painter

The **Project Painter** allows you to create and maintain the objects in your PowerBuilder project. Once defined, you can rebuild your application with a single click from this painter. Building a project object for your application can greatly reduce the amount of time spent creating an executable, as it defines all your PowerBuilder Dynamic Libraries (PBDs) and PowerBuilder Resource Files (PBRs) required to generate the executable.

Other Painters

The other painters that are available from the opening PowerBuilder screen allow you to run and debug applications.

Help

Help displays a standard, context-sensitive, Windows hypertext help file providing detailed syntax, examples of PowerBuilder commands and other useful information for PowerBuilder developers. Like Preferences, this is only useful in the development environment.

Run

You guessed it – the **Run** icon allows you to execute the current PowerBuilder application.

Debug

The **Debug** painter allows you to view the execution of the current application step-by-step, simplifying the discovery of the bugs in your application. It is very powerful and comes to the fray with all the debugging facilities you will ever need.

Placing the PowerBar

When you invoke PowerBuilder, you will be placed into what PowerBuilder refers to as PowerBar mode. You can place the PowerBar wherever you want on the screen by selecting File/Toolbars... and selecting the appropriate button in the Move box:

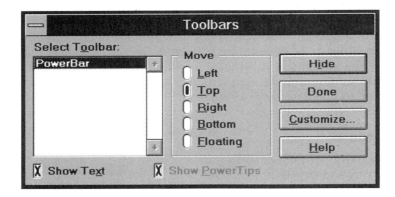

As you can see, the other available options are Show Text, which displays the labels beneath toolbar icons and Show Power Tips which displays micro help in the status bar at the bottom of the window.

Clicking on the Hide button hides the selected toolbar and the text of the button changes to Show. The Customize... button allows you to customize the PowerBar, a task we'll cover in a later chapter.

The PowerPanel

You can also invoke the various painters from another source, the PowerPanel. To invoke the PowerPanel, select File/PowerPanel:

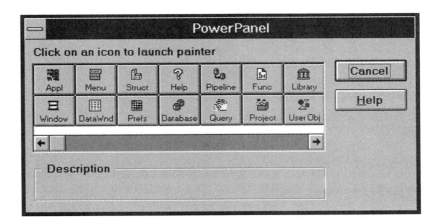

Note that this version of PowerPanel will only appear if you have the
Show Text selected for the dialog. If you haven't got this option selected,
the dialog will still function correctly, but will appear slightly different.

In this mode, all the toolbar icons are displayed in a response window which
can't lose focus until you select an icon or close it down.

If a window is responding like this, it is said to be modal.

Switching to PowerPanel mode doesn't hide the PowerBar, but you can't click on
a PowerBar icon until you close PowerPanel.

The PowerPanel versus the PowerBar

The differences between the PowerPanel and the PowerBar can be summed up
in the following table:

PowerPanel	PowerBar
Can't hide the icon labels.	Can hide the icon labels.
Can't change the location of the PowerPanel except by moving the window.	Can place the PowerBar anywhere on the PowerBuilder screen.
Can't be customized.	Can be customized.

The PainterBar

When you invoke a painter from the PowerPanel or PowerBar, the relevant PainterBar will be displayed. For example, the following screenshot shows the options available when painting a window with the Window painter:

Like the PowerBar, the PainterBar can be positioned anywhere on the screen. To change the position of a painter bar, either select Window/Toolbars... to display the Toolbars dialog box as before:

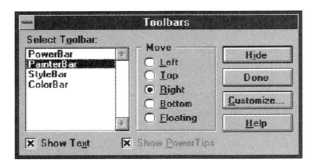

or you can right-click on the PainterBar and select the appropriate position from the pop-up menu.

As you can see, the same options apply to the PainterBar as the PowerBar; you can customize the toolbar, as well as opting whether or not to display the icon labels and the PowerTips. Each of the options available on a PainterBar are also available from the Controls menu:

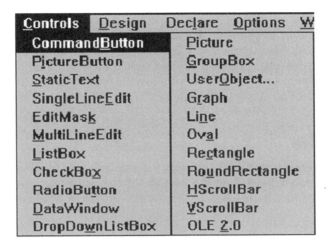

There are two other toolbars that you can use when working with a painter: the StyleBar and the ColorBar. You can attach either of these toolbars to either the window frame or the painter frame, simply by selecting from the Options menu:

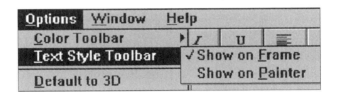

The StyleBar

As the name indicates, the StyleBar allows you to change the style of any control or object. This tool allows you to change the size, shape and appearance of any text in the selected item:

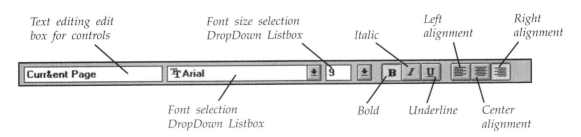

If you don't have a control or object selected, the first box won't be visible. This displays the text that appears on the control. The second box is used to change the font of the text. The drop-down list allows you to select from the available fonts, while you can change the font size using the third box. The next six icons are the standard windows text options allowing you to select bold, italicized and underlined text and to have left, center or right alignment.

The ColorBar

The ColorBar allows you to set the selected control's text, background and border colors. It is displayed at the bottom of the screen or at the bottom of the current painter window:

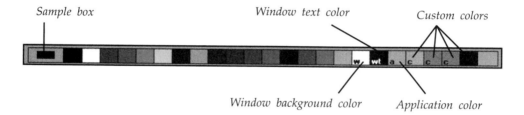

Sample box   *Window text color*   *Custom colors*

Window background color   *Application color*

When you select an object, the background and foreground colors display in a sample box at the extreme left of the ColorBar. To change the background color of an object, select the object by clicking on it with the left mouse button, then click with the right mouse button on the required color. To change the foreground color, click with the left mouse button.

Any icons on the ColorBar that appear with letters in the bottom left-hand corner denote derived colors from the Windows environment. The letters stand for the following colors:

Letter	Color
w	Window color
wt	Windows Text color
a	Application color
c	Custom color

The Window color, Application color and Window Text color options equate to 'set these colors to those set by the user via the Windows control panel'. For example, selecting 'a' will change the object's color to that defined by the user as the Application color in the control panel.

To see how this works, open a window, select an object and change the background color to the Application color by clicking on the 'a' on the ColorBar. Now, *Alt+Tab* to the Windows Control Panel and change the color scheme. When you change back to PowerBuilder, you'll see that the new colors have been applied to the object you selected.

This is a powerful feature as it allows you to give users an application that has exactly the same color scheme as the rest of their Windows applications. Hard-coding colors isn't considered good programming practice. Some of your users may be color-blind or simply dislike certain colors; effectively allowing the user to select the color scheme is considered to be a good and user-friendly practice.

Defining Custom Colors

You can define custom colors by double-clicking on one of the 'c' boxes and defining the color using the color palette that is then displayed:

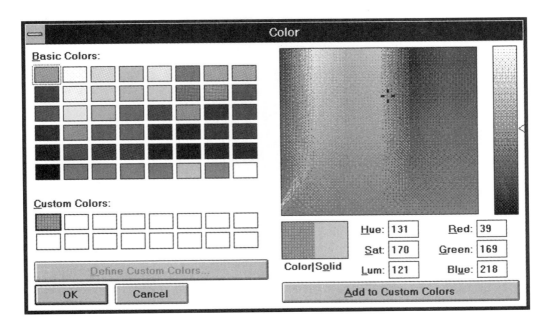

You can define up to 16 custom colors, displaying up to four of them at a time in the available custom color boxes on the ColorBar. Once you have defined the color, click on the Add to Custom Colors button to commit your color to the generated set. After defining all the custom colors you require, click on the OK button and you will see the first four colors on the ColorBar.

> If you want a specific color to be displayed on the ColorBar and it is not one of the first four that have been designed, select the color before leaving the Color Palette and PowerBuilder will replace the custom color on the ColorBar that you double-clicked upon to get to the Color Palette.

Context-Sensitive Popup Menus

The standard menus along the top of the window are drop-down menus but PowerBuilder also provides a Popup menu that can be activated anywhere on the PowerBuilder screen, simply by clicking on the right mouse button. For example, if you right-click on a painter bar, you will get a Popup menu similar to this:

The options available on the menu relate to the painter bar. In Chapter 4, we'll look at how to create Popup menus in your applications, while in Chapter 9, we'll look at how to implement them using PowerScript.

Customizing Toolbars

PowerBuilder allows you to add or remove icons in the PowerBar and your painter bars. This can be very useful as it allows you to run other applications from within PowerBuilder. For example, if you frequently need to invoke the Windows File Manager, it's much easier to execute it from within PowerBuilder rather than by changing the focus over to Program Manager and clicking the File Manager icon.

To customize the PowerBar, right-click on it and select the Customize... option. You'll be presented with the Customize dialog box which allows you to drag-and-drop icons from the selected palette onto the current toolbar:

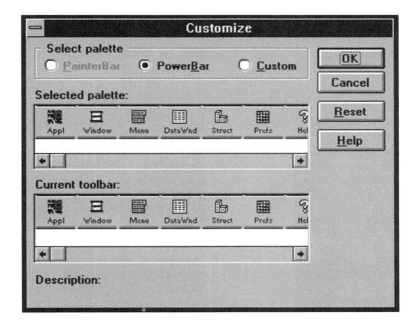

If you scroll along the Selected palette:, you'll see other PowerBuilder specific options which allow you to run reports, open windows, browse objects and so on.

> *Note that these icons are pre-defined and you can't change the action that will take place when they are selected.*

To add a custom-defined icon click on the Custom button. This displays the icons that are available in the custom palette:

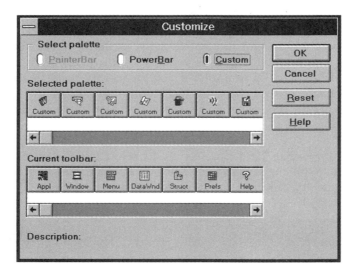

If you drag one of the custom icons into the PowerBar, the Toolbar Item Command dialog box will appear allowing you to specify the Command Line, Item Text and Item Microhelp for that icon.

The command line is the full path to the **.COM** *or* **.EXE** *file that you wish to run, the item text is the word(s) that will appear under the icon if this option is selected and the item microhelp is the text that appears in the status bar when the mouse pointer is placed over the icon.*

For example, if you wanted to run File Manager, enter the following in the dialog box:

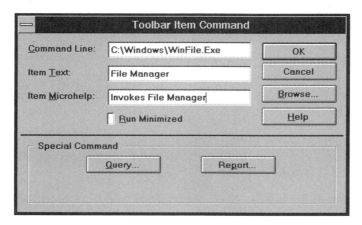

From the PowerBar, there are three types of command you can specify for a custom icon:

- An external command
- A PowerBuilder query
- A PowerBuilder report

For some of the PainterBars, a fourth option is also available, namely a UserObject, and if you are using the DataWindow Painter, you can also use:

- A format name
- A function name

Assigning a Query to a Toolbar Icon

To specify a query to run from a toolbar icon click on the Query... button to bring up the Select Query dialog box:

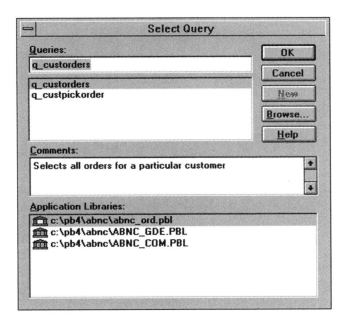

To assign the query to the toolbar, simply select the appropriate query from the selection and click on OK. Now when you select the icon, the Query Painter will open and load the specified query, execute it and display the results. However, you can't change the definition of the query when the results are displayed.

Assigning a Report to a Toolbar Icon

In the same way, you can assign a report to a toolbar icon. If you want to see how this works, select the Report button in the d_example_detail (available in the pb_examfe library). You can use the following options to supply arguments with reports:

Argument	Description
/l	library name
/o	report name
/r	runs report

An example of how you can use these arguments is illustrated below:

```
Report  /l  c:\pb4\examples\pbexamfe.pbl  /o  d_categories  /ro
```

This entry at the command line for an icon would cause a report, located in the library called **PBEXAMFE.PBL** in the **C:\PB4\EXAMPLES** subdirectory, called d_categories to run when the icon is selected.

Assigning a UserObject to the PainterBar

The procedure for assigning a UserObject is the same as for specifying a query or a report. However, unlike queries and reports, when you select the icon, the specified UserObject is placed in the Window painter. As another consideration, the icon is only available when a Window or UserObject painter is active.

Assigning a Menu Item to a Toolbar Icon

As you might notice, after you have been using the PowerBuilder interface for a while, not all the menu items are afforded icons on the associated toolbar. Due to the flexibility that Powersoft has instilled into its product, PowerBuilder allows you to customize the toolbars with references to the associated menu bars.

To add this extra functionality to the interface, select the option to Customize... the appropriate Toolbars... from the menu. Change the focus of the icons to Custom and drag-and-drop the icon you want to add to the toolbar onto the lower pane, taking care to release it where you wish it to appear, in respect of the other icons.

When you drop the icon at the required position, you are presented with the following dialog:

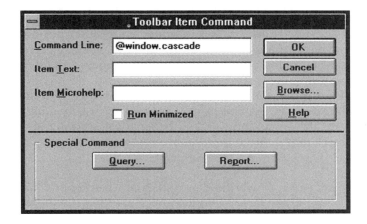

To power up the icon, we can make use of the Command Line, using the following syntax to refer to a menu option:

@menubaritem.menuitem

In our example:

`@window.cascade`

causes PowerBuilder to invoke the functionality provided by Window/Cascade when you click on this icon.

> Instead of placing the textual reference to the menuitem that you wish to emulate with this icon, you can also place a numerical reference to the item. For example, instead of the word 'cascade', you could use the number '4' as it's the fourth item on the **Window** listing.

By filling in Item Text and Item Microhelp, you can provide context-sensitive help for the labels that appear under the icon when the mouse pointer passes over it and for the status bar at the bottom of the screen respectively.

All icons that are added to the PowerBar are only available when the PowerBar is active. They (temporarily) disappear when you switch to the PowerPanel mode.

Application Development Flow in PowerBuilder

There are no hard and fast rules for PowerBuilder application development, especially in view of PowerBuilder's flexibility towards where painters can be invoked from - anywhere! However, we recommend a bottom-to-top approach.

Since windows make up the main point of interaction between the user and the application, and almost all of the objects you create in PowerBuilder are either placed or called from those windows, it is a better idea to create all of the objects that will be related to the windows, before creating the windows themselves.

If you have not developed a PowerBuilder application before, and therefore you have not developed any class libraries containing your most frequently used PowerBuilder objects, we suggest you follow these recommendations:

- Depending on the nature of the applications you will be developing, spend some time putting together the required class libraries. This will save development time now and in the future.

- By using (inheriting and customizing) the above developed class libraries, develop a specific class library for your current project.

We recommend the following steps for the application development, assuming that you have taken on board all of the concerns about class libraries and the visual aspects of application development:

1 Create the required Libraries.

2 Create the Application and specify defaults.

3 Create dummy windows with no objects in them. This allows you to refer to the window names in other objects.

4 Develop the Structures. This allows you to use the structures in the script.

5 Develop the Queries. Query names can be referenced in other objects. This allows you to use a Query as a data source for a DataWindow object.

6 Develop the Functions.

7 Develop the DataWindow objects and specify DropDownDataWindow edit styles to database columns wherever it is required (See Step 2).

8 Develop UserObjects.

9 Develop the Menu objects.

10 Develop Data Pipeline Objects.

11 Develop the Windows.

12 Develop the Project Object.

> *The steps that are outlined over the following chapters concerning the development of an application refer to a PowerBuilder application (the library and the objects held in it). At this point, we are assuming that you have already produced a database to connect with or you have set up the connect to a server based back-end. For more information on how to do this task, please refer to Chapter 6 on the Database Painter.*

This method requires a great deal of forethought and planning. A well planned project reduces maintenance costs and helps to develop an efficient system, as well as speeding project development.

> *For more discussion on application development guidelines, see Appendix A: Application Development Guidelines.*

Summary

PowerBuilder is an object-oriented graphical interface for developing Client/ Server applications and incorporates a powerful fourth-generation script language called 'PowerScript'.

One of PowerBuilder's primary advantages is that its applications can serve as front ends to more than one data source simultaneously. PowerBuilder uses painters to paint menu items, screens and reports, all of which are objects for the PowerBuilder developer to manipulate. In all there are fourteen different painters, covering such features as the development of applications, windows, menus, DataWindows, structures, databases, queries, functions, libraries and user objects as well as features for developers such as debugging.

The PowerBuilder interface consists of a PowerPanel/PowerBar with painter and other icons, a PainterBar, a StyleBar, a ColorBar and context-sensitive Popup menus. The PowerBar and the PainterBar are customizable through the ability to add and remove icons.

PowerBuilder also offers you the ability to execute external commands, reports and queries from the PowerBar, simply by adding and customizing icons to it. In the same way, you can execute all the PowerBar commands from the PowerPanel and you can specify formats and place functions from the Painter Bar.

CHAPTER 2

Library Painter

When you've written a program, you'll usually want to save it. You will proceed to save the program to disk and, in fact, to an operating system file. For example, a program written in the 'C' language is stored in a file with a `.c` extension, while dBase programs get a `.PRG` file extension.

In exactly the same way, an application developed in PowerBuilder is stored in an operating system file with a `.PBL` extension (pronounced 'pibble'). This is a PowerBuilder library file and it is used to store all the objects that you create, such as windows, menus, DataWindows and so on.

To manage this file and the objects it contains, PowerBuilder provides the Library Painter, which is the subject for this chapter.

In this chapter, we will cover:

- Creating, deleting and optimizing libraries
- Managing PowerBuilder objects
- Browsing the class hierarchy and its objects
- Working in a multi-user environment
- Version control management
- Creating DLLs
- Migrating from version 3.0

Introduction

Welcome to the most fundamental component of any PowerBuilder application, the Library, and the painter that is used to create and maintain it. Any object that you create must be stored in a PowerBuilder library making the **.PBL**s into one of the basic application building blocks.

> *For an idea of how the Library fits into the PowerBuilder hierarchy, take a look at the inside front cover for Wrox's interpretation of what makes up a PowerBuilder application.*

Any one application can reference objects from any library, whether its own or one on the other side of the world, as long as the library remains in the system's sight while the application is running.

PowerBuilder ships a sample application called 'exampl40' along with version 4.0. This sample application object is stored in **PBEXAMFE.PBL**, but also refers to objects that are stored in other libraries.

You can save your objects into one of these sample libraries, but we recommend that you create a new library before you start developing an application. Remember that this is not a necessity, but rather a matter of tidiness. With your own library, your objects will be easy to locate and you will be well on the road to creating your first custom library.

> **Note that there are essentially two different types of library. One contains an application and the objects that are specific to that application, while the second type holds generic objects. These generic objects could support a company logo or a menu structure, allowing you to maintain a consistent look and feel to your applications.**

Before you look at how to maintain your libraries, let's take a look at how to create one using the Library Painter.

Invoking the Library Painter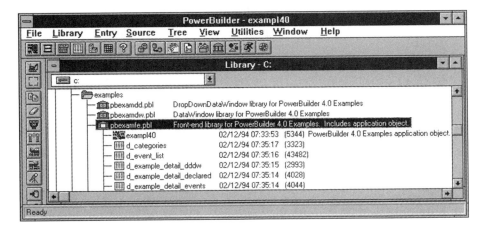

To invoke the Library Painter, click on the Library icon from the PowerBar or double-click the Library icon held in the Power Panel. When you invoke the Library Painter, the library that contains the current application object opens by default - we'll look at how to change this in a moment.

> If you get a File Error Message when you first invoke the library painter, just click the **Close** button and click **OK** to the warning message. The library painter will open as normal. Don't worry about these messages - we'll discuss why they occur in the section on Version Control.

When you invoke the painter, it allows you to see what goes on inside those mysterious pibbles. A typical Library Painter may look like this:

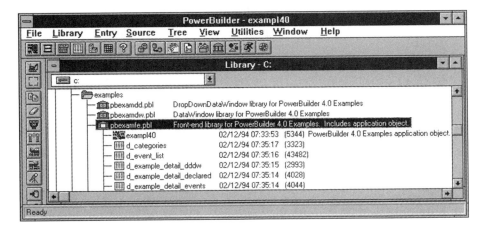

You can see that the display looks like the tree structure of Window's File Manager. You can see all the directories and sub-directories on any of your drives, but the files that you can see are restricted to those used by PowerBuilder, held in the Library files.

When you double-click on a library name, the file expands or contracts (just like the Windows File Manager), allowing you to look at all the objects stored in that library or reducing it down to one entry for compactness. In the previous figure, you can see that **PBEXAMFE.PBL** is expanded and that several objects are contained in it, including:

▲ The application object - exampl40

▲ A DataWindow - d_categories

▲ Another DataWindow - d_event_list

On a generic front, a library may contain any of the following objects:

▲ Application objects - used to contain application defaults.

▲ DataWindow objects - used to retrieve and display data.

▲ Function objects - collections of frequently used PowerScript procedures.

▲ Menu objects - the menus that apply to your application.

▲ Query objects - used to select specific sets of data from your database.

▲ Structure objects - collections of related variables.

▲ UserObject objects - custom, user-defined PowerBuilder objects.

▲ Window objects - the screens that appear in your application.

▲ Project objects - used to contain information about building executables.

▲ Data Pipeline objects - used to copy data from one database to another.

Each of these objects can be part of the jigsaw that is your PowerBuilder application. The specifics behind what each of these objects does, how they are created and maintained and where and why you would use them is the subject matter for the first section of this book.

If you scroll down this library tree, you will also see some of the other objects that are held in this library:

▲ A Structure - example_report_structure

▲ A UserObject - u_search

▲ A Window - w_main

▲ Another Window - w_dw_print_options

If you flick over to File Manager, you can only see the library filename; the objects that are contained in that library are hidden from view unless you use the PowerBuilder painters to view them.

Refining the Library Painter Output

Beside each object in the library is an icon which identifies the painter in which the object was created. Along with the object definition, PowerBuilder stores a lot of other useful information, such as the date and time the object was created, the size of the object and any comments that you have made about the object since it was created. You can select what information you want to see by choosing from the options available in the View menu:

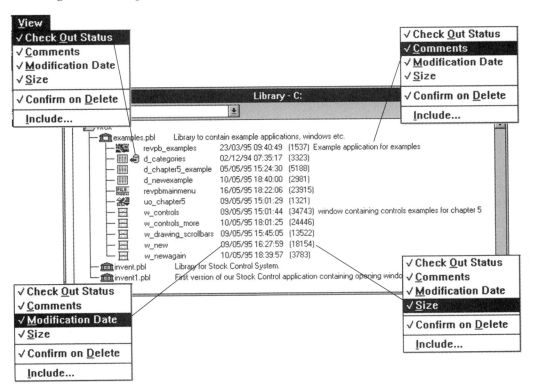

The Library PainterBar

The various menu options specific to the Library Painter are also available from the Library PainterBar:

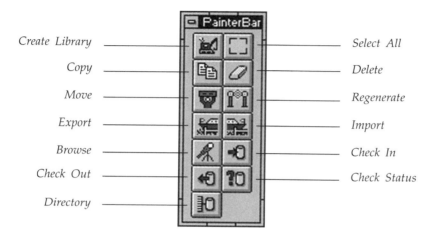

Create Library — Select All

Copy — Delete

Move — Regenerate

Export — Import

Browse — Check In

Check Out — Check Status

Directory

Now that we have seen how to control the Library Painter, let's look at how to create your first library using the tools that PowerBuilder provides.

Creating a Library

Creating the libraries required for your project is the first step in the application development. For an opening example, let's create a library for the Stock Control System that we are building up throughout the book. This is quite a small application, so we'll only need a single library, but for large applications, you may want to keep different objects in various different libraries.

> Clearly, if you want to reuse your objects in many different applications, it makes sense to store them in different libraries, grouped by some related property.

To create a library, select Library/Create... or click on the Create Library icon. In the case of our example application, call the library **INVENT.PBL**:

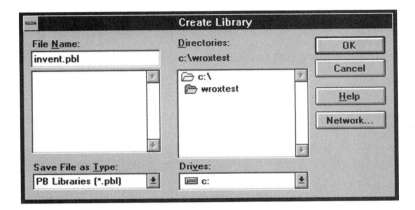

*In order to differentiate between the complete sample application that you have installed on your system from the accompanying CD-ROM and the application you will create in these chapters, we have provided you with a **WROXTEST** directory into which you can place your creations. This will appear on your system on the drive earmarked for the source code when you install the CD-ROM.*

Specify the name and location of the library that you wish to create and click the OK button.

*If you don't specify a **.PBL** filename extension, PowerBuilder will automatically add it for you. This is the recommended option, because if you get the file extension wrong, you'll get the following error:*

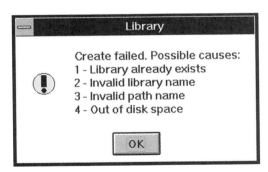

You can't change the name of a library from within the Library Painter, but you can change it in File Manager.

This opens the Modify Library Comments dialog box, which allows you to specify comments for the library. It is always a good idea to add comments to the objects that you create in your application; it allows you to easily identify what each object does, a task that can sometimes be difficult if you just work with the names.

Following the idea of creating the library for the sample application, specify 'Library for Inventory Management System' in the Comments box and select the OK button. You may choose to add comments after the creation is complete by selecting Library/ Modify Comments, but you should make a practice of writing comments at the time:

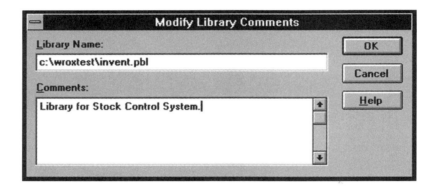

When a library is first created it is empty; it doesn't contain any objects.

> Remember that a PowerBuilder library is used to store your application and any objects that go towards its make-up, which means that most, if not all, of your application will be stored in one file, even though PowerBuilder is an object-based development platform.

As you add objects to the library, they are saved in two forms:

1 Source format

2 Compiled format, the binary representation of the source format

Whenever you save an object, PowerBuilder automatically compiles the object. When you create a run-time executable, ready for the distribution of your application, you'll also create a PowerBuilder DLL. This DLL holds all the compiled versions of your objects, ready for use in the application by the executable.

By compiling the objects when they are created, PowerBuilder automatically has up-to-date versions ready for conversion into the DLL and it can also use the objects in previews of your application before the executable is created. This process of object compilation is completely hidden from the developer and you have no access to that format.

Opening an Object

One of the most common options that you will use against the objects in your libraries is that of opening them to modify or review their contents. At the moment, our library doesn't contain any objects to open, so we suggest that you select the sample library that ships with PowerBuilder to review this operation.

> *This library is called* **PBEXAMFE.PBL** *and is available in*
> **C:\PB4\EXAMPLES** *if you select the default installation options.*

To open an object from the Library Painter, either double-click on the object or highlight the object and press the *Enter* key. You can open any object from any library, but there are some limitations to opening objects directly from the Library Painter:

1 If a menu, window or UserObject is open, you won't be permitted to open another application object:

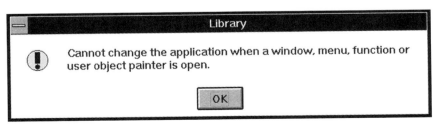

2 If you open and make changes to an object which isn't in the current application's library, you can't save those changes unless the library that contains the object is in the application's library list:

We'll take a detailed look at using library lists in the following chapter on the Application Painter, but in summary, an application's library list is the list of libraries that the application is aware of, i.e. the libraries that hold the objects that you wish to use in your finished product.

3 If the ancestor object is not present in the application library's library list, the inherited object can't be opened from the Library Painter.

> *Following one of the basic principles of object-orientation, it is possible to create general, basic objects and then derive more specific versions of the objects from them, adding more and more features and specialities until the required object is achieved.*
>
> *In PowerBuilder, the derived object is referred to as being inherited, while the object from which we have inherited the basics of the new objects is referred to as the ancestor object.*

Organizing the Objects in Your Libraries

One of the consequences of PowerBuilder's flexibility is that you need the ability to move objects between libraries. This requirement surfaces when you are putting together an application library using generic objects held in base libraries, producing slim-line resource libraries for specialized applications or simply tidying up after a creative session.

The PowerBuilder Library Painter offers you the three common tools for object maintenance:

Copying

Moving

Deleting

Through the use of these tools, together with the ability to create new libraries and objects, you will now be able to organize all of your PowerBuilder components as you wish.

Copying a Library Entry

One effect of copying objects from one library to another is that once the task has been completed, there isn't a link between the original and the copied version. This means that any changes that are made to the original don't affect the copy.

> *This is one of the major reasons behind Powersoft's decision to allow you to access objects in other libraries, as long as the library appears in your application's library list. If you use this method of getting the object into your application, any changes made to the original will be reflected in your application, because it is the original that you are using.*

As an example of how easy it is, let's copy an object from **PBEXAMFE.PBL** into our **INVENT.PBL** library.

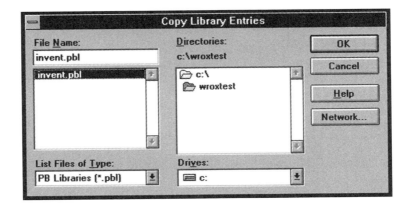

1 Place the mouse pointer over **PBEXAMFE.PBL** and double-click on it to expand the library.

2 Select an object and click on the copy icon. This opens the Copy Library Entries dialog box to accept the destination library.

3 Select the destination library from the library list, in this case **INVENT.PBL**, and select the OK button.

Note that PowerBuilder preserves the timestamps of any objects that you move or copy between libraries. The timestamp represents the time and date of the last modification to the object it is associated with:

Timestamp

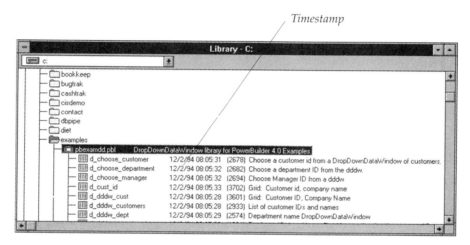

Moving a Library Entry

Moving an entry between two libraries is just as simple a task to accomplish:

1 Expand the library that contains the object you wish to move.

2 Highlight the object and click on the Move icon.

3 Select the destination library from the Move Library Entries dialog box:

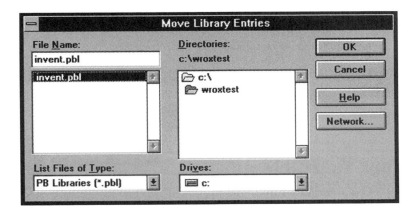

4 Hit the OK button and PowerBuilder will perform two operations: a copy to transfer the object to the new library and a delete to remove it from the original library.

Deleting a Library Entry

The third use of this object maintenance tool is for tidying the contents of your libraries. As usual, the method for performing this task is quite simple:

1 Expand the library that needs tidying.

2 Select the object you want to delete and either press the *Delete* key or click on the Delete icon.

PowerBuilder will then confirm your action with the following prompt, before it deletes the selected object:

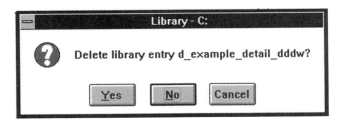

You may not receive this prompt when you try to delete an object because the library preference variables may be set against this option. We'll discuss how to get at and alter these variables later in the chapter.

If you want to delete the library itself, you will have to select the library and select Library/Delete from the menu. Make sure that the library you are trying to delete is not a member of your application's library list, otherwise PowerBuilder will object.

Converting Your Objects

Not only does PowerBuilder offer you the ability to maintain the objects in your libraries, it also allows you to convert them to another more readable format, that of ASCII text.

This ability to export your objects is offered to you as a developer for a number of reasons including:

▲ A reduced file size for transportation.

▲ A basic format that can move cross-platform.

▲ A basic format that doesn't encounter readability problems over services such as the Internet (it removes the need to UUEncode your files).

▲ This feature only affects objects and not the parent libraries. This allows you to transport just the objects you need as opposed to the whole library.

▲ There are occasions when you need to edit the ASCII text file version of the object to get the required results.

▲ By looking at an object's declaration statements, you can get a better understanding of how PowerBuilder is using the concepts behind object-orientation.

▲ To alter your objects in a manner that the traditional PowerBuilder functions don't allow. For example, to alter a DataWindow data source to 'Stored Procedure' from 'SQL Select', convert to ASCII text format, alter the appropriate sections and convert back. If you have changed the correct sections of the ASCII text file (discovered through your own research), the DataWindow data source will have 'magically' changed to 'Stored Procedure'.

Exporting a Library Entry

If you have identified an object that you wish to export to ASCII text file, follow these steps:

1 Expand the appropriate library and select the object.

2 Click on the Export icon from the toolbar to open the Export Library Entry dialog box:

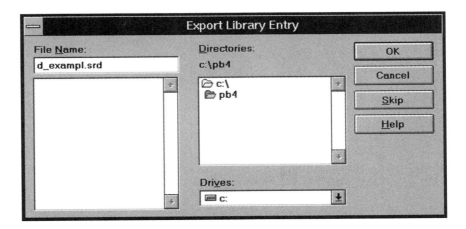

Accept the default filename or enter another in the File Name box before clicking the OK button.

> *PowerBuilder uses the first 8 letters of the object name for the default filename. The last letter of the extension is the object type; for a window, the extension will be .SRW, for a menu .SRM and so on.*

PowerBuilder now converts the object to the required format, creating the file on your system at the location indicated in the dialog. The exported version of the object is not displayed in the Library Painter, but you can display and edit the exported ASCII file using the file editor that ships with PowerBuilder.

> **To invoke the PowerBuilder file editor, press *Shift+F6*.**

The PowerBuilder File Editor

When you ask PowerBuilder for the services of the file editor, you are presented with this dialog:

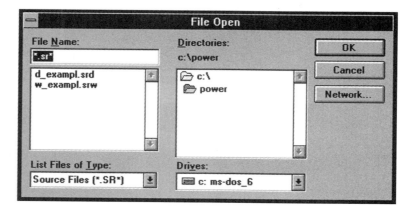

When you select the filename of the exported object, the editor will display the ASCII file. For example, if you export the d_example_detail_dddw DataWindow from exampl40 using the default options for the filename, you'll be presented with the following text file:

```
File Editor - D_EXAMPL.SRD

$PBExportHeader$d_example_detail_dddw.srd
release 4;
datawindow(units=0 timer_interval=0 color=16777215 processing=0 print.documentn
header(height=89 color="536870912" )
summary(height=1 color="536870912" )
footer(height=1 color="536870912" )
detail(height=65 color="536870912" )
table(column=(type=char(258) name=compute_0001 dbname="compute_0001" )
 column=(type=char(128) name=xref_info_object_ref_type dbname="xref_info.object
 retrieve="SELECT ~"xref_info~".~"object_ref~"|| ', '|| substr(event,1,length(ev
text(band=header alignment="0" text="DropDown && Nested DataWindows"border="4"
column(band=detail id=1 alignment="0" tabsequence=32766 border="0" color="0" x=

                                                                      0013:0002
```

Importing a Library Entry

When you import a PowerBuilder object from an ASCII file, PowerBuilder creates the object from the source file. When importing from the ASCII file, there is no need to specify the destination object name as PowerBuilder gets all the required information from the headers in the ASCII file. When you click on the Import icon, you'll be prompted for the name of the file you want to import:

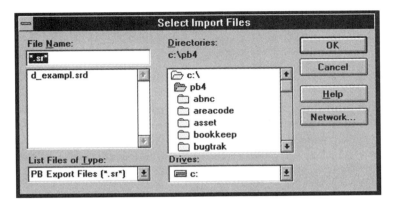

When you've selected the file, you'll be prompted for the name of the library where you want to place the object. The list of libraries on offer in this dialog box is restricted to the libraries that appear in your application's library list:

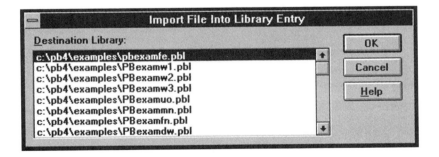

If something goes wrong with the importation, PowerBuilder will supply you with this dialog:

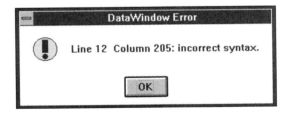

In this dialog, PowerBuilder identifies the problem area of the file. If you are experienced with this format, you might be able to rescue the error by altering the file using an ASCII text editor. However, by getting this error, the file is probably very corrupt and you should resign yourself to throwing the object away and starting anew.

Printing Definitions

You may have gathered that the information contained in a library is useful for any maintenance you have to perform against your applications. PowerBuilder allows you to keep a record of a library's contents by printing out individual object definitions along with the actual library structure.

Printing an Object Definition

To print an object definition, highlight the object and select Entry/Print... from the menu. PowerBuilder lets you select which object properties you want to print and also allows you to print multiple copies:

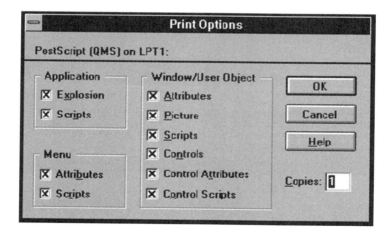

The full printout for the d_example_detail_dddw DataWindow looks like the following:

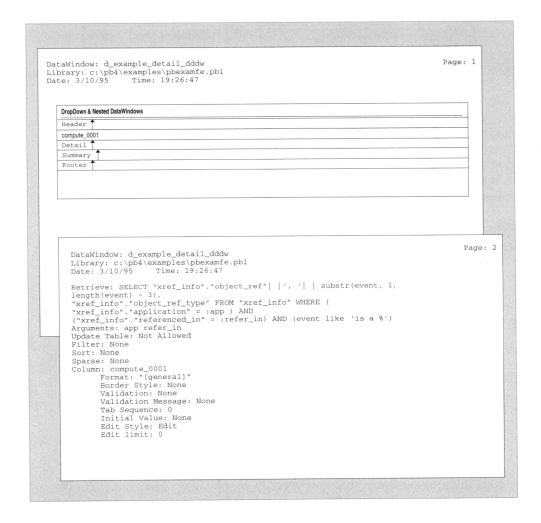

```
DataWindow: d_example_detail_dddw                                    Page: 1
Library: c:\pb4\examples\pbexamfe.pbl
Date: 3/10/95      Time: 19:26:47


 ┌──────────────────────────────────────────────────────────────────┐
 │ DropDown & Nested DataWindows                                      │
 ├──────────────────────────────────────────────────────────────────┤
 │ Header                                                             │
 ├──────────────────────────────────────────────────────────────────┤
 │ compute_0001                                                       │
 ├──────────────────────────────────────────────────────────────────┤
 │ Detail                                                             │
 ├──────────────────────────────────────────────────────────────────┤
 │ Summary                                                            │
 ├──────────────────────────────────────────────────────────────────┤
 │ Footer                                                             │
 └──────────────────────────────────────────────────────────────────┘
```

```
                                                                     Page: 2


    DataWindow: d_example_detail_dddw
    Library: c:\pb4\examples\pbexamfe.pbl
    Date: 3/10/95      Time: 19:26:47

    Retrieve: SELECT "xref_info"."object_ref"| |', `| | substr(event, 1,
    length(event) - 3),
    "xref_info"."object_ref_type" FROM "xref_info" WHERE (
    "xref_info"."application" = :app ) AND
    ("xref_info"."referenced_in" = :refer_in) AND (event like 'is a %')
    Arguments: app refer_in
    Update Table: Not Allowed
    Filter: None
    Sort: None
    Sparse: None
    Column: compute_0001
          Format: "[general]"
          Border Style: None
          Validation: None
          Validation Message: None
          Tab Sequence: 0
          Initial Value: None
          Edit Style: Edit
          Edit limit: 0
```

Printing a Library Structure

To print the structure of a library, select Library/Print Directory... You'll be prompted for the name of the appropriate file from the Print Library Directory, as shown in the following screenshot:

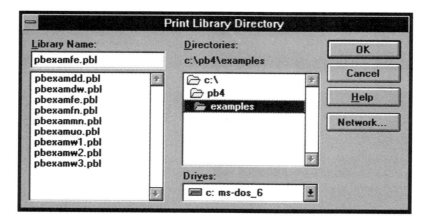

PowerBuilder prints all the details for the library grouped by the type of object. On the opposite page there is an example of the library printout for the **PBEXAMFE.PBL**.

Regenerating Objects

Sometimes your objects may be corrupted, for example through errors during linking, or you may want to update them to a new version of PowerBuilder. To accomplish either of these tasks, simply regenerate them.

> *Apart from through developer error (you pressed the wrong key!) or physical disk errors, the source code for an object can't be affected. The effects that we are considering here affect the compiled versions of the objects that PowerBuilder uses to run your application.*

However, this doesn't mean that you have to repaint the object from scratch. PowerBuilder regenerates the object by recompiling from the source code and replaces the old version of the object, updating the timestamp due to the modifications.

```
Dirctory Report.                                                        Page: 1
Library: c:\pb4\examples\pbexamfe.pbl
Date: 3/13/95          Time: 16:15:34


*----------------------------------*
Application entries.
*----------------------------------*
Name                              Date          Time          Size
exampl40                          12/2/94       07:33:53      (5344)


*----------------------------------*
DataWindow entries
*----------------------------------*
Name                              Date          Time          Size
d_categories                      12/2/94       07:35:17      (3323)
d_event_list                      12/2/94       07:35:16      (43482)
d_example_detail_dddw             12/2/94       07:35:15      (2993)
d_example_detail_declared         12/2/94       07:35:14      (4028)
d_example_detail_events           12/2/94       07:35:14      (4044)
d_example_detail_functions        12/2/94       07:35:13      (4291)
d_example_report                  12/2/94       07:35:13      (4988)
d_example_report_main             12/2/94       07:35:18      (8619)
d_function_list                   12/2/94       07:35:11      (100839)
d_new_example_list                12/2/94       07:35:04      (84197)
d_object_list                     12/2/94       07:35:01      (32732)
d_search_event_list_dddw          12/2/94       07:35:00      (8806)
d_search_events                   12/2/94       07:35:02      (2817)
d_search_objects_ddw              12/2/94       07:35:05      (38751)
d_search_object_ref               12/2/94       07:35:12      (2776)
d_search_results                  12/2/94       07:35:13      (2754)

*----------------------------------*
Structure entries.
*----------------------------------*
Name                              Date          Time          Size
example_report_struct             12/2/94       07:34:25      (525)

*----------------------------------*
UserObject entries.
*----------------------------------*
Name                              Date          Time          Size
u_search                          12/2/94       07:34:31      (21158)

*----------------------------------*
Window entries.
*----------------------------------*
Name                              Date          Time          Size
w_dw_print_options                12/2/94       07:34:35      (24791)
w_example_report                  12/2/94       07:34:40      (15790)
w_main                            12/2/94       08:34:27      (66476)
w_main_backdrop                   12/2/94       07:34:59      (3565)
```

A Directory Report for a Specific Library

This directory report is generated, based upon the options that you select, to display the objects that are contained in a specifc library. The options allow you to select what information is displayed, such as the name of the object, when it was created and how big it is. For clarity, the objects are organized based upon their type.

There are two main instances when regeneration of an object may be necessary:

- Linking errors
- Problems with inheritance

Let's look at how each of these problems can occur, thus allowing us to avoid the situations that create them.

Linking Errors

For an example of how a linking error can occur consider the following situation:

Suppose that you declared a global variable and referred to it from an object, which we'll call Window A. For some reason, while painting another window, Window B, you delete this variable and save Window B. If you don't update the code in Window A which refers to the deleted variable, then when you create an executable, you'll get linking errors.

PowerBuilder won't display the errors while creating the DLL, because during the construction it doesn't recompile all the objects in a library. However, if you regenerate Window A, PowerBuilder will see the problem and display the error.

Problems with Inheritance

Following a similar line to linking errors, if you work with inheritance between objects, you may also experience problems that require regeneration. For example, suppose you make an alteration to an ancestor object without realizing that scripts in the descendant object are affected by that action. If you open the descendant object, PowerBuilder, recognizing that something is awry, will display the following warning:

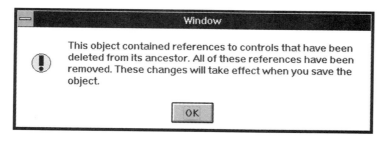

However, if you don't open the descendant object before attempting to create a DLL, the problem will again avoid detection. The error will only be displayed while you attempt to create the executable itself, forcing you to return to fix the problem and recreate the DLL before carrying on with the executable.

For this reason, if you use a lot of inheritance between your objects, it is a good idea to regenerate all the required objects before attempting to create a DLL. This reduces the chance of errors appearing while creating `.EXE` files.

When using inheritance, it is a good idea to use the class browser to locate any ancestor objects so that you can regenerate them ahead of the descendants. The class browser, which is discussed in detail later in this chapter, allows you to example the relationship between the objects in your library.

One other point that you should consider while making changes to an object is to regenerate any descendant objects. This ensures that any changes that you have made don't affect descendant objects.

> *In Chapter 12, we look at the use of object-oriented concepts such as inheritance and polymorphism in more depth.*

How to Regenerate Your Objects

The process of regenerating any given object is simple:

▲ Select the object

▲ Click on the Regenerate icon

PowerBuilder handles all the compilation of the source code, replacing the old version with the new updated version.

> *When you upgrade an application from an older version of PowerBuilder, all the objects referred to in the application will automatically be regenerated. You can upgrade your old PowerBuilder applications to v4.0 simply by attempting to open it using the new software. PowerBuilder will automatically detect the older version and take you through the conversion process.*

Optimizing a Library

Over a period of time as you add, modify and delete objects, libraries can get fragmented. At any one time, there may be a large amount of unused fragmented space that is too small for new objects to soak up, all of which amounts to objects getting stored in non-contiguous areas of your hard disk.

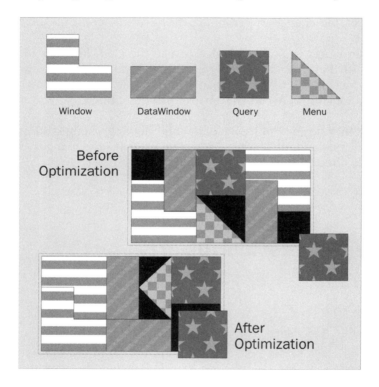

This can have a tremendous effect on the performance of your application. The Library/Optimize... option can be used to rectify this problem. Optimizing a library doesn't recompile the objects in the library, but simply removes the unused space and defragments the storage of objects. Since PowerBuilder doesn't recreate the objects, the timestamps don't change.

When you select Library/Optimize..., you are presented with the following dialog box to select the library to optimize:

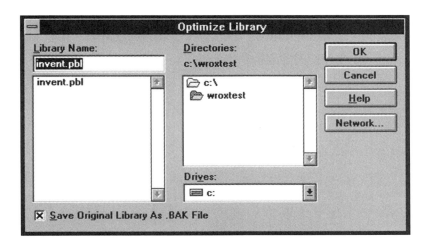

We recommend that you always check the Save Original Library As .BAK File option so that you have a backup copy of the optimized library, just in case anything goes wrong with the optimization.

Creating a Dynamic Link Library

A Dynamic Link Library (DLL) is a collection of functions, resources or data that is available to any program. DLLs are different from regular applications as they can't be executed by themselves; they are always called from another application or DLL.

The main advantages that can be gained by using a DLL are:

- Their ability to be shared by many independent applications at the same time.

- They provide a high level of abstraction. An application doesn't need to know how the DLL works to use it.

- DLLs are very easy to use.

- High upgradeability. If a new version of a DLL is released, you should be able to use the new one immediately, without modifying, recompiling or re-linking your software.

▲ Calling functions in a DLL has the same effect as calling the corresponding functions in the underlying language.

▲ DLLs are only loaded in memory when required. This differs from using **.EXE** files which are loaded into memory when the application is run.

The major advantages that a Dynamic Link Library has over its cousin, the Static Link Library, include the ability to share their functionality with several callers at the same time, saving on redundant code and the memory required for several copies of the library, one for each caller.

PowerBuilder DLL files are stored with the **.PBD** extension. You can only create one DLL for each library and you can't select which objects to include in the DLL - all the objects are included.

> **A useful tip for larger applications is to break down your libraries into specialized collections of objects, which has the effect of producing several smaller DLLs.**

If you update your application by changing just a few object definitions, by simply compiling those new definitions into a new DLL, you can update your distributed applications by supplying the new DLL to your customers. By naming the new DLL with the same name as the old one, your customers only need to copy the new one over the old to update their application.

Suppose that you have three DLLs associated with your application's executable. If you update two objects, each one from a different DLL, you will need to recompile both DLLs and supply them both to update a customer's application.

Resource Files

If you have dynamically changing objects, bitmaps or icons in your application then these files will never be included in a Dynamic Link Library.

Take the example of two DataWindows, dw_1 and dw_2, that are held in the same library. Suppose that you assign dw_1 to a Window when you initially paint it, while dw_2 is only assigned to the Window at run-time under certain conditions.

While creating the DLL from the library, dw_2 won't be added to the DLL. In the development environment, this application will work fine, but when you create the **.EXE** file and run it on any machine, PowerBuilder will display a blank area on the Window in place of dw_2.

Similarly, if you are referring to bitmaps or icons, the location of these files should be identified by a reference in your DOS path, found in your **AUTOEXEC.BAT**, or a full path should be given to the file, otherwise they won't be displayed in the application.

The solution to any of these problems is to create a **resource file**. A resource file is an ASCII file with the **.PBR** extension, containing references to all the additional resources that your application needs to run correctly.

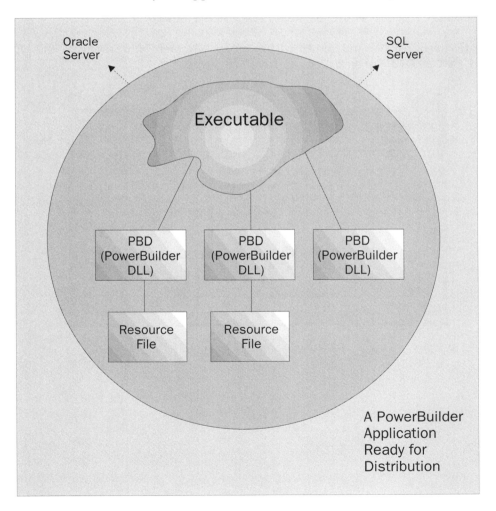

Using the File Editor

You can use the file editor to create a **.PBR** file. Press *Shift+F6* to invoke the editor and supply each entry name on a separate line. For all external objects specify the file name with its full path. For example, to add the **BEACH.BMP**, you would add the following line to your resource file:

C:\WROX\ICONS\BEACH.BMP

For PowerBuilder objects, you need to specify the library name and the object name. For example, to specify DataWindow 'd_example_detail', you would put:

C:\WROXTEST\INVENT.PBL   (DW_FOR_ITEM_MASTER_QUERY)

Save the resource file and return to the Library Painter. Now to create the DLL, select Utilities/Build Dynamic Library... from the menu:

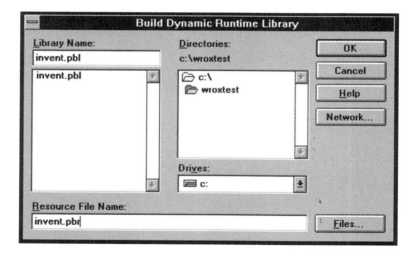

Select the library name and either type the resource file name in the Resource File Name box or click on the Files... button to select the resource file name. Selecting the OK button creates the DLL.

Note that you can only have one resource file for each DLL that you create.

The DLL is given the same name as the library with the `.PBD` extension. You should not change this name. If you compare the `.PBL` and `.PBD` files you'll notice that the `.PBD` file is smaller. This is because the DLL only contains the compiled versions of the objects and not the source code.

At run-time, DLLs must be in one of the following directories:

▲ The current directory

▲ The Windows directory

▲ The Windows\System sub-directory

▲ Directories on the DOS path

Multi-User Environment

When a team of developers are working together on a project, creating, improving and maintaining the same libraries, there is always a possibility that two developers may be working on and altering any given object at any one moment in time. If the first developer makes changes to and saves an object while the second developer has the object open, and then the second developer saves his version of the object, all the changes that the first developer made to the object will be lost.

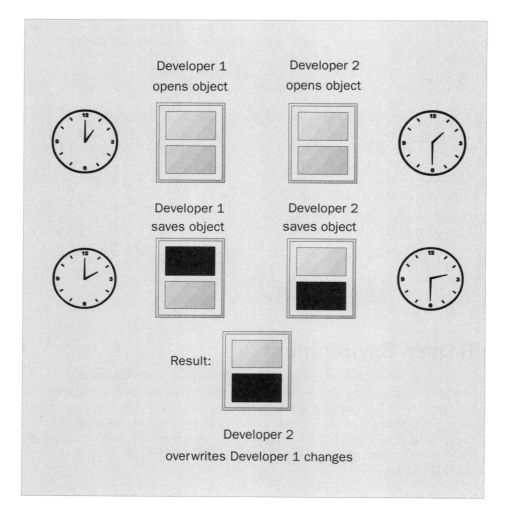

Developer 1
opens object

Developer 2
opens object

Developer 1
saves object

Developer 2
saves object

Result:

Developer 2
overwrites Developer 1 changes

Since all of the objects that the developers are working on are part of a PowerBuilder library, granting and revoking permissions to that library file at the operating system level won't work. To get around this problem, PowerBuilder provides **Check In** and **Check Out** facilities.

There are three options available from the Library Painter relating to the control of the objects held in your libraries in a multi-user environment:

▲ Check Out

▲ Check In

▲ Version Control

Note that these options are only available in the PowerBuilder Enterprise version - not in PowerBuilder Desktop.

Check Out

When you need to edit an object exclusively, you should check out the object to a local working library:

▲ Select the object from the Library Painter

▲ Click the Check Out icon on the toolbar

If you are doing this for the first time after installing PowerBuilder, you will be prompted for a User ID:

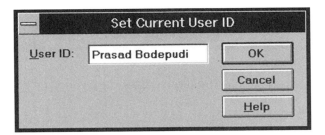

The User ID that you supply is stored in the **PB.INI** file and is used whenever you check out objects in the future. When you have set the entry in the **PB.INI** file, you will be presented with the following screen to nominate the library to hold the checked out object while you work on it:

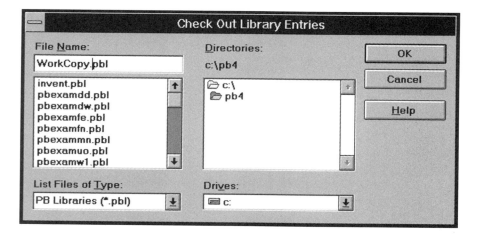

When an object is checked out, if other developers attempt to open the original object, PowerBuilder displays a warning message indicating that it is checked out by another user:

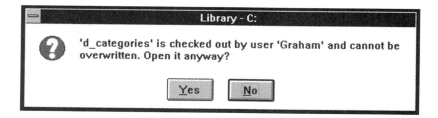

You can still open the object and make changes, but you won't be able to save any changes to the object.

Viewing an Object's Check Out Status

When an object is checked out by a user, PowerBuilder displays a locked symbol before the checked out entry in the source object library and the checked out symbol before the object in the local library. You can view all the details about the checked out entries by selecting the Chk Stat icon from the toolbar.

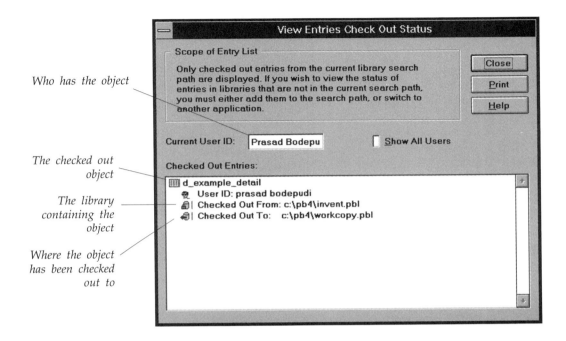

Who has the object

The checked out object

The library containing the object

Where the object has been checked out to

Check In

When you have finished working with the checked out copy of the object, you can use the Check In feature to replace the original entry in the source library. Select the working copy and click on the Check In icon from the toolbar. PowerBuilder already knows the source of the checked out object, replaces the original entry and deletes the working copy.

Clearing an Object's Check Out Status

As long as you don't check in the object, other users can't make changes. Sometimes, you may decide not to apply the changes done in the working copy. In that case, you can clear the check out status by selecting the working copy and choosing Source/Clear Check Out Status from the menu. At this point, PowerBuilder will offer you the opportunity to delete the working copy from your local library before clearing the original object's status.

Version Control

Version control allows you to maintain the different versions of an object that grow up through a library's developmental lifetime. Using version control means that even though you are always editing the new version, you will be able to retrieve old versions of an object at any time. Clearly, such a process is closely associated to the Check In/Check Out facilities that we have just explored.

Version control packages work by keeping a record of changes made to the original object rather than storing several complete versions of an object. This saves space but means that, if you retrieve an old version of an object, it reads the original version and applies the changes before presenting it to you.

> The advantages of version control can be subdivided into two categories, undo and mutli-developer control. The undo advantage allows the developer, at any time during the creation process, to return to a previously tried and tested version of the object, throwing away any changes that they have tried, failing to get the added functionality they were looking for.
>
> The multi-developer control advantage means that instead of locking the other developers out with Checking In and Checking Out, each developer can work on the same object concurrently and not risk the loss of any changes. Each version of the object that the developers saved is registered as a different version, ready for the team leader to draw together the different copies into one release. The Checking In/Checking Out feature would now come into its own, allowing the team leader to work unhindered.

Version control features are not built-in to PowerBuilder, but from v3.0, PowerBuilder shipped with a fully integrated version control package from a third-party software developer. PVCS (Polytron Version Control System) is a tightly integrated product in v3.0, and with the release of v4.0, Powersoft took the opportunity to add more third party products.

If you install a version control package before you install PowerBuilder, PowerBuilder automatically enables some options relating to version control under the Source menu. The options that appear due to the presence of a version control package are the currently grayed out options in the screenshot:

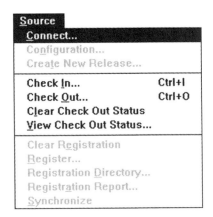

Connecting to a Version Control Package

To connect to a version control package after you've installed PowerBuilder, simply select Source/Connect... and choose the package name from the drop-down list:

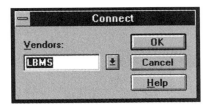

PowerBuilder currently supports five version control packages:

- CCC
- ENDEVOR
- LBMS
- PVCS
- RCS

As we mentioned at the start of the chapter, you may get warning messages when you first invoke the Library Painter. This is because when you first call upon the painter, PowerBuilder looks for a default version control package. If you don't have any installed upon your system, you will get the error messages. To avoid this annoying dialog box, you can change the default Source Vendor to blank in the Library Painter Preferences. We look at all of the library preferences at the end of the chapter.

Browsing

From the Library Painter, PowerBuilder allows you to browse object properties, strings and the class hierarchy. This gives you another way of touring your .PBL, while allowing you to copy and paste values that are related to your application's objects straight into your script.

Browsing Objects

When using the Library Painter, you can see all the PowerBuilder supplied objects, properties, object level functions, declared instance variables and so on. Selecting Utilities/Browse Objects... opens the Browse Objects dialog box:

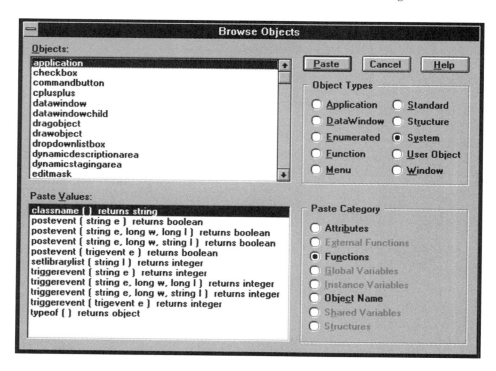

By using the Browser, you can focus your review onto a select band of objects, based on one of the generic groupings, i.e. all DataWindows or all UserObjects. By default, PowerBuilder displays the system objects, but you can easily select the type of objects you want to browse, by choosing the appropriate category.

This feature is particularly useful when writing scripts as it also allows you to paste object names, functions and so on into your scripts, by clicking on the Paste button or double-clicking on the value.

Browsing Library Entries

This is a very useful utility that helps to locate occurrences of a given string in the selected objects. For instance, you may want to find all the objects and events that refer to the window called 'w_main_window'.

You wouldn't want to open every object and check every event of every control for the string, so instead of this slow, monotonous task, you can select the objects you want to search in and click on the browse icon:

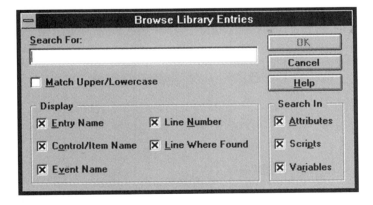

You can specify the string you want to search for, what you want to be displayed and where you want to search. The search string need not be a full string and it need not start with the leading characters. The string can include any valid character, but PowerBuilder doesn't recognize wildcards in this dialog box. You can make the search case-insensitive by selecting the Match Upper/Lowercase checkbox.

For example, if you search for the string 'pen' in the exampl40 application, you'll get the following reply:

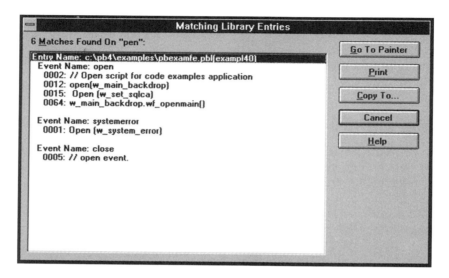

You can see that PowerBuilder has returned all the entries that include the string 'pen'. If you want to open one of the matched entries, you can double-click on the object name in the Matching Library Entries dialog box, or select the object name and click on the Go to Painter button.

You can also print out the list of matching entries, by selecting the Print button, or save the listing as a text file by selecting the Copy to... button.

Browsing Class Hierarchy

PowerBuilder implements all of the object-oriented concepts and allows you to create objects by inheriting attributes from others; for example, the standard objects provided by PowerBuilder are inherited from the PowerObject. When using inheritance, it is useful to be able to see the hierarchy of the objects, simply so that you can see which objects are inherited from which others.

You can view the class hierarchy in the Library Painter by selecting Utilities/ Browse Class Hierarchy... from the menu:

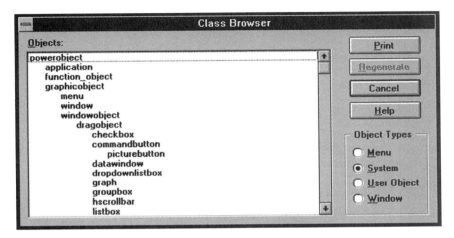

By default, this option displays the system class hierarchy, but PowerBuilder supports inheritance with three specific types of objects: Menus, Windows and UserObjects.

Due to this subdivision, PowerBuilder allows you to change the selection in the Object Types group box, so focusing upon a group of user-defined objects in the current application.

> **You can also regenerate objects from here. This is an obvious place to do this as you can see the ancestor/descendant relationship between all the objects in your application.**

Library Painter Preferences

Every painter has certain default attribute values. You can change these default values by clicking on the Preferences icon and selecting the relevant painter or by changing the values in the painter itself. When you set options in the painter, those values are retained and used when you next invoke the painter:

All preference variables related to the Library Painter are available in the Variable listbox when the Library icon is selected in the Preferences window. Clicking on the variable name shows the default value.

The Library Painter preferences can be divided into the following logical groups:

- Printing preferences
- Library entry details display preferences
- Library entry display preferences
- Other general preferences

Printing Preferences

The following variables determine whether the associated elements should be included in the reports printed from the Library Painter. They will be included if the variable is set to 1 and excluded when set to 0:

- Application explosion
- Application scripts
- Menu attributes
- Menu scripts
- Window attributes
- Window objects
- Window object attributes
- Window object scripts
- Window scripts
- Window picture
- NormalFont - this is the font used to display the text on the controls in a window.

It is worth playing around with these settings to get the format and feel of the report that you require, tailoring the information on the printed report to that which you require.

> *Note that you can set these preferences when you elect to print out a given object's report. Any alterations that you make to these preferences in this dialog are reflected in the Library Painter Preferences.*

Library Entry Details Display Preferences

The following variables determine whether the associated details are to be included in the reports printed when you select Library/Print Directory from the menu. They will display in the Library Painter environment if they are set to 1 and they will be suppressed if they are set to 0. Turning these options on and off from the View menu will also automatically set these values:

- Display comments - comments associated with a library or object.
- Display dates - last modified date and time.
- Display sizes - object size.

Library Entry Display Preferences

The following options determine the type of objects you want to display in the Library Painter. These options can also be set from the View/Include menu and the settings of 1 or 0 have the same effect as before:

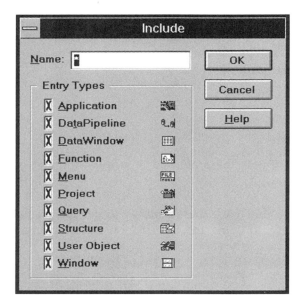

Other Preferences

The other Library Painter preferences that PowerBuilder makes available to you include:

- ▲ UserId - the user ID is used in the Check Out and Check In options. This is also recorded in the **PB.INI** file.

- ▲ DeletePrompt - when set to 1, PowerBuilder asks for confirmation before deleting an object.

- ▲ SaveBackupsOnOptimize - when set to 1, PowerBuilder makes a backup file before it optimizes the library.

- ▲ SourceVendor - the name of the default version control package.

Summary

We've now completed the first step in the application development cycle; the creation of a library to contain all the objects for our example application. We've covered quite a lot of advanced topics such as DLLs and Resource files, and we'll return to them later in the book as we develop our application. However, it is important to understand how PowerBuilder uses these files and why they will appear later on in the book.

Application Painter

Now that we understand how the library fits into the PowerBuilder developmental hierarchy, let's look at the next component that you need to create: the application object.

The Application Painter is used to create this object, as well as being the tool that defines certain default properties that are used throughout your application. This painter also allows you to perform some other ancillary tasks here such as defining an icon to represent your application and maintaining your application's library lists.

One point of interest is that the Application Painter can also be involved in the final stage of development, as it can be used to create the executable version of your application.

In this chapter, we will cover:

- Creating an application object
- Setting application wide defaults
- Creating an executable
- Setting application preferences

Introduction

When you are developing in the PowerBuilder environment, you must always have an application open. This is one of the reasons that creating an application at the start of a project is such a vital step. An application object in PowerBuilder is similar to a **main()** function in C or a control program in COBOL. It is from here that you call all other modules in an application.

In this chapter, not only will we look at how and why you should use the Application Painter, we will also create an application object for our Stock Control System and look at how we can go about creating an executable version of our application, ready for distribution to our users.

Invoking the Application Painter

To invoke the Application Painter, click on the icon in the PowerBar and PowerBuilder will open both the painter and the last application that the software was used to modify. If you are invoking the Application Painter for the first time after installation, 'exampl40' is the default application:

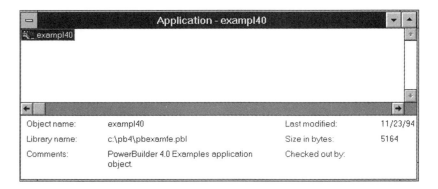

At the bottom of the screen, PowerBuilder also displays the following details about the selected application:

▲   Object name - the name of the current open application.

▲   Library name - the name and full path of the library to which the application belongs.

▲   Comments - any comments that you have made about the application.

▲   Last modified - the date and time of the last saved modification.

▲   Size in bytes - the size of the application object.

▲   Check out status - whether the application has been checked out by another developer or not.

The Application PainterBar

The options concerning an application are also available from the Application PainterBar:

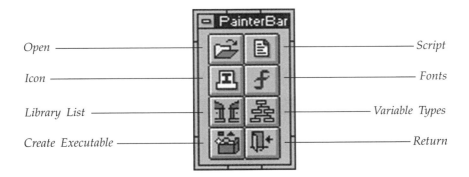

Creating a New Application Object

To create a new application object for our example stock control system, select File/New... from the menu or click on the Open icon and select the library where you want to create the application. In our case, this is the **INVENT.PBL** library:

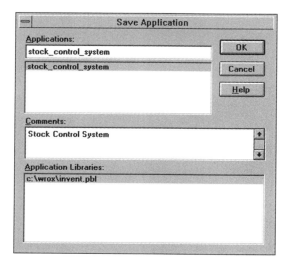

You must supply a library name, before you can create an application object, because any object that you create must be associated with a library. Once you have selected the library, you are prompted for the name of the application (you can also add any comments about the application at this stage):

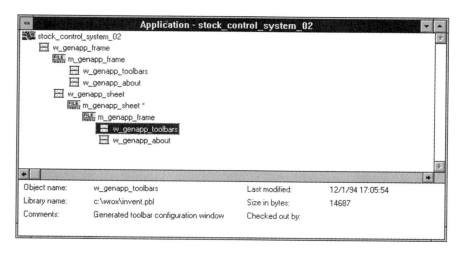

The following naming conventions must be adhered to when titling an application object:

- ▲ A maximum of 40 characters.

- ▲ The name must start with a letter.

- ▲ The name can include letters, digits and any of the following characters; dash (-), dollar ($), percent (%), hash (#) and underscore (_).

- ▲ PowerBuilder application object names are case insensitive.

- ▲ You can't use spaces in the name of an application object.

The library that you specify for the application will now become the default application library and any objects that you create from now on will be stored in this library. This application will now become the default application object and will be opened the next time that you invoke the PowerBuilder Application Painter.

You can change the default library in the Application Preferences, which we'll be looking at later in the chapter.

When you click on the OK button, you'll be asked if you want PowerBuilder to create a template for the application. If you select Yes (don't do this for the example application), PowerBuilder automatically creates some window and menu objects for your application:

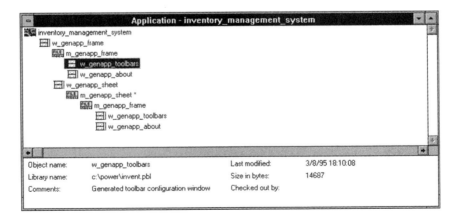

Note the asterisk (*) beside the second **m_genapp_sheet** *object. This means that the object is a descendant object. If you right-click on it, you can select the* **Object Hierarchy...** *option to view the hierarchy:*

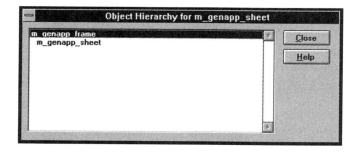

You can see that the **m_genapp_sheet** *is a descendant of the* **m_genapp_frame**. *The object-oriented features of PowerBuilder are discussed in greater detail in Chapter 12.*

As we only need a single window for the time being, select No and we'll go on to create the window ourselves in a moment. For now, let's look at some of the other features that PowerBuilder offers the developer to customize the application object.

In the later chapter on Multiple Document Interfaces (MDI), we'll look at creating full Windows-like applications with more than one single window.

Customizing Your Application Object

Up until now, we have been looking at the idea of an application object with a view towards creating our Stock Control System. However, to see the results of any customization that you can perform against the application object, you have really got to use a working application, with a full complement of objects.

Due to this requirement, we are introducing a new library with all the functionality required to achieve its purposes up and running. This new library is called **MENUEXAM.PBL** and can be found on the accompanying CD-ROM.

This application's task is based around the display of the Wrox Press logo, a task that it begins when you first execute the program:

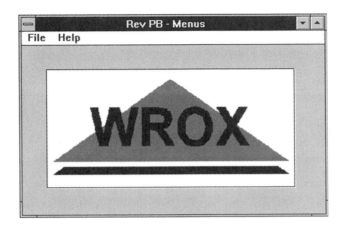

We'll explain more about the functionality of this little application as we go on, but first let's look at some of the custom features that PowerBuilder allows you to add to your application object.

Specifying an Icon for the Application Object

In the same way that you can minimize a Windows application to an icon, you can minimize a PowerBuilder application, so you need to associate it with a representative icon. To associate an icon with your application, click on the Icon icon and select the graphic that you want to represent your application:

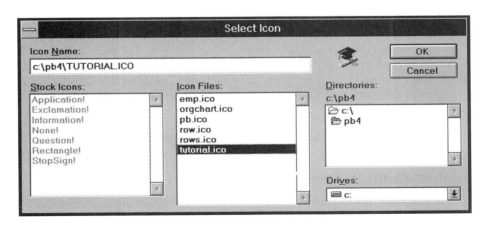

A number of icons ship with PowerBuilder for this purpose - the `TUTORIAL.ICO`, for example. If you can't find an icon you like, you can create a new one using an image editor such as the Watcom Image Editor.

> *Remember that you will have to include the full path name to the icon in the resource file as we discussed in the last chapter.*

The icon you specify is used at run-time, so if you click on the Run button and then minimize your application, you'll see the icon. If you minimize the application at development time your icon is not used - PowerBuilder uses its generic application object icon.

At the moment, you can't run the Stock Control application for two main reasons:

▲ To run an application, you must provide it with some script associated with its open event to tell PowerBuilder what needs to be calculated and what needs to be displayed to get the application moving.

▲ So far, we haven't added anything to the application, so we can't refer to anything in that opening script.

This is one of the circumstances in which our specialized application that displays the Wrox Press logo comes into its own - being a fully functional application means that you can see the results of adding an icon to your application object.

Open up the application, select the Edit/Application Icon... and you'll be able to see the icon that we have associated with it. Try running the application and *Alt+Tab* around your other running programs - the icon will be displayed with the title of the currently open window. If you minimize all your applications, you will also be able to see the icon at work at the bottom of the screen.

> *The icon that you specify for your application object is also used by Windows if you create a Program Item for your application.*

Specifying Default Fonts

In order to save on development time (and costs!), PowerBuilder allows you to set a variety of defaults. These defaults are applied to any objects that you create for this application and apply to:

▲ Font types for text, data, headings and labels

▲ Point sizes for text, data, headings and labels

▲ Ink used for the text

▲ Background colors

You can modify these defaults at any time, without affecting any objects that have already been created; in other words, if you use the defaults to paint one window, then you change them to paint another window, the first window's fonts and colors won't change to the new defaults.

To set the application defaults to your own custom settings, click on the Fonts icon:

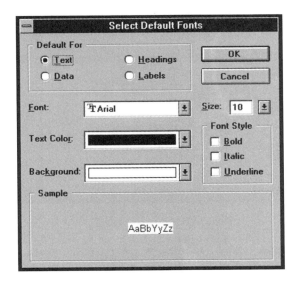

This dialog box allows you to set any of the defaults simply by selecting which type you wish to modify, either Text, Data, Headings or Labels, and by choosing your own personal settings from those available in the drop-down lists.

The Sample box shows what the defaults will look like if you accept the current choice.

Specifying the Library List

Although an application is created in a library, it is possible to refer to objects in other libraries. By default, PowerBuilder will search for objects in the application's library, so when you want to refer to objects in other libraries, you have to specify which libraries PowerBuilder should also search.

To specify the other libraries for an object search, click on the Library List icon to bring up the Select Libraries dialog box:

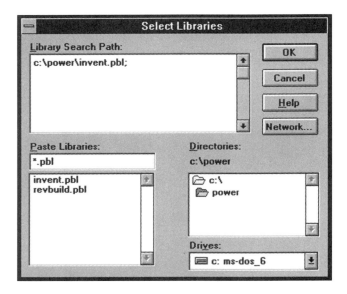

To add a library name to the Library Search Path, double-click on the library name in the Paste Libraries box; to remove a library name from the library list, highlight the library name in the Library Search Path and press the *Delete* key.

The Network... button allows you access to your network administrator. For example, if you are running on a NetWare based system, selecting this option would deliver to the usual screen:

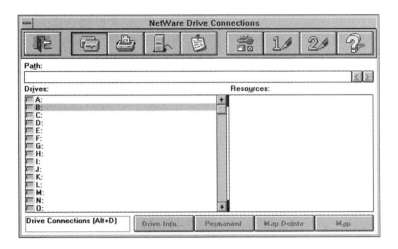

This button allows you to check and develop your network connection, assign printers to your station, observe the users that are currently logged onto the system and much more.

Clicking the OK button confirms the library search path definition and returns to the application painter.

For a working example of how the library list is used, take a look at the one associated with our logo application:

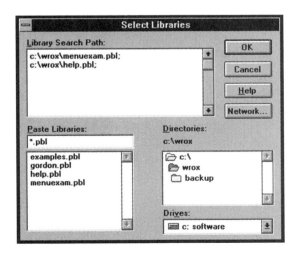

As you can see, this application uses two libraries, **MENUEXAM.PBL** and **HELP.PBL**. The main library where most of the application's objects and functionality is stored always appears first on the list and is the library containing the application object - in our case, this library is called **MENUEXAM.PBL**.

Any other libraries are used to hold generic application development objects. The other library on the list, **HELP.PBL**, contains two windows that are being used as the generic entries for any help that we add to any of our applications.

> Two points of interest surround an application's library list. The first is the order that PowerBuilder searches for the required object. It looks in the first library in the list, and then moves to the next if the search is unsuccessful and so on down the list.
>
> Due to this search pattern, if you wish to optimize your application, make sure that the libraries with the greatest number of regularly referenced objects appear closer to the top of the list than those that contain less used objects.
>
> One consequence of this search order is the reason behind the second point of interest. If you have two different objects with the same name (clearly, they must be held in the two different libraries), PowerBuilder will always use the one found in the library closest to the head of the application's library list. The other object will never be referenced.

Creating an Executable

When you want to deliver an application to an end user, you have to create a DLL, a resource file (if necessary) and an executable file. We've already looked at creating a DLL and resource file in the previous chapter, but to create an executable, click on the Create Executable icon:

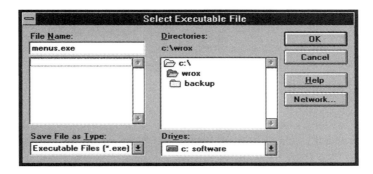

By default, PowerBuilder takes the first 8 characters of the application name to build the executable filename. You can change this name as you wish, but when you click the OK button, you'll be asked to specify the name of the appropriate resource file:

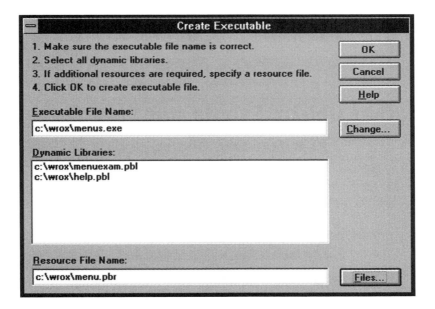

You can't edit the list of libraries in the Dynamic Libraries box because PowerBuilder automatically defines this list from your application's library list. If you misspell the name of the resource file, you won't get an error now, so you should always use the Files... button to bring up the standard file select dialog box, rather than typing in the filename.

When you click on the OK button, PowerBuilder will create an executable, providing there are no compile errors. You can run the application from the File Manager or create a Program Item in Program Manager with the name of the `.EXE` file as the command line.

> You can try to create this executable using the resource file that we have supplied on the CD-ROM, based around this logo application. Rename the executable because we have already created `MENUS.EXE` for you.

If you try running our application, nothing will happen as PowerBuilder doesn't know what to do now. To inform PowerBuilder of the steps you would like to take when a user attempts to run the executable, we must provide a script, the subject of the next section.

Application Object Events and Scripts

There are four events that are connected with an application object. Before you can run an application, you have to write scripts for at least one of these events - Open. If you let PowerBuilder create a template for your application, some of the scripts will be written automatically, in particular the opening script, and you will be able to run the application.

To write a script for one of the application object events, click on the Script icon:

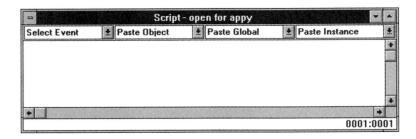

Selecting this icon opens PowerBuilder's script editor, allowing you to type in code for any of the available events. The four events that can be associated with an application object are:

- Open
- Close
- Idle
- System Error

The Open Event

The **Open** event occurs when the user runs the application. Some typical actions you would code into the **Open** event are initializing the application, connecting to databases, invoking log-in screens and displaying the main window and menu.

This event is essentially designed to fire off all of the preparatory work that your application requires to function correctly, including provisions for the unknowledgeable user.

Again, if you return to our example logo application, you can see that we have used the **Open** event to begin our application with the window called w_intro. This window is opened to let the user know that the application has started and to give the user something to react to:

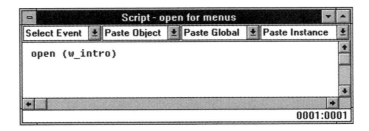

In this case, it just presents the user with an opening screen and calls the appropriate menu to allow the practical demonstration to initialize. However, with a live application, you might use this to inform your users of events, initialize global variables or any of the other tasks that you need to accomplish before the user begins work with the application:

```
=                    Script - open for exampl40                  ▼ ▲
Select Event        ± Paste Object    ± Paste Global    ± Paste Instance    ±
|
 // Open script for code examples application

 string first_time, showtext
 environment  le_environment

 // If it's the first time the application is being run, prompt the
 // user for database connection information. In any case, set all the
 // SQLCA variables from the example.ini file.
 first_time = ProfileString("example.ini","sqlca","firsttime","")

 open(w_main_backdrop)
 if Upper(first_time) = "YES" then
     SetProfileString ("example.ini","sqlca","firsttime","no")
     Open (w_set_sqlca)
     if message.doubleparm = -1 then
        halt close
        return
     end if
 else

     SetPointer (HourGlass!)
```

`0001:0001`

This is the opening script for the example application that ships with
PowerBuilder. You may find it useful to take a look at some of the example
scripts that are provided with the other example applications. Don't worry about
the syntax of the script, we'll cover that in Chapter 9 on PowerScript -
concentrate more on the comments to see what is possible, rather than how it is
performed.

The Close Event

The **Close** event occurs when the user closes the application. Usually, the script
for the **Close** event takes care of disconnecting from the database, any log
writing procedures and saving previous session preferences.

Again, this event is designed to clean up any loose ends that remain, a tidying
up process that allows the application to close down without causing any
problems.

Our logo application uses an API call to generate the playback of a .WAV file. Again, don't worry about how this works at the moment, we'll cover it later:

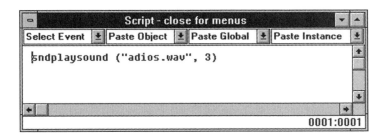

If you can't stop yourself, take a look at the Declare/Global External Functions... that are defined for this application to get an idea of what our function definition looks like for the .WAV playback functionality.

The Idle Event

The Idle event occurs when a specified time has elapsed after the **Idle function** has been called and no mouse or keyboard activity has been registered.

One example of where this function could be used is when it is necessary to disconnect the application from the back-end database after the user has finished accessing the available information. The function is called when the user connects and when the user leaves with their desire for information satisfied, no user activity is registered and the idle event causes the disconnection.

This could be motivated by a need to restrict active access to an overloaded database or to remove data from an unattended screen for reasons of security.

System Error Event

This event is triggered if an error occurs in the application. It is typically used to offer the user the options of logging or printing the error, closing the application or continuing with the execution of the application. If you don't write any script for this event, by default, PowerBuilder will display the error and the application will terminate.

Note that if the error is a system-level General Protection Fault (GPF), you wouldn't be able to continue with the execution of the application.

Setting Default Global Variables

Global variables are used in conjunction with global objects to give you more freedom to achieve the results that you require. PowerBuilder allows you to customize the standard objects that are on offer to you as a developer, to create new specialized objects to handle the tasks that are specific to your application.

The subject of declaring new global variables, their use and their interaction with customized objects is complex and is covered in more detail in Chapter 9. For now, let's leave the subject with a look at the global variable values that PowerBuilder defaults to and how to get a look at them.

By selecting Edit/Default Global Variables..., PowerBuilder provides you with access to this dialog, offering the opportunity to review and modify these default values:

We'll look into what these variables are used for later on.

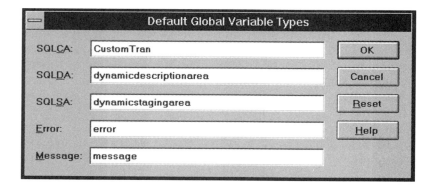

Application Painter Preferences

The Application Painter has three preferences that define the manner in which the tool operates, all of which you can modify using either the Preferences painter or by directly editing the **PB.INI** file. Click on the Preferences icon to bring up the Preferences dialog box:

There are four different types of preference that you can alter, including:

- DefLib
- AppLib
- AppName
- All the possible members of an application's library list

DefLib

This is the name of the default library that PowerBuilder uses to store any objects that you create.

AppLib

This is the name of the default library that PowerBuilder uses to store the current application object.

AppName

This is the name of the application which PowerBuilder will invoke by default when it is opened.

Library List

The preferences also display a list of all the available libraries that an application can refer to. If you scroll down the list, you'll see all the example libraries that ship with PowerBuilder and, tagged onto the bottom of that list, you'll find any new libraries that you've created.

Summary

We've now looked at most of the initial steps in developing an application. We've created a library to contain our application, created the application object itself and we've also specified some defaults that will be used throughout the application.

We've seen how to create an executable of our application so that we can distribute it to the end users and we've also seen how to define an icon for our application.

Over the next few chapters, we'll look at the details behind putting an application together, following the development guidelines that we've already laid down, concentrating on each of the important objects that go forward to make a professional PowerBuilder application.

Menu Painter

The common look and feel of any software package from one of the big software companies means that anyone who has used a Windows application will be familiar with the File and Edit menus and with the various options that they'll be able to find under these menus.

PowerBuilder offers you the ability to add your own custom menus to your application and, in this chapter, we'll see how you can create menus to emulate these 'default' menu styles, while retaining control over what the user can and can't do. To illustrate the techniques that you can use to create these menus, we'll construct the various menus that we use in our example application and we'll also look at some of the other options available in the Menu Painter.

In this chapter, we will cover:

- The various types of menu
- Creating menus
- Specifying accelerator and shortcut keys
- Menu preferences
- Menu design guidelines

Types of Menus

You can create three different types of menus in PowerBuilder:

- DropDown menus
- Cascading menus
- Popup menus

DropDown and Cascading menus can be attached to windows in your application. To use Popup menus, you have to write script for an event, typically the right mouse button down event.

DropDown Menus

DropDown menus are displayed when you select an option from a menu bar along the top of a window. The available options are grouped into logical collections and the group names are displayed horizontally in the menu bar:

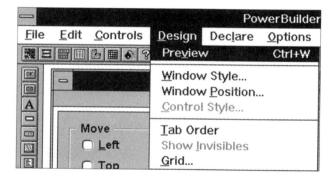

You can associate an icon to any of the options and add this icon to the toolbar, so giving your user another shortcut to get the required result, the shortcut key (e.g. *Ctrl+P* for the PowerPanel) being the other option. There are three standard formats used in DropDown menus:

Format	Meaning
Ellipses (...)	Selecting this option will bring up a response window to get more information.
Tick Mark (✓)	This option works in toggle mode, so selecting this menu entry either turns the feature on or off, the current state being denoted by a tick mark.
Right Arrow Head (▶)	Selecting this option will invoke a further cascading menu offering more choices.

Cascading Menus

A Cascading menu can display many more menu options than a menu item in the DropDown menu. In the following example, Show on Frame and Show on Painter are additional options available for the Text Style Toolbar menu option:

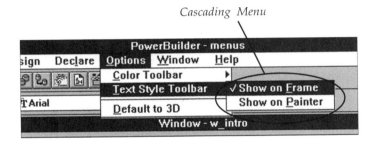

Cascading Menu

Clearly, these menus are usually used in conjunction with the DropDown type.

> *Notice the Default to 3D option that operates in toggle mode as we discussed in the last section.*

Popup Menus

A Popup menu is displayed in response to a specific event. Unlike DropDown menus, a Popup menu is not displayed in any fixed place, but pops up at the current mouse position. You can activate a Popup menu for any event, but the usual way of activating these menus is with the right mouse button:

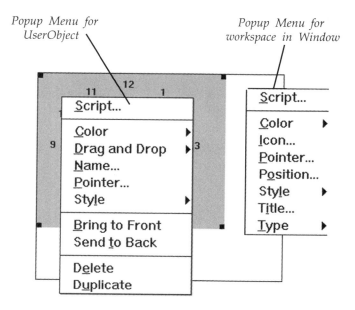

Popup Menu for UserObject

Popup Menu for workspace in Window

As you can see, Popup menus use the same ellipses, right arrow head and tick mark conventions as DropDown and Cascading menus. However, Popup menus are more versatile than the other types of menu as they don't have to be associated with a particular window and can offer different options depending on the object that the pointer is over at the time the right mouse button is clicked.

Creating Popup menus is no different from creating other menus, but the increased functionality does mean that you have to write some script.

The Menu PainterBar

Just as with the other painter, the Menu Painter can be controlled using a PainterBar. All of the functions that the painter has to offer can be called upon using this toolbar:

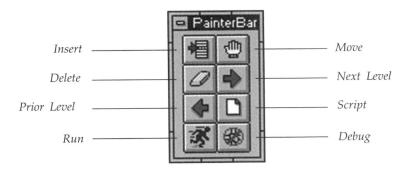

Insert ———————— Move

Delete ———————— Next Level

Prior Level ———————— Script

Run ———————— Debug

Looking at an Example Menu

When you invoke the Menu Painter from the PowerBar, the Select Menu dialog box prompts you for the pre-defined menu that you wish to open. If the menu that you require is not available, you can create it by selecting the New button:

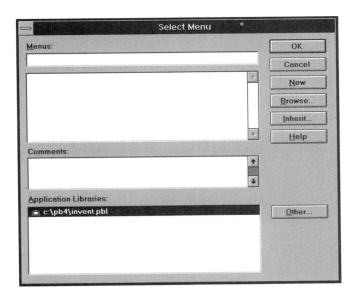

Before we create the menus for our application, it is useful to look at an example of a fully working menu. By coincidence, our logo application has such a menu and is therefore the natural choice. Click on the Other... button and select the **MENUEXAM.PBL** library, which should be in the **C:\WROX** directory if you accepted the defaults during installation:

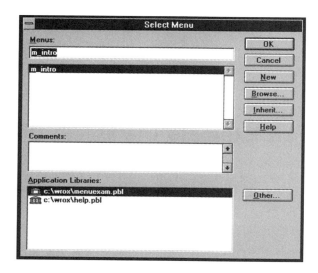

Select the m_intro menu and click on the OK button to bring up the painter:

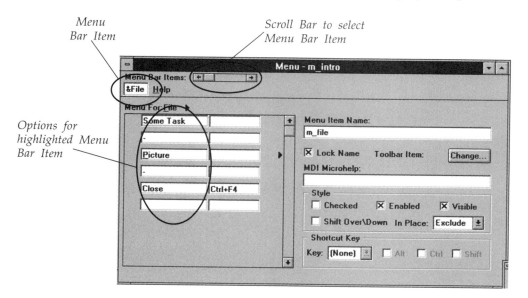

Menu Bar Item

Scroll Bar to select Menu Bar Item

Options for highlighted Menu Bar Item

As you can see, there are many different options that can be specified when painting a menu. Along the top of the window there is a list of the menu groups and down the left hand side the options for the highlighted group are displayed. You can see that the options for the File group are Some Task, Picture and Close.

> You might also notice a small right facing arrow at the end of the Picture entry. This denotes that a cascading menu has been designed for this entry. You can take a look at the menu in the same way that you would create it - double click on the arrow.

To see the options for the other groups, you can click on the group you want to inspect or you can use the scroll bar to move the focus between the groups.

> You can also use the scroll bar to return you to the top of a cascading menu when you have finished reviewing or modifying the entries.

Menu Item Name

This is the name that PowerBuilder uses to reference the menu groups. PowerBuilder automatically creates the menu item name as you type in the name of the menu group and adds the prefix **m_**.

You'll see how this works later in the chapter when we paint the menus for our example application.

You can call your menu groups whatever you like as there is no restriction on the type of characters you can use, but you are restricted to 64 characters. Obviously, you want your menu bars to look neat, so in practice you wouldn't want to make the text that long.

> When PowerBuilder creates the menu item names it strips out any spaces that you have included and limits the length of the name to 40 characters.

Locking an Item Name

By default, PowerBuilder locks a menu item name when you go to the next item:

When a menu item name is locked, even if you go back and change the item text, it doesn't change the menu item name. To change the name, you have to de-select the check box. The benefit of locking a menu item name is that any references to the menu item in your application are still valid even if you change the text of the menu item.

Assigning an Icon to the Menu Item

Each menu option that you install upon your custom menu bar can also appear on a toolbar. To enable this feature, you must provide PowerBuilder with a representative icon and some text to display as tooltips. To assign an icon to a menu item, click on the Change... button:

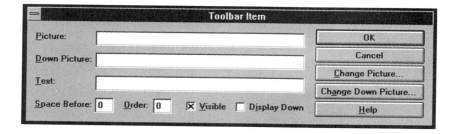

In this dialog, PowerBuilder allows you to specify two pictures for each menu item, one to represent the menu item on the toolbar and another one, the Down Picture, to represent the menu item when it is selected. You specify the picture by clicking on the Change Picture... or Change Down Picture... buttons:

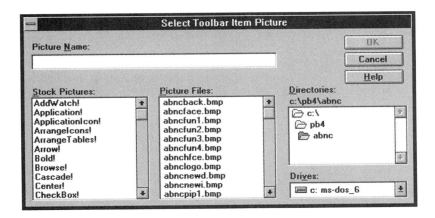

PowerBuilder ships with several Stock Pictures and there are also various Picture Files which are used in the example applications. If you create your own icons, you should ensure that they are 16x16 or 32x32 pixels so that they are displayed properly as icons.

> *Remember, as before, if you specify icons other than the stock pictures that ship with PowerBuilder, you will have to include a reference to the file in the resource file for the application.*

If you supply any text, this will be displayed under the icon in the toolbar if the 'ShowText' option is turned on. This option is set from Window/Toolbars... where you can click on the appropriate toolbar and select or deselect ShowText.

In our logo example, we have added two icons to represent the changing state of the logo; one is to make the logo visible, while the other reverses that action. We have used Custom010!, a small video camera, for the visible action and Custom009!, a cross mark, for the invisible action:

The selection of the icons can be crucial, as the user should be able to identify the action that the icon represents by the picture displayed upon it.

> *These icons short-circuit the cascading menu. Most users are more at home using the cascading menus when they first approach an application, but will soon be singing your praises if you provide such icons.*

We have also added some text to the icons to illustrate the functionality that they hold, enabling the user to quickly reassure themselves if they don't immediately understand the pictures.

Specifying Microhelp

If you are using MDI windows in your application, then you can specify help text that will be displayed in the status bar at the bottom of your windows by filling in this window with an appropriate phrase:

You can enter text for each menu item in a menu bar and it will be displayed when the menu item is selected. In our logo application, we have assigned microhelp to all the entries in the menu:

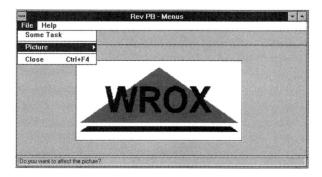

The advantage that Microhelp has over the PowerTips that you can specify for your custom icons is that it appears in the status bar no matter how you attempt to invoke the functionality to which it is attached. The PowerTips are restricted to only appearing when the mouse comes to rest over the appropriate icon.

Assigning an Accelerator Key

An accelerator key is the underlined letter in the text of a menu item or window object. The user can access the menu items or objects using the keyboard by pressing the specified key, instead of using the mouse. A well designed application should make use of this feature - offering full keyboard compatibility is a must for all professional applications.

The ampersand character (&) is placed in front of the letter to be used as the accelerator key. For example, if you look at the m_intro menu, you can see that the accelerator key for the Eile menu bar item is F:

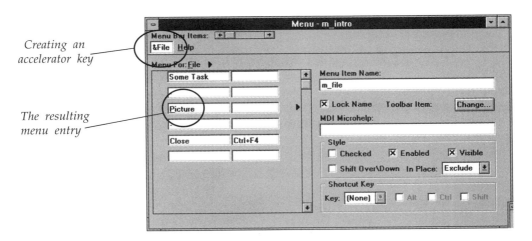

Creating an accelerator key

The resulting menu entry

Note that to select a menu bar item you must press the *Alt* key along with the specific letter. However, when a menu is open, you only have to press the specified letter to request the required option.

Assigning a Shortcut Key

A shortcut key is a single key or a combination of keys that can be used to select a menu item directly, without having to first open the relevant menu. If you look at the Close option on the File menu item, you can see that *Ctrl+F4* has been added as a shortcut key:

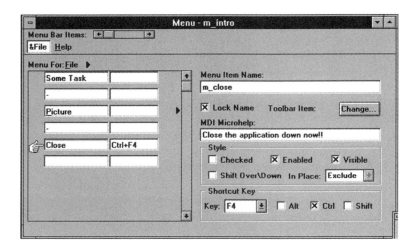

The full list of available shortcut keys includes all the function keys, letters of the alphabet and the specialized *Ins* and *Del* keys, and they can also be used in conjunction with any combination of the *Alt*, *Ctrl* and *Shift* keys.

> *Note that for the highlighted menu item, the selected shortcut key is displayed in the box next to the menu item text.*

Painting a Separator Line

You can divide a menu group into logical sections by using separator lines. For example, under a File menu bar item, you can group all the print options together, all the save options together and so on. In the m_intro menu, you can see that the File menu group uses two separator lines:

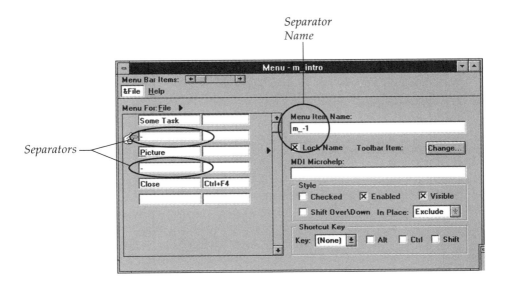

To specify a separator line, you simply supply a hyphen as the menu item text. PowerBuilder will automatically give the separator line a name, like any other menu item, with an identification number.

> *This number is calculated based on the number of separator lines you've specified in the menu up to that point.*

Adding Script to a Menu Option

For any of the menu options, you can write script that will be executed when the menu option is selected. You do this by clicking on the Script icon from the PainterBar. For example, if you highlight the Picture/Visible option in the above menu and click on the script icon, the following script window will open:

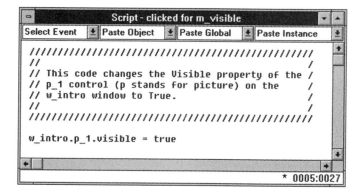

```
┌─────────────────────────────────────────────────────┐
│ ═     Script - clicked for m_visible        ▼  ▲ │
├────────────┬────────────┬────────────┬─────────────┤
│Select Event ±│Paste Object ±│Paste Global ±│Paste Instance ±│
├─────────────────────────────────────────────────────┤
│ ///////////////////////////////////////////////  ▲│
│ //                                             /   │
│ // This code changes the Visible property of the / │
│ // p_1 control (p stands for picture) on the     / │
│ // w_intro window to True.                       / │
│ //                                             /   │
│ ///////////////////////////////////////////////  │
│                                                    │
│ w_intro.p_1.visible = true                      ▼│
├─────────────────────────────────────────────────────┤
│ ←                                              → │
├─────────────────────────────────────────────────────┤
│                                    * 0005:0027 │
└─────────────────────────────────────────────────────┘
```

As you can see, this script is associated with the click event for the m_visible menu item and it is used to change the p_1 control on the w_intro window visible property to true.

> When you print out the script, you also get a header describing the event that the script is associated with and, perhaps more importantly, the menu object that contains the menu item that the script is related to.
>
> Due to this feature, it is a good idea to fully comment your code with a 'path' to the script, i.e. the menu object, the menu bar item, the menu item and the event that it is associated with - organizing your code in this manner will pay dividends in the future!

Creating Menus for Our Application

For our Stock Control application, we need several different menus to offer increased functionality to our users. One of the advantages that PowerBuilder offers to the developer is the two stage menu creation process. This split process allows us to paint the menus now and add the actual functionality through scripts in a later chapter.

These menus can be found in the invent1 application in the **INVENT1.PBL** *library on the accompanying CD-ROM, but it is a good idea to paint them from scratch yourself.*

Main Menu

The main menu that dominates our sample application is called m_main_menu and it contains the following options:

File	Edit	Module	Window	Help
Close	New	Item Master	Tile	Help
Save	Delete	Transactions	Tile Horizontal	About
Save As		Item Images	Layer	
Query		Consumption Report	Cascade	
Retrieve		Current Stock Report	Toolbar	
Sort		Month Beginning Stock Report		
Filter		Custom Report		
Printer Setup				
Print Preview				
Print				
Exit				

Open the menu painter and begin the process of painting your first menu. The following screenshots show what the two main options, File and Module, should look like while you are painting them.

The File Option

This contains all the usual File menu options that you would expect in a Window's application, as well as some of our own:

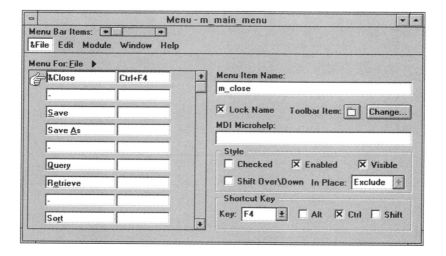

If you scroll down the list, you'll see the other options that we have on offer. The final option, E*x*it, has the *Alt+F4* shortcut assigned to it.

The Module Option

This menu contains most of the options that are relevant to our application, including requests to display the various reports that we will be designing:

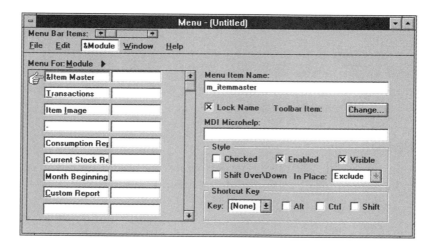

Note that none of the available options have been assigned any shortcut keys.

The other menu options for the main menu are painted in a similar way. If you wish to see how they are put together, have a look at the other menus that invent1 has to offer.

Previewing a Menu

When you have finished painting your menu you can check that the structure is correct by reviewing the menu in a simulated run-time condition by using the Design/Preview option. It should look something like this:

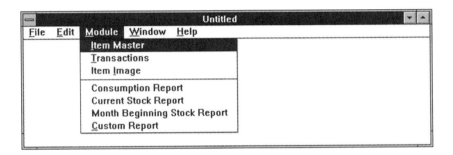

We've only shown the Module options here, but you can click on any of the menu options and the resulting DropDown menu should contain the relevant options. None of the options will do anything as yet because we haven't written a script for each of the individual events. Save this menu as an m_main_menu and we'll move on to the other menus.

Popup Menus

As an extension to the menu functionality we have explored up to now, we also need to add two Popup menus to our application. The actual process of painting a Popup menu is no different from that of other menu types, so we won't go through the whole process again. Here's what the final menus should look like:

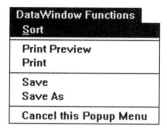

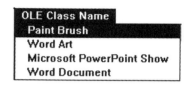

Save the left one as m_dw_func and the right one as m_oleclass. The real power behind Popup menus is the added scripting which gives the menus that extra flexibility, so improving their usefulness.

> *The point that we are trying to make here is that even though Popup menus seem to be different from those found on the menu bar, when it comes to creating them, they are virtually identical until you start coding.*

Creating Toolbars for Your Application

Now that we have painted all the menus which will allow the user access to the application's functionality, let's look at how to create a toolbar to short-circuit them. Each of the icons that we add to the toolbar will reflect the actions that are activated by one or more selections from the menus.

For our example application, we are going to create the following toolbar:

To simplify the creation process, we have used some of the stock bitmaps that have been shipped with PowerBuilder, but you can design your own images with any drawing package that supports the **.BMP** file format.

The following table shows which options these represent, in order, from left to right:

Menu Option	Bitmap File
File/Close	Custom039!
File/Save	Update!
File/Save As	Custom008!
File/Query	Query!
File/Retrieve	Retrieve!
File/Sort	Sort!
File/Print	Print!
File/Exit	Exit!
Edit/New	Insert!
Edit/Delete	Custom094!
Window/Tile	Horizontal!
Window/Layer	Layer!
Window/Cascade	Cascade!

To create this toolbar, open up the m_main_menu again, go to each of the above menu options and click on the Change... button:

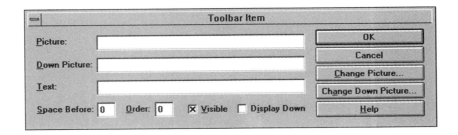

Click on the Change Picture... button and select the appropriate icon from the set of stock bitmaps:

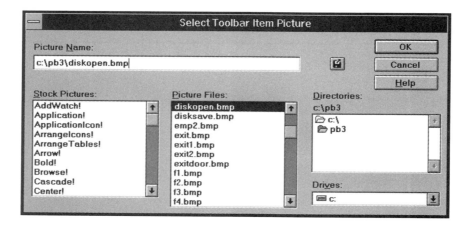

The icon you've selected will be displayed at the end of the Picture Name control for you to review. When you have decided upon an appropriate icon, click the OK button and that icon will be associated with that menu option. When you have done this for all the menu options, you can preview the menu again to see the toolbar:

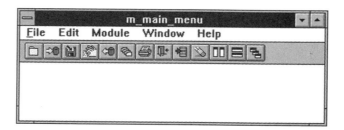

As you can see, the creation of the menus and toolbars that you need to add to your application is very easy to accomplish. However, as you'll notice in the Preview of the menu, selecting any of the menu items doesn't produce any visual effects. This is because all we have done is draw the elements on screen - we haven't assigned any PowerScript to the menus or the toolbar icons and as this is the engine behind the controls, the application won't respond to your requests.

Menu Painter Preferences

The Menu Painter has only one preference variable associated with it - the menu name prefix. The text that is shown here will automatically be added, as a prefix, to any menu bar items and menu items that you create:

The prefix can be comprised of up to sixteen characters.

Menu Guidelines

Now we have seen the mechanics behind the menu creation process, let's look at some of the implications of using custom menus in your application. You should be aware of these implications because, as opposed to adding more functionality, you might be adding holes to your application if you don't take them into account.

The following list documents some of the important points concerning the creation of custom menus for your application:

▲ If the currently active sheet doesn't have its own menu, the menu and toolbar associated with the last active sheet remain in place and operative, while that sheet remains open. If the currently active sheet has a menu but no toolbar, the previous toolbar will still be displayed.

▲ Menu toolbars only work in MDI frame type windows and MDI sheet windows. If you open a non-MDI window with a menu that has a toolbar, the toolbar won't be shown.

▲ Menu toolbar buttons map directly to menu items, so clicking a menu toolbar button is exactly the same as clicking its corresponding menu item.

▲ Disabling a menu item will disable its toolbar button as well, but won't change the appearance of the button.

▲ Hiding a menu item doesn't cause DropDown or Cascading menu item toolbar buttons to disappear. However, it does disable them, with the accompanying graying out of the button.

▲ Hiding an item on a DropDown or Cascading menu doesn't cause its toolbar button to disappear or be disabled.

▲ A double toolbar effect can be achieved if you have a menu with a toolbar on both the frame and the sheet. You can assign these toolbars any way you like.

▲ Enabling and disabling a menu item or menu bar is less overhead to the system than Hiding/Showing. In the case of Hiding/Showing, PowerBuilder destroys the current menu and recreates the original toolbar, excluding the hidden item or menu bar item. So whenever possible, it is better to use the Enable/Disable options.

This method of altering the states of controls at run-time is dealt with, in more depth, in the chapter on PowerScript.

▲ Menu item names are unique throughout a menu and if you use the same text for different menu options, you will get an error message.

Summary

We've seen the differences between the various menus that you can use in PowerBuilder and we've created some of the menus that we need for our Stock Control application.

We're starting to get into the nitty-gritty of creating an application and in the next chapter, we'll move on to creating some windows to which we can then attach our menus.

Window Painter

No matter what kind of application you have used, it is the user interface that has been your best friend. Without this cohort, you would have been powerless to interact with the software, whether it be to apply formatting to a document, calculate your tax return or interrogate the information in your local database.

To address this basic requirement, PowerBuilder provides you with an object that operates in the customary manner to display information or accept it from the user and, in combination with others of its own type, to be used to guide the user through the task that they wish to complete.

The object that PowerBuilder provides is called a **Window** and the basic building blocks of the user interface are designed, maintained and customized using the Window Painter.

In this chapter, we will cover:

- Types of window
- Window controls
- Placing controls on a window
- Window properties
- Window preferences

Windows: PowerBuilder Objects

The whole subject of producing a professional and friendly user interface is based around the PowerBuilder window object. However, there are several different ideas that must be introduced when you start to look more deeply into the task, including the notions of controls, events and the fundamentals of the window itself.

Before we can move on to these concepts, let's take a look at the window itself and the different types of window that are available to you, the PowerBuilder developer.

Types of Window

There are six basic types of window available in PowerBuilder. They are all created in the same way, but each has a specific task for which it should be used. You don't have to specify the type of window before you create the window, but it is useful to look at the different types before we start, so that you have an idea of what is possible.

Main Window

A **Main Window** is a stand-alone window, which acts independently of all others. This type of window can be minimized, maximized and resized; it can also overlap and be overlapped by other windows. It is usually used as the opening screen that your application presents, but can also be used as a sheet in an MDI application.

> *Sheets are basic child windows; they only exist inside a parent window. This has no great functionality by itself, but as they tend to appear in packs, roaming around MDI applications, they can be used to present a professional overall effect.*

Popup Window

A **Popup Window** is typically opened from another window, which is then said to be the Popup window's parent:

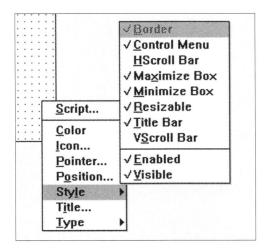

The Popup window is dependent on its parent window, but it can be displayed without opening the parent window. Parent windows will not overlap a Popup window, but if a parent is minimized, the Popup will be hidden.

> *You can create a Popup window that is not opened from another window, but it will generally behave like a main window.*

Response Window

A **Response Window** is the PowerBuilder equivalent of a Windows dialog box; it is used to accept responses from the user to a given question. A response window demands action from the user and once active remains active until the user has answered the demand.

> **If a window behaves in this manner, it is said to be modal.**

When a response window is opened, you can't move to another window in the application, nor can you resize, minimize or maximize it. You can switch to any other application that you have open under Windows, but when you return to the current application, the response window will still be active.

A typical example of where you might encounter this type of window is when you want to save a new document using your favorite wordprocessor. When you click on the save option, the wordprocessor can't save the file as the document is as yet untitled and therefore displays a 'Save As' window, asking for the required information:

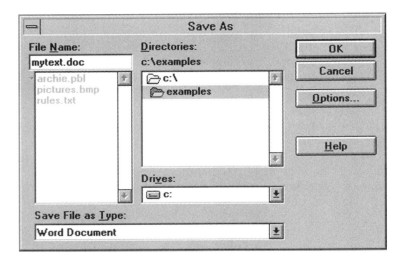

Until you answer this question, the wordprocessor will not allow you to continue with any work, unless you click on the Cancel button and throw away the whole idea of saving the document.

Child Window

In the same way as Popup windows, a **Child Window** can only be opened from another window, which then becomes its parent. If you try to move a child window outside of its parent, only the part of the child that remains inside the parent is displayed. On the other hand, if you move the parent, the child window will maintain its relative position within the parent:

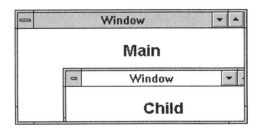

You can't associate a menu with a child window, but it can still have a title bar. When you minimize a child window, the minimized icon is displayed at the bottom of the parent window and when it is maximized, it occupies the entire parent window. A child window is never considered as an active window, so when you close the parent window, any children that are related to it are also closed automatically.

MDI Frame Window

An **MDI Frame Window** allows you to open multiple windows as sheets inside it. To open a window as a sheet in an MDI Frame window, you use the **OpenSheet()** function instead of the usual **Open()**:

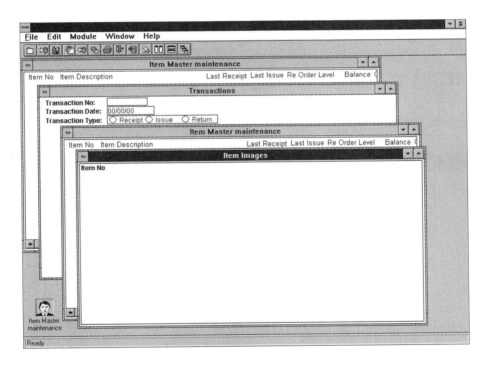

> The Child Window technology is a hang-over from previous versions of PowerBuilder. MDI Frame Windows are their replacement, including added window management functionality. The current version of PowerBuilder includes both as a compromise between backwards compatibiliiy and progressive programming.

When a window (sheet) inside the MDI Frame window minimizes, the minimized sheet icon is displayed at the bottom of the MDI Frame window.

> *An in-depth discussion of MDI Frame windows and their properties can be found in Chapter 13.*

MDI Frame with Microhelp

This window is exactly like an MDI Frame except that it has the additional feature of a status bar at the bottom of the window. This status bar is used to display context-sensitive help as well as the current time.

The PowerBuilder opening window is a good example of this type of window. When you move the mouse over the toolbar icons, Microhelp is displayed on the status bar giving you an idea of what the icon is used for.

Creating a Window

To create a new window, click on the Window icon from the PowerBar and select the New button in the Select Window dialog box:

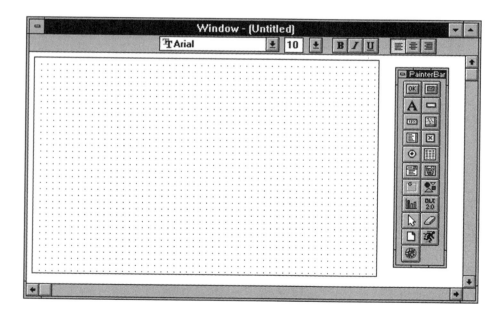

The dotted rectangle is your workspace and you can resize it as required. To paint a window, you add controls to the workspace and write scripts as responses to window and control events.

> *By resizing this window's workspace, not only are you defining your design area, but you are also defining the size of the window when the application is run. Clearly, if you have enabled the Maximize, Minimize and Resizable properties of the window, you will be able to alter this sizing at run-time, but when the window is initially opened, it will be displayed at these proportions.*

In the rest of this chapter, we'll concentrate on the first of these steps and look at all the various controls that can be placed on a window. Programming for the window and control events is covered in a later chapter.

Using Window Controls

PowerBuilder provides a wide selection of controls that you can place on your windows. All of these controls, once placed on a window, can be resized and customized and PowerBuilder also allows you to design your own user-defined controls, if you need to perform a specialized task.

To see the full list of available controls, select the Controls menu:

Controls	
CommandButton	Picture
PictureButton	GroupBox
StaticText	UserObject...
SingleLineEdit	Graph
EditMask	Line
MultiLineEdit	Oval
ListBox	Rectangle
CheckBox	RoundRectangle
RadioButton	HScrollBar
DataWindow	VScrollBar
DropDownListBox	OLE 2.0

To add a control to a window, simply select the control from this menu and click on the workspace at the position that you want the control to appear.

139

The Window PainterBar

As with most of the other painters, PowerBuilder provides you with a Window PainterBar with which you can quickly select the controls that you want on your window:

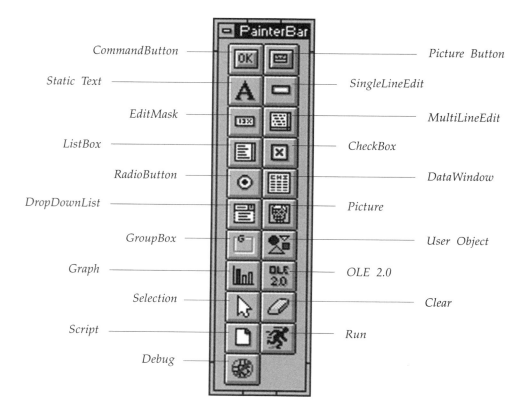

Naming Controls

When you place controls on a window, PowerBuilder automatically names them using standard prefixes and a number to uniquely identify them. The full list of controls and naming prefixes is as follows:

Control	Naming Prefix
CommandButton	cb_
PictureButton	pb_
StaticText	st_
SingleLineEdit	sle_
EditMask	em_
MultiLineEdit	mle_
ListBox	lb_
CheckBox	cb_
RadioButton	rb_
DataWindow	dw_
DropDownListBox	ddlb_
Picture	p_
GroupBox	gb_
Graph	gr_
Line	ln_
Oval	oval_
Rectangle	r_
RoundRectangle	rr_
Horizontal ScrollBar	hsb_
Vertical ScrollBar	vsb_
OLE 2.0	ole_

You can rename any of the controls, but it's a good idea to keep the prefixes so that it is easy to identify any objects that appear in your scripts. These prefixes allow you to name collections of related objects of different types with the same title, without losing the uniqueness that PowerBuilder demands for object names.

As an example of this collective naming convention, suppose that you created a window and a menu that always appeared with that window, saving them as w_test1 and m_test1. The prefix denotes the type of object, but the common suffix indicates that these two objects are related. As you can see, this example can easily be extended to the objects that are placed upon a window.

Control Events

There are various events that can be associated with window controls, for example, a CommandButton has a **Click** event when a user clicks on the CommandButton. The following table summarizes some of the more common events

Events	Description
Clicked	This runs when the control is clicked.
Constructor	Runs immediately before the Open event occurs in the window.
Destructor	Runs immediately after the Close event occurs in the window.
DragDrop	Runs when a dragged control is dropped on the control.
DragEnter	Runs when a dragged control enters the control.
DragLeave	Runs when a dragged control leaves the control.
DragWithin	Runs when a dragged control is within the control.
GetFocus	Runs before the control receives focus.
LoseFocus	Runs when the control loses focus.
Other	Runs when a Windows message occurs that is not a PowerBuilder event.
RButtonDown	Runs when the right mouse button is pressed when on the control.

Every control has its own events peculiar to the way it functions. For example, a vertical scrollbar has line up and line down events when you click on the up and down arrows.

The Controls

In this section, we'll take a closer look at each of the controls that PowerBuilder has on offer. As we take a look at each different type of control, we'll also investigate what makes them useful and what special features they have on offer.

CommandButton

A **CommandButton** is used to allow the user to trigger an action. You'll probably be familiar with the OK and Cancel buttons used in standard Windows dialog boxes, allowing the user to take control of whether or not a task is completed.

PowerBuilder allows you to pass on this functionality to your users by providing CommandButtons that can be customized to emulate these buttons, while allowing you to modify the code behind each button to perform the options that you have on offer.

If you look at the w_controls window in the revpb_examples application (the application that holds all the examples in this chapter), you'll see that we've added a couple of CommandButtons to the window:

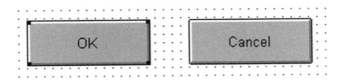

If you double-click on one of the CommandButtons, you'll be able to see the properties associated with that object:

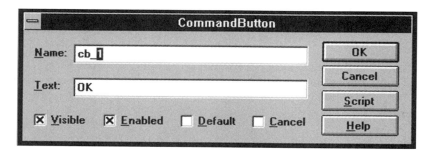

You can see that PowerBuilder has named the control cb_1 following its naming conventions. The Text field contains the lettering that you wish to appear on the button. As you can also see, we've deleted the default entry, i.e. none, and customized the look of the button with some more appropriate text.

Four other properties are displayed for type of control, which can either be selected or not, depending on whether you require them for this CommandButton:

Property	Description
Visible	When this property is selected, the CommandButton will be visible on the window. If a CommandButton is invisible, it can't be clicked on and therefore can't generate the associated Click event.
Enabled	When this option is selected, the CommandButton will be enabled. This means that it will respond to being clicked by generating the Click event. Any code that you've written for this control's Click event will then be executed.
Default	If this property is selected, the CommandButton can be operated by the *Enter* key as well as by being clicked. This is useful when you have two buttons in a dialog box, one of which is the usual response to the question - clearly, this option is generally used when the buttons are placed on a response window.

Continued

Property	Description
	If the user wants to accept the default response, rather than moving the mouse pointer over the button and clicking the left mouse button, they can now simply hit the *Enter* key.
	This option can be of particular use when you arrive at a mission-critical event such as overwriting a file. In this case, the pessimistic option would be to make the Cancel button into the default, so that user error will not cause permanent damage to the system.
Cancel	This is similar to the Default option, but instead of the *Enter* key, the *Esc* key is nominated as the activating key. Again, this can be seen in Windows applications, where the *Esc* key selects the Cancel option.

*If you choose to make the CommandButton invisible, the button disappears from the design workspace as well as the run-time window. If you wish to return the button to sight, select the control name from **Edit/Control List...**, choose the **Control Style** button and check the control's visible property.*

Due to this feature, it's a good idea to deselect a control's visible property nearer the completion of the window design, rather than at the beginning because, unfortunately, a combination of the Control List and a lot of mental energy is the only way of telling if you have any invisible controls on your window.

PictureButton

A **PictureButton** works exactly like a CommandButton, except that instead of displaying text on the face of the button, it allows you to display a bitmap, a Run Length Encoded file or Windows metafile picture on the button.

We've put a PictureButton on our example window:

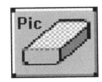

As with the CommandButton, if you double-click on the PictureButton, you'll see the properties associated with the button:

> *If you have not defined a file for the PictureButton to display when it is*
> *enabled, double-clicking on the control will take you directly to the dialog*
> *box to select this file, before taking you to the properties.*

PowerBuilder allows you to display different bitmaps when the PictureButton is either enabled or disabled. When you disable the PictureButton with some script, PowerBuilder automatically displays the picture you specified for the Disabled File.

> **Remember to add these filenames to the resource file, otherwise**
> **neither of the pictures will be displayed.**

PictureButtons have one more advantage over CommandButtons - the ability to display multiple lines of text on the button and to format them around the button as you require. You can set the alignment of the text by using the Horizontal Alignment and Vertical Alignment properties.

> **If you select the MultiLine option from the Vertical Alignment**
> **property and resize the PictureButton so that the text can't fit on**
> **one line, PowerBuilder will wrap it onto the next one. Generally,**
> **this will not happen and text will be lost as it paints off the end**
> **of the control.**

Checking the Original Size property changes the picture to its original dimensions, i.e. those dimensions that the picture was given when it was first created. Even if you check this option, you can still resize the control and the picture will stretch to fit the size of the button. If you do this and look at the properties of the button again, you'll see that PowerBuilder has unchecked the Original Size option.

StaticText

A **StaticText** control is used to display text. For instance, on our example window, a text control is being used to display the words Enter Item Number:

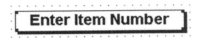

If you double-click on this control, you'll see its various properties:

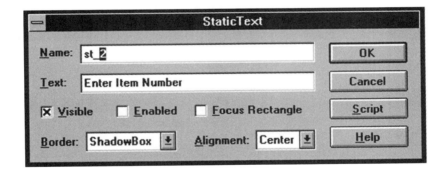

In this properties dialog, PowerBuilder allows you to change the border style of the control and the alignment of the text within it. With the Enabled and Focus Rectangle options, you can enable the StaticText control's events and allow the control to receive the focus if the user clicks upon it.

You can then write scripts for control events by clicking on the Script button. We'll only use StaticText controls to display text in this application, so we won't be writing any scripts for them.

SingleLineEdit

A **SingleLineEdit** control is a box that allows the user to input data. On our example window, we have a SingleLineEdit control beside our StaticText control so that we can allow the user to enter the Item Number:

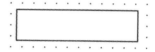

To see what this control will let you do, select Design/Preview and try typing something in the control:

The control should let you type in a maximum of five characters, each of which is displayed as an asterisk. You may think this looks familiar if you've ever had to log onto a password-protected system or application. Go back to design view and look at the control's properties:

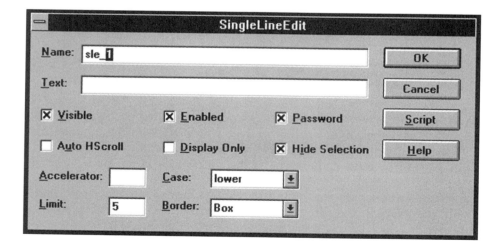

You can see that we've checked the <u>P</u>assword option, so that what you typed in isn't displayed and that we've set the <u>L</u>imit to 5 characters. The default limit is zero, which allows the maximum number of characters (or in other words, the string of characters that is as long as the width of the control) to be entered.

The Text Field

Any text that you type into this field will appear, by default, in the SingleLineEdit control, when the window is first opened.

The Hide Selection Option

By default, this option is selected. If you deselect it, when you highlight some text in the control and then move the focus to a different part of the window, the highlighted text will remain highlighted. This allows you to begin editing the text, move elsewhere to check on some other attribute, return and still be able to continue where you left off, without reselecting any text.

The Case Option

This option allows you to control the case of the text the user can enter. The user can enter text in either case, but if you specify UPPER or lower, the text will be displayed in that relevant case.

The Auto HScroll Option

The Auto HScroll option should be checked if there is a lot of text to be entered. With this option selected, the text will automatically scroll as the user enters it, until a pre defined limit is reached. This means that you don't have to use up lots of screen space with large SingleLineEdit boxes when you want the user to enter a lot of text.

> *When designing windows and sizing controls, you should also keep in mind the various size and type of fonts that may be used.*

The Display Only Option

If you select this option then the SingleLineEdit control will only be used to display data; it will not accept input from a user.

The Accelerator

This option allows you to associate a hot-key with the SingleLineEdit control, which causes the focus to jump to it when the accelerator is pressed at any time, apart from when you select the accelerator while entering text into another control.

EditMask

The **EditMask** control is similar to the SingleLineEdit control, but is used to accept input from the user, formatting it to a pre-defined mask as the user types. If the user tries to input information into this control that doesn't conform to the mask, PowerBuilder refuses to accept the keystrokes. There is an EditMask on our example window which is formatted to accept a date:

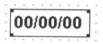

If you preview the window and try typing into the EditMask control, you'll find that it restricts you to typing a date in the month/day/year format:

```
02/23/95
```

Go back into design view and look at the properties for the EditMask:

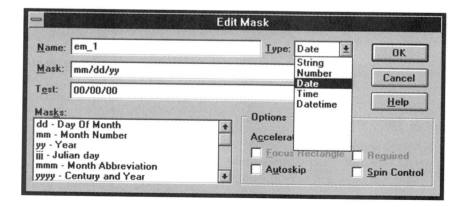

We've shown the drop-down list of available data types and for each of these there is a different set of masks available. For example, if you select the String data type, you can format the data in upper case (!), lower case (^), number (#) and alphanumeric (a) characters.

> Note that the formatting of data is only used for display purposes. PowerBuilder doesn't store text data in mixed case and in particular date type data is not stored in the format in which it is displayed. Dates are usually stored as a number representing the number of days from a fixed date. This allows PowerBuilder to easily swap between formats by simply applying the rules for the given format to this base number, rather than performing two conversions and remembering what format the date is currently stored in.
>
> For example, if the fixed date is 1st January 1994, then 3rd January 1994 would be stored as 2 and the 25th December 1993 would be stored as -7.
>
> The point is that it doesn't matter to us how PowerBuilder stores the date as long as we see it in a format that we understand and require.

You can build up your mask by double-clicking on selections from the list of available masks and you can test out the formatting by typing into the Test box.

The AutoSkip Option

If you check this option for an EditMask control, when the user has completely filled the mask with their input, the focus will automatically jump to the next control in the Tag List.

Spin Control

The Spin Control property is most often used with numeric data to allow the user to increase or decrease the value in the EditMask control by clicking on the arrows that appear at the end of the control. To see how this works change the data type to Number and select the Spin Control option:

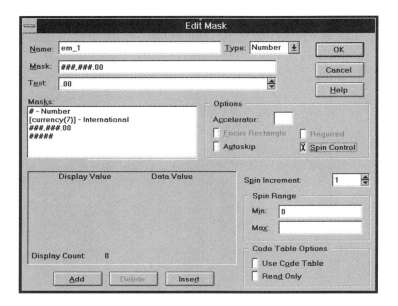

Enter a value in the T<u>e</u>st box and click on the up and down cursor keys. By default, the value in the T<u>e</u>st box will increase or decrease by one. You can specify the minimum and maximum values for the control and the size of the increment, which must be a whole number, by entering the relevant information in the appropriate fields that are now available.

> *You can also use the spin control option with date type fields. In this case, only one part of the date will increment or decrement depending on the cursor position.*

We've put a spin control EditMask on our example window to show you what it looks like. This has been set up to accept a three-digit number between 1 and 200 and to increment and decrement in steps of one. Preview the window and type a number into the EditMask control:

You won't be able to click on the arrows because you are only previewing the window and so the cursor changes as soon as you enter the control, but you can achieve the same effect by using the up and down cursor keys. When you use the control at run-time, the mouse pointer will work as you would expect.

If you type in a value which is outside the allowable range then, as soon as you try to increment or decrement it using the spin control, the value will change to the minimum or maximum value and won't allow you to move outside this range.

Code Tables

If you want to use spin controls with string-type data, you must provide a **Code Table**. We've included an example on our window, which allows you to select a state from three possibilities. Preview the window, click on this control and use the up and down cursor keys to go through the list of options:

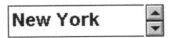

Now go back into design view and bring up the properties for the control:

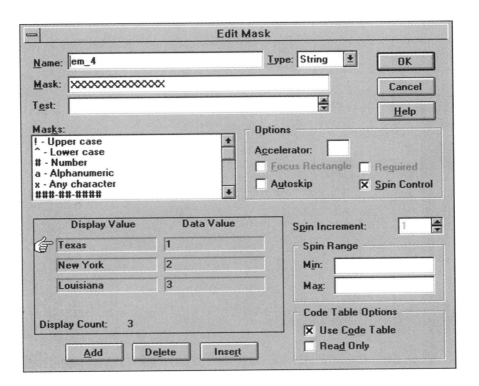

You can see that we've entered the names of three states that we want to be displayed and given each of them a data value. We only see the display value, but PowerBuilder saves the information using the smaller, more robust data value. If you don't supply a data value then PowerBuilder will automatically use the display value to save the information.

> *You could also use code tables with numeric or date values but we can't think of a good example of when you might want to do this. One of the beauties of PowerBuilder is freedom of choice.*

MultiLineEdit

A **MultiLineEdit** control is similar to the SingleLineEdit, but it lets you enter or display multiple lines of text. Our example has a vertical scrollbar which allows you to scroll down to see the rest of the text that we've entered:

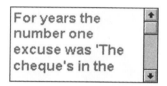

Looking at the properties for the control you can see that you can select horizontal and vertical autoscrolling, scrollbars, limit the number of characters and so on:

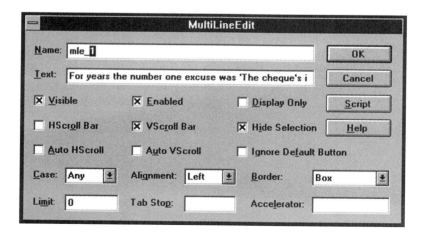

One important property is the Ignore Default Button option. If this is selected, then it will allow the user to hit the *Enter* key to start a new line of text without triggering any CommandButtons whose Default options have been set.

The Tab Stop property allows you to display text in a table format and will be covered in greater detail in the chapter on PowerScript.

ListBox

A **ListBox** control is used to display a list of options from which the user can select one or more options. Our example shows a list of states with a vertical scrollbar to scroll through the list:

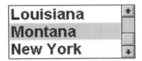

You select from the list by clicking on one of the states. By looking at the properties of the control, you can see that we've typed in the options that we want to be displayed in the Items box:

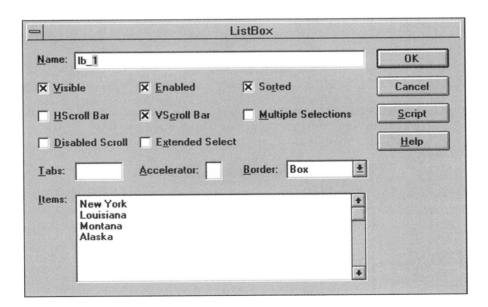

The list of options is in the order in which we typed them, but when you previewed the window, you may have noticed that the list was in alphabetical order, because we've checked the Sorted option.

> *Note that when you are typing in a list of options, to move on to the next line, you have to use* Ctrl+Enter *rather than just the* Enter *key.*

The Disabled Scroll option will automatically turn off the vertical scrollbar if there is enough room in the control for all the options.

Allowing Multiple Choices

There are two ways to allow a user to select more than one choice from a list. Checking the Multiple Selections option allows any number of options from the list to be selected by clicking on them. Clicking on a selected option will then deselect it.

You can also allow multiple selections using the standard Windows conventions of the *Ctrl* and *Shift* keys by enabling the Extended Select option.

CheckBox

A **CheckBox** is used to either select or deselect a given option. Our example might be used on an insurance questionnaire to determine whether or not the user is married:

If required, a CheckBox can also have a third state, that of undecided. This option is activated by checking the control's Three State property.

The default value of a CheckBox is unchecked, but you can change this by selecting the Checked or Third State options:

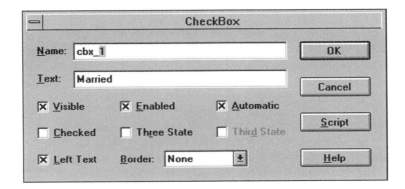

The Left Text option displays the text to the left of the CheckBox. Deselecting it reverses the order, placing the CheckBox on the left of the text.

RadioButton

A **RadioButton** is similar to a CheckBox, but whereas a number of CheckBoxes can be checked at once, in any given group of RadioButtons only one can be selected. This option makes sense, as in our example, because you can't be single and married at the same time!

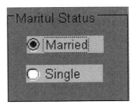

157

*If you select one RadioButton when another is selected, the first
RadioButton will be deselected before your button is activated.*

The properties for RadioButtons are similar to those for CheckBoxes.

If you want to put more than one group of RadioButtons on a window you
have to enclose them in a GroupBox, otherwise only one RadioButton on the
window can be selected at any one time.

GroupBox

The **GroupBox** control is used to group related objects together, but it is
generally used to group sets of related RadioButtons together. We have
enclosed our two sets of RadioButtons in GroupBoxes, so that you can select a
button from each group:

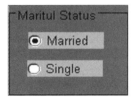 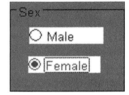

DropDownListBox

A **DropDownListBox** is used to display a list of available options when you
click on the down arrow at the side of the box. Again, this can be used to
save space on your window, as it only takes up the same amount of space as
a SingleLineEdit control, but allows you to select from a fixed range of
options. Our example is used to select from the same list of states as before:

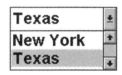

You can select the state by clicking on the one you want, or you can start to type and the list will scroll down to the first entry that starts with the letters you type in. This is an important feature as it allows you to put a great number of entries in a DropDownListBox, but still allows the user to quickly find the one they want.

If you look at the properties of our control, you'll see that the list of options is typed in like a standard ListBox:

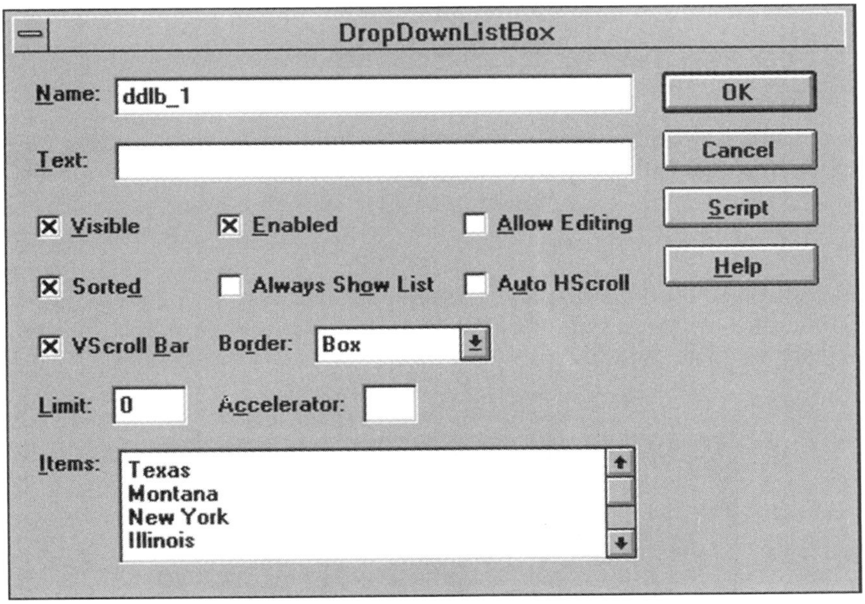

Again, you can choose to have the list Sorted and can enable or disable both the horizontal and vertical scrollbars. If you don't have a vertical scrollbar, you can still select from a long list using the cursor keys.

The Allow Editing option allows the user to type a new entry into the control. If Allow Editing is enabled and you supply some Text, then this is displayed in the control and becomes one of the selectable options. However, it is not permanently added to the list, which means that if you select another option from the list and then decide to change it back, you will have to type it in manually.

If you allow editing of a DropDownListBox, it will be displayed slightly differently with the down arrow detached from the actual box:

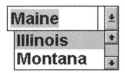

The Always Show List option means that the list of options will always be displayed, so the control effectively becomes a standard ListBox.

Picture

A **Picture** control is used to display a bitmap, Run Length Encoded file or Windows metafile on your window. We have an example of a Picture control on our w_controls_more window:

When you first place a Picture control on a window, you must specify the filename of the picture together with the format of the file that you want to use:

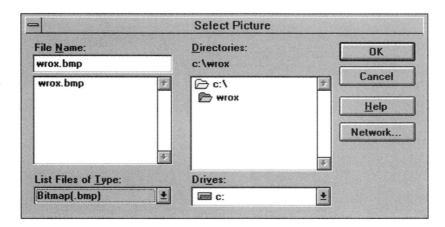

You can change the file at any time, by clicking on the Change... button in the control's properties.

You can specify a Border style, choose to have the image converted back to its Original Size or you can Invert the image by selecting from the available options.

OLE 2.0

An **OLE 2.0** control is used to add functionality to your application by allowing you to add objects from another package such as wordprocessors, spreadsheets or presentation packages. When you add an OLE 2.0 control to a window, you must specify which type of object you want to add:

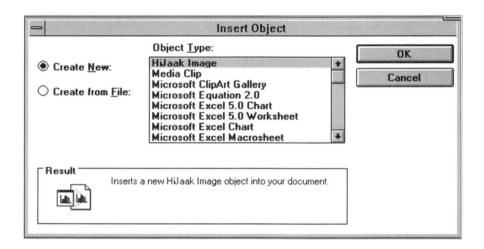

The list of objects depends on the packages that you have loaded on your computer. You can choose to create a new object directly from the parent package or you can create an object from an existing file. If you create a new object, PowerBuilder will automatically launch the required package and let you create the object. The example on our w_controls_more window (still in the rev_pbexamples application) was created in Microsoft PowerPoint:

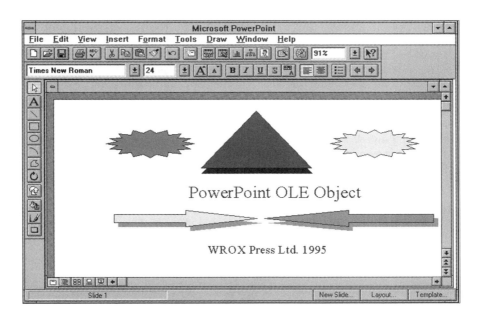

When you have finished creating your object, by closing down the application, you will be returned to PowerBuilder with your new object being placed in the OLE control.

There are several options that you can set relating to OLE objects. We won't go into a full explanation of all the available options here as they are covered in a later chapter, but you can change some of the options by looking at the control's properties:

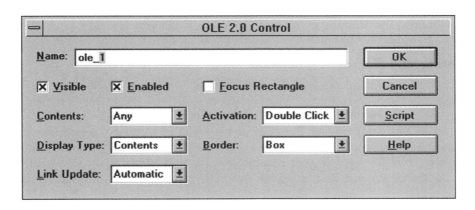

The Contents option allows you to specify whether the object should be linked, embedded or either.

> Basically, the difference between linking and embedding an object is that a linked object is saved as a file in its own right and can be changed outside the PowerBuilder environment, while an embedded object is saved internally and can only be changed through PowerBuilder. We'll discuss these differences and the advantages and disadvantages of both in the chapter on DDE and OLE.

The Display Type option allows you to display either the contents of the object or an icon representing the object. For example, if we changed this option on our control, we'd get the following icon:

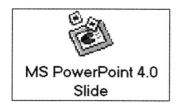

MS PowerPoint 4.0
Slide

Updating Links

The Link Update option works with linked objects and allows you, if you want, to specify the object to be updated automatically or manually. If you specify automatic updating, when changes are made to the source file, the object that is used by PowerBuilder will be updated at the same time. Otherwise, you have to handle the updating yourself, by coding the process into your scripts.

Activating the Server Application

The Activation option allows you to specify how you want to activate the OLE object's application at run-time. You can specify Double Click, Get Focus or Manual. We don't recommend using the Get Focus option as it would activate the server if the user tabs to the control by mistake - clearly, activating and de-activating other applications can take a long time and can become quite monotonous for the user. If you request Manual activation, again you will have to handle the activation of the server by coding the process into your scripts.

Graph

Through the use of this type of control, PowerBuilder allows you to add a **Graph** to your window, based upon any of the common graphical formats for presenting numerical data. We've added a graph to our w_controls_more window:

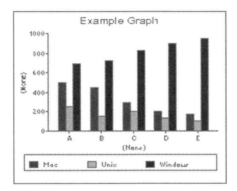

If you look at the properties for this control, you can see that there are numerous options relating to titles, legends and axes, as well as the type of graph:

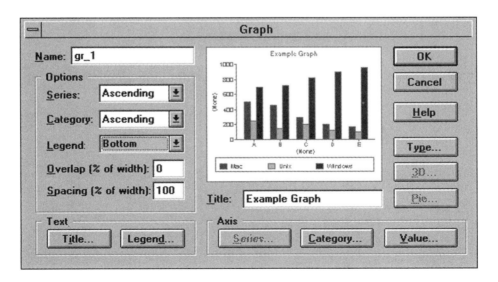

We won't go into all of these details now as they are covered in a later chapter, but if you click on the Type... button, you'll see the full range of graphs that PowerBuilder allows you to create:

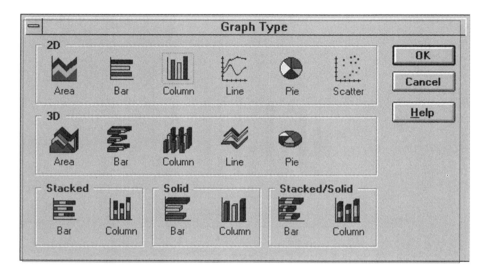

DataWindow Control

A **DataWindow** control is used to display data from a table or query in a database. To use a DataWindow control, you must:

1 Create a DataWindow object which contains data from the source.

2 Add a DataWindow control to your window.

3 Associate the control with the object.

DataWindows are one of the most important features offered by PowerBuilder for database-related tasks and we'll look at them in much greater depth in Chapters 7 and 8. For now, you can look at the DataWindow control that we've placed on our example window:

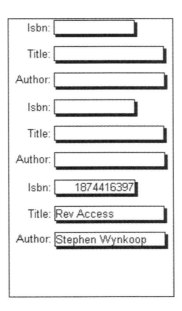

If you look at the properties for this control and click on the Change... button, you'll see where the data comes from:

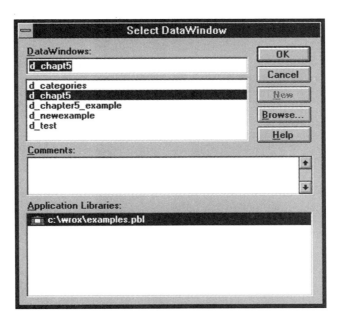

Note that the highlighted DataWindow is the current source of information for the control.

UserObject

A **UserObject** is an object that you have defined yourself to solve a specific task and to speed up your developmental process. For example, if you had a certain piece of text that you wanted to appear on every CommandButton, you could create a standard visual UserObject of that type and enter the text you required, once, into this object. Now, whenever you want to put a CommandButton with this text on a window, you could use your customized UserObject with no need to retype the text.

If you look at our w_controls_more window, you'll see that there are two CommandButtons with the same text entry appearing on their face:

These look like standard CommandButtons, but if you look at their properties, you'll see that they are in fact UserObjects inherited from the uo_chapter5 object:

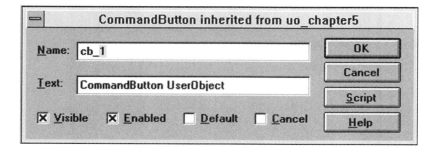

We created this object using the UserObject Painter and now that it is defined, we can add as many of these buttons to a window as we like, just by clicking on the UserObject icon from the PainterBar and specifying the name of the customized object that we want to use.

> We will look at defining UserObjects in a later chapter.

Drawing Controls and Scrollbars

To improve the appearance of your windows, you can also add drawing controls and independent scrollbars. These are selected from the Control menu and, by default, they are not available from the PainterBar:

Controls	
CommandButton	Picture
PictureButton	GroupBox
StaticText	UserObject...
SingleLineEdit	Graph
EditMask	Line
MultiLineEdit	Oval
ListBox	Rectangle
CheckBox	RoundRectangle
RadioButton	HScrollBar
DataWindow	VScrollBar
DropDownListBox	OLE 2.0

Drawing Controls — Line, Oval, Rectangle, RoundRectangle

Scrollbars — HScrollBar, VScrollBar

In our example library, you'll find another window, w_drawing_scrollbars which illustrates these controls:

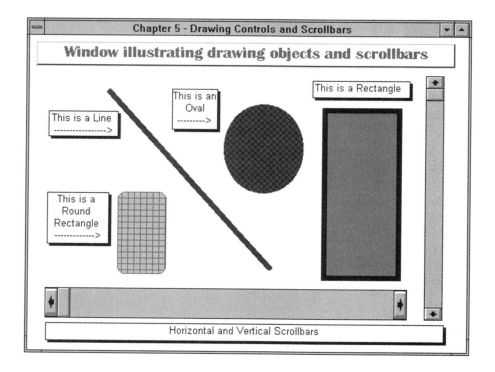

You can change the appearance of all the drawing controls by changing the colors, fill patterns and line styles, simply by right-clicking on the control and selecting from one of the options from the pop-up menu:

Changing Colors

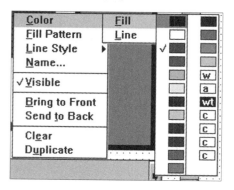

Changing Fill Pattern

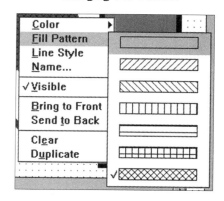

Changing Line Style

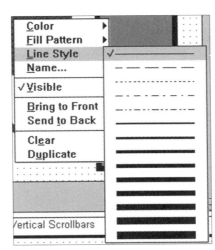

The only drawing control that has any interesting properties is the RoundRectangle:

The Corner Height and Corner Width options allow you to specify the degree of roundness that should be applied to the corners. The Corner Height option defines how far from the corner on the vertical edges the curve begins, while the Corner Width option affects the same thing, except that it affects the horizontal edge.

Given those starting points, two for each corner, PowerBuilder calculates the smoothest possible curve between the two points closest to each corner, so producing a rounded rectangle.

Manipulating Controls

Now that we've covered all the possible controls that you can place on a PowerBuilder window, we now need to look at the wide range of tools that PowerBuilder provides us with to manipulate and generally tidy up the appearance of the window and the controls on it.

Selecting Multiple Controls

There are two ways of selecting more than one control. The first of these methods involves holding down the *Ctrl* key while clicking on the controls you require, or you can click on the window and drag a box to surround the controls you want to select.

The screenshot below shows an example of selecting multiple controls:

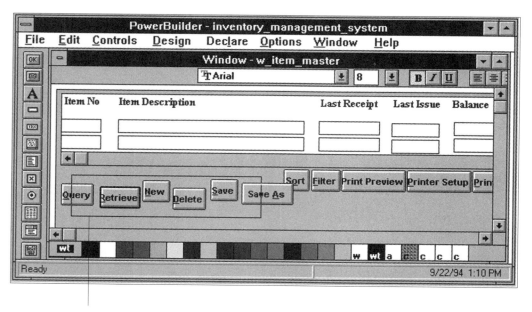

Selection Box

In this case, the Query, Retrieve, New, Delete, Save and Save As buttons are selected.

> *Note that for a control to be selected, it doesn't have to be completely enclosed by the box.*

When you select a control, the corners turn black to show that it is selected and you can then affect any changes against it that you wish. This holds true for multiple control selections, but the actions that you can perform against such selections are less numerous.

Some of the actions that you can perform against a multiple control selection include:

- Moving them
- Aligning them, based upon one axis
- Resizing them, based upon the size of one of the controls
- Spacing them, based upon the current spacing between two controls

Moving Controls

This is the easiest action to perform against a multiple control selection. To move all of the controls so that they retain their relative positions, simply select the controls that you wish to move, click on one of the controls and move it to its new position.

PowerBuilder will indicate where the controls will end up at any one moment through the use of an image of the controls moving around the window until the left mouse button is released.

Aligning Controls

To align a group of controls, select the controls using one of the methods outlined above, and then select Edit/Align Controls and choose one of the following methods of aligning the controls:

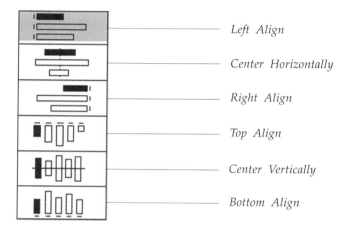

Left Align

Center Horizontally

Right Align

Top Align

Center Vertically

Bottom Align

> **If you use the *Ctrl* method of selecting the controls, PowerBuilder will always use the first control that you select as the reference point. The reference point is the control that doesn't move and all other controls conform to.**
>
> **If you use the box swipe method of highlighting multiple controls, the reference control is the last one that is selected.**

Spacing Controls

To make the spaces between your controls equal, you can select Edit/Space Controls and select either horizontal or vertical spacing:

Horizontal Spacing

Vertical Spacing

PowerBuilder takes the first two controls that you select and uses the space between them as the default to space all the other controls.

Note that you should use the Ctrl key method of selecting controls, otherwise PowerBuilder won't be able to determine the first two controls and when it spaces them you will not get what you want!

Sizing Controls

If you want to make several controls the same size you can select the required controls and select Edit/Size Controls:

Same Width

Same Height

> The note that was made for aligning controls also applies here. Use the *Ctrl* method of selecting the reference control for the sizing to be based upon.

The Grid

Using these tools to manipulate your controls can take a while to get used to and, when they do become second nature, they can still be a little unwieldy. To help out with this problem, and to speed up the process, you can use the Window Painter's grid as a basis for your controls positioning.

The Window Painter's grid is turned on by default when you first begin to create a window.

To look at the properties that PowerBuilder has associated with the grid, select Design/Grid...:

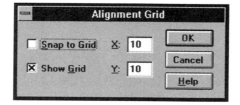

You can change the horizontal and vertical spacing of the grid by changing the X and Y values and, if you check the Snap to Grid option the size controls will snap to the nearest grid point when you move them. This enables you to size, space and align controls very quickly.

Duplicating Controls

If you want to add several similar controls to a window, you can use the duplicate tool. Select the control you want to duplicate and press *Ctrl+T* or right-click on the control and select Duplicate:

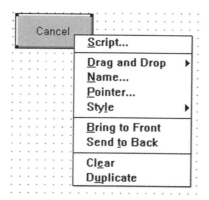

Another control of the same type is created and placed below the original control. The new control gets all the appearance properties such as text, colors, font, font size, borders and so on, and is named with the next available control name. Unfortunately, any scripts or user events that were created for the original control aren't copied to the new control.

Copy and Paste

Another way of duplicating a control is to use the Copy and Paste options from the Edit menu, or use the *Ctrl+C* and *Ctrl+V* shortcut keys. When you use this method of copying controls, all the properties of the original control will be copied including any scripts and the name of the control. For example, if you copy one of the CommandButtons on the w_controls window, you'll get the following warning:

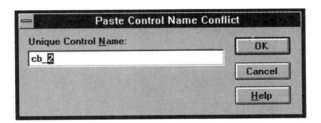

You can't have two controls with the same name on the same window, so you have to type in a new name before PowerBuilder will create the new control. The control is copied directly on top of the original control, so you'll have to move it to verify that it is there!

You can also use the Copy and Paste method to copy controls between windows. PowerBuilder does allow you to have two controls with the same name in different windows, so you won't get a naming conflict warning when you attempt this.

Listing Controls

As we have just seen, when you copy and paste a control, it appears directly on top of the original. Back in the section on CommandButtons, we saw that when you deselected the visible property, the control disappeared from both the run-time and the design view.

Both of these situations can cause you to 'lose' some controls and to get around this problem, PowerBuilder allows you to see a list of all the controls that you have placed upon a window. This catalog of controls is called the **Control List** and you can call it up by selecting Edit/Control List...

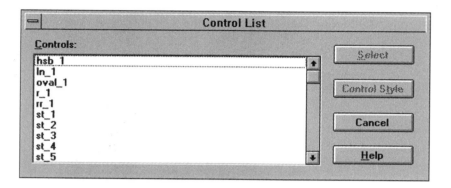

You can select all of the controls on your window from here, and you can affect changes against any of the properties of that control by selecting the Control Style button to take you to the relevant properties dialog.

> *PowerBuilder also offers you a function to help you with invisible controls. By selecting **Design/Show Invisibles**, PowerBuilder will paint all the controls that you have placed upon your window, no matter what their visible property is set to. PowerBuilder will continue to do this until you deselect this function.*

Defining Tag Values

A **Tag Value** is used to hold the text that will appear on the status bar whenever the mouse moves over a particular control and context-sensitive help is enabled. To see the various tag values that are currently set, select Edit/Tag List from the menu:

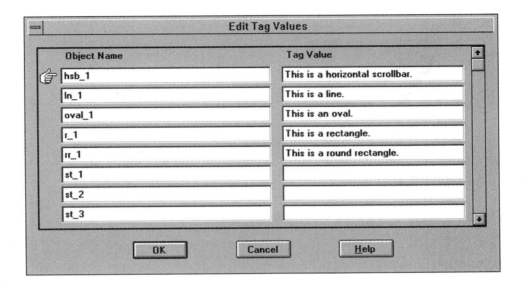

Note that this will only work at run-time. It will not work when designing or previewing a window.

Specifying the Tab Order

A window's **Tab Order** is the sequence which focuses the changes from one control to another when the *Tab* key is pressed. It is vitally important to provide a smooth and well disciplined tab order, so that the user can easily follow the motion of the focus around the window. Your applications will quickly be condemned as unfriendly if you don't provide a sensible tab order.

To see the current tab order, select Design/Tab Order. The tab order for our w_controls_more window looks like this:

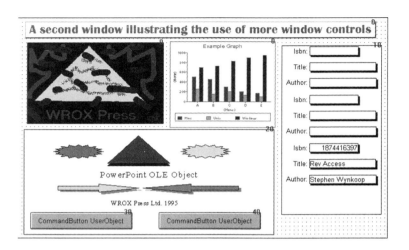

As you can see, the control tab order for this window is:

1 DataWindow

2 OLE 2.0 Object

3 UserObject No. 1 (CommandButton)

4 UserObject No. 2 (CommandButton)

The following controls are not included in the tab order, or in other words, have been assigned a value of zero:

- StaticText
- Graph
- Picture

PowerBuilder automatically creates a tab order which matches the order in which you placed controls on the window, spaced out with increments of 10.

If you have ever programmed in BASIC, back in the good old days before PCs, you might remember numbering your program lines with increments of 10 so that you could add extra lines later without having to re-number all your lines. The same principle applies with the tab order set by PowerBuilder.

You can't tab into drawing objects or StaticText controls, so PowerBuilder gives these a default tab value of zero, which means that they are not included in the tab order. This also applies to any RadioButtons or any other mutual exclusive controls that you place on a Window.

These defaults are generated for two main reasons:

▲   If you tab to StaticText or drawing object, you can't change anything, so why would you want to tab to it?

▲   If you change a set of mutually exclusive controls to have an 'active', non-zero tab order, as each control receives the focus, it is also selected. As you might guess, this can cause some consternation among your users.

Due to its flexibility, PowerBuilder does allow you to alter these tab orders, but you should understand the effect that this will have upon your application and even the underlying information in your database.

If you place a custom UserObject containing more than one object in a window, when you tab to the UserObject, each time you press the Tab key you will move within the UserObject until every control in the UserObject has been visited. After that, continued tabbing will take you to the next control on the window.

To alter the tab order values, click on the relevant number and retype the new value. Once you have highlighted one value, the *Tab* key will move you around the controls in the new tab order.

Window Properties

We've looked at all the controls and control properties and seen how to manipulate these controls on a window. However, the window itself has properties that we can review and modify. To see the properties for a window, select Design/Window Style...:

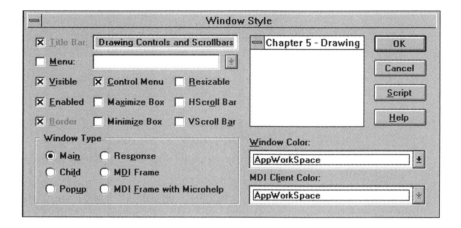

This is where you can specify the type of window, associate menus to the window, specify window colors and so on. You can also choose to turn on or off various standard Windows features such as scrollbars and the maximize and minimize buttons.

> *If you specify the type of window as* **MDI Frame** *or* **MDI Frame with Microhelp***, you will also have to supply the name of a menu to associate with the window.*

Window Size and Position

You can also change the size and position of a window, simply by selecting Design/Window Position...:

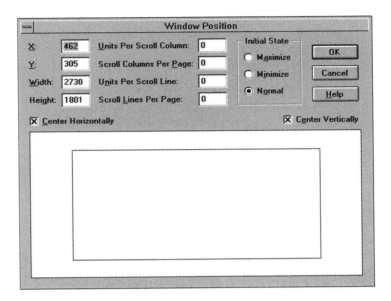

The $\underline{X}$ and $\underline{Y}$ values specify the position of the top left-hand corner of the window and you can choose how to open the window: maximized, minimized or normal size. You can also choose to open the window centered horizontally and/or vertically.

To change the size or position of the window, you can alter the values of $\underline{X}$, $\underline{Y}$, $\underline{W}$idth and Height or you can grab the edge of the window and drag it to the required size and position.

The scrolling options allow you to specify how the standard Windows scrollbars will work. The defaults are as follows:

Scrollbar	Default	Value
Horizontal	Units Per Scroll Columns	0 - 1/100th of the width of the window
	Scroll Columns Per Page	0 - 10 columns
Vertical	Units Per Scroll Line	0 - 1/100th of the height of the window
	Scroll Lines Per Page	0 - 10 lines

Window Preferences

To bring up the preferences for the Window Painter, so allowing you to further refine the painter to your own requirements, click on the Preferences icon from the PowerBar and select Window:

All the control preferences relate to the default prefixes that PowerBuilder gives the controls. At the bottom of the list are the following preferences:

Variable	Description
Default3D	When set to 1, controls are displayed with a 3D interpretation by default.
GridOn	When set to 1, both the grid and the <u>S</u>nap to Grid option are checked by default when you open the Window Painter.
GridShow	When set to 1, this option just turns the grid display on.
GridX	Grid width in pixels. The default is 8 pixels.
GridY	Grid height in pixels. The default is 8 pixels.
Status	When set to 1, this option causes the Object Status window to be displayed when the Window Painter is open.

Testing a Window

We've already seen how you can preview a window to see what it will look like and how the controls will behave at run-time. Unfortunately, by previewing a window, you are giving up the chance to run any scripts that you have coded against control or window events. To test these out, you have to run the window, an option that is not supported by the menus.

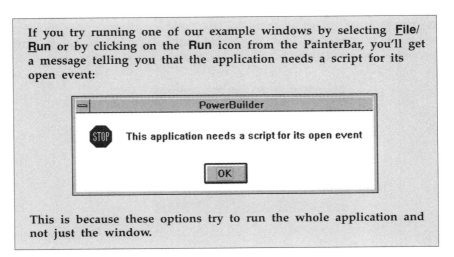

If you try running one of our example windows by selecting **<u>F</u>ile/ <u>R</u>un** or by clicking on the **Run** icon from the PainterBar, you'll get a message telling you that the application needs a script for its open event:

> **PowerBuilder**
>
> STOP This application needs a script for its open event
>
> OK

This is because these options try to run the whole application and not just the window.

To run a window, you have to use the shortcut keys *Ctrl+Shift+W*. This is a system-wide shortcut which will work from any of the painters. It will bring up the Run Window dialog box allowing you to select the window you want to run:

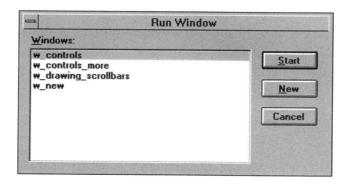

Simply highlight the window that you want to test and click on the Start button.

Painting the Windows for Our Application

For our Stock Control application, we need to create three windows. One of these windows is used to let us login to our database, the second allows us to see the information contained in that database and the third is use to present error information. When finished, they should look like this:

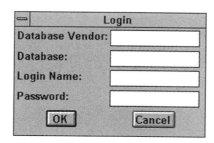

The Login window is quite easy to paint and the only things to note are that the Password: SingleLineEdit control has its Password option turned on and that the OK and Cancel CommandButtons are set as Default and Cancel respectively.

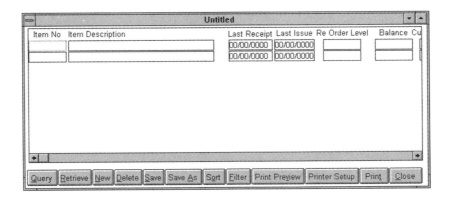

The second window is more difficult. All of the CommandButtons are set up as Visible and Enabled, but you won't be able to paint the top half of the window as this is a DataWindow control and we haven't painted any DataWindow objects yet. For now, you can simply add a DataWindow control to the window and size it to the correct size:

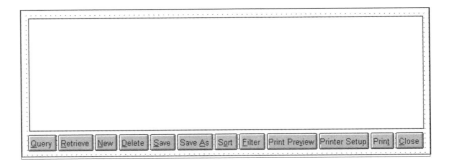

The third window is used to display any associated error information when something goes wrong in our application. This window will be called by the PowerBuilder error handlers to help us with any problems that occur in the application. It is a run-time debug tool, which allows your users to actively report problems back to you after you have left the facility.

The window is composed of two major components, a DataWindow object held in a DataWindow control in the top half of the window and a selection of buttons for the user to choose what to do with the information. We'll look at how to add the functionality behind this window in a later chapter:

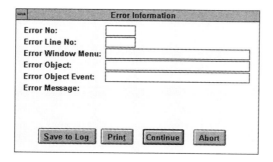

You can see the full definition for these three windows in the invent1 application that is part of the **INVENT1.PBL** library on the CD-ROM. We'll build on these windows in later chapters and, at each stage of completion, we'll provide you with a new version of the application up to that point.

Summary

Windows are the interface between your users and your application. We've looked at all the various window controls and properties and have created a couple of windows which we will use in our Stock Control application.

We'll add increased functionality to these windows in later chapters as we learn more about DataWindows and PowerScript, but before we cover these areas, we need some data to work with. In the next chapter, we'll look at the Database Painter and how you can create the tables that we need for our application.

Database Painter

Up until now, we've been creating objects in our PowerBuilder application. However, without a source of data, the application will be a little redundant and so, in this chapter, we will be concentrating on this minefield and how it can dramatically improve the usefulness of a PowerBuilder application.

The Database Painter is used to perform any operation involving the creation of and the connection to PowerBuilder-compliant databases. PowerBuilder can connect to many different types of databases, but for our Stock Control application, we'll be creating a local Watcom database.

In this chapter, we will cover:

- The creation and maintenance of database tables, indexes and keys
- Referential Integrity constraints
- Retrieval and manipulation of data from tables
- The transfer of data between PowerBuilder and several other popular formats
- PowerBuilder's System Tables

Introduction

PowerBuilder 4.0 ships with the Watcom 4.0 database engine and all the example applications that ship with PowerBuilder use this database format. Whilst your primary reason for buying PowerBuilder may not have been to connect to Watcom databases, it is a very useful prototyping feature, allowing you to test your application against a local database before connecting to your production database, be it Sybase, Oracle, SQL Server or whatever.

This isn't a book on database design, so we won't go into the details of designing fully normalized relational databases. We will, however, provide definitions of some of the key features of a relational database such as keys, indexes and referential integrity, as they relate to PowerBuilder.

Invoking the Database Painter

To invoke the Database Painter, click on the database icon from the PowerBar. The Select Tables dialog box will appear, illustrating the existing tables and views in the database you are connected to:

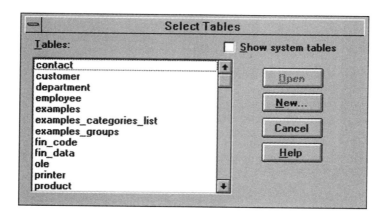

When you invoke the Database Painter for the first time, PowerBuilder will automatically connect to the **PSDEMODB.DB** example database. If the Select Tables box doesn't appear with these contents, it is likely that you aren't connected to the right database. To remedy this problem, select Powersoft Demo DB from File/ Connect.

*You can check the **Show system tables** box to see all the database tables that are used for administration purposes. Normally, you won't want to see these tables, but if you need administration information for use in your scripts, such as the names of the fields in a given table, PowerBuilder does allow you access to these tables, although not the right to change their design.*

You can add any of the tables in the database to the display by double-clicking on the table name or by selecting the table and clicking the Open button. The following screenshot shows some of the example database's tables that we've chosen to view:

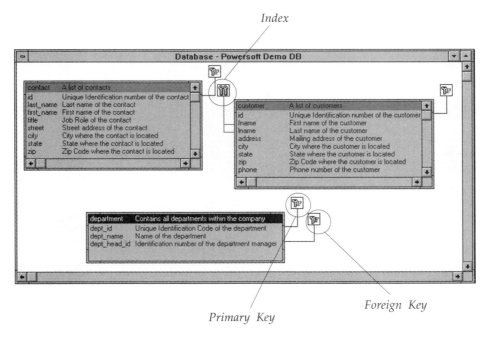

As you can see, each table is composed of a number of fields; a description of what the developer thought the fields would be used for is also included. The key symbols represent the various indexes and primary and foreign keys that have been set up for each table.

The ideas behind indexes and keys, both primary and foreign, are discussed in more depth when we take our first look at creating a database.

Field Attributes

Each field in a table has a range of possible attributes. When you are creating tables, you specify the fields contained in the table and various attributes relating to each field. This allows you to fully specify the type of data that can be held in your database, together with the structure that the data must be supplied in to get into the database. To view the design of the contact table, double-click on its title bar:

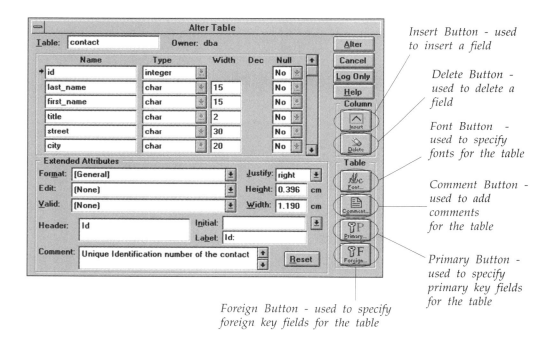

Insert Button - used to insert a field

Delete Button - used to delete a field

Font Button - used to specify fonts for the table

Comment Button - used to add comments for the table

Primary Button - used to specify primary key fields for the table

Foreign Button - used to specify foreign key fields for the table

For each field in a table, you can specify four main attributes:

1 Name

2 Type

3 Width

4 Null

Name

This is the name that you must use to refer to this field and can contain any alphanumeric characters, spaces and the underscore character. You don't have to worry about using invalid characters, as PowerBuilder will give you an error message if you try to do this:

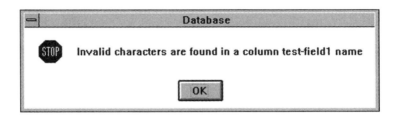

It is a good idea to use some form of naming convention for field names, so that you can quickly identify them in your script. In our example application, we've used the underscore character to separate words in our field names. Table and field names are case insensitive, so everything you type will appear in lowercase.

Type

This attribute defines the type of data that will be stored in the field. For a database based upon the Watcom engine, there are 13 possible data types:

These include most of the common types such as char, numeric, date and time. For an explanation of some of the more obscure data types, you should either check the PowerBuilder on-line help for the Watcom engine or the appropriate manual for another source. The list of possible data types will change depending on the type of database you are connected to.

Width

This defines the width, or maximum number of characters, that a field can contain. It is a good idea to limit the width of each field, limiting the amount of memory assigned to data storage. This use of memory can be very wasteful, if large amounts are allocated to store small amounts of data.

For example, if you know that the surname of all your contacts will never exceed 30 characters, limit the field to this size. If your field is numeric, there is a supplemental attribute called Dec which defines the number of decimal places that should be allowed into the field.

> *Note that not all field types will allow you to specify a width. For example, you can see that the* id *field in the* contact *table is an* integer *type and has no value under the* Width *heading. This is because an integer field is restricted to storing whole numbers between -32,768 and 32,767.*

Null

This is a Yes/No option which is used to determine whether or not the field accepts a NULL value. A NULL is an empty, undefined value, which shouldn't be confused with zero-length string.

> *Both NULLs and zero-length strings are used to indicate that an entry has not been made. The distinction between the two entries is based on the reason for the omission.*
>
> *A NULL entry indicates that the information is unknown, while using a zero-length string shows that the information is definitely not available. For example, you would use a NULL in a Phone field if you don't know whether your contact has a telephone, but a zero-length string if your contact definitely doesn't have one.*

The default is to reject NULLs, but if you scroll down the list of fields in the example contact table, you'll see that it will accept NULLs for the phone and fax fields. This means that you don't have to know all the details about a contact, before entering a new record in the table.

Extended Attributes

As well as the main attributes, you can also define extended attributes for any field. These additional options allow you to provide formatting information for the window layout at the table level, as well as covering some of the data entry criteria:

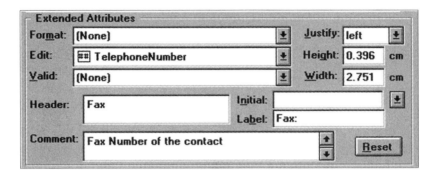

The following table illustrates these extended attributes with a description of their usage:

Attribute	Description
Format	This is used to alter the format of the data when it is displayed. An example of a well-used format style is the alteration of European date format to the US style of presentation.
Edit	This can be used to specify an edit mask for the field. An edit mask allows you to define a template that the user fills in, formatting the data in a pre-defined manner.
Valid	This can be used to specify a validation rule for the data; all numbers must be less than 31, for example.
Justify	You can specify left, right or center justified text.
Height	Used to specify the height of the box, which displays the data.
Width	Used to specify the width of the box, which displays the data.

Continued

Attribute	Description
Header	You can specify a header for the field which is different to the field name - the header is used in Tabular and similar presentation style windows.
Initial	You can specify a default value for the field. An good example of how to use this field would be the insertion of today's day, if the user left the field blank.
Label	You can specify a label for the field which is different to the field name - the label is used in Freeform and similar presentation style windows.
Comment	In this attribute, you can add comments for the field.

PowerBuilder will automatically fill in the Header and Label text using the field name, replacing underscore characters with spaces and capitalizing the first letter of each word.

> You should always try to define as many options at the earliest possible stage of your application development. This allows these options to be used as defaults for all the following stages. They can always be overwritten if necessary, but if you can decide on certain styles, fonts and so on, defining them at the earliest possible stage will speed up your development time.

We'll look at the other extended attributes in more detail when we come to create the tables for our Stock Control application.

The Database PainterBar

The tools available in the Database Painter can also be selected from the Database PainterBar:

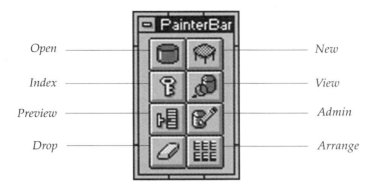

In this chapter, we will be covering five of these options, but the others, Drop, View and Arrange, may still come in handy.

The **Drop** facility allows you to delete a table from a database, using the basic SQL statement of the same name.

A **View** is similar to a query. It creates a virtual table that you can use as normal, except that you can't update the information that it presents - but the information is automatically updated if the base table information is altered. The advantage to creating Views is that, as they exist with the database rather than your PowerBuilder application, they are available to one and all. Remember that queries are stored in your PowerBuilder application!

The **Arrange** option is purely a presentation tool which allows you to organize your tables in the database window so that they are all visible, but don't overlap.

Creating Our Database

We need to create four basic tables for our Stock Control System. You can create these tables in the existing database, but it is a better idea to create a new database to hold the tables for our example. We'll use a Watcom database,

which you can create on your local machine, as PowerBuilder ships with the
Watcom database engine.

> *In the next chapter, we'll show you how to connect to other databases
> and, in a later chapter, we'll look at connecting PowerBuilder to a SQL
> Server database.*

To create a new database, select File/Create Database... and for our example,
give the database the name Invent:

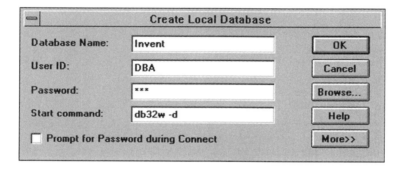

PowerBuilder automatically supplies the User ID as DBA and Password as SQL
(remember, each asterix takes the place of a letter in a Password field). Later,
we'll see how you can set up users and permissions for a database, but for
now let's enjoy the power of a **DataBase Administrator** and keep the application
out of the hands of our users. PowerBuilder also generates the necessary
information to start the Watcom database engine, placing it in the Start
command box.

You can click on the More>> button to identify other specific database options
and you can also check the Prompt for Password during Connect box at this stage.
This option allows you to force the user to type in the password each time
they connect to the database. During development, it is a good idea to disable
this feature, so click on the OK button and we'll move on.

Creating Our First Table

To create a new table, click on the New icon. This invokes the Create Table
dialog box:

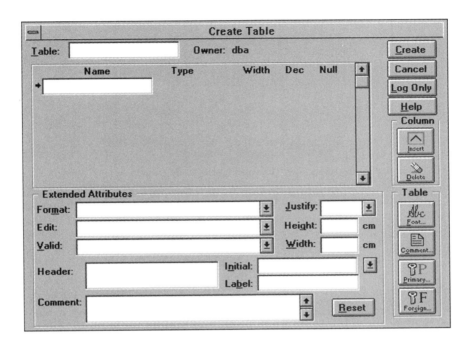

Supply the name of our first table - the item_master table - and create the field definitions as follows:

Name	Type	Width	Dec	Null
item_no	numeric	5	0	No
item_description	varchar	30	-	No
last_receipt_date	date	-	-	No
last_issue_date	date	-	-	No
re_order_level	numeric	8	3	Yes
balance	numeric	8	3	No
measuring_unit	char	1	-	No
current_price	numeric	8	2	No

Click on the Create button to create the table. You should get a dialog box asking if you want to create a Primary Key:

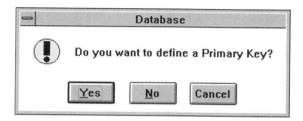

In order to define a Primary Key, we need to understand what indexes and keys mean to the PowerBuilder environment. As the Watcom database engine allows you to define a Primary Key at any time, click on the No button and we'll return to this later.

Using Logs

If you want to see the SQL (Structured Query Language, pronounced 'sequel') statements which are used to create a table, you should be interested in logs. To see the statements that created the item_master table, select Objects/ ExportTable/View Syntax To Log.... When the dialog box asks you to specify the data source, click OK and the Activity Log icon should appear at the bottom of your screen:

If you double-click on the icon, it will bring up the SQL syntax which was used to create the table:

```
Activity Log

CREATE TABLE "dba"."item_master"
    ("item_no" numeric(5,0) NOT NULL,
    "item_description" varchar(30) NOT NULL,
    "last_receipt_date" date NOT NULL,
    "last_issue_date" date NOT NULL,
    "re_order_level" numeric(8,3) ,
    "balance" numeric(8,3) NOT NULL,
    "measuring_unit" char(1) NOT NULL,
    "current_price" numeric(8,2) NOT NULL);

insert into "dba".pbcattbl
    (pbt_tnam,
    pbt_ownr,
    pbd_fhat
```

You can scroll down the screen to see the full syntax and you'll appreciate how much easier it is to create a table using the Database Painter rather than using SQL!

You might wonder why you'd want to look at these SQL statements. Well, if you're not familiar with SQL, it is a good way of learning how the language works, but there is a more practical reason - it allows us to copy tables from one database to another.

Copying Tables Between Databases

The table that we've just created is designed to work with three other tables in our example application. Rather than repeating the creation process in this new database, PowerBuilder allows you to save development time by simply running the creation log associated with our table. This will cause an exact copy of our table to be created in the new database.

> *PowerBuilder doesn't provide you with the ability to 'cut and paste' tables from one database to another. You must either manually reproduce the tables or use the logs to automatically recreate them.*

On the CD-ROM, we've included a database, **INVDUMMY.DB** which contains the other three tables required for our Stock Control system. To illustrate how easy this process can be, let's save our item_master table definition and import it into this dummy database.

Select Options/Save Log As... and call it **CREATE.SQL**. Now, to connect to our dummy database, we'll have to create a database profile.

Creating a New Profile

Database profiles are the gateways between your application and the database that you are trying to connect to. They contain all the necessary information required by the application to both find the database and access the data, no matter what security has been placed around it.

If the profile is fully completed, you will have immediate access to the database, but as more and more information is left out of it, more and more information is required from the user - this is the way that security and the user interact in your final executable.

We'll quickly show you how to create a new database profile and in a later chapter, we'll look at the process in more depth. Select File/Configure ODBC...

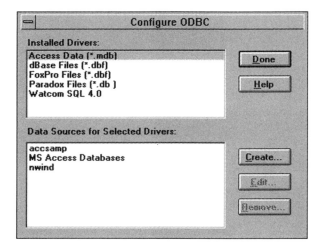

This lists all the installed drivers and allows you to select or create data sources for any of the available data source drivers.

> *The list of drivers on your system may differ depending on the software that you have on your machine and the options that you selected when installing PowerBuilder.*

Select Watcom SQL 4.0 and click on the Create... button:

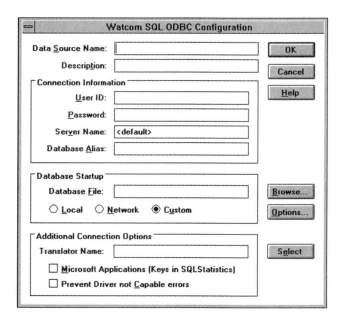

The quickest way to fill in all the details is to select the database by clicking on the Browse... button and specifying its filename. Assuming that you copied all the files from the CD-ROM into `C:\WROX`, then the full path to the file is `C:\WROX\INVDUMMY.DB`.

PowerBuilder will automatically fill in the Data Source Name and Database Alias using the name of the database. You should also select the Local radio button as the database is on your local drive and type in the User ID as 'DBA' and Password as 'SQL'. The full definition looks like this:

You don't have to fill in the User ID and Password options, but if you don't, then every time you connect to this database you will be prompted for your User ID and Password. When you distribute this application, the database profile that the application uses is very important for purposes of security - you only want passworded users to get access to your database!

Click the OK button and then the Done button to save the configuration. PowerBuilder creates a database profile based on this information and this allows you to connect to the database by selecting from the File/Connect menu option:

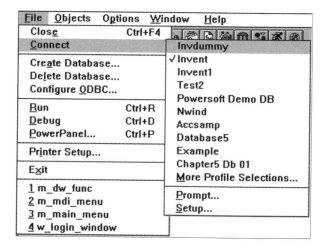

Select the Invdummy profile and PowerBuilder will connect you to the dummy database, throwing up this dialog. It allows you to see the tables that currently exist in the database as well as allowing you to select the tables that you wish to see in more detail:

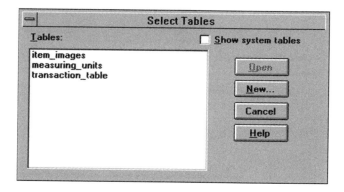

As you can see, the other three tables are here already, awaiting the final table. Now, to import our item_master table, we've to go to the Database Administration Painter.

Database Administration Painter

Cancel the dialog and select the Admin icon from the Database PainterBar:

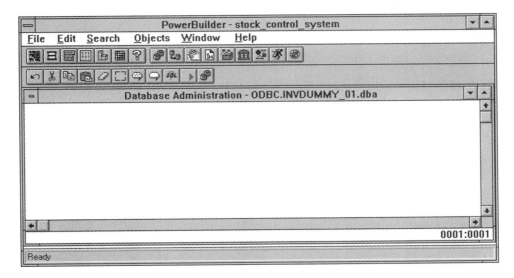

Open the **CREATE.SQL** table definition by selecting File/Open... and then run the SQL statements by clicking on the Execute icon:

If you return to the database window and click on the Open button, you'll see that the item_master table has now been added to the list:

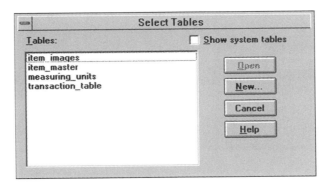

Now we've completed the creation of the tables that we need for our Stock Control system, we need to refine the new table by defining some keys, indexes and extended attributes. Double-click on item_master and it will be added to the database window, ready for you to work on it.

Primary Keys

A **Primary Key** is used to uniquely identify each record in a table. When you apply a primary key to a field in a table, you are forcing each entry in that field to be unique - the database engine will reject any entries into this field which would duplicate any that already exist.

Keys are important because they are used to join tables in a database. In our example table, we want to make the item_no field into a primary key field, as it uniquely identifies the items in the table.

> You don't have to define a primary key for every table, but if you don't, you won't be allowed to enter data into the table from the data manipulation screen in the Database Painter.

To do this, double-click on the title bar of the item_master table to bring up the table definition and click on the Primary... picture button to bring up the definition dialog box:

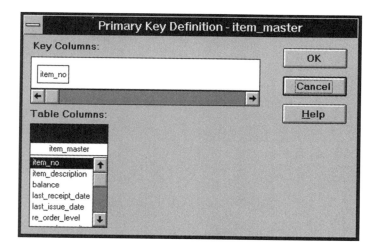

Click on the item_no field to add it to the Key Columns box. If you were defining multiple primary keys, you simply double-click on another field from the list.

> *On some occasions, you may want to compose your primary key from the contents of two or more fields - Department and Position in the Department, for example - rather than creating a field that specializes in being unique. This is quite acceptable as long as the fields that you choose will create a unique identifier for each record. In this example, if there are two Dogsbodies in the Editorial Department, the multiple field primary key wouldn't work!*

Foreign Keys

A **Foreign Key** is used to link a table to the primary key of another table. In our item_master table, there is a field called measuring_unit which has a familiar in the measuring_units table that holds the position of primary key. We only want to allow an entry in the item_master table that exists in the measuring_units table, so we will make it a foreign key field in the item_master table to enforce this.

Click on the Foreign... picture button and then click on the New... button:

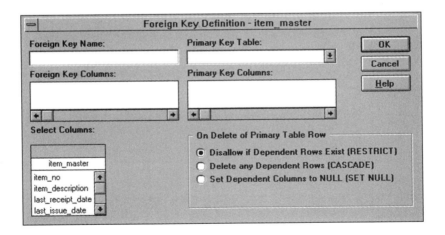

Give the key the name measuring_unit_fk and click on the measuring_unit field from the item_master table. Select the measuring_units table from the drop-down list of primary key tables and PowerBuilder will automatically add the measuring_unit field to the Primary Key Columns box. The final definition looks like this:

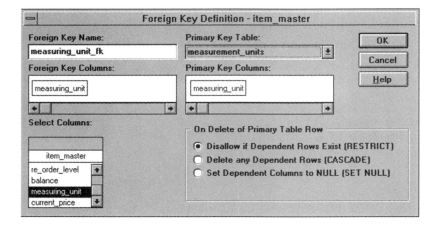

The radio buttons allow you to specify what will happen if a record in the Primary Table is deleted. There are three options:

Option	Description
RESTRICT	If you select this option, PowerBuilder won't allow you to delete a row in the measurement_units table, if there are dependent rows in the item_master table.
CASCADE	This option will delete dependent rows in the item_master table, if a row is deleted in the measurement_units table.
SET NULL	Selecting this option means that, if a row is deleted in the measurement_units table, then a NULL value will be placed in the measurement_unit field of any dependent rows in the item_master table.

In our example, we want to restrict the deletion of rows in the measurement_units table, so select the first option, RESTRICT. Click the OK button to define the foreign key and click the Alter button to add it to the table.

Indexes

Indexes are used to speed up the selection of data from a table by restricting the number of records that have to be searched. For example, if you had a table of contacts with a gender field and assuming you had equal numbers of male and female contacts, then indexing this field would roughly halve the number of records that had to be searched on a query.

> **It makes sense to add indexes to fields that contain a large number of unique values.**

We've just made the item_no field a primary key to uniquely identify records in the item_master table, so this is the logical choice for an index. Click on the title bar of the item_master table and click on the Index icon:

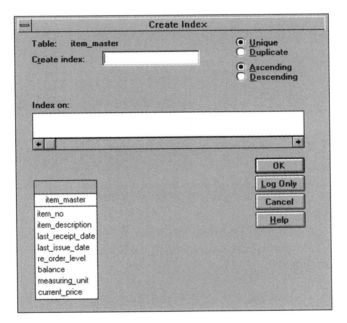

Name the index as item_master_index1 and click on the item_no field. You can specify that the indexed field must contain unique values or that it should allow duplicates and you also have the option of indexing in ascending or descending order. We want a unique and ascending index, so accept the defaults and click on the OK button to add the index to the table.

We now have all our tables with all the keys and indexes defined. If you open all the tables, you should have a diagram that looks something like this:

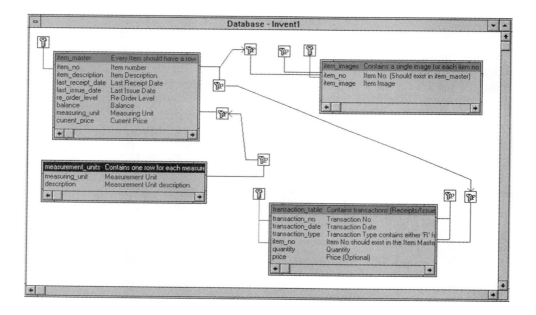

We've moved the tables around to simplify the picture. It may look quite daunting, but you can see immediately which tables rely on which and how the database is structured.

We've almost finished creating our database; the only thing left to do is to add some extended attributes to the item_master table. Before we do that, let's look at some of the extended attributes which have already been defined for you in the other three tables.

Format Styles

Right-click on the item_no field in the item_images table and select Display... from the pop-up menu:

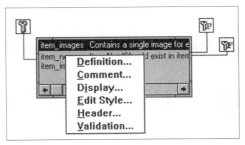

This will take you to the Column Display Format window, which displays the pre-defined formats that are available for this field:

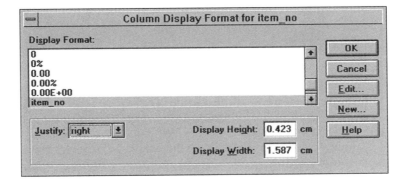

You can see that there is a display format called item_no for this field. Click on the Edit... button to look at the definition of this format:

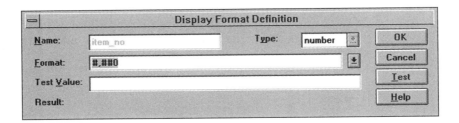

The # (hash) sign represents a numeric character, the comma indicates that we want a thousand separators inserted into the number and the zero means round the number so it won't display decimal values.

> Note that the Format attribute doesn't limit the number of characters in the field - we've already done this by specifying the width of the field to be 5 in the table definition.

You can see what the formatting will do by typing a number into the Test Value box and clicking the Test button. PowerBuilder will apply the formatting and display the result:

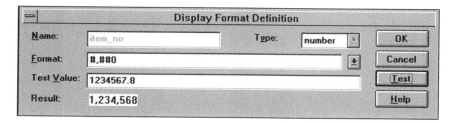

As you can see, the test value has been rounded to the nearest whole number and commas have been inserted to improve the display.

The symbols you can use in the format mask depends on the data type that you've already defined for the field. The symbols you can use for string and number data types are as follows:

Symbol	Numeric Data Type	String Data Type	Meaning
#	X		Numeric character - this symbol also rounds trailing integers automatically.
$,£,%,-,.,/	X	X	Displays the appropriate punctuation character.
@	X	X	Any character.

Continued

Symbol	Numeric Data Type	String Data Type	Meaning
'....'	X	X	Used to display the characters between the quotes.
(....)	X		Used to specify a different format for negative numbers.
;	X		Used to separate formats such as for positive and negative numbers.
[GENERAL]	X		Lets PowerBuilder choose a suitable format.
[CURRENCY]	X		Lets PowerBuilder choose a suitable format based on the current Windows International settings.
[BLUE]	X	X	Used before the format mask to display in the specified color.

As an example of the kind of effects that you can use these formatting symbols to achieve, take the following:

```
$#,###.##;[RED]($#,###.##)
```

This formatting will display an positive numeric input with a dollar sign, thousand separators and two decimal places in the default font color. Any negative inputs use the same formatting except that the font color is now red.

For more explanation of these and examples of how they work you should look in PowerBuilder's on-line help.

Date and Time Formats

For date and time data types, there is an extra set of formats that can be used to display the data in the way that you want. The following table lists these extra formats:

Symbol	Date Type	Time Type	Meaning
d	X		Day as a number
dd	X		Day as a number with leading zero
ddd	X		Day name abbreviation
dddd	X		Full day name
m	X		Month as a number
mm	X		Month as a number with leading zero
mmm	X		Month name abbreviation
mmmm	X		Full month name
yy	X		Two digit year
yyyy	X		Four digit year
h		X	Hour
hh		X	Hour with leading zero
m		X	Minutes
mm		X	Minutes with leading zero
s		X	Seconds
ss		X	Seconds with leading zero
ffffff		X	Microseconds
AM/PM		X	Displays AM or PM as applicable
am/pm		X	Displays am or pm as applicable
A/P		X	Displays A or P as applicable
a/p		X	Displays a or p as applicable

Again, check PowerBuilder's on-line help for more information and some examples of how to use these formats. We don't use any formats for any of our date type fields, but we do use edit styles, so let's move on to take a look at this extended attribute.

Edit Styles

An **Edit Style** is used to limit the type of data that can be entered into a field, while also affecting how the data is entered. For example, you could limit a date field so that the user had to enter the date in the format month/day/year. We've added this limitation to the transaction_date field in the transaction_table and you can take a look at this definition by right-clicking on the transaction_date field and selecting Edit Style...:

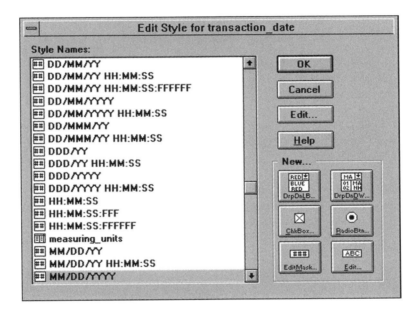

As you can see, this attribute uses the same syntax as the formatting of date and time fields. The measuring_units edit style is a custom-defined style and if you scroll down the list, you'll also find a transaction_type style. Select this one and click on the Edit... button:

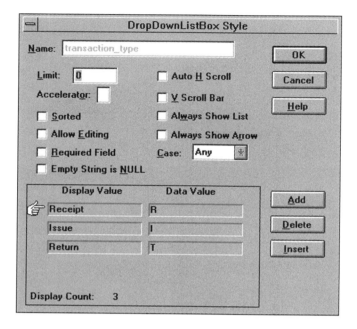

As you can see, this edit style is a DropDownListBox and is defined in a similar way to the Window control that we looked at in the last chapter. It allows the user to select from three possible values for the transaction_type field.

You can define six different types of edit style:

- DropDownListBox
- DropDownDataWindow
- CheckBox
- RadioButton
- EditMask
- Edit

Each of these is defined and behaves in a similar way to the related window control.

This is a very useful feature as it means that you can define how a field will appear on a window at the database level and not, as some other tools would have you format the field, at the presentation level.

Validation Rules

We haven't defined any validation rules for any of the fields in our tables, but to see how it works select Objects/Validation Maintenance... and then select New... from the Validation Rules dialog box:

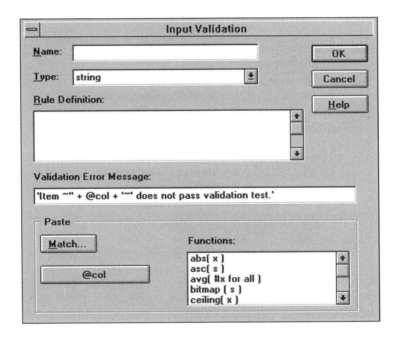

Suppose we had a table containing book details. Clearly, we would wish to force the user who was entering these details to provide ten characters for the ISBNs, which is where a validation rule would help. We need to give the rule a name, say item_no_rule, and specify the data type, which is number in this case. We can then define the rule using the @col button, mathematical operators and the functions in the function list.

The full definition would be:

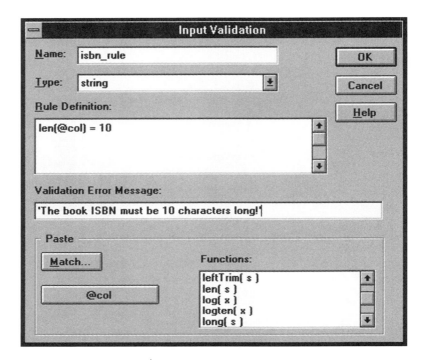

The @col stands for the value that the user types in, so the rule states that the length of the entry must be equal to 10 characters. If the validation rule is broken, it is useful to display an error message that guides the user towards the type of input that we are looking for. This message is fully customizable and you should try to make it as informative and useful, providing as much information as possible.

The Match Option

Another facility that PowerBuilder provides for string data types is Match. With this you can specify a range of specific values for a particular position in the string. To see how this works, click on the Match... button:

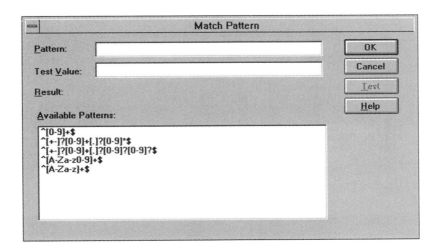

The ^ (hat) symbol represents the beginning of the pattern, the dollar sign ($) represents the end of the pattern and you can specify exact values or ranges of values for any of the characters in between. We could use this feature to refine our previous validation rule.

For example, the ISBN that corresponds to Wrox Press books is 1874416 followed by three digits, although in certain circumstances the last one could be an 'X'. The validation rule to test for one of our ISBNs would be as follows:

```
^1874416+[0-9]+[0-9]+[0-9X]$
```

We can test the rule by typing a value into the Test Value box and clicking on the Test button:

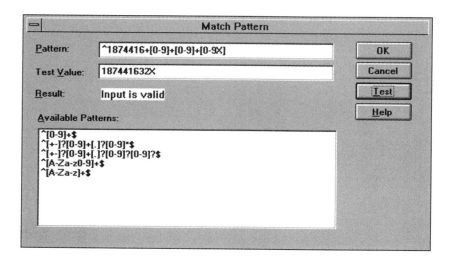

In this case, you can see that the ISBN 187441632X (which incidentally, you may be interested to know, is our forthcoming title 'Revolutionary Guide to Games Programming') is a valid input.

If the input isn't valid, the test will detect it:

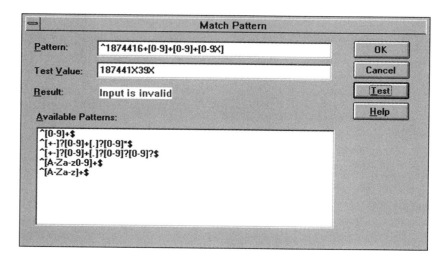

Extended Attributes for the item_master Table

To complete our database design, you should add the following extended attributes to the item_master table:

Field	Format Style	Edit Style
item_no	item_no	-
last_receipt_date	-	MM/DD/YYYY
last_issue_date	-	MM/DD/YYYY
re_order_level	[General]	-
balance	[General]	-
measuring_unit	-	measuring_units
current_price	[General]	-

This completes the database design stage. The next step is to add some actual data to our tables.

Data Manipulation

To view the data that is stored in a table, or even to alter/manipulate it, click on the Preview icon from the PainterBar. When viewing data, PowerBuilder uses a default presentation style, but you can use a different style by selecting Objects/Data Manipulation from the menu and selecting the appropriate presentation style from the cascading menu:

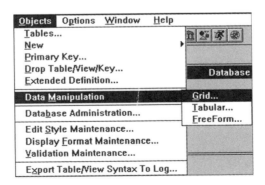

Once you are in the Data Manipulation window, you can insert new, change existing or delete old data from the table. The toolbar allows you to perform all of these tasks:

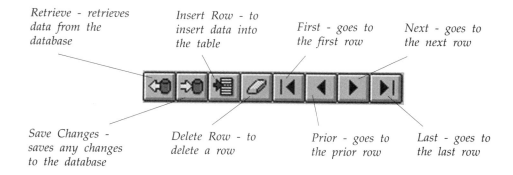

Retrieve - retrieves data from the database

Insert Row - to insert data into the table

First - goes to the first row

Next - goes to the next row

Save Changes - saves any changes to the database

Delete Row - to delete a row

Prior - goes to the prior row

Last - goes to the last row

> Any data that you add, or any changes to existing data, are held at the client site, that is, in your local memory. To make the changes permanent in the back-end database, you have to click on the **Save Changes** icon.

Go into the Data Manipulation window for the measurement_units table, click on the Insert Row icon and type in the following data:

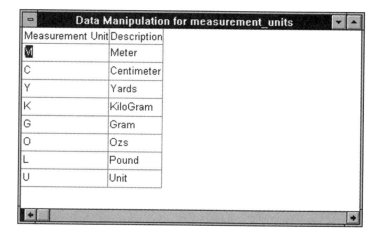

Measurement Unit	Description
M	Meter
C	Centimeter
Y	Yards
K	KiloGram
G	Gram
O	Ozs
L	Pound
U	Unit

Click on the Save Changes icon to save the information to the database. Our other tables contain much more information than this one, so to save you typing in all the data, we'll show you how to import data from a tab delimited text file.

Importing Data

At the moment, PowerBuilder only supports importing data from two types of file format, tab delimited text and the **.DBF** format. However, it is likely that in future releases, more file formats will be supported.

To import the data for the item_master table, go into the Data Manipulation window and select Rows/Import...:

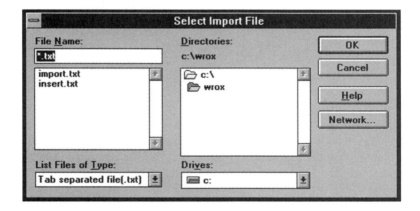

Select the **IMPORT.TXT** file and click OK. This should be in the **C:\WROX** directory if you copied all the files from the CD-ROM.

> *For each row that you import, PowerBuilder creates an INSERT statement and sends it to the database when you click on the Save Changes icon. This is a logged operation so, if you are importing large amounts of data, first consider the memory on your local machine and the log space that is required. If you are connected to SQL Server, you should consider using a Bulk-Copy Program (BCP).*

PowerBuilder will import the information from the text file and display it on the screen:

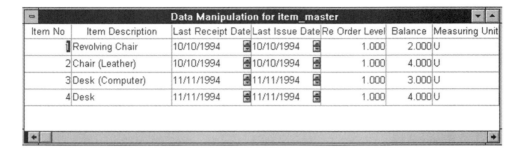

When you save the changes, the data will be written to the database. We've included two more text files on the CD-ROM, **IMPORT2.TXT** and **IMPORT3.TXT**, which contain the data for the item_images and transaction_table tables. Import these in the same way and we'll have a database, awash with information, ready for interrogation.

Exporting Data

We've just seen how you can import data from a tab delimited text file. It may occur to you that it would be useful to export data from a table into some other format. PowerBuilder allows you to do this, by providing you with the tools to support several popular file formats.

To see how this works, go to the Data Manipulation window for the measurement_units table and select File/Save Rows As...:

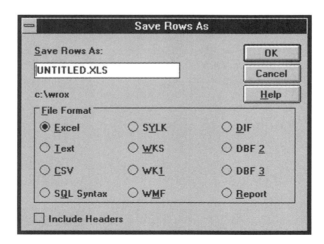

As you can see, PowerBuilder provides you with a wide choice of file formats. For our example, choose Excel with the Include Headers option selected, so that we know what the data refers to, then give the file a name, say **UNITS.XLS**, and click the OK button.

Now *Alt+Tab* out of PowerBuilder and open up the spreadsheet:

	A	B	C	D
1	measuring unit	description		
2	M	Meter		
3	C	Centimeter		
4	Y	Yards		
5	K	KiloGram		
6	G	Gram		
7	O	Ozs		
8	L	Pound		
9	U	Unit		
10				
11				
12				
13				
14				

UNITS.XLS — UNITS

You can see that we have all the information from the measurement_units table in a standard Excel spreadsheet.

> The *.XLS* file format which PowerBuilder creates isn't the latest version, in fact it is an Excel 2.1 worksheet. Fortunately, Microsoft operates a backwards compatibility program, so Excel 5.0 will read the file. However, if you attempt to save any changes to the 2.1 version format, you'll be informed that it isn't the latest version and asked if you want to update it.

As you can imagine, this exporting feature can be very useful. In the same way that we copied the table definition of our item_master table into our example database, you could export the actual data from a table into SQL Syntax or a text file and then import it into another table.

Sorting Data

From the Data Manipulation window, you can force PowerBuilder to sort the displayed data into alphabetical or numerical order. Look at the measurement_units table and select Rows/Sort...:

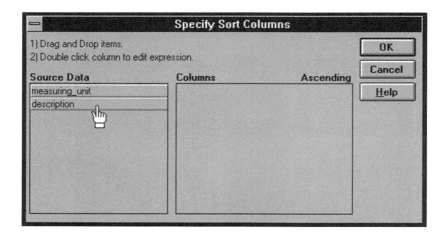

Drag the description field from the Source Data column into the Columns column and click on the OK button. The data will now be displayed in alphabetical order:

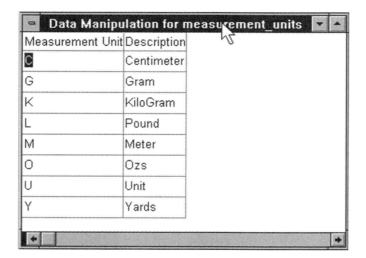

You can also alter the sorting expression so that we sort based on the length of the description field. The data would then be displayed in numerical order of length.

Filtering Data

As well as sorting the displayed data, we can also filter it. To perform this task, select Rows/Filter...:

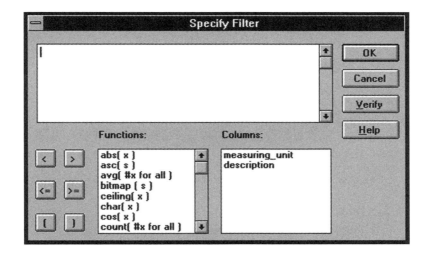

You can build an expression using any of the available functions from the list, fields in the table and the selection of mathematical operators. For example, if we only wanted to display the rows with a description of less than six characters long, we would use the following expression:

```
len( description ) < 6
```

Applying this filter would produce the following output:

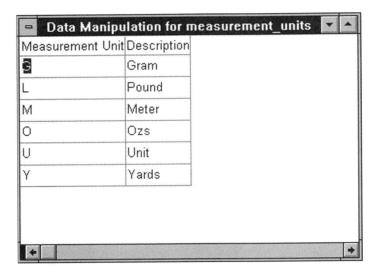

Only those rows that pass the filter criteria are displayed, but you should note that all the data is still available to us on our local machine and we've not made any changes to the back-end database; we could remove the filter and all the data would be displayed again.

When you are building an expression, you can test its validity by clicking on the __Verify__ button. Obviously most of the available functions are used with a particular type of data, so you need to verify that your expression makes sense.

Displaying Row Description

When you have been sorting, filtering, deleting and modifying data in the Data Manipulation window, it may be useful to see a summary of what you have done to the rows. You can see this by selecting Rows/Described...:

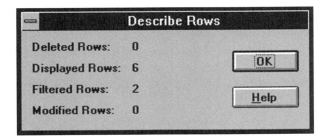

Zooming

When you have sorted and filtered data, you may want to change the size of the display on screen. To do this select Display/Zoom...:

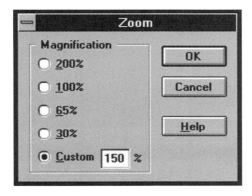

You can select from one of the pre-defined magnifications or type in a custom value. When you click the OK button, the display will change to the specified size:

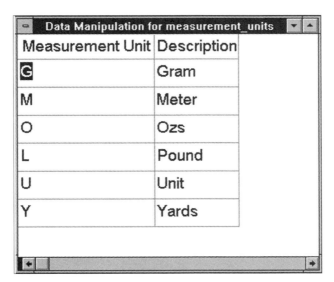

Printing the Data

You can print or preview the current display using the standard File menu options of Print... and Print Preview. In Print Preview mode, you can turn on the Print Preview Rulers to let you adjust the margins and you can alter the magnification by using the Print Preview Zoom... feature.

Drag these arrows to adjust the margins

The zoom feature allows you to adjust the magnification

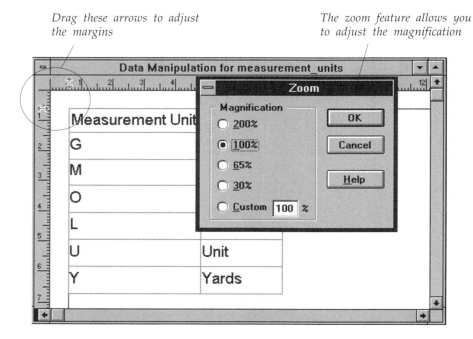

Both of these options are selected from the File menu. Note that any magnification changes that you make in Print Preview mode are discarded when you turn Print Preview off; the display returning to the size it was before the Print Preview.

PowerBuilder Attributes and System Tables

We've now completed our review of the Database Painter, including a look at connecting to a back-end database, administration of the database from your PowerBuilder application and the actual process of creating and populating new tables.

Unfortunately, this flexibility may cause you some problems. In order to enhance the relationship between your PowerBuilder application and the database, PowerBuilder uses system tables to store some of the important attributes concerning the layout and internal structure of the database that the application is currently associated with.

The crunch comes when you consider that the database structure and content may have been altered by the native database engine outside of your PowerBuilder application. If any alterations are made to the database between PowerBuilder connections, the system tables can fall out of sync with the actuals in the database. It is this problem that you will need to solve before the PowerBuilder application can work properly with the out of sync back-end database.

Getting the System Tables Back in Sync

At the start of this chapter, we mentioned that you could choose to view PowerBuilder system tables by checking the appropriate option in the Select Tables dialog box:

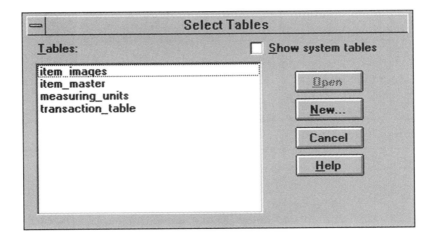

If you check this option, a whole series of system tables will be displayed and you can look at the information contained in any of these, simply by selecting them onto the Database Structure window and opening them as usual.

We are particularly interested in five of these tables, the ones starting with the prefix pbcat:

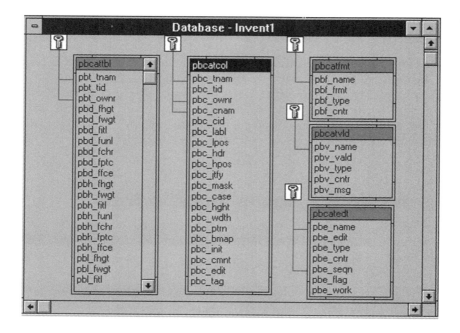

These tables contain information about the various extended attributes that are available or have been defined for our database.

System Table	Description
PBCATTBL	Contains all the font information for the text, labels, headers and so on
PBCATCOL	Contains details of all the extended attributes for each column in each table in the database
PBCATFMT	Contains definitions of available formats
PBCATVLD	Contains definitions of validation rules
PBCATEDT	Contains definitions of edit styles

In most cases, you won't use PowerBuilder to create and alter table definitions. In fact, you will probably only use PowerBuilder as a front-end tool to display data from existing databases. In such situations, the extended attributes that are offered by PowerBuilder are not used at all.

On the other hand, it is possible to create tables with PowerBuilder and then alter them outside of the PowerBuilder environment. For example, we could alter the definition of our PowerBuilder produced tables using Watcom's Interactive SQL tool. In order to rectify this situation, PowerBuilder supplies the option to synchronize the attributes from the Options menu.

If there aren't any differences between the attribute definitions, PowerBuilder will display a message telling you that synchronization isn't required:

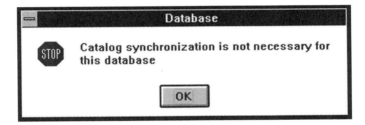

Summary

We've now completed the set up of the database that we'll use throughout the application that we are building. We've shown you how to create tables, define attributes and enter data into your tables. We've also covered a little bit of database design theory, so you should be more confident when designing and creating your own databases.

You've already seen how to sort and filter the data that is displayed from the data manipulation screen. In the next chapter, we'll look at one of the cornerstones of PowerBuilder - DataWindows, and show you how to query the data in our tables.

DataWindows: Retrieving Data

The idea of a DataWindow is one of the cornerstones that PowerBuilder is built upon and, perhaps coincidentally, it is one of the most extensively used components when creating an application.

In this chapter, the first of two devoted to this subject, we'll introduce the DataWindow Painter environment and see how DataWindows are used to retrieve information from a data source. We'll investigate the various methods of retrieving data and cover some of the options which relate to these methods.

We will look at:

- Building a DataWindow
- Connecting to a database
- Importing and exporting data
- Using stored procedures

Introduction

A DataWindow is a data aware object and is used to retrieve, manipulate and display data from a database. DataWindows reduce to a minimum the need for code which has been specially developed to get the data from a database into a presentable format on screen, by internally creating native database related commands for you.

There are two main parts to a DataWindow - the retrieval of data from the database and the display of that retrieved data. In this opening appraisal of the idea of a DataWindow, we are going to cover the process behind the retrieval of the data from the database, ready for the following chapter on display.

Objects and Controls, Data and Users

There are 4 main steps to creating a DataWindow and using it in your applications:

1 Select a data source and presentation style, or in other words, the way that you want to extract some data from a database and the general format that the data should be displayed.

2 Define the appropriate SQL statements which will provide the information that you wish to supply to the user; this is sometimes referred to as the Data Source definition.

3 Paint the DataWindow to appropriately display the information.

4 Associate the DataWindow object with a DataWindow control on a window, so that the data held in the object can be displayed to the user.

To illustrate how PowerBuilder uses a data source, DataWindow objects, DataWindow controls and the user interface, take a look at the following diagram:

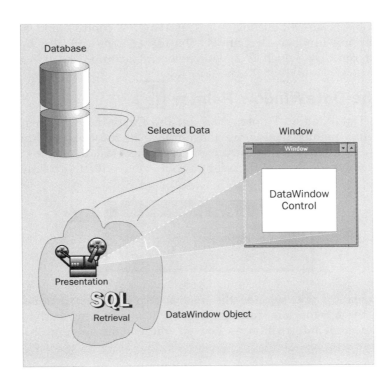

The DataWindow object definition consists of any display information, initial values, validation rules and SQL statement definitions required to present the user with the appropriate data, ready for alteration or review. Once a DataWindow object has been defined, it has to be associated with a DataWindow control that has been placed on a Window.

In the simplest terms, the role of a DataWindow object is one of data retrieval. It contains all the information necessary to retrieve the data you wish to see in your window, the formatting that you wish to apply to that information and the manner in which you want it passed to the DataWindow control. Remember that the difference between a DataWindow object and a DataWindow control is that the control simply displays the information, while the object gets the appropriate information and formats it as required.

DataWindow objects are independent of DataWindow controls and so can be associated with any number of controls. The associations can also be changed dynamically at run-time which is a very powerful feature.

Invoking the DataWindow Painter

To invoke the DataWindow Painter, click on the DataWindow icon from the PowerBar. As this painter deals with the retrieval of information from a database, PowerBuilder automatically connects to the last database you were using. At this stage, PowerBuilder might supply you with the following dialog:

This dialog appears if you selected the Prompt before connecting option as you were defining the appropriate database profile. It allows you to dynamically define the connection information as you go, rather than relying on statically created database profiles.

> Connecting and disconnecting to databases takes a noticeable amount of time and uses valuable system resources. Therefore, we advise you to set the **Database Stay Connected** preference to 1, so that the connection to a database remains open until you specifically change the database connection or physically shut down PowerBuilder.

Once you have connected to your database, you are ready to review your current DataWindows or create new ones. To get more of an idea of what is behind a DataWindow object, let's look at how they are created.

Creating a DataWindow

When you are connected to your database, create a new DataWindow by clicking on the New button. PowerBuilder presents you with the following dialog, allowing you access to stage one of the creation process:

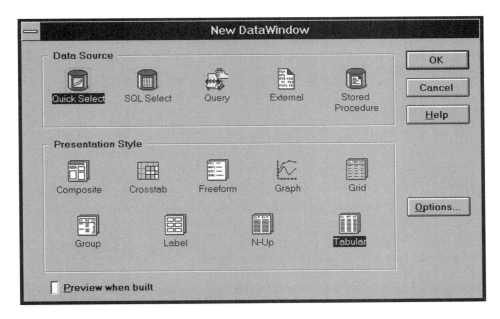

When you begin to create a DataWindow, the first task you must complete is the declaration of a DataSource and a Presentation Style. Clearly, the former affects the selection of information from the database, while the latter affects how the data will be presented. Throughout this chapter, we will be using the default presentation style of Freeform, while we examine the various data sources that are available.

Before we move on to look at the different options that PowerBuilder has to offer when considering the data source that you are going to use, it is useful to take a quick tour of the various views of the DataWindow object that you will be encountering.

Viewing a DataWindow

There are three main views of a DataWindow that you will encounter:

▲ Preview

▲ Design

▲ Select

Each of these views are used to look at the contents of the DataWindow in a different format. Using Preview, you can take a look at the data you have chosen from the database with the commands in the Select view, in a format defined in the Design view.

Preview

You can use this view of a DataWindow object for two main reasons:

▲ To check out the subset of data that the SQL statements that you have defined.

▲ To review the layout of the data - this is the layout that will appear in the DataWindow control on your window.

An example of Preview in action is shown below:

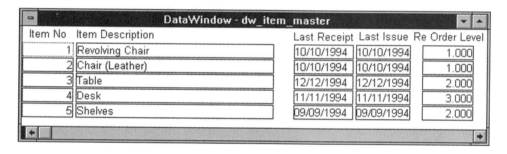

If you check the Preview when built option, when you have completed the definition of the data source, PowerBuilder retrieves the data with the default settings and presents the data in this view, as the user will see it. If you leave this option unchecked, PowerBuilder takes you straight into Design view.

Design

This view of the DataWindow illustrates how the data will be presented to the user. The default layout of the DataWindow is heavily based upon the selection that you make for the Presentation Style.

By a combination of headers and footers and the layout of the specific fields in the different areas of the window, you can produce any of the formats that are offered here. We'll look at how to get the most out of this arrangement in the next chapter, but for now, take a sneak preview of what you might encounter:

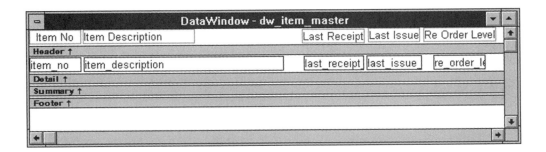

Select

This view of the DataWindow is the basis for the data that will be presented to the user. Based upon the SQL statements that are defined here, PowerBuilder sends appropriate requests for specific subsets of the information contained on the database.

Through the various options that are available, you can choose to define criteria to narrow the selection, sort the returned information by some set of rules, compute some extra information from the returned information and much more.

We'll be concentrating on this part of the DataWindow in the rest of this chapter, as well as how it interacts with the data source and the method of interrogation that you select from the earliest stages of defining a DataWindow:

Connecting to a Data Source

Now that we have completed a quick tour of the DataWindow Painter, let's return to the creation of a DataWindow. One of the fundamental objectives of a DataWindow is the collection of information from a database and the method by which it performs this task is a complex issue that is worth investigation.

PowerBuilder provides you with five methods of connecting to a data source, each of which has a different structure and a different effect on the overall application. These five methods are:

- Quick Select
- SQL Select
- Query
- External
- Stored Procedure

Let's look at each of these in turn, concentrating on how each should be used and when it is most appropriate to use that method.

Quick Select

This method is most often used when you want to select data from a single table, although you can select from multiple tables. It allows you to quickly define the data source, simply by selecting the table and corresponding fields you want to see, followed by a sort order and selection criteria to obtain and organize a specific set of data. To see how this works, select Quick Select and click on the OK button:

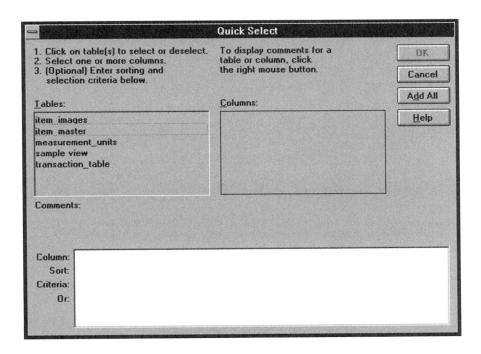

All the available tables and views are listed in the Tables ListBox and when you highlight one of these entries, the related fields will be displayed in the Columns list. Right-clicking on a table or field name will display any comments associated with the component without highlighting it.

> *The right-click allows you to obtain just the information that you require (the comments associated with the component) without wasting valuable time and resources adding the whole component to the DataWindow. This functionality is very user-friendly and resource conservative - two good reasons to use the idea in your own applications.*

When you have selected the table that you are interested in, by highlighting its associated fields, PowerBuilder will add them to the box at the bottom of the window, so starting the selection process. You can then opt to specify a sort order (either ascending or descending) for each field and any selection criteria that is used to further refine the information that is returned to the PowerBuilder application.

The following example is the d_chapter7_quick_select DataWindow in the **EXAMPLES.PBL** on the CD-ROM:

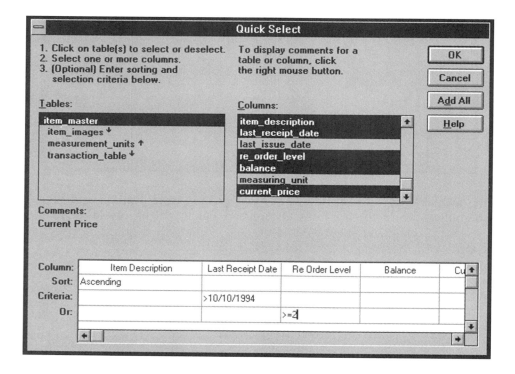

Remember that this is the Select view of the DataWindow which you must create as your first task. When you open this from the CD-ROM, PowerBuilder will automatically take you to the Design of the DataWindow:

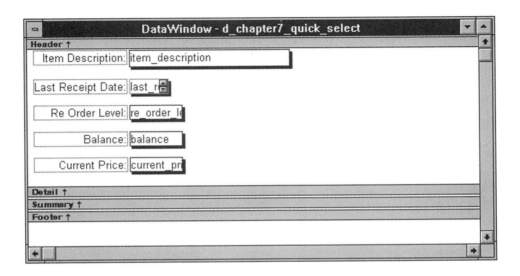

Looking at the Results

As you can see by reviewing the Select view of this DataWindow, we've asked for item_description, last_receipt_date, re_order_level, balance and current_price from the item_master table to be displayed. We've specified an ascending sort order on the Item Description field and the criteria that the Last Receipt Date should be greater than 10/10/1994 or the Re Order Level should be greater than or equal to two.

If there are two or more criteria in the Criteria row then all the conditions in the row must be met - this is known as a logical **AND**. The Or row is used to specify **OR** conditions, or in other words, where one thing or another (or both) must be met. By using one or both of these commands, you can quickly refine the information that you wish to see by compiling more and more complex criteria.

You can also use the keywords AND and OR in a criteria for a single column. As you will see in a moment, PowerBuilder automatically converts this graphical definition into SQL syntax before requesting the information from the database. While it performs this conversion, it looks at the layout of your criteria and places AND and ORs in the appropriate places in the SQL statement.

For example, if we wanted the Last Receipt Date to be between 10/10/1994 and 12/12/1994, we would use in the appropriate column:

```
>10/10/1994   AND   <12/12/1994
```

> *The criteria that you specify can contain the names of other columns in the table. This allows you to compare two 'dynamic' values, rather than having to stick with a static entry. For example, we could have specified a criteria that required the Re Order Level to be greater than the Balance.*

If you select Design/Preview... you'll see what information the DataWindow has retrieved from the database:

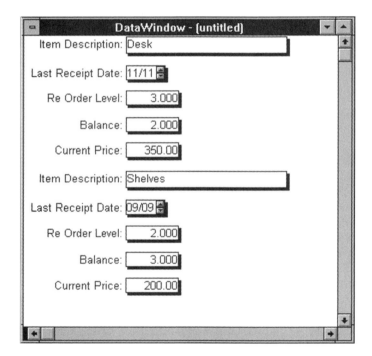

This is similar to the Data Manipulation view in the Database Painter. You have the same toolbar options to move through the data and the same menu options to filter, sort, export, print and so on.

SQL Select

This is the most flexible and extensively used way of creating a DataWindow because it gives you greater control over the SQL statement without you needing to know the syntax of SQL. As an example of how this type of data source works, we've created a DataWindow called d_chapter7_sql_select, which is in the **EXAMPLES.PBL** on the CD-ROM:

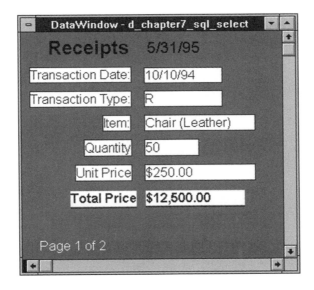

If you scroll down, you'll see that there is a second and third page to this DataWindow. The DataWindow is based on the transaction_table and item_master tables and displays the receipts with the name of the date, name of the item, quantity and price. The third page contains the grand total of all the receipts:

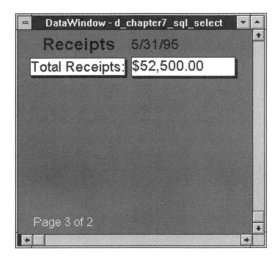

You can see that the page numbering is a little strange. This is because the **Page()** function which we added to the footer only counts the pages which contain a record. The consequence of this is that the final page which contains summary information isn't included in the total page count.

To see how we created this DataWindow, select Display/Design... and then Design/Edit Data Source...:

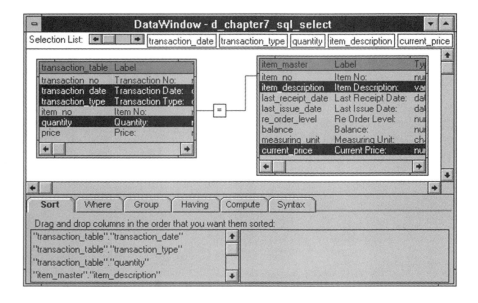

This shows our two tables joined automatically and the highlighted fields are the ones that we've selected to display in the DataWindow. They also appear in the Selection List at the top of the window. PowerBuilder creates the appropriate SQL statement based upon this information combined with that supplied in the various tabbed dialog boxes in the bottom half of the window.

Sort

This is where you specify a sort order for the fields that you want to display:

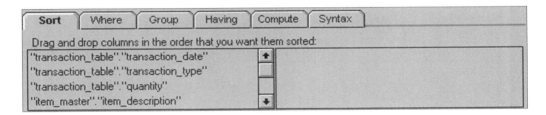

When you click on a field from the tables, it is added to the list on the left-hand side. By dragging the fields from the left to the right, you can define the manner in which the information that PowerBuilder has retrieved from the database is sorted.

For example, we could sort based on transaction_date, simply by dragging it from the left to the right column:

When you specify a field to sort on, you can select either ascending or descending for your sort order by checking or clearing the Ascending checkbox.

> If you specify more than one sort order, PowerBuilder will sort on the first field in the list, then the second and so on from top to bottom.

Where

The **WHERE** clause of the SQL SELECT statement allows you to specify criteria for the data that you want to display:

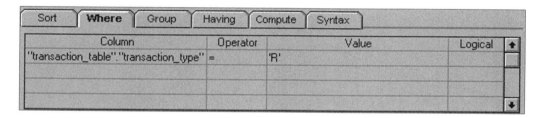

This is similar to the Criteria row that appears when you create a Quick Select style DataWindow. You can select fields from a drop-down list, using operators to specify the type of comparison that you require. In this example, you can see that we've specified that the transaction_type should be equal to 'R'. The Logical column allows you to build up complex criteria with AND and OR statements.

> *Note that you don't have to supply the quote marks around the value. PowerBuilder will decide if it needs them based on the type of data and will automatically add them as necessary.*

If you right-click in the Value box, a pop-up menu will allow you to select various options:

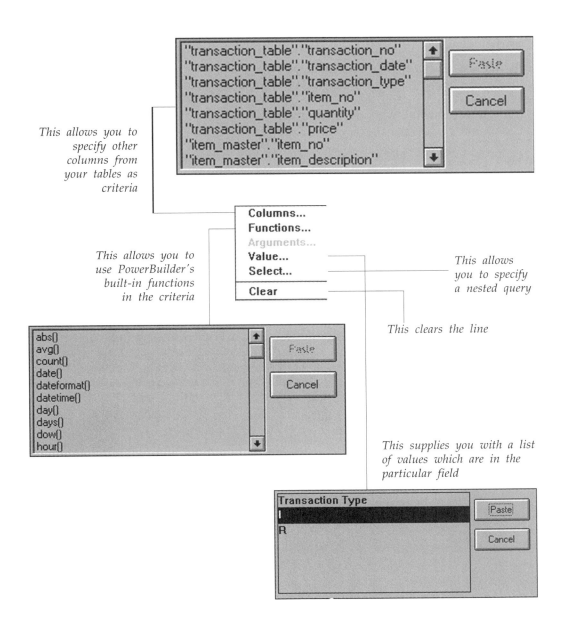

This allows you to specify other columns from your tables as criteria

This allows you to use PowerBuilder's built-in functions in the criteria

This allows you to specify a nested query

This clears the line

This supplies you with a list of values which are in the particular field

There is another - Arguments...- which you can use if you have set up any **Retrieval Arguments**. We'll show you how to use these arguments in a moment.

Group

This allows you to group your data based on one or more fields. For example, you might choose to group your data based on transaction type. This might be useful for different departments in a company who are only interested in one particular transaction type. The grouping allows you to put more structure into the data simply by rearranging it.

When using a Watcom database, you must include every field that is to be displayed in the DataWindow in the GROUP BY clause:

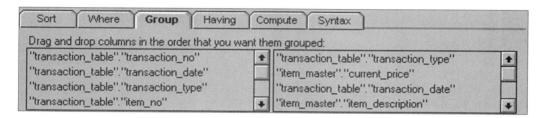

This effectively invalidates the usefulness of grouping data, but with other databases, it isn't necessary to include all the fields in the GROUP BY clause.

Having

This is created in the same way as the WHERE clause, but is used to specify criteria for a group. So, as an illustration, we could further refine the above example to only select records for each transaction type which fall between certain dates.

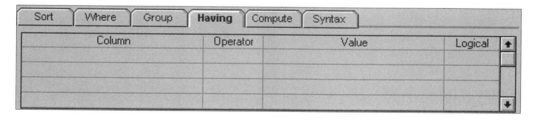

You can see that the structure is exactly the same as the WHERE clause. Our DataWindow is quite simple so we don't need to specify any extra criteria here. With a Watcom database and its poor support for the GROUP BY clause, this clause is virtually unused.

Compute

This allows you to define computed fields based on one or more existing fields. In our example, we've defined a computed field to display the product of the quantity and the current_price fields. This gives us the total amount of money for each transaction:

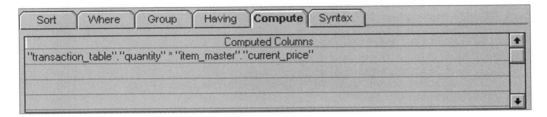

As before, by right-clicking in the Computed Column, PowerBuilder brings up a menu which allows you to select fields from your tables as well as predefined PowerBuilder functions.

> It is always a good idea to create computed fields dynamically at run-time rather than storing them as part of your database. Whilst our example application is quite small, if you had a proper enterprise application with possibly thousands of records, storing an extra field in your database would be a significant use of memory.

Syntax

The final tabbed dialog box displays the SQL statement which PowerBuilder creates, based upon the entries that you have made in the other tabbed dialog boxes:

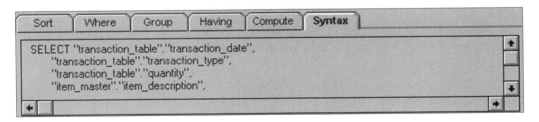

You can't edit the SQL statement from here, but if you do know SQL and prefer to type in the syntax rather than going through the visual steps we've described, you can select Options/Convert To Syntax to display the full editable SQL:

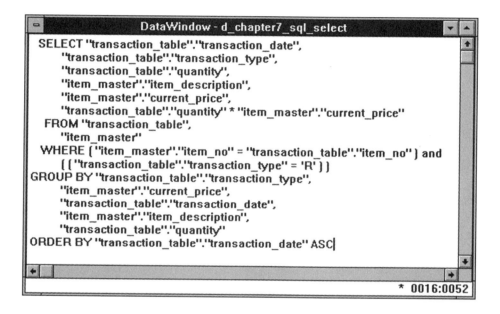

```
DataWindow - d_chapter7_sql_select

SELECT "transaction_table"."transaction_date",
    "transaction_table"."transaction_type",
    "transaction_table"."quantity",
    "item_master"."item_description",
    "item_master"."current_price",
    "transaction_table"."quantity" * "item_master"."current_price"
  FROM "transaction_table",
    "item_master"
  WHERE ("item_master"."item_no" = "transaction_table"."item_no") and
    (("transaction_table"."transaction_type" = 'R'))
GROUP BY "transaction_table"."transaction_type",
    "item_master"."current_price",
    "transaction_table"."transaction_date",
    "item_master"."item_description",
    "transaction_table"."quantity"
ORDER BY "transaction_table"."transaction_date" ASC

                                              * 0016:0052
```

Structured Query Language is a powerful, yet easy-to-learn language and just by looking at the SQL statements that PowerBuilder creates, you will quickly pick it up.

The DISTINCT Clause

When you are creating a SELECT statement, you can ensure that no duplicate records are displayed by specifying Distinct from the Options menu. PowerBuilder adds the word DISTINCT after SELECT and will only return unique rows in the resulting subset of information.

> You should be aware that if you compare two columns for equality in a WHERE clause and both the columns have NULL values, then you won't get a match. If you are using one of the more flexible database engines, you can get around this problem by using the DISTINCT clause.

When using WATCOM SQL, specifying DISTINCT automatically sorts the result sets, but this isn't true with SQL Server and is something you should note when porting applications from one database to another.

Retrieval Arguments

If you don't want to hard code a SQL SELECT statement's criteria at design time, but instead want to allow the user some control over the criteria at run-time, then you can use **Retrieval Arguments**.

In our example, we can allow the user to type in the transaction_type at run-time. Select Objects/Retrieval Arguments..., supply the name trans_type and specify the data type as String:

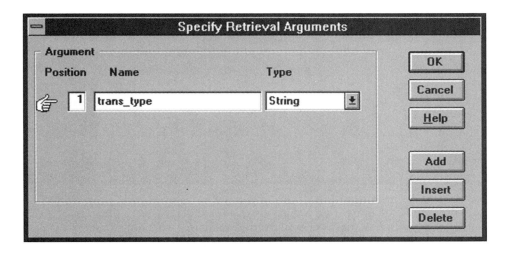

Now go back into the design view for our DataWindow and in the Where dialog box right-click in the Value column. You'll see that the Arguments... option is now available and, if you click on it, you'll be able to paste the retrieval argument that we've just created into the Value column:

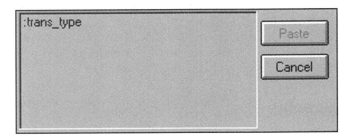

With this stage complete, if you try previewing the DataWindow, you'll be prompted to supply the argument for the WHERE clause:

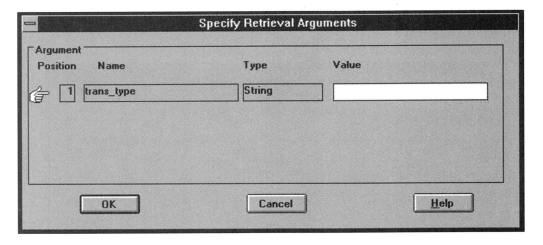

You can now type in either 'R' for receipts or 'I' for invoices and the relevant data will be retrieved. If you type in something else, an entry that PowerBuilder doesn't recognize, you'll simply get a blank DataWindow.

> Note that once you've specified a retrieval argument, the same argument will be used until you close your current session or requery the database by clicking on the Retrieve icon from the PainterBar.

SQL Differences

Unfortunately, there are several different flavors of SQL and each is constantly updated. In an attempt to resolve this potentially explosive minefield, the American National Standards Institute (ANSI) set up the SQL standards committee for just that task - to standardize the various versions of SQL that are currently being used by the major database servers.

Due to the lack of standards in the past, there are some significant differences between standard SQL and the versions in use in the real world. The following table summarizes some of the differences with Microsoft SQL Server:

Clause	Standard SQL	SQL Server
GROUP BY	Columns in a select list must also be in the GROUP BY expression or they must be arguments of aggregate functions. A GROUP BY expression can only contain column names that are in the select list.	A select list that includes aggregates can include columns that are not arguments of aggregate functions and are not included in the GROUP BY clause. The GROUP BY clause can include columns or expressions that aren't in the select list.
HAVING	Columns in a HAVING expression must be, for instance, single-valued-arguments of aggregates and they must be in the select list or GROUP BY clause. A query with a HAVING should have a GROUP BY clause, but if omitted, all the rows not excluded by the WHERE clause are considered to be a single group.	The HAVING clause can include columns or expressions not in the select list and not in the GROUP BY clause.
ORDER BY	No restrictions.	Restricted to a maximum of 16 columns.

When you are porting your applications from one platform to another, it is vital that you understand the differences between the two versions of SQL that you are moving between - if not, you could be in for some long evenings surrounded by huge text books, reams of computer print-out and far too many empty coffee cups:

Joining Tables

The join operation is the hallmark of the relational database model. More than any other feature, a join distinguishes relational database management systems from other types of DBMSs. We've already seen how PowerBuilder automatically joins database tables which have the appropriate primary and foreign keys defined, a process that is graphical reflected in our SQL SELECT DataWindow between the item_master and transaction_table tables:

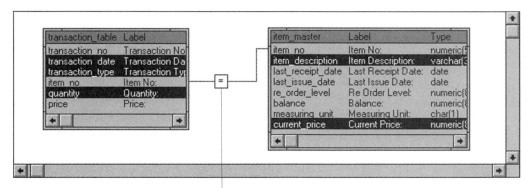

Join Box - note the symbol inside the box

There are basically four types of join:

Join	Description
Equi or Natural	A relationship between two tables where the values in the two critical columns are compared on the basis of equality, with all the columns in both tables appearing in the results set. Note that only one of the two joined columns is included, as they are identical. This is the default type of join which PowerBuilder creates automatically.
Theta	Theta joins use the comparison operators as the join condition. Comparison operators include equal (=), not equal(!=), greater than(>), less than(<), greater than or equal to (>=) and less than or equal to(<=).
Self	A join used for comparing values within a column of a table. Since this operation involves a join of a table with itself, you need to give the table two temporary (correlation) names. The correlation names are then used to qualify the column names in the rest of the query.

Continued

261

Join	Description
Outer	A join in which both matching and non-matching rows are returned. The operators *= and =* are used to indicate that all the rows in the first or second tables should be returned, regardless of whether or not there is a match on the join column.

If primary and foreign keys are not defined for the tables, PowerBuilder will try to join the tables based on common column names. You should be aware of this, but it isn't too bad as you can easily delete any unwanted joins.

If you want to change the type of join or determine the type of joins in someone else's database, you can double-click on the join box:

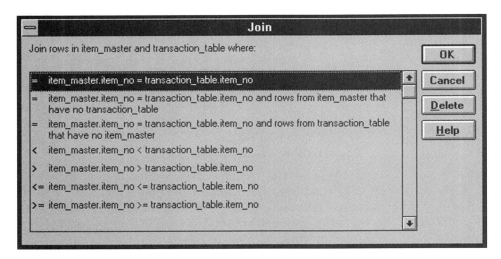

As well as displaying the type of join, this gives an explanation of exactly what will be selected from both tables. You can see that in the first case only rows that are equal in both tables will be selected, whereas the next option - an outer join - allows all the rows from one table with equivalent rows from the other. The bottom four represent the various theta joins that are possible.

Saving as a Query

Once you have defined a SQL SELECT statement, you may want to save it for future use. The simplest way to do this is to save it as a query which can then be re-used. Select File/Save Query or File/Save Query As... from the menu:

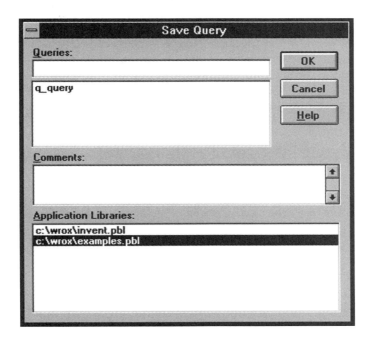

The query is stored in your PowerBuilder library, along with all the other objects from the current application, as opposed to saving it as a text file containing the SQL statements themselves.

You can also create queries outside of the DataWindow Painter; this environment is called the Query Painter. You can then choose to create a DataWindow based on an existing query. We'll look at this next.

Query

Queries are created in exactly the same way as SQL SELECT statements, except that they have their own Painter and are created outside the

DataWindow environment. Using Queries means that you can base multiple DataWindows on the same SQL statements without having to repeat the definition.

Create a new DataWindow and this time select Query as the data source. PowerBuilder asks for the name of the query that you want to base the DataWindow on. Select the query that we just saved and click OK. If you preview this DataWindow the Specify Retrieval Arguments window will pop up asking you to specify the transaction type. If you type in 'R', PowerBuilder will show a preview of the DataWindow:

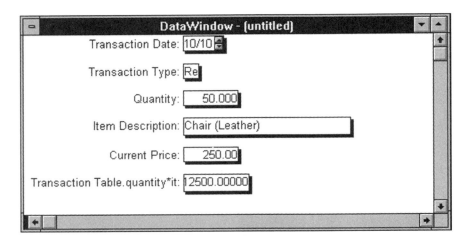

You can see that this shows the same basic information as our previous example, but has none of the nice touches. In the next chapter, we'll look at the various presentation styles that you can use in a DataWindow and we'll explore some of the user interface design aspects relating to them.

When you select a query as the basis for a DataWindow, you aren't creating a dynamic link between the two components. This means that if you then make changes to the query or to the DataWindow definition, the changes made to one object won't be reflected in the other.

External

When you consider the topic of data retrieval, you automatically begin to think about databases, SQL and queries. However, a database isn't the only means of storing data; you can also retrieve data from an external source such as a text file.

When you create a DataWindow using an external data source, the first thing you have to do is declare the result set definitions:

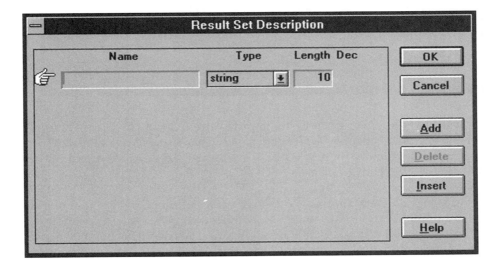

This is exactly like the database table definitions, providing you with column names, data types and lengths. You populate an external DataWindow programmatically using file functions or embedded SQL statements in your PowerScript code.

We need an external DataWindow for our Stock Control System, so create an external DataWindow and declare the following result set:

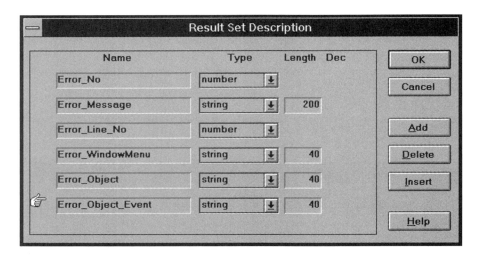

In the next chapter, we'll see how to improve the look of the DataWindow and, in the scripting chapter, we'll look at how we use this DataWindow in our application. Switch to design mode by selecting Display/Design and save the DataWindow as dw_error_information.

We'll be using this DataWindow to display error information if something goes wrong in our application. We could use window controls such as StaticText, SingleLineEdit and MultiLineEdit instead of this DataWindow, but if we did, we would have to call a whole string of print functions to output the error information. Using the DataWindow means that we can output all the information with a single print function. We'll go into the details of this in the scripting chapter.

Stored Procedures

A stored procedure is essentially an SQL statement that is stored at the database level. When you create a stored procedure, an execution plan is prepared which makes subsequent execution very fast.

> An execution plan is a compiled version of the SQL statement that you wish to execute. Each back-end database uses its own internal format for the compilation, so you may have to regenerate the stored procedures if you move a database between platforms.

Also, since the stored procedure is stored in the database, the client application only needs to send the stored procedure name and any associated parameters. This can drastically reduce network traffic and also help to speed up execution.

We'll look at stored procedures in depth in the later chapter on embedded SQL, but for now, we can show you the steps involved in the creation of a stored procedure based DataWindow:

1 Select the Stored Procedure Data Source.

2 When the Select Procedure screen comes up, select one of the predefined stored procedures:

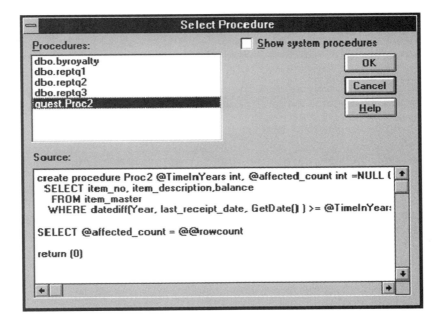

When you select a stored procedure, the SQL source code is displayed in the bottom box.

3 Click on the OK button to bring up the result set definition dialog box:

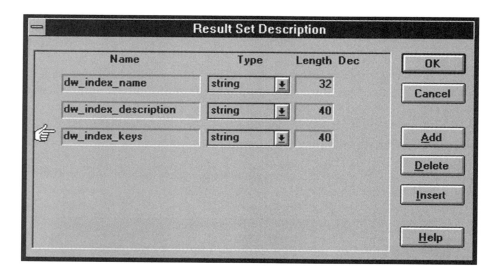

PowerBuilder automatically detects the stored procedure result definition but still allows you to manually alter it. Clicking on the OK button completes the DataWindow.

> Note that the stored procedure option is only available if the database to which you are connected supports stored procedures.

By completing this stage, you are providing your DataWindow with one of the most advanced and speediest sources for data retrieval in the new Client/Server environment.

Summary

In this chapter, we have covered the DataWindow Painter environment, with a particular focus on the data retrieval side of the equation. We have looked at each of the sources through which you can obtain data, whether it is held in your back-end database or simply held in a plain text file, whether you are using PowerBuilder derived SQL statements or the more advanced stored procedures.

In the next chapter, we are going to review the other half of the DataWindow experience, the manner in which you organize and present the data to the user, including a look at the default presentation styles that PowerBuilder has to offer.

DataWindows: Presentation Styles

So far, we've covered how to retrieve information for your DataWindow, but that is only half the story. Once you have your data, you need to consider how to display it, both in terms of graphical simplicity and enhancing the type of data that you are using.

To accomplish this task, we will look at the various presentation styles that are already built-in to PowerBuilder, as well as how and when each style should be used. By the end of the chapter, you should be producing easy-to-understand, impressive looking DataWindows which communicate data efficiently to your users.

In this chapter, we will cover:

- DataWindow presentation styles
- The DataWindow Design environment
- DataWindow options
- DataWindow preferences

Introduction

Just as there are several ways of populating DataWindows, there are several ways of displaying that population. PowerBuilder provides us with nine different presentation styles, each of which can be used in different situations to provide the best layout for your information:

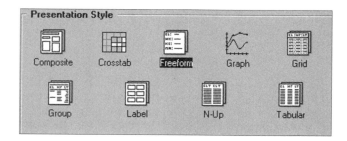

We will look at each of these, in turn, before going on to look at the design view of the DataWindow Painter, creating some DataWindows that we will use in our Stock Control application.

Freeform Presentation Style

We've been using the **Freeform** presentation style in the previous chapter, so you've already seen some examples of it:

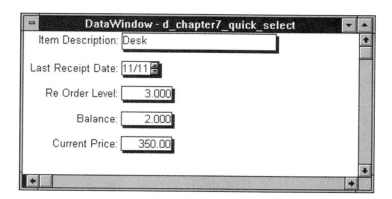

This style is similar to that of database forms, so it is best suited to data entry rather than data display. However, if you want to display records one at a time, for purposes of close-up examination, this style is back in the running.

Tabular Presentation Style

The **Tabular** presentation style displays data in columns with headers like a two-dimensional table:

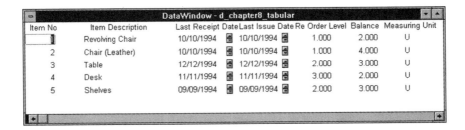

This style is often used for reports, grouping columns and for DropDown DataWindows. The number of columns and rows displayed on the screen at any one time depends on the size of the DataWindow control.

Grid Presentation Style

A DataWindow generated with the **Grid** presentation style is similar to the Tabular style, except that its rows and columns are separated by grid lines:

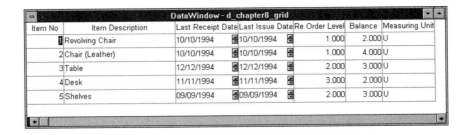

The added advantage associated with the Grid style is that at execution time, users can resize columns and even move entire columns around by clicking and dragging the column heading.

Unlike the Tabular and Freeform styles, you can't move headings and columns in the design view of a Grid style DataWindow. If you add new columns in the SELECT list by editing the data source, they will always be appended to the existing columns even if placed between existing columns in the SELECT list. To reorder the columns, switch to preview, move the columns and switch back to design view. Any changes you make will be reflected in the design view.

PowerBuilder makes this style even more flexible by allowing you to alter the basic Grid characteristics. You can choose to:

▲ Turn off the grid lines completely

▲ Only have them on when printing or previewing

▲ Restrict row resizing and column moving

To select these options, simply right-click in design view and choose the Grid menu option:

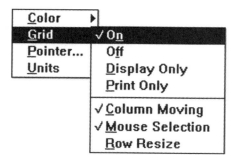

Selecting the Grid Off option automatically disables column moving. Note that under the right conditions, the Grid presentation style acts exactly like the Tabular style.

Group Presentation Style

The **Group** presentation style allows you to perform the necessary grouping of data at the client side of the machine rather than at the database side - the database side grouping occurs when you use the **GROUP BY** clause in a **SELECT** statement.

We've already mentioned the problem with the **GROUP BY** clause and a Watcom database, so this also allows us to get round the problem and still be able to present grouped sets of data:

	DataWindow - d_chapter8_group						

Item Master Report
6/13/95

Item No	Item Description	Last Receipt Date	Last Issue Date	Re Order Level	Balance	Measuring Unit
		09/09/1994				
5	Shelves		09/09/1994	2.000	3.000	U
		10/10/1994				
1	Revolving Chair		10/10/1994	1.000	2.000	U
2	Chair (Leather)		10/10/1994	1.000	4.000	U
		11/11/1994				
4	Desk		11/11/1994	3.000	2.000	U
		12/12/1994				
3	Table		12/12/1994	2.000	3.000	U

Page 1 of 1

When you build a DataWindow with the Group presentation style, the **GROUP BY** clause isn't added to the SQL statement. PowerBuilder automatically adds trailers containing the sum of grouped columns, together with title information, the current date and page numbers.

> *Note that the trailer summations are always added to the DataWindow, even if the data that is presented doesn't warrant such an addition. Fortunately, we can modify any of the presentation styles and so it is possible to remove the useless trailers.*

N-Up Presentation Style

The **N-Up** presentation style displays data in a similar format to that of newspaper columns, allowing you to use space efficiently by displaying more than one record across the page.

DataWindow - d_chapter8_nup					
Item No	Item Description	Balance	Item No	Item Description	Balance
1	Revolving Chair	2.000	2	Chair (Leather)	4.000
3	Table	3.000	4	Desk	2.000
5	Shelves	3.000			

PowerBuilder displays the data from left to right and then top to bottom as you can see in the example above. PowerBuilder doesn't allow you to alter this organization, as there isn't an option to display the data top to bottom and then left to right.

Label Presentation Style

The **Label** presentation style allows you to create labels from existing data:

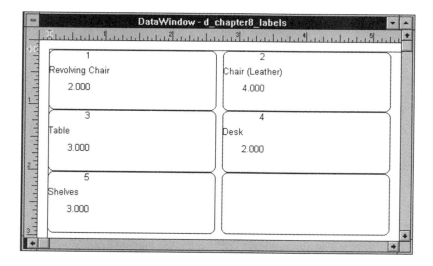

You can choose from a vast selection of pre-defined label sizes or create a custom label size. You can also alter the spacing, number of labels per page and specify top to bottom or left to right display.

Crosstab Presentation Style

A **Crosstab** is a special kind of query which is most often used to display data over a period of time. For example, a publishing company might want to display their sales figures for all their books broken down by month:

Crosstab Quantity Sold Per Month									
Title	Price	Author	1	2	3	4	5	Grand Total
Beginner's Visual Basic	29.95	Peter Wright	1100	2000	800	1745	1000	6645
Instant Delphi	24.95	Dave Jewell			1750	1020	2070	4840
Rev Access	44.95	Stephen Wynkoop	2240	1000		2650	1065	6955
Rev PowerBuilder	49.95	Prasad Bodepudi	900	1200	3300	2190	1050	8640
Grand Total			4240	4200	5850	7605	5185	27080

We've used the **Month()** function to group the data by months 1, 2, 3, 4 and 5. To create this type of query using SQL would be very complicated because of the varying number of days in a month. PowerBuilder automatically adds summary Grand Total rows and columns to the output for you.

There are three parts to a crosstab: columns, rows and values. When creating a crosstab DataWindow, you specify which fields you want to appear where:

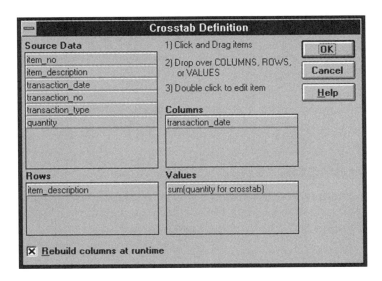

You click and drag fields from the source data into the relevant boxes and then double-click on the fields to create an expression. So, for our example, we created the expression **Month(date)** for the column to split up the data by month.

Graph Presentation Style

PowerBuilder allows you to retrieve data and display it as a **Graph**, with or without the data itself appearing in the DataWindow. Whilst the graph engine might not be as powerful as those bundled with some spreadsheet packages, it should be able to produce enough variety for most of your business needs:

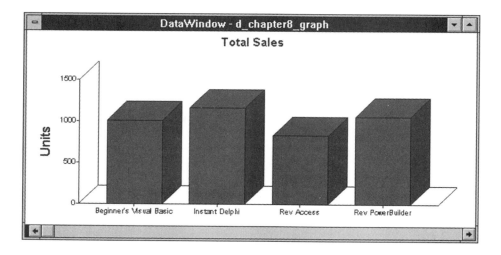

All the options relating to colors, labels, fonts and types of graph are the same for DataWindow graphs as for the graph control which we looked at in the Window Painter chapter.

Composite Presentation Style

The **Composite** presentation style allows you to produce a DataWindow based on multiple existing DataWindows. For example, we can combine the Crosstab and Graph examples onto one single DataWindow:

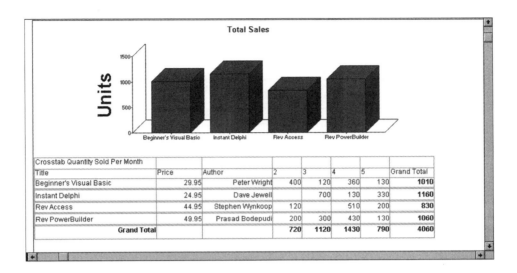

This type of DataWindow is most useful for displaying nested DataWindows. This is a technique commonly used for one of two reasons:

▲ To display more exact information with a graphical representation that has been designed to present the overall picture, rather than the details.

▲ To display a one-to-many relationship. For example, as a book distributor, you might have the book details (one side) at the top of the DataWindow and the details of all the bookstores who have ordered that book (many side) in the lower part of the DataWindow.

We use this latter use of nested DataWindows in our Stock Control application, where we display item details from the item_master table and display receipts for the current item in a second DataWindow. We'll see how to create this report later in the chapter.

DataWindow Design View

Now that we've had a brief look at the various presentation styles that are on offer, let's take a detailed look at the DataWindow Painter view where you will be doing most of the work to improving the presentation of your data: Design view.

Design View allows you to define what goes where in your DataWindow. It is split into several bands depending on the type of presentation style you are using.

Band	Description
Header	Displays a title at top of each page
Header group	Used in Crosstab and Group styles to display group headers
Detail	Contains the main body of information
Trailer group	Used in Crosstab and Group styles to display group trailers
Summary	Can be used to display summary information
Footer	Displays further information at the bottom of every page

Most of the standard window controls can also be placed on a DataWindow to improve the presentation. These can be selected from the Design view PainterBar:

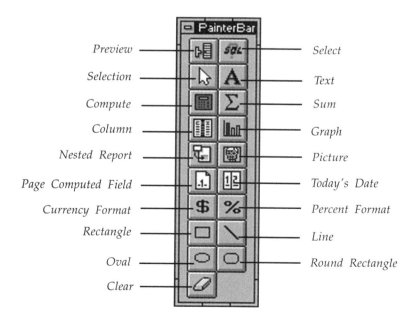

It is a good idea to try to produce consistent DataWindows with perhaps a company logo, descriptive text and date in the header band and the page number in the footer band. If you keep your DataWindows consistent then it makes it much easier for a user to find the information they want.

> **If you encounter problems with disappearing data in a DataWindow, this can be due to too much space being left between the border of the detail band and the bottom most data or text control. To counter this problem you should move the detail band to just below the last control on the DataWindow or increase the height of the DataWindow control in the window.**

Creating DataWindows for Our Applications

The best way to see what is possible with DataWindows is to create some examples and review the results. Our Stock Control application employs several DataWindows of differing formats, so let's review how these objects are created and what effect they can have on an application.

dw_item_master_free_format_for_query

This is a Freeform DataWindow which simply displays all the information from the item_master table. You can use a Quick Select to create it:

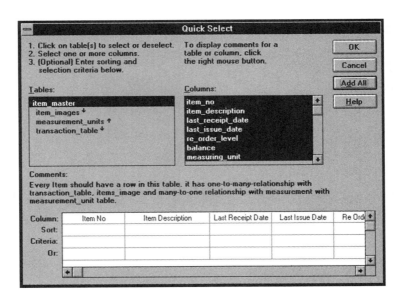

We don't need to specify any criteria as we want all of the information that the table has to offer, so when you've added all the fields from the item_master table, go into Design view and rearrange the fields so that they look like this:

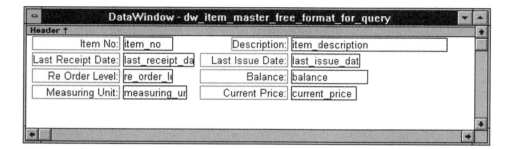

dw_consumption_report

This DataWindow displays transaction information for every item on each distinct date in a given month. The easiest way to create this is to use a Tabular DataWindow - we don't want the user to be able to alter the appearance of the information at run-time, hence we avoid the Grid presentation style.

We need information from the item_master and transaction_table tables, so we must use a SQL Select data source:

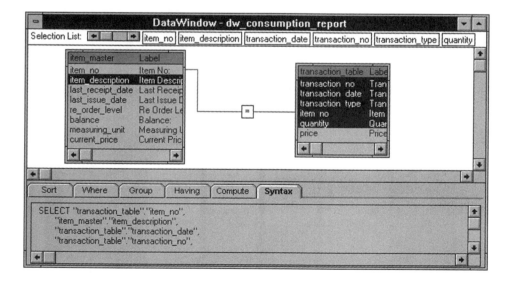

We want to allow the users to enter a month and year for the data that they want to see, so we have to specify a couple of retrieval arguments. Select Objects/Retrieval Arguments... and define the following arguments:

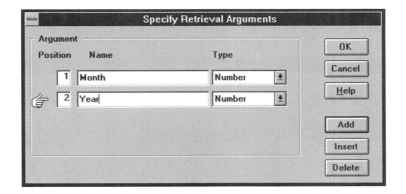

Now define the **Where** clause as follows:

You can right-click in the Column column to select the month() and year() functions and in the Value column to select the :Month and :Year arguments which we defined above. If you preview this statement, you should get something like the following:

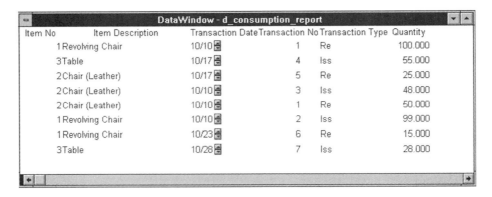

This displays all the information we want, but there are some things we can improve. For example, the full date and transaction type aren't visible, the column headings could be improved and we don't know what we are looking at - it needs a heading and a date.

Go into Design view and we'll improve our report:

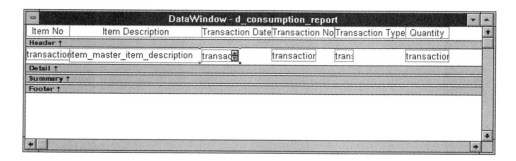

Right-clicking on the controls allows you to change the various attributes, edit styles and so on. Change the Transaction Date edit style from Edit Mask... to Edit... and accept the defaults, then change the Transaction Type edit style to Edit... and select the following options:

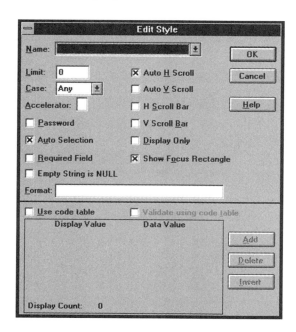

Now let's create a new header which gives us some idea on what the DataWindow is showing us and also allows us to improve the column headings. Delete the existing header and add the following to the header band:

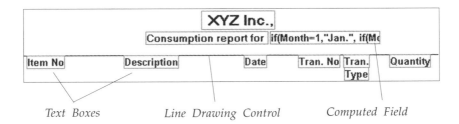

Text Boxes   *Line Drawing Control*   *Computed Field*

Computed Fields

We've used a computed field to display the month which the DataWindow relates to. Computed fields allow you to produce very complex expressions using any of PowerBuilder's built-in functions. However, the definition for our field is really quite simple:

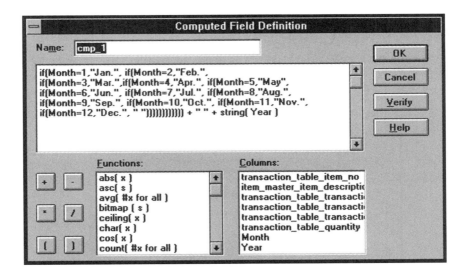

This is just a series of **if** statements which converts the numerical version of the **Month** to the text version and adds the **Year** to the end. Now if you preview the DataWindow, you will have something like this:

```
┌─────────────────────────────────────────────────────────────┐
│ □          DataWindow - d_consumption_report        ▼ ▲ │
├─────────────────────────────────────────────────────────────┤
│                      XYZ Inc.,                                │
│              Consumption report for  Oct. 1994                │
│                                                               │
│  Item No    Description      Date      Tran. No  Tran.  Quantity
│                                                   Type        │
│  ─────────────────────────────────────────────────────────── │
│       1   Revolving Chair   10/10/94      1      R    100.000 │
│       3   Table             10/17/94      4      I     55.000 │
│       2   Chair (Leather)   10/17/94      5      T     25.000 │
│       2   Chair (Leather)   10/10/94      3      I     48.000 │
│       2   Chair (Leather)   10/10/94      1      R     50.000 │
│       1   Revolving Chair   10/10/94      2      I     99.000 │
│       1   Revolving Chair   10/23/94      6      R     15.000 │
│       3   Table             10/28/94      7      I     28.000 │
│                                                               │
│ ◄                                                          ► │
└─────────────────────────────────────────────────────────────┘
```

As you can see, this is much more visually appealing than the original version. Now, let's look at a few more DataWindows which illustrate some of the other presentation styles.

dw_ole_for_item_images

This is a Freeform DataWindow which is used to display the images for each of the item numbers in the item_images table. You can use a Quick Select data source and select just the item_no field from the item_images table:

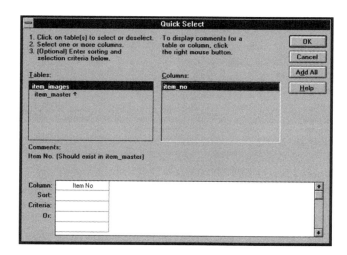

Now go into design view and move the controls around so you have the following layout:

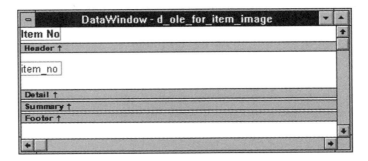

We want to add an OLE control which will contain a bitmap image of our item.

Adding a BLOB

BLOB is an acronym for **Binary Large OBject** and can be used to contain any number of OLE objects depending on the software packages you have installed on your computer. There is no support for BLOBs in the Watcom database engine, so you can't define this field at the database level - it has to be done at the DataWindow level. From the Objects menu, select OLE Database Blob and define the object as follows:

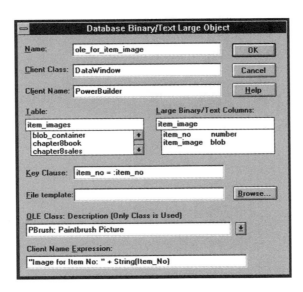

287

The most important options here are Client Class, Client Name and OLE Class. These entries define the type of client and the specific OLE object that we want to display in it. We've specified the client to be a PowerBuilder DataWindow and the OLE object type to be a Paintbrush Picture.

> *We won't go into all the details of OLE objects now, as we cover the use of OLE in depth in a later chapter.*

To finish the DataWindow we can add a border around the BLOB. To do this, we draw a rectangle over the top of the control, lining up all the edges, specifying a black line color and transparent fill color.

> *The transparent color option is only available to controls in a DataWindow.*

The final DataWindow should look like this:

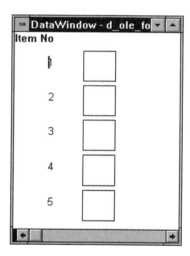

When you run this DataWindow, double-clicking in one of the boxes will start Paintbrush and allow you to create the image for the relevant item:

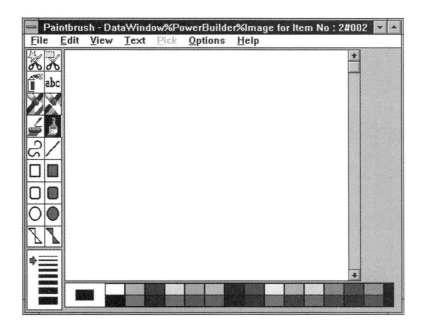

You can see that the titlebar displays the client name and class, together with the item number of the image that we are editing. When you close Paintbrush, you will be prompted as to whether you want to save changes to the image:

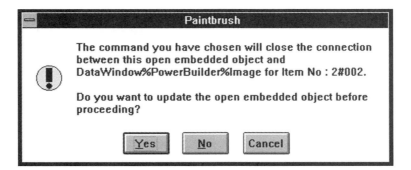

dw_tran_header

This displays the transaction number, together with the date and type of transaction and is used to create a transactions report which we use in our application. It is a Freeform, Quick Select DataWindow with the following definition:

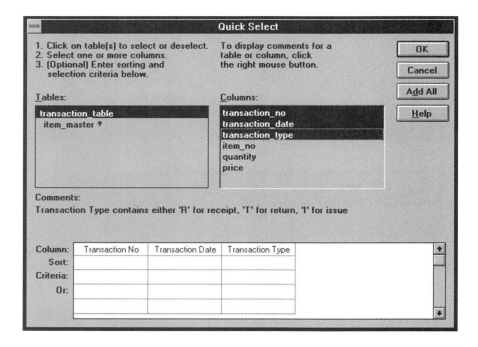

When you've set up the SQL statement, go into Design view and make the following changes:

1 Go into the edit style of Transaction Date and turn off the spin control option.

2 Change the edit style of Transaction Type to RadioButtons with 3 columns across.

3 Change the borders on the controls to boxes.

Now resize the controls so that the final design looks like this:

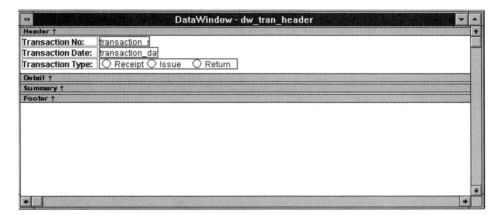

We've now shown you how to create four DataWindows which we will use in our Stock Control application. We won't go through the design of the other DataWindows we need, but these are all contained in the **CHAPTER8.PBL** library. Take a look through them to see how they are created and copy them into your working library.

Finishing Off Our Windows

Now that we've created some DataWindows, we can finish off the design of our windows by linking the DataWindow Controls on the windows to the DataWindow objects. If you remember in Chapter 5 we painted three windows: a login window, an item master window and an error information window. Both the item master and error information windows had DataWindow controls on them, so go into the window painter now, open these windows and link the DataWindow controls to the DataWindows dw_item_master and dw_error_information. If you then run the w_item_master window you should see the following:

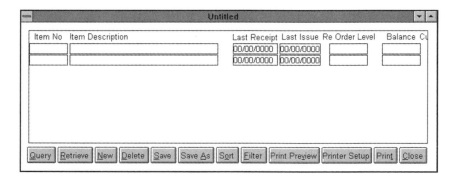

We also want to add another DataWindow Control to this window which will allow us to query the database.

Add another DataWindow Control exactly the same size on top of the existing control and link it to the dw_item_master_free_format_for_query DataWindow. Now hide this DataWindow by selecting Edit/Send to Back. This will hide it behind the original DataWindow - it is still there, but this is a neat way of allowing us to display the DataWindow only when we need it.

There is still one problem with this - it doesn't display the information contained in the database. We can fix this problem by telling PowerBuilder what information to retain when it saves the DataWindow.

Specifying Data to Be Retained

Go back into the DataWindow Painter and open the dw_item_master DataWindow. In design view, select Rows/Data... and click on the Retrieve button to bring in the data from the database:

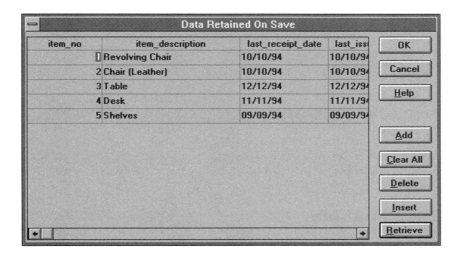

This displays the data from the database and you can add, insert or delete any of the information which is saved in the DataWindow.

> Note that any changes you make to the information at this point won't affect the data which is contained in the database. This is simply another layer of data control which allows you to refine the information displayed in the DataWindow. In most cases, you would never want to alter the data at this level as you should have already refined your data set in the appropriate SQL statement.

If you now go back into the Window Painter and preview the w_item_master window, you'll see that it now displays the data from the database:

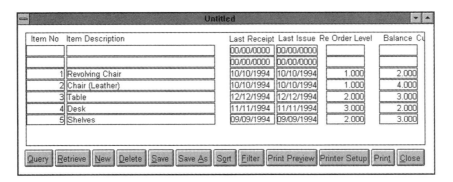

As you can see this works fine, but for our application this step is unnecessary. This is because we will query the database programmatically at run-time when the user clicks on a CommandButton. We will see how to do this in Chapter 10.

DataWindow Options

You should now be confident when creating your own DataWindows using the various presentation styles and data sources. In this section, we'll run through some of the other options which are available in both Design view and Preview.

Print Specifications

You can specify printer parameters to print a DataWindow in two places: in the design view of the DataWindow painter or in the script before printing. It is a good idea to set up the options in the DataWindow Painter as this means that each DataWindow can have its own set of custom parameters.

> Note that you could use the script option as the place to set your own defaults for all the print jobs, giving specialist parameters to each DataWindow through the painter.

To display the print specifications for a DataWindow, select Design/Print Specifications...:

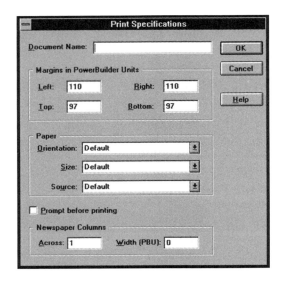

If you supply a document name, this will be what appears in the print queue. You also have the standard margin and paper print options, but you should be aware that the margins will be in PowerBuilder Units by default. You may want to change this to a more understandable form by selecting Design/ DataWindow Style... and changing the units:

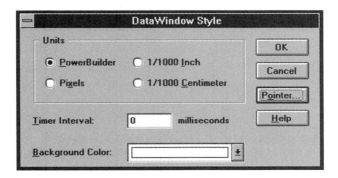

You can also change the timer interval here, a function that can be used when you have fields derived from the **time()** function. For example, you can add a computed field to a DataWindow and specify the expression as **time(today())** to effectively display a clock on your DataWindow. You can then change the Timer Interval so that the clock is updated every second, minute or whatever. We've provided an example of this in the **EXAMPLES.PBL** library called dw_clock:

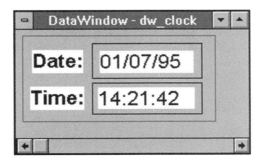

This displays the current date and time. If you look at the Timer Interval for this DataWindow, you'll find that it is set at 1000 milliseconds (one second), so the time is updated every second. If you changed this to 2000, the time would only be updated every two seconds and so on.

Columns Specification

You can see all the details of selected columns in a DataWindow by selecting Rows/Column Specifications.... This lists the column names, types, initial values, validation expressions, validation messages and database names:

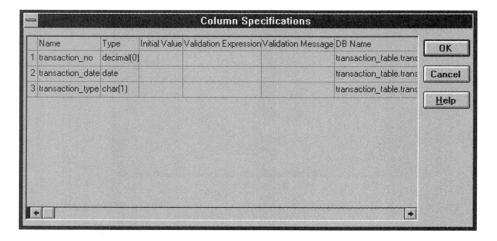

You can't change the data type or width here, but you can add validation rules or initial values. However, you should note that anything added here won't affect existing data in the database. This makes sense from a data integrity point of view - you wouldn't want to overwrite existing data.

> *Validation rules or initial values which you set up in a DataWindow will only apply to that DataWindow. If you create another DataWindow containing the same data and specify different validation rules or initial values then they will apply to any new data entered through this DataWindow.*

Preview Options

When previewing a DataWindow, you have all the same zoom and row description options that were available in the Data Manipulation view in the Database Painter. One extra option available is the ability to divide the DataWindow into two horizontal areas which can scroll independently of each other.

Split Horizontal Scrolling

To split a DataWindow you move the cursor over the black rectangle at the bottom left hand corner of the DataWindow:

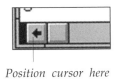

Position cursor here

When the cursor changes to a double arrow, click and drag to position the split where you want it:

Date	Tran. No	Tran. Type	Quantit	Item No	Description	
0/10/1994	2	I	$99.(	1	Revolving Chair	0/
0/10/1994	1	R	$100.(	1	Revolving Chair	0/
0/23/1994	6	R	$15.(	1	Revolving Chair	0/
0/10/1994	3	I	$48.(	2	Chair (Leather)	0/
0/10/1994	1	R	$50.(	2	Chair (Leather)	0/
0/17/1994	5	T	$25.(	2	Chair (Leather)	0/
0/17/1994	4	I	$55.(	3	Table	0/
0/28/1994	7	I	$28.(	3	Table	0/

DataWindow - dw_consumption_report

'Z Inc.,   XYZ

port for Oct. 1994   Consumption repoi

This feature is most useful when you have a lot of information going across a page and you need to relate something at the far right-hand side to something on the left-hand side of the page.

DataWindow Preferences

PowerBuilder provides a plethora of preferences for the DataWindow Painter, covering such subjects as the default presentation style, the default print preview characteristics and the workspace for the painter itself.

In this section, we have provided two tables for your reference, each covering some of the preferences that PowerBuilder has to offer, together with some suggested options for them:

Preference	Description	Option
new_default_datasource	The default data source for a new DataWindow object.	1. SQL Select 2. Query 3. Stored Procedure 4. Script 5. Quick Select
new_default_presentation	The default presentation style for a new DataWindow object.	1. Tabular 2. Freeform 3. Grid 4. Label 5. N-Up 6. Crosstab 7. Graph 8 Group

This table illustrates some of the generic preferences that apply to any new DataWindows that you create:

Preference	Description
new_form_color	Default background color for a freeform DataWindow
new_grid_text_color	Default text color for new grid DataWindow
new_label_column_color	Default column color for a label DataWindow
new_tabular_column_border	Default column border for a tabular DataWindow

There are many more preferences associated with the DataWindow Painter. Fortunately, they tend to be very intuitive, but if you have any problems, please refer to the PowerBuilder help system.

Summary

We've looked at all the presentation styles available for creating DataWindows, set up the DataWindows which we will use in our example application and looked at some of the options available in design and preview. You should now be confident of producing the right DataWindows to display the information you want and to produce intuitive DataWindows which are easy to use.

We've now looked at the major components of a PowerBuilder application. In the next chapter we'll look at the glue which binds all these components together - PowerBuilder's programming language, Powerscript.

PowerScript

In previous chapters, you have learnt about painting the various objects that make up a PowerBuilder application, but this is only part of the application development process. You'll also need to write code using PowerBuilder's 4th generation language PowerScript.

This is a powerful object-oriented language and you'll find that in many cases one line of code is all that is needed to accomplish much added functionality. We'll be looking at where you should add code to get the desired effects, the simplicity of the coding language and the flexibility of the scripting environment.

In this chapter, we will cover:

- The scripting environment
- Creating, compiling and saving scripts
- Adding scripts to our existing objects
- Implementing Popup menus
- Implementing error handling in our application

Introduction

Taking COBOL as an example of a procedural programming language, there are four different divisions to the source code: Identification, Environment, Data and Procedure. Each of these sections is executed in order, line by line, until you reach the end of the source code. The result is 'pre-defined' for a given entry and all stages must be completed before a result is produced.

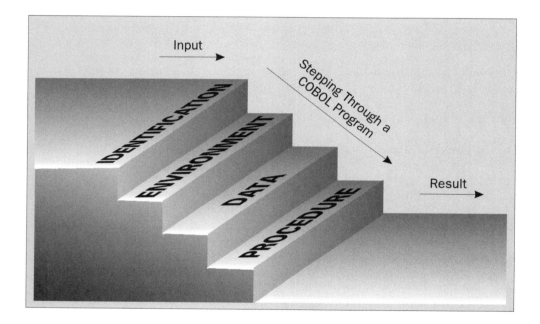

PowerBuilder is based around the concepts of Object Orientation and handles this problem in a very different way.

Event Driven Programming

Coming from this environment to PowerBuilder may be a bit of a cultural shock. In this environment, you write code for **events** which are triggered by the system whenever something happens - this is called Event Driven Programming. For example, opening a window triggers the **Open** event.

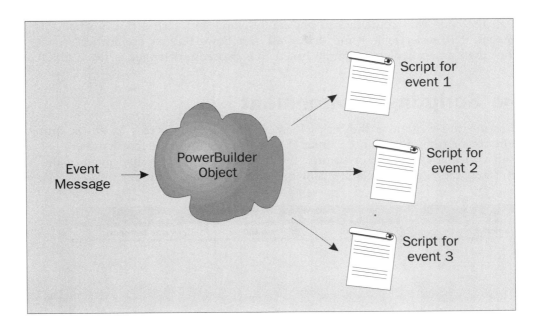

When using Event Driven Programming, you provide scripts for each of the events that you want an object to respond to. When you release the object into the programming soup, it floats around waiting for an event message to be forwarded to it and then runs the appropriate script, if it exists.

If the script doesn't exist, the object does nothing and goes back to waiting for the next event message.

You don't have to run all the options and only that code needs to be completed to get the desired result.

This is known as 'defensive' programming as you're often completely relying on the user to select the next course of action, rather than guiding them through a strict series of actions in the program. On the other hand, you are now allowing the user to take control of the program, choosing what happens in which order, rather than having to stick to a rigid and predefined order of events.

Apart from the events created by the user's interaction with the basic PowerBuilder objects, there are also internal or system events for which we can write code. For example, the **PrintStart** event occurs whenever you print a report and the **RetrieveRow** event occurs whenever PowerBuilder retrieves a row from a database.

As all the code isn't contained in one large listing and each script is small and compact, it is easier to test and debug all of a PowerBuilder application's code rather than an equivalent example based in a procedural language like COBOL.

The Scripting Environment

All scripts are written in the Script Painter. You can gain access to this scripting environment from any object painter if that object supports event handlers. When you invoke the Script Painter, the title bar will display the name of the object and the relevant default event name that you are coding:

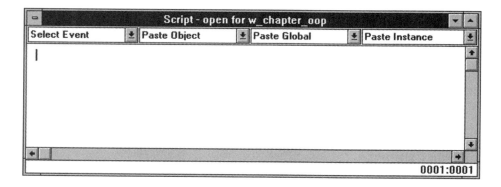

In this case, we are about to code the open event for the w_chapter_oop window. The four DropDown ListBoxes allow you to:

▲ Select the various events that this object supports.

▲ Paste references to other objects directly into your code.

▲ Paste the names of declared global and instance variables into your code.

Each of these options allows you to speed up the development of your code and helps to avoid typing mistakes.

> *The objects that are available from **Paste Objects** are only those that are referenced by the object you are working in. In the example above, the objects available are the controls which appear on the **w_chapter_oop** window.*

As with the other painters in the PowerBuilder environment, the Script Painter is supported by a PainterBar. The options on the Script PainterBar are also designed to aid your script writing:

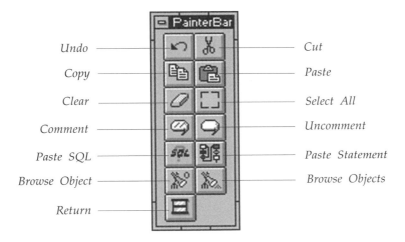

Undo — Cut
Copy — Paste
Clear — Select All
Comment — Uncomment
Paste SQL — Paste Statement
Browse Object — Browse Objects
Return

The Browse Objects option lets you paste any objects that are contained in the whole application as opposed to those on offer from the DropDown ListBox:

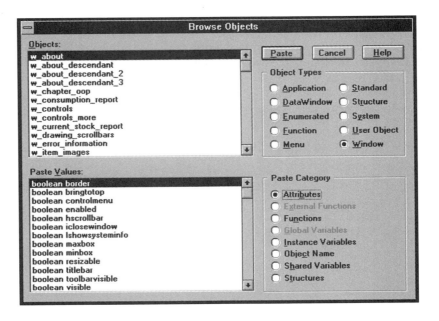

You can browse all the various object types and both view and paste any of the categories for the chosen object type into your script.

Scripting Guidelines

Before you start coding, it's a good idea to establish some naming conventions, a few guidelines about writing comments and any other basic things that control the look and feel of your scripts. Here are some general guidelines.

Identifiers

Keep the following guidelines in mind when you're working with the various identifiers in your system:

- They must start with a letter and can have up to 40 characters.

- Spaces are not allowed.

- They are case insensitive.

- They can include letters, digits and the following special characters: dash (-), Dollar ($), Percent (%), Hash (#), Underscore (_).

Comments

It is always a good idea to comment your code as much as possible. There is nothing more frustrating than trying to debug someone else's code (or even your own old code!) which doesn't have comments.

PowerBuilder uses the same two methods of designating comments as C++:

1 The double slash method (//). This comments out text on a line-by-line basis. For example:

```
// This is a comment which uses the single
// line comment style. We have to put the comment
// characters at the start of each line.
```

2 The slash and asterisk method (/* ... */). This is the commenting method used to comment out a block of text which may cover several lines in the editor. For example:

```
/*
This is the comment style which is used to
comment out a large block of text. We don't have to
put the comment character at the start of each line,
only at the start and end of the comment.
*/
```

The Comment and Uncomment options on the PainterBar allow you to quickly comment and uncomment lines of code. This is useful when you are debugging a script and want to comment lines out to try to find errors in your script.

Line Continuation Character

PowerBuilder allows you to split a command over more than one line through the use of the special ampersand character (&). This should be the last character in the line and you should note that you can't split a variable name between two lines:

```
MessageBox("Save","Do you want to save" + &
"changes? ", Question!, OkCancel!,2)
```

When you are using SQL statements in your PowerScript, there is no need to use a continuation character. By default, everything after the SQL keyword is considered to be a single line until it encounters a semi-colon. For this reason, it is vitally important that you don't forget to add a semi-colon to the end of your SQL statements. For example:

```
select description into :litem_description
from item_master
where item_no = :vitem_no;
```

Statement Separator

You can write more than one command on a single line by separating the statements with a semi-colon:

```
SQLCA.dbms = "Sybase"; SQLCA.ServerName = "SQLServer1"
```

Generally, it isn't a very good idea to put more than one statement on a single line simply because it makes your code more difficult to read. It also causes the process of code debugging to become more complex as any debug error messages refer to line numbers, not specify commands. If you have multiple statements on a line, you will still have to determine which statement is causing the error.

To avoid this problem, you should put each statement on a separate line, especially as there is no difference in efficiency from the PowerBuilder standpoint. This also has the added advantages of improving the readability of your code, while easing any maintenance worries.

Scripting Structures

PowerBuilder supports several common coding structures for looping and decision making. To see the structures that are supported, click on the Paste Statement icon:

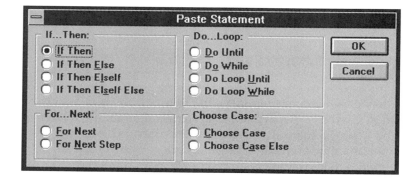

This allows you to paste a skeletal framework of the required statement into your code, which has the effect of providing a uniform layout for your code and a reduction in development time. For example, if you paste the If Then Elself statement into your code you'll get the following:

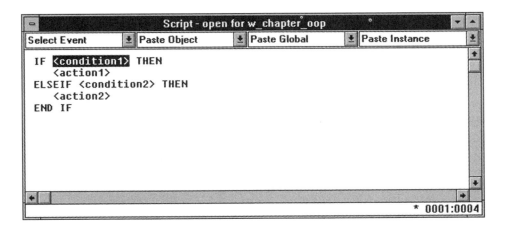

You can then make changes to the statement, substituting your specific variables, test conditions and so on, as needed.

Functions

PowerBuilder has a vast range of built-in functions which you can use in your scripts - we've already seen some of these when creating validation rules for your database tables. Again, to save you having to remember the exact function names, PowerBuilder allows you to paste functions from a generated list into your code simply by selecting Edit/Paste Function...:

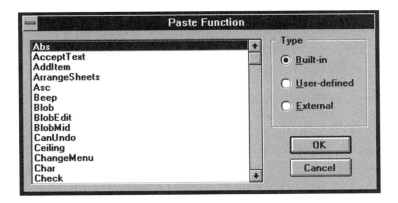

As you can see, you can also paste user-defined and external functions into your code from this feature.

Standard Data Types

There are two types of data in PowerBuilder: standard and enumerated. The following table lists the standard data types:

DataType	Range
Boolean	TRUE or FALSE.
Character (char)	A single ASCII character.
String	Any ASCII character. Length: 0 to 60,000.
Integer (int)	-32,768 to +32,767.
Long	-2,147,483,648 to + 2,147,483,647.
Real	Single floating point, six digits of precision, range 1.17 E -38 to 3.4 E +38.
Decimal	Single decimal numbers with up to 18 digit.
Double	Single floating point, 15 digits precision, range: 2.2E-308 to 1.7E+308.
Date	Includes full year (1000 to 3000).
DateTime	Date and Time together.
Time	Time in 24-hour format - supports fraction of a second (up to six digits).
UnsignedInteger (UInt)	0 to 65,535.
UnsignedLong (ULong)	0 to 4,294.967,295.
Blob	Binary large object (No limit).

Enumerated data types are used as arguments in functions and to specify the attributes of objects. To see which enumerated data types are supported, browse the objects again and select Enumerated object types:

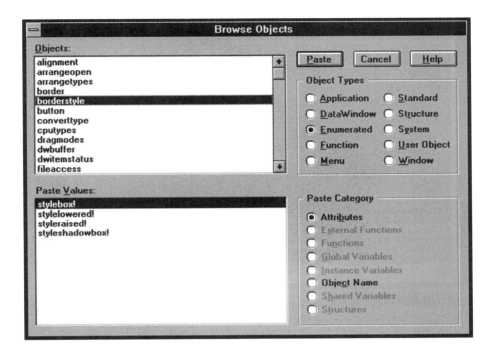

You can see that the borderstyle object has four available enumerated data types, each representing a different type of border style.

Variable Declarations

Variables have to be declared as a data type before they can be used in your PowerScript code. If you try to use a variable which hasn't been declared, you'll get the following error message when you try to compile the script:

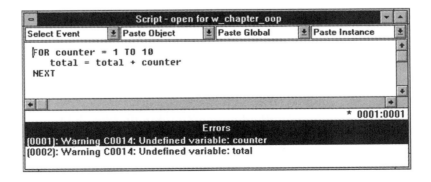

Variables can be declared in four different places depending on the scope you wish to associate with them. A variable's scope indicates its lifetime and the influence that it can have over the rest of your application during that time.

By employing the idea of scope, you can 'overload' a variable name. This is the process of naming different variables with the same name, their uniqueness being preserved by the scope you associated with them. There are four levels of scope:

▲ Local

▲ Global

▲ Shared

▲ Instance

Local

Local variables are declared in the script itself and they are only available in the script where they are declared. You can't refer to this variable in any other events or functions. The method of declaring a variable in a script is as follows:

<Data Type> <Variable Name> = <Variable Value>

For example, in the above script, we would want to declare the counter and total variables as integers:

```
integer counter
integer total = 0
```

The variable value is optional and in our example, we could have left off the initial value of the **total** variable as PowerBuilder assigns a default value of zero to integer data types.

> *By default, string data types are assigned an initial value of "" and Boolean data types are assigned an initial value of FALSE.*

Global

Global variables can be referred to from anywhere in your application. They become available when the application is opened and are destroyed when the application is closed. You should only use Global variables where absolutely necessary and should take care when naming them so that they don't conflict with other variables.

> *It is a good idea to adopt a naming convention for your variables which highlights their scope so that naming conflicts are avoided. In Appendix A, we suggest some naming guidelines for all PowerBuilder objects.*

To declare Global variables, select Declare/Global Variables... and enter the declaration in the same manner that we used for Local variables:

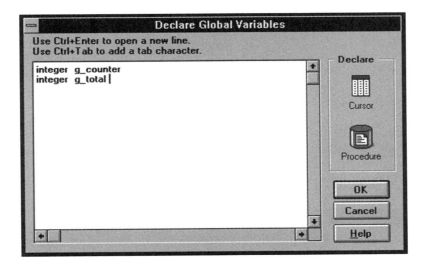

> Note that to add more than one declaration you have to use *Ctrl+Enter* to start a newline as simply hitting the *Enter* key closes the declaration dialog box.

Shared

Shared variables are stored in an object's definition and are available for all instances of a particular object. When you open an object that has a shared variable, it is initialized and exists until you close the application. The value of the variable persists even if the object is closed.

> Based around the idea of scope comes the ability to open more
> than one instance of any object. By requesting that a new instance
> of an object is created, PowerBuilder creates a new copy of the
> object, internally handling the management of the object and
> supplying it with newly initialized instance variables and access to
> any associated shared variables.

One example of how you could use this type of variable is when you want to
count the number of times an object has been opened in an application. Each
time that a new instance is opened, the shared variable is incremented by one,
and the destruction of an instance has no effect on the value or the existence of
the variable itself.

If you open multiple instances of an object, then the same value is used by all
instances and if the value of the variable is changed in one instance, the change
will be reflected in all other instances of the object.

Shared variables can be declared for Applications, Menus, Windows and
UserObjects. No matter which kind of object the shared variables are associated
with, they are declared using Declare/Shared Variables... while the appropriate
object is available in the painter:

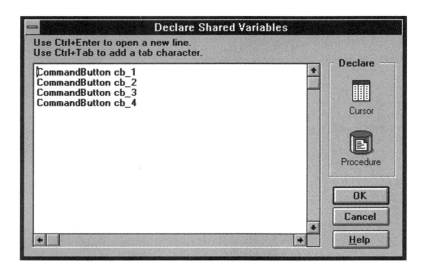

Instance

Instance variables are similar to shared variables in that they are created when an instance of an object is opened. The difference is that they are destroyed and are no longer available when that instance of an object is closed.

> *If you open more than one instance of an object, the value of the instance variables can be different in each case.*

Like shared variables, instance variables can be declared for Applications, Menus, Windows and UserObjects. When declared for windows or UserObjects, they are available to any objects which are part of these objects. For example, if you declare an instance variable at the Window level, you can refer to it in the script of any controls that you have placed on that Window. Instance variables are declared like global and shared variables by selecting from the Declare/ Instance Variables... menu.

Arrays

PowerBuilder supports single and multi-dimensional arrays. Each dimension can have up to 65K elements; the only limit to the number of dimensions is the size of your computer's memory.

To declare an array, you must use the following syntax:

`<Data Type> <Array Name> [ <Number of Elements> ]`

All the standard data types can be used in the definition of an array, but PowerBuilder doesn't allow you to use enumerated data types for the same task. For example:

```
Integer totals [6]
Char letters [10,10]
```

Initializing Arrays

When using single dimension arrays, you can assign initial values to the array simply by supplying a list following the declaration. For example, if we wanted to assign initial values for the above integer array, we could do it as follows:

```
Integer totals [6] = {1,2,3,4,5,6}
```

Single dimension arrays can also be dynamic. This enables you to use single dimension arrays when you don't know how many elements there will be. By default, PowerBuilder inserts the elements into the array starting from 1. Following this principle, the values shown in the example above would be referred to as totals[1], totals[2] ... totals[6].

You can alter this default action by specifying starting and finishing values for your array as follows:

```
Integer totals [3 To 8] = {1,2,3,4,5,6}
```

Note that this is still a 6-element array. The elements are now labeled from 3 to 8 rather than 1 to 6.

You can apply both of these methodologies (initialization and start/finish label values) to multi-dimensional arrays, but you should be aware that PowerBuilder works in a top to bottom and then left to right manner. As an example of this, take the following initialization:

```
Integer totals [1 to 3, 2 to 3] = {1,2,3,4,5,6}
```

PowerBuilder performs this allocation in the following order:

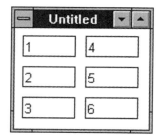

When you start to interrogate the array, you may find it useful to programmatically identify the limits of the array. PowerBuilder provides two functions which you can use to determine the upper and lower boundaries: **UpperBound()** and **LowerBound()**.

If you refer to an array element outside the declared size, it will cause a run-time error which will terminate the application unless you have written error handing scripts. We'll cover more about those in a later section in this chapter.

Errors and Warnings

Before you can run any scripts, they must be compiled. PowerBuilder will automatically compile a script if you try to exit the Script Painter and have made changes to it. However, PowerBuilder also allows you to compile a script yourself by selecting Compile/Script:

When you compile a script, PowerBuilder will display any errors and warnings at the bottom of the screen and won't let you save any changes to the script until it compiles without any problems:

```
                              Errors
[0001]: Error C0001: Illegal data type: ffor
[0002]: Warning C0014: Undefined variable: total
[0002]: Warning C0014: Undefined variable: count
[0003]: Error C0031: Syntax error
```

Errors are caused by statements which PowerBuilder doesn't understand, but warnings can be caused by, for example, undeclared variables. You have the option of turning off the Compiler and Database warnings, which allows you to save a script even if warnings are generated.

Unfortunately, PowerBuilder overrules these options if you try to save the actual object and will display any compiler warnings at this stage if they were generated:

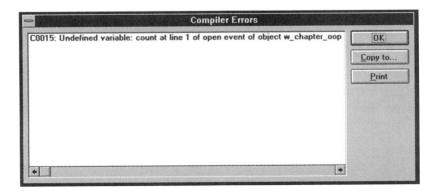

Note that you have the option to either print out or copy the errors to a text file at this stage.

Special Characters

When you need to use special characters such as tab or new line in a string, you need to prefix the special reserved character with the tilde character (~). The following table contains a list of special characters:

To denote these special characters...	...use these character combinations
Newline	~n
Tab	~t
Vertical tab	~v
Carriage return	~r
Formfeed	~f
Backspace	~b
Tilde	~~
Decimal number	~nnn
Octal number	~oxxx
Hexadecimal number	~hyy

This completes our overview of the scripting environment provided by PowerBuilder. We've described some of the neat features that this environment uses to speed up your application development. In the next section, let's move on to examine some practical uses of PowerScript.

Some Code Examples

One of the best ways to learn a programming language is by example, so let's analyze some of the simple code samples that we've put together. These are all contained on the w_code_examples window in the **EXAMPLES.PBL** file on the CD-ROM.

There are three basic examples:

▲ Quotes - illustrates how to use built-in functions in your code.

▲ Calculate - illustrates data type conversion.

▲ Picture - illustrates how to use property values in decision making.

Run the window using the *Ctrl+Shift+W* keys and we'll look at each one in turn:

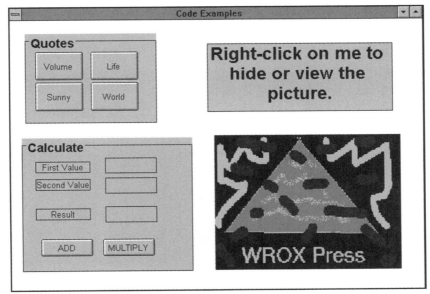

The Quotes Example

This consists of four CommandButtons, each of which throws up a message box containing a relevant quote:

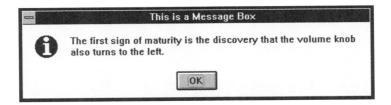

The following code is placed in each of the CommandButtons clicked events:

```
// Object: Volume CommandButton
// Event: clicked
MessageBox("This is a Message Box","The first sign of maturity" + &
" is the discovery that the volume knob also turns to the left.")
```

This simply uses the `MessageBox()` function to display a message box with the title 'This is a Message Box' and an appropriate textual quote. Note that the syntax of this function demands that you separate the title text from the message with a comma.

The Calculate Example

To see how this works, type in an integer into the First Value and Second Value EditMasks and click on one of the CommandButtons:

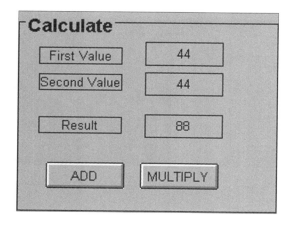

Obviously, we've clicked on the ADD button in this case, the Result indicating that the answer to the sum is 88. If you look at the code for the `clicked` event of the ADD button, you'll see how it works:

```
// Object: ADD CommandButton
// Event: clicked

number_one = integer(em_first.text)
number_two = integer(em_second.text)
em_result.text = string(number_one + number_two)
```

We use the **integer()** function to assign the integer value of whatever is typed into the two EditMasks to the variables **number_one** and **number_two**. The final line stores the string value of the sum of the two variables in the **em_result** EditMask.

> Note that the contents of the EditMasks are referred to by the Text property. As you would expect, the values produced by this property are Strings. Therefore, before you can use math functions upon them, you must convert them to their integer values. PowerBuilder allows you to quick perform this action using the **Integer()** function. This is known as **Data Type Conversion**.

Before this will work, we have to declare the necessary variables. We could have declared them in the code as local variables, but this would mean they were only available for this code. As the MULTIPLY CommandButton uses the same variables, we can declare them as instance variables and so save having to declare the same variables twice:

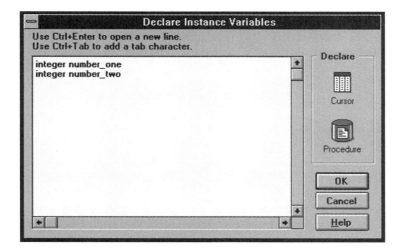

The Picture Example

This works when you right-click in the large StaticText control and turns the picture on or off. The code is in the **rbuttondown** event for the text control:

```
// Object: Toggle Text Box
// Event: rbuttondown

IF p_wrox_picture.visible = TRUE THEN
    p_wrox_picture.visible = FALSE
ELSE
    p_wrox_picture.visible = TRUE
END IF
```

This simply tests the visible property of the picture control and toggles it between **TRUE** and **FALSE** depending on the current state.

These three examples are very simple, but they do illustrate the concepts of event driven programming, PowerScript's dot notation and how to use some common PowerBuilder functions. As we said at the beginning of the chapter, a few lines of code are all that is needed to give your applications much more functionality, so let's put together some scripts which will get our example application up and running.

Adding Script to Our Application

The first script we have to add to our application is the initial script which will actually run the application. When the user runs the application, the first thing we want them to do is login. When they have successfully navigated this security level, we want to display w_item_master, the real opening window for our application. The script that we need to accomplish this task is given below:

```
// Object: Stock Control Application
// Event: Open

Open (w_login_window)
Open (w_item_master)
```

This simply opens w_login_window and then w_item_master. If you save this and then run the application, you'll see the login window flash up on the screen and then the item master window opens immediately. This is because we haven't added any script to the login window yet.

We'll add this script in the next chapter when we look at database connectivity. This script will force the user to move through the security associated with the database before allowing them to move into the rest of the application. For now it's enough to have our application actually doing something.

You'll find that you can't close the application because we haven't added code to any of the menu options. This isn't a problem - if you use the *Alt+Tab* keys to switch back to PowerBuilder, you'll get the following message box:

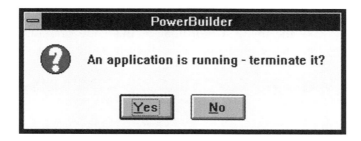

This allows you to close down the application and return to the development environment.

Implementing the Popup Menu

If you remember back to Chapter 4, we created some menus to control our application. One of these, the m_dw_func menu, was a Popup menu - let's look at the code required to implement this menu.

To display a Popup menu, we first have to create an instance of the menu. To do this, we declare an instance variable **iDataWindowMenu** in the w_item_master window:

```
m_dw_func iDataWindowMenu
```

In the **open** event for the w_item_master window, create an instance of this menu as follows:

```
// Object: w_item_master
// Event: Open

iDataWindowMenu = Create m_dw_func
```

Now for the **rbuttondown** event of the dwc_1 DataWindow control, add the following script:

```
// Object: dwc_1
// Event: RbuttonDown

iDataWindowMenu.PopMenu( PointerX( Parent ), PointerY( Parent ) )
```

We have used the instance variable together with the PowerBuilder function **PopMenu()** to invoke the menu. Unfortunately, this code presents the whole menu, including the menu bar item, rather than just the menu items:

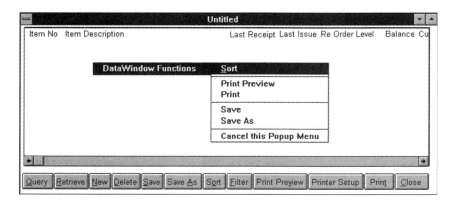

In order to remove the menu item bar from the picture, you must include a reference to the menu bar item in your code:

```
// Object: dwc_1
// Event: RbuttonDown

iDataWindowMenu.m_datawindowfunctions.PopMenu( PointerX( Parent ), &
PointerY( Parent ) )
```

The right mouse click will only produce this menu when the mouse pointer is over the DataWindow control. In order to reinforce this, we display the menu at the current pointer position by using the functions **PointerX()** and **PointerY()**. These functions return the X and Y co-ordinates of the mouse pointer relative to the object that is specified as the argument.

We specify the argument as **Parent** - a PowerScript reserved word - which refers to the object that holds the current one. In this case, this is the w_item_master window.

PowerScript Reserved Words

When you are working with controls and windows, there are three very important reserved words that you will find very useful:

Important Word	Description
This	Represents the object for which you are writing the code. For example, if you write **Close(this)** for a window event, it closes the window. Writing the same code for a window control would produce an error as you can't close a window control.
Parent	Represents the object that contains the object you are working in. Following the same example from above, the Parent for a window control is the window which contains the control.
ParentWindow	This is used exclusively in menu scripts and refers to the window to which a menu is attached.

Using these reserved words can save you a lot of time as they can make your code far more reuseable. For example, you can write a generic script which closes a window and use it for all your windows.

In Chapter 12, we'll look at the concepts of object-oriented programming in detail and see how it can be used to speed up the application development process.

Error Handling

The Error object is one of the built-in global objects used by PowerBuilder. Whenever an error occurs, PowerBuilder stores all the error information in this object. It has the following structure:

Property	Data Type	Meaning
Error.Number	Integer	PowerBuilder error number.
Error.Text	String	Error message.

Continued

325

Property	Data Type	Meaning
Error.WindowMenu	String	Name of the Window or Menu object in which the error occurred.
Error.Object	String	Name of the object in which the error occurred. If an error occurs in a window or menu then this string will be the same as Error.WindowMenu.
Error.ObjectEvent	String	The name of the event where the error occurred.
Error.Line	Integer	The line number where the error occurred.

When an error occurs, the **SystemError** event is triggered at the Application level, PowerBuilder displays its default error message and in most cases the application will terminate. We don't want our application to terminate every time we get an error, so we can trap these errors by writing some code for the **SystemError** event.

Even a few lines of comments added to the **SystemError** event will allow us to continue executing our application. Unfortunately, this still doesn't help us if the error is a General Protection Fault (GPF). In this case, there is little you can do but close the application.

Open our application and add the following code to the **SystemError** event:

```
// Object: Application
// Event SystemError

Open(w_error_information)
```

This simply opens up w_error_information which we painted in Chapter 5 to display error information - it is the code behind this Window that handles the error information and keeps the application alive:

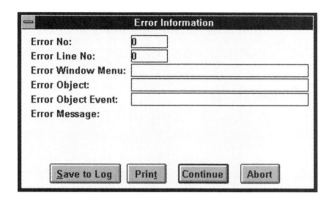

Adding Code to the w_error_information Window

The key code behind this window is that which is found associated with the
dwc_1 DataWindow control, which draws its information from the
dw_error_information DataWindow. Add the following code to the **open** event of
this control:

```
// Object: w_error_information
// Event: Open

long lNewRow
lNewRow = dwc_1.insertrow( 0 )

dwc_1.SetItem( lNewRow,  "Error_No", error.Number )
dwc_1.SetItem( lNewRow,  "Error_Message", error.Text )
dwc_1.SetItem( lNewRow,  "Error_Line_No", error.Line )
dwc_1.SetItem( lNewRow,  "Error_WindowMenu", error.WindowMenu )
dwc_1.SetItem( lNewRow,  "Error_Object", error.Object )
dwc_1.SetItem( lNewRow,  "Error_Object_Event", error.ObjectEvent )
```

We declare a local variable, insert a new row into the dwc_1 control and assign
values from the error object. This effectively copies the error information into the
various controls on the Window.

> *Notice the lack of code to abort the error. PowerBuilder automatically aborts
> the error and so saves the application from termination simply because of
> the existence of this code.*

Now we have to add some functionality to the CommandButtons on the window. We have four CommandButtons which allow us to continue with the application, abort the application, print the error messages or save them to a log file.

The Continue CommandButton

To continue with the application, we simply want to close the w_error_information window:

```
// Object: cb_continue in w_error_information
// Event: Clicked

Close (Parent)
```

Once PowerBuilder executes the script written for the application's **SystemError** event successfully, it continues with the execution of the next statement after the error line. As we don't have any more script in the **SystemError** event, closing this window will allow the user to continue the application.

The Abort CommandButton

If the user wants to abort the application, we call the **close** event for the application, causing it to gracefully close down:

```
// Object: cb_abort in w_error_information
// Event: Clicked

Halt Close
```

Simply using the **Halt** command without the **Close** parameter would terminate the application immediately. By adding this parameter, we force PowerBuilder to execute any code that we have added to the application's **close** event.

The Print CommandButton

For the Print CommandButton, we want to print out the DataWindow control using the Print property:

```
// Object: cb_print in w_error_information
// Event: Clicked

dwc_1.Print( TRUE )
```

This will print the contents of the DataWindow control to your current default printer.

The Save to Log CommandButton

This button will allow the user to append the latest error information to an error log. To accomplish this task, we need to handle several different jobs. These jobs include opening an external log file, appending information and then closing the file.

The script for this task is more complicated than the others:

```
// Object: cb_Save_To_Log in w_error_information
// Event: Clicked

Int lFIleHandle

lFIleHandle = FileOpen( "Invent.Err", LineMode!, Write!, &
   LockWrite!, Append!)
If lFileHandle = -1 Then
   MessageBox( "Save to Log", "Error in opening          Invent.Err file!")
   Return
End If


/*
Some databases accept userid and some expect logid. If you take care of
checking, you can use this script in any application irrespective of the
database connection.
*/

If SQLCA.UserId <> "" Then
   FileWrite( lFileHandle,"User: " + SQLCA.UserId)
Else
   FileWrite( lFileHandle,"User: " + SQLCA.LogId)
End If

FileWrite( lFileHandle, "Time:" + String(String( Now(), &
   "m-d-yy h:mm am/pm")
FileWrite( lFileHandle, "Error No:" + String( &
   dwc_1.GetItemNumber( 1, "Error_No")))
FileWrite( lFileHandle, "Error Message:" + &
   dwc_1.GetItemString( 1, "Error_Message"))
FileWrite( lFileHandle, "Error Line No:" + &
   String(dwc_1.GetItemNumber( 1, "Error_Line_No")))
FileWrite( lFileHandle, "Error Window Menu:" + &
   dwc_1.GetItemString( 1, "Error_WindowMenu"))
FileWrite( lFileHandle, "Error Object: " + &
   dwc_1.GetItemString( 1, "Error_Object"))
```

```
FileWrite( lFileHandle, "Error Object Event: " + &
    dwc_1.GetItemString( 1, "Error_Object_Event"))

FileClose( lFileHandle )
```

The first section of code opens a log file - **INVENT.ERR** - and enables linemode, which means each **FileWrite** will put text on a new line. We also enable writing and appending to both enable us to put text into the log and to ensure that each line of text is appended to the file. The **LockWrite!** option ensures that when we have the file open nobody else can write to it.

The next six lines of code writes the UserId or LogId into the file depending on which is relevant and then writes in the date and time.

The main section of the code reads all the error information using the **GetItemString()** function and writes it into the log file. The final line closes the log file.

Error Signaling

When you want to test your error handler, you can do so by using the **SignalError()** function. Simply assign some values for the Error object and call the **SignalError()** function. This causes an application level **SystemError** event to be triggered, allowing you to review and test your application's error handling.

To see how this works, you can write the following script in the **rbuttondown** event for one of the CommandButton:

```
// Object: cb_query for window w_item_master
// Event: rbuttondown
//
// This is test code which enables you to
// test out the error information window
//

error.object = "window"
error.text = "This is an error"
error.line = 10
SignalError( )
```

This simply assigns some values to the error object and calls the
`SignalError()` function. When you run the application, you can right-click on
this button and the Error Information window will be displayed with the
values we've assigned to the error object:

```
┌─────────────────────────────────────────────────────────────┐
│ ─              Error Information                              │
├─────────────────────────────────────────────────────────────┤
│  Error No:            │0          │                          │
│  Error Line No:       │10         │                          │
│  Error Window Menu:   │                                    │ │
│  Error Object:        │window                              │ │
│  Error Object Event:  │                                    │ │
│  Error Message:       │This is an error                    │ │
│                                                               │
│                                                               │
│      ┌───────────┐ ┌───────┐ ┌──────────┐ ┌───────┐          │
│      │ Save to Log│ │ Print │ │ Continue │ │ Abort │          │
│      └───────────┘ └───────┘ └──────────┘ └───────┘          │
└─────────────────────────────────────────────────────────────┘
```

Summary

We've shown you how to navigate around the scripting environment and
explained some of the variable declarations and basic scripting guidelines. We've
also shown you some simple examples of PowerScript, before moving onto
adding functionality to our application by adding a start-up script, showing you
how to implement our Popup menu and adding the necessary code for our
error handling.

In the next chapter we'll look at database connectivity and show you how to
create profiles and configure ODBC connections. We'll also discuss `.INI` files and
get into some more advanced scripting when we add the necessary script to our
Login window.

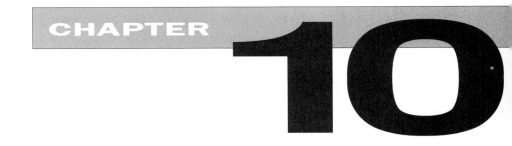

Database Connectivity

In the last chapter, we started adding functionality to our application, by writing some initial scripts to set our application running and to handle any errors which might occur during the execution. In this chapter, we'll be concentrating on how to connect to the back-end databases, what you've got to do and what you can expect in return.

We'll also be completing the scripts for our login window to allow us to connect to our database and writing the scripts for all the CommandButtons on our w_item_master window.

In this chapter, we will cover:

- How to create and use database profiles
- The **PB.INI**, **ODBCINST.INI** and **ODBC.INI** files
- How to set up your database security
- An overview of ODBC, the Microsoft standard for Open DataBase Connectivity
- How to control the connection to our database
- The completion of the scripts for our w_item_master window

Database Profiles

We already know that PowerBuilder uses profiles to control the connections between our application and the databases that we wish to connect to, and we've briefly seen how to create a profile when we connected to the **INVDUMMY.DB** database in Chapter 6.

Now, let's take a more detailed look at what is contained in these profiles and how we can control them to get the desired results. All the profiles are controlled through the Database Painter and in particular, the File/Connect/Setup... menu.

Select the Invent profile from the list and click the Edit... button:

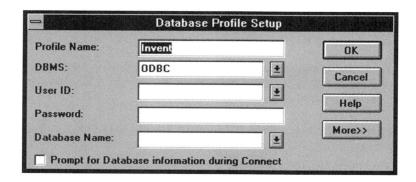

There are five sections to the database profile:

Section	Description
Profile Name	This is the name that you give to the profile and is used whenever you want to connect to the database.
DBMS	The name of the database system. For example, it could be Sybase, Oracle, Access etc. For Watcom databases we use ODBC.
User ID	This is an ID which is used to identify the user.
Password	A security password.
Database Name	The name of the file that the database is held in. For example, our database is held in a file called **INVENT.DB**.

*By default, the User ID, Password and Database Name won't be displayed
when you edit the profile, but you can get them automatically inserted by
PowerBuilder by editing your* **PB.INI** *file, as we'll see later.*

There are also several extra connection options which you can view by clicking
on the More>> button:

These entries are optional depending on the type of DBMS that you are
connecting to. For example, if you are connecting to an SQL Server, you will
have to supply a Server Name, a Login ID and a Login Password, as opposed to
User ID and Password.

The last prompt in the dialog box is DBPARM, which is used to specify any
database specific parameters. For example, you can specify a **TimeOut** for the
client or a **Locks** isolation level when connecting to SQL Server. For our Invent
profile, the DBPARM section simply contains a connection string specifying the
name of the database. This is automatically completed when we create a
profile, so don't worry about it.

*Any additional entries that you can add to DBPARM are in the realms of
SQL Server rather than PowerBuilder. Please refer to the SQL Server or
other back-end database server manuals for more information.*

You don't have to create separate profiles for every database that you want to
connect to. If you check the Prompt for Database information option on the profile
setup screen, then whenever you connect using that profile, you'll be prompted
to select the name of the database you want to connect to:

For security reasons, we wouldn't recommend the use of this option for any profiles in a production ready system, as it allows a user to see all the databases on your system. However, as a tool that provides you with flexibility at design time, this feature is very useful.

> Remember that a database profile is primarily a vehicle for connecting your application to the correct ODBC driver for your back-end database. The ability to connect to a specific database is a bonus feature.

The PB.INI File

Every database profile is stored in the **PB.INI** file, which is located in your PowerBuilder directory. The [DBMS_PROFILES] section of **PB.INI** contains a list of the current default profile, all the currently available profiles and a history of which profiles have been used:

```
[DBMS_PROFILES]
CURRENT=Invent1
PROFILES='Invent1','Invent','Invdummy','Test2','Powersoft Demo
DB','Nwind','Accsamp','Database5','Example','Chapter5 Db 01','ABNC Main DB
(v4)','Chapter5 Db','ABNC Sales DB (v4)'
History='Invent1','Invent','Invdummy','Test2','Powersoft Demo
DB','Nwind','Accsamp','Database5','Example','Chapter5 Db 01','ABNC Main DB
(v4)','Chapter5 Db','ABNC Sales DB (v4)'
```

As you can see, we have several versions of the Invent profile and various examples and test profiles that were used during the production of the examples on the CD-ROM. These are intermingled with the profiles that shipped with PowerBuilder itself.

Each profile also has its own section in the **PB.INI**, which contains any specific connection information required to access our database. The entry in our **PB.INI** for the Invent profile looks like this:

```
[PROFILE Invent]
DBMS=ODBC
Database=
UserId=
DatabasePassword=
LogPassword=
ServerName=
LogId=
Lock=
DbParm=Connectstring='DSN=INVENT'
Prompt=0
```

As we said above, if you want the Database Name, User ID and Password to appear in the Profile Setup screen, you can manually type them into your **PB.INI** file. However, you should be aware that PowerBuilder stores the password in the **PB.INI** file in exactly the same manner in which you supply it. This means that it is freely accessible and totally unencrypted to anyone who has access to this **.INI** file.

Database Security

PowerBuilder's database security uses the concepts of groups, users and privileges. A user is anyone who can have access to tables in a database, and a group is a collection of users. Privileges are assigned at the table level and you can assign any of the following privileges to a user or group:

- Alter
- Delete
- Insert
- References
- Select
- Update

When you create any new databases with PowerBuilder, the software automatically assigns a default User ID of 'DBA' and a Password 'SQL'. This allows you to gain access to the database and modify the security to your own requirements.

337

We've used the same User ID and Password conventions for our example databases to simplify matters, but you can, and should, set up proper security for your databases by maintaining users and groups, together with their associated privileges.

You can perform this maintenance from the Database Administration Painter by selecting the appropriate option from the Objects menu:

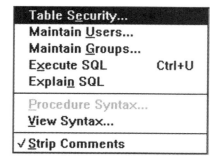

The three options we're interested in are Table Security, Maintain Users and Maintain Groups.

The first thing you have to do is set up users.

Maintaining Users

If you select Maintain Users..., PowerBuilder will display a list of the current users:

All registered users must be included in this list, even if the user names actually refer to groups. As you can see, we have editorial, marketing and production users - these users are actually groups.

At this stage, you can add a new user, or else delete or modify existing entries:

When adding a new user, you must supply a User ID and a Password. After creating all your users, the next step is to specify which users belong to which groups.

Maintaining Groups

When you select the Maintaining Groups... option, you'll see the following dialog box which allows you to create new groups and assign users to groups:

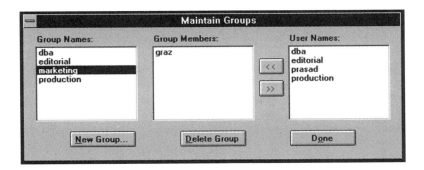

You should be aware that you can only create a new group if it has already been set up as a user. To assign other users to this group, highlight the group and the user that you wish to move and select the arrow that corresponds to moving users into or out of the group.

As you can see, we've assigned the user graz to the marketing group. Once you've assigned the users to groups, the final stage is to set privileges for both sets of users.

Assigning Privileges

The Table Security option brings up the dialog box which lets you assign privileges to your users and groups:

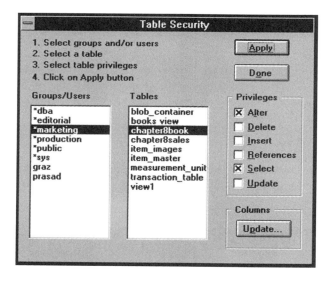

PowerBuilder's security works at the table level. This means that you can set different privileges for different tables against different users and groups.

> *If you set up privileges for a group, all of the users that are associated with that group automatically inherit them.*

For example, you can see that we've assigned Alter and Select privileges to the marketing group on the chapter8book table. This means that the user graz, will automatically be assigned these privileges, as he is part of the marketing group.

PowerBuilder's table security features are both powerful and flexible; they allow you to mix and match group-wide and individual privileges. For example, you might assign a marketing manager extra privileges which the rest of the marketing group didn't have.

You can also provide the marketing manager with extra privileges in another way. Any user may be a member of more than one group. This means that the marketing manager could be a member of the marketing group and the managing group to get the required set of privileges.

Once you have assigned the necessary table privileges to a user, if you create a profile for a user and force them to use that profile through passwording the database, their privileges will be taken into account when they try to do anything to the tables in the database.

For example, if someone in the marketing group tried to preview the chapter8sales table, they would get the following error message:

Note that to be able to set up users, groups and privileges, you must be logged in as 'dba', or otherwise have full access rights to the database whose security you are setting up.

Now that we have covered the security issues that are involved with a database profile, let's take a look at the other major component of this code, the ODBC connection.

ODBC

Microsoft's Open Database Connectivity standard defines a standard SQL grammar and two sets of function calls that are based upon the SAG CLI specification. These two sets of function calls are named core grammar and core functions respectively. It allows you to connect to a vast array of database systems.

ODBC Architecture

In general, the realm of ODBC can be split into four major components:

1 Application

2 Driver Manager

3 Driver

4 Data Source

Each of these components fits together, making a bridge between the two resources that need to exchange data:

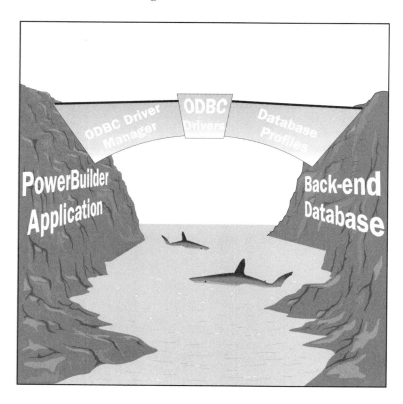

Let's look at each of these components in detail.

Application

This is the program that is used to access data from the back-end database typically running on the Windows operating system. For example, a PowerBuilder application which accesses data from Sybase SQL Server can be considered as the application when looking at the ODBC setup. Any ODBC functions that you need to call are made from the application.

Driver Manager

This is a DLL which controls the loading of the necessary drivers to connect to the required database system. When an ODBC call is made from an application, the Driver Manager scans the necessary `.INI` files to determine which driver to use and where it is located.

Driver

The driver is the heart of ODBC. It takes care of any network protocols that are required to connect to the data source and it also translates and submits the SQL statements to the data source:

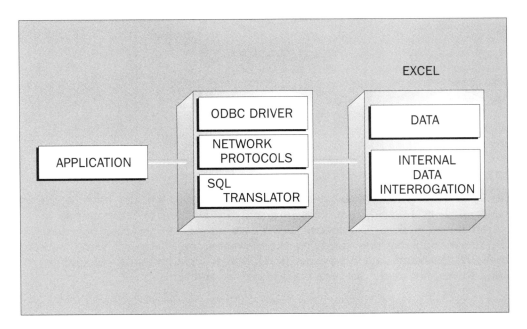

Note that there are currently three standards for SQL, ANSI '86, ANSI '89 and ANSI '92. This has lead to a proliferation of 'flavors' of SQL and prompted the need for this ODBC translation layer. It is therefore sometimes necessary for the ODBC driver to translate between these standards and flavors, for the application and the database to communicate effectively.

Generally, the back-end database system processes the actual SQL statements passed to it by the driver, but in the case of text files and some DBMSs which don't support SQL, the driver actually takes care of processing the SQL statements and sends the results back to the application:

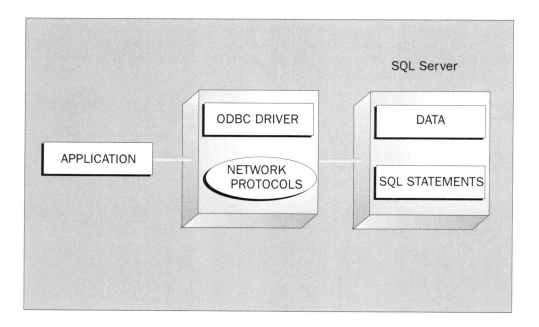

Data Source

This is an ASCII file, which contains the DBMS name and any other necessary details, such as Login Name, Password and the location of the database to connect to, as well as any specific DBMS parameters. In the case of Sybase SQL Server, you may be specifying the Server Name, Database Name, Server Login ID, Password and other specific DBMS information, such as application name, to display in the server's connection list and so on.

> ODBC takes care of finding the SQL Server address on the
> network and connecting to the SQL Server.

As an application developer, you only deal with two components: the function
calls from the application and the data source details. When using
PowerBuilder, the data source details are the database profiles which we've
already looked at.

The most interesting feature of ODBC is that you can connect to more than
one data source from the same application at the same time, simply by using
another profile.

The ODBCINST.INI File

When you first install PowerBuilder, you are prompted to select which ODBC
drivers you want to install. The selected drivers are installed in your **WINDOWS/
SYSTEM** directory, and the **ODBCINST.INI** file, which contains a list of installed
drivers, gets updated. The [ODBC Drivers] section of this file contains a list of
the installed drivers:

```
[ODBC Drivers]
Access Data (*.mdb)=Installed
FoxPro Files (*.dbf)=Installed
dBase Files (*.dbf)=Installed
Paradox Files (*.db)=Installed
SQL Server=Installed
Excel Files (*.xls)=Installed
Text Files (*.txt; *.csv)=Installed
Btrieve Data (file.ddf)=Installed
Watcom SQL 4.0=Installed
PB Q+E dBASEFile=Installed
PB Q+E ParadoxFile=Installed
PB Q+E NetWareSQL=Installed
PB Q+E Btrieve=Installed
PB Q+E Paradox5File=Installed
```

Each installed driver also has a section in the **ODBCINST.INI**, which contains
the full path name for the required driver:

```
[Watcom SQL 4.0]
Driver=c:\windows\system\WOD40W.DLL
Setup=c:\windows\system\WOD40W.DLL
```

PowerBuilder uses this information to set the driver options, which are available when you configure ODBC.

The ODBC.INI File

There is one other **.INI** file which we should look at - the **ODBC.INI** file. This is also contained in your **WINDOWS/SYSTEM** directory and contains the full connection information for all your databases. The [ODBC Data Sources] section specifies the DBMS to use for all of your databases, defined by either the manufacturer of the ODBC driver or by your profiles:

```
[ODBC Data Sources]
MS Access Databases=Access Data (*.mdb)
FoxPro Files=FoxPro Files (*.dbf)
dBase Files=dBase Files (*.dbf)
Paradox Files=Paradox Files (*.db)
NWind=dBase Files (*.dbf)
Powersoft Demo DB=Watcom SQL 4.0
ABNC Main DB (v4)=Watcom SQL 4.0
ABNC Sales DB (v4)=Watcom SQL 4.0
Mmrmgmt=WATCOM SQL 4.0
BookKeep=WATCOM SQL 4.0
Bug tracking 4.03=WATCOM SQL 4.0
Powersoft Cashtrak DB=WATCOM SQL 4.0
Contact=WATCOM SQL 4.0
DbPipe=WATCOM SQL 4.0
Diet=WATCOM SQL 4.0
Expense=WATCOM SQL 4.0
PowerPim=WATCOM SQL 4.0
Skills=WATCOM SQL 4.0
Wrkflow=WATCOM SQL 4.0
Invent=Watcom SQL 4.0
market=Watcom SQL 4.0
```

For each of these definitions, the **ODBC.INI** also has a separate section which contains the complete connection information for that database. For example, the [Powersoft Demo DB] section looks like this:

```
[Powersoft Demo DB]
DatabaseFile=c:\pb4\examples\PSDEMODB.DB
DatabaseName=PSDEMODB
UID=dba
PWD=sql
Driver=c:\windows\system\WOD40W.DLL
Start=db32w -d -c512
```

When you specify ODBC as the DBMS in a profile, the ODBC Driver Manager scans this file for the profile name and loads the appropriate driver.

This is probably the most important `.INI` file, as it contains the fullest information, including passwords, about all of your database connections. Due to this consideration, it is important that this file is protected on your system and not freely accessible to everyone.

> We would warn you against manually altering any of the entries in any of the `.INI` files which we've looked at, as doing so can have a serious effect on your ability to connect to your databases.

Please refer to the inside front cover of this book to get an idea of how all these elements fit together to create the mechanism required to get data to and from your application and back-end database.

The Transaction Object

The Transaction Object contains the information required to connect to the database and to return any results of the executed SQL. Before connecting to a database, the Transaction Object has to be populated with the database connection information. PowerBuilder supplies a global Transaction Object called SQLCA (Structured Query Language Communication Area). This is available when an application starts and is automatically destroyed when execution completes. The Transaction Object has 14 attributes, as shown in the following table:

Attribute	Data Type	Description
DBMS	String	Database vendor name, such as Sybase, ODBC...
Database	String	Database Name
UserId	String	User Name or User ID
DBParm	String	DBMS specific
DBPass	String	Database Password
Lock	String	The isolation level

Continued

Attribute	Data Type	Description
LogId	String	Login ID for the server
LogPass	String	Server Password
ServerName	String	Server Name
AutoCommit	Boolean	True/False
SQLCode	Long	The success or failure code of the most recent operation
SQLNRows	Long	The number of rows affected
SQLDBCode	Long	Database vendor's error code
SQLErrText	String	The database vendor's error message
SQLReturnData	String	Database vendor-specific information

When you want to connect to a database, you must populate the Transaction Object and use the **connect** statement to cause the Transaction Object to attempt the connection. If an error occurs, for example, if an invalid password is detected or the database isn't available, then the SQLCode attribute will contain a value other than zero and the SQLErrText attribute is populated with an error message.

If an error is received, you can display it and prompt the user whether to try again. We'll use this feature in the code for our login window to handle this error event.

Adding Code to our Login Window

When a user runs our application, the first thing we want them to do is login, using the correct profile. We've already written the script for the **open** event of the application so that it opens the login window:

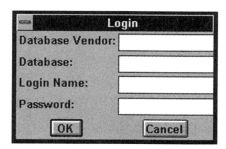

Now, let's add some code to the login window itself to handle the connection to our database. There are three events for which we need to write scripts:

▲ The w_login_window **open** event

▲ The cb_ok on w_login_window **click** event

▲ The cb_cancel on w_login_window **click** event

The Open Event for the Window

Our login window requires the user to type in four things: the Database Vendor, Database, Login Name and Password. To save the user having to type these in every time they want to use the application, we can read the values from an **.INI** file which we can distribute with the application.

> Note that the **PB.INI** entries are read automatically, whereas any custom **.INI** files that you distribute with your application must be programmatically interrogated at run-time.

We've included an **.INI** file on the CD-ROM called **STOCK.INI**, which contains the following information:

```
[inventory profile]
DBMS=ODBC
database=invent
userid=dba
logpass=
dbparm=Connectstring='DSN=invent'
```

To read this information in our script, we use the **ProfileString()** function and supply the name of the **.INI** file, the section which contains the data and the variable name. Following these instructions means that the **open** event of w_login_window should look like this:

```
// Object: w_login_window
// Event: open

sle_DatabaseVendor.text = ProfileString( "c:\wrox\stock.ini" , &
"inventory profile" , "dbms" , "" )
sle_Database.text = ProfileString( "c:\wrox\stock.ini" ,&
"inventory profile" , "database" , "" )
sle_LoginName.text = ProfileString( "c:\wrox\stock.ini" , &
"inventory profile" , "userid" , "" )
```

This assigns the values in the **STOCK.INI** file to the SingleLineEdit controls on our window. However, on a database security note, we still force the user to enter a password.

You may wonder why we didn't simply hard code the DBMS, database and userid in the **open** script. If we did this and anything changes, for example, you moved your database to Sybase SQL Server, then you need to physically open up all of the **open** scripts for all the applications that you have distributed, in order to modify the code and reflect this change. If you use an **.INI** file, all you need to do is distribute a new one containing the updated information.

The OK CommandButton

When the user has entered all the connection information and clicks on the OK CommandButton, we want to populate the Transaction Object (SQLCA) and connect to the database.

The code for the clicked event of the OK button is as follows:

```
// Object: cb_ok in window w_login_window
// Event: clicked

int lUserAnswer
SQLCA.dbms = sle_databasevendor.text
SQLCA.database = sle_database.text
SQLCA.userid = sle_loginname.text
SQLCA.dbpass = sle_password.text
SQLCA.dbparm = ProfileString( "stock.ini", &
"inventory profile", "dbparm", "Connectstring='DSN=invent'" )
connect;
if SQLCA.sqlCode <> 0 then
lUserAnswer = MessageBox("Login Error", &
SQLCA.SqlErrText + "~r" + &
"Do you want to try again ? ", Question!, &
YesNo!, 2 )
   if lUserAnswer = 2 then
halt
   else
return
end if
else
close( parent )
end if
```

The first section populates the SQLCA attributes with the values in the SingleLineEdit controls on our window. We then **connect** to the database and check if the **sqlcode** attribute is zero or not:

```
if SQLCA.sqlCode <> 0 then
```

If **sqlcode** isn't equal to zero, then an error has occurred in the connection and we use the **MessageBox()** function to display the error message. This dialog box also asks the user if they want to try again. If they answer 'no', then we **halt** the execution, but if they answer 'yes', we return to the login window for them to try another combination.

> *As this loop is handled progammatically, it is very easy to count the aborted attempts to connect to a database. If this number becomes excessive, it is possible that someone is attempting to hack into one of your databases. At this point, you might attempt to alert the network administrator to this fact, so that the necessary steps can be taken to safeguard the databases.*

If there are no connection errors, we close the window and the application will continue execution at the next line of code in the **open** script for the application - it opens the w_item_master window, the proper opening window of our application.

The Cancel CommandButton

The only other code we have to add to the login window is the code for the **clicked** event of the Cancel CommandButton. If the user clicks on this, we simply want to stop the execution of the application:

```
// Object: cb_cancel in window w_login_window
// Event: clicked

Halt
```

Test the login window by using the *Ctrl+Shift+W* keys to run it. You should see the connection information filled in automatically:

351

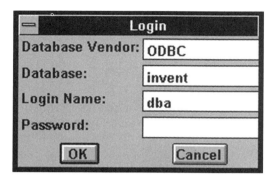

You can simulate a connection error by not typing in a password or changing one of the other values. When a connection error occurs, you'll get a message box telling you what the error is and asking if you want to try again:

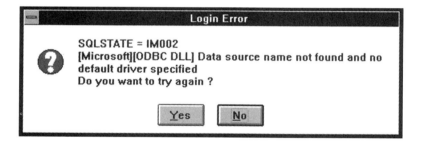

If your users are on a Novell network, you can automatically get their user information by using the Novell Network Bindery Service function call `nwDSWhoAmI()`, or by using the Windows SDK call `GetEnvironmentVar()`. These would enable you to distribute a single `.INI` file for all users, calling the relevant function rather than reading the hard coded userid from the `.INI` file.

> To use these functions, you need to purchase additional Novell Network Bindary Service DLLs from Powersoft. Register the DLLs with your application by declaring them as local or global external functions. You can then call them like any other user-defined function in your script. We'll look at how to use Windows SDK calls in a later chapter, when we cover how to declare external functions.

If you don't specify the full path for the `.INI` file name, PowerBuilder first looks in the directory from where PowerBuilder was started and then looks in the working directory specified when you created the relevant program item. This is only true when you are running the application under the development environment, that is, from within PowerBuilder.

When you create an `.EXE` file and run it independently, PowerBuilder first looks in the working directory specified for the `.EXE` file program item. If the file isn't found in that directory, it then searches in the directories appearing in your `AUTOEXEC.BAT` path.

We've now completed all the scripts for the login window, so let's move on to the w_item_master window and look at the scripts we have to add to it, to complete the functionality of our application.

The w_item_master Window

This is the main window of our application which allows us to view and manipulate the information in our database:

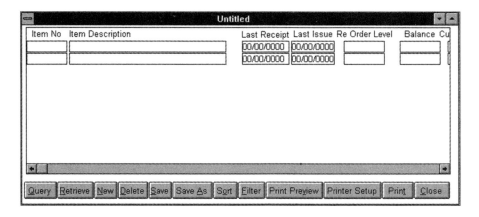

When we first open this window, we have to specify where the DataWindow control is supposed to get its information from, or in other words, to which Transaction Object it should be referring. This might seem strange, as we've already defined the data source for the DataWindow object, but there are two main benefits to this:

1 **Database Independence**: As long as the result set is the same, the same DataWindow can be used to manipulate data from many databases. For example, you may have a production database and a historic database with the same table structures and permissions. You could use the same DataWindow to connect to both of these, simply by changing the database attribute of the SQLCA object.

2 **Multiple Database Support**: This allows you to connect to multiple databases at the same time within an application. You can create multiple Transaction Objects and connect to various databases for each DataWindow.

We do this in the **open** script for the window by using the **SetTransObject()** function. So you should add the following lines to the **open** event script for the w_item_master window:

```
dwc_1.SetTransObject( SQLCA )
dwc_2.SetTransObject( SQLCA )
```

Note that there is another function which allows you to set the transaction object - **SetTrans()**. If you use this function, you have no control over the transaction management and an application is automatically connected or disconnected to the database whenever the **Retrieve()** or **Update()** functions are called.

> The major problem with using this function is that continually connecting and disconnecting to a database takes both time and processor power.

Before we start adding the functionality to the CommandButtons on our window so that we can manipulate the data in our database, let's look at the way that PowerBuilder's DataWindows store information.

DataWindow Buffers

Internally, PowerBuilder maintains one edit control and four buffers for each DataWindow control. These buffers include the:

▲ Original

▲ Primary

▲ Deleted

▲ Filtered

These buffers are used to contain the data from the database and reflect any changes that are made to that data before they are saved back to the database. When data is retrieved from the database, it is retrieved into the Primary buffer and it is the contents of this buffer which are displayed in the DataWindow:

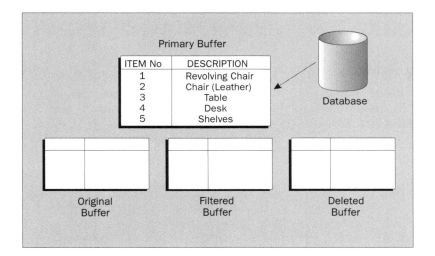

Adding Rows

Rows can be added to the DataWindow using the `InsertRow()` function. This will add a row to the Primary Buffer, but it has no effect on the other buffers:

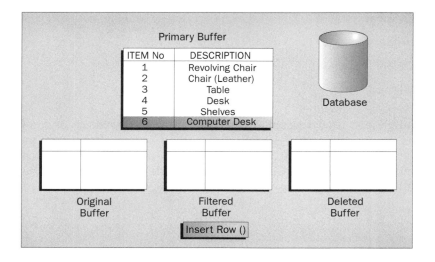

Deleting Rows

When you delete a row with the **DeleteRow()** function, the row is transferred from the Primary buffer into the Deleted buffer. If we deleted item 5, the buffers would look like this:

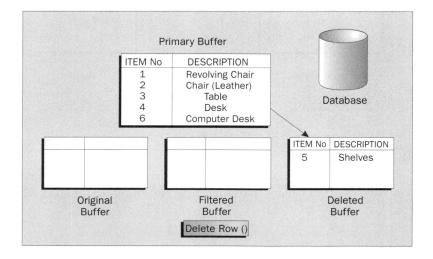

Filtering Rows

When rows are filtered using the **SetFilter()** function, all rows that don't match the filtered condition are moved to the Filtered buffer. If we filtered on the criteria that the item_no was greater than 3, the buffers would look like this:

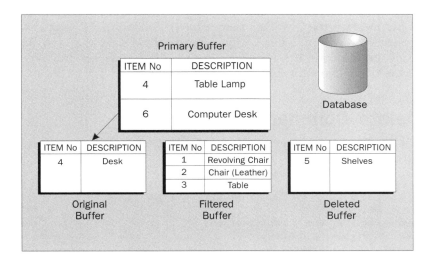

Modifying Rows

If you modify a row in the DataWindow, the row in the Primary buffer is modified and the original value is copied into the Original buffer. If we changed the description of item_no 4 from a desk to a table lamp, the buffers would look like this:

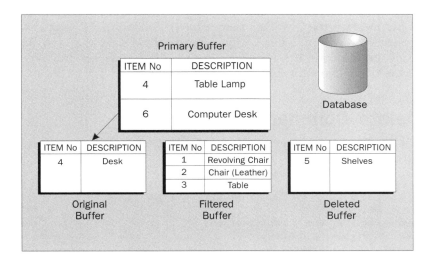

> Note that this is only the case for rows which were originally retrieved from the database. If we modified **item_no** 6, nothing would be copied to the Original buffer, because this row was added to the results set after the data was retrieved from the database

All of these changes to the data will have no effect on the data in the database until the **Update()** function is called. It is at this stage that the necessary SQL statements are created to delete, insert and modify the existing data in the database.

Now that we have an idea of how the DataWindow controls the data, it's time to add functionality to our CommandButtons.

The New CommandButton

This button adds a new row to the DataWindow using the **InsertRow()** function. The code is as follows:

```
// Object: cb_new in window w_item_master
// Event: clicked

Long lInsertedRow
lInsertedRow = dwc_1.InsertRow( 0 )
dwc_1.ScrollToRow( lInsertedRow )
```

The row number returned by the **InsertRow()** function is a long data type and represents the row number of the new record. Using the zero parameter for the function appends the new row to the end results set and we use the **ScrollToRow()** function to move to that row.

The Delete CommandButton

This script for the **clicked** event of the Delete CommandButton is as follows:

```
// Object: cb_delete in window w_item_master
// Event: clicked

long lDeleteThisRow
int lUserAnswer, lItemNo, lUpdateStatus
lDeleteThisRow = dwc_1.GetRow()
If lDeleteThisRow > 0 then
```

```
lItemNo = dwc_1.GetItemNumber(lDeleteThisRow,1)
lUserAnswer = MessageBox("Delete","Do you " + &
" want to delete Item No: " + String(lItemNo),&
StopSign!, YesNo!, 2 )
if lUserAnswer = 1 then
dwc_1.DeleteRow( lDeleteThisRow )
lUpdateStatus = dwc_1.update()
if lUpdateStatus = 1 then
Commit ;
else
RollBack ;
MessageBox( "Delete", "Error in deleting " &
+ String( lItemNo ) + "Error Message: " &
+ SQLCA.SqlErrText )
return
end if
end if
end if
```

We use the `GetRow()` function to return the current row and if it exists, then we ask the user to confirm the deletion. If they confirm it, we call the `DeleteRow()` and `Update()` functions and commit the deletion. If there are any problems, we roll it back and display an appropriate error message.

> You may not be familiar with the words commit and rollback. This is transaction processing in action. When using the Transaction Object, we have to take care of committing or rolling back any changes to the database. If we use the commit statement, then changes are confirmed and made to the database. If we rollback the changes, then the database returns to the state it was in before the `update()` function was called.

The Retrieve CommandButton

The script for the Retrieve button simply calls the `Retrieve()` function for the DataWindow control dwc_1:

```
// Object: cb_retrieve in w_item_master
// Event: Clicked

dwc_1.retrieve()
```

All the information you defined in the DataWindow will be retrieved and displayed in the DataWindow control. If you have a lot of information to be retrieved from a database, you can choose to only display the amount of information which will fit in the DataWindow control.

Retrieve Only as Needed

This option is available in the DataWindow Painter from the Rows menu and you must select it when you paint the DataWindow. The amount of data retrieved will depend on the size of your DataWindow control. PowerBuilder automatically performs this calculation for you and modifies the result if you change the size of the control.

When the user starts scrolling down the DataWindow, PowerBuilder will retrieve another screen full of data. A possible disadvantage of this method is that if you print the DataWindow, only the displayed rows are printed. This also has an effect if you try to determine the number of rows in the table; you'll only receive a count of the number of current records.

Another effect of using this method is that the remaining information is held in the back-end database's memory, and this may use a lot of system resources and affect the server's response time.

You can get round these problems by dynamically changing the Retrieve Only As Needed status. For example, you could add the following line in the `clicked` event of the Print CommandButton:

```
dwc_1.dwmodify( "datawindow.retrieve.asneeded = false" )
```

This cancels the Retrieve Only As Needed option, so that all the information would be printed. You should note that you would need to perform the retrieval again for this code to have any overall effect on your application.

> Note that if you specify a sort order using the **Rows/Sort** option, or if you use any aggregate functions such as `sum()` or `avg()` in the DataWindow Painter, then the **Retrieve Only As Needed** option will be ignored.

The Save CommandButton

The code for the Save button is as follows:

```
// Object: cb_save in window w_item_master
// Event: Clicked

int lUserAnswer
int lUpdateStatus
lUserAnswer = MessageBox( "Update", &
"Apply Changes ?", Question!,YesNo!,2)
if lUserAnswer = 1 then
SetPointer( HourGlass! )
lUpdateStatus = dwc_1.Update()
if lUpdateStatus = 1 then
commit ;
else
SetPointer( Arrow! )
RollBack ;
MessageBox( "Update", "Error in update" + "Error Message: " + &
SQLCA.SqlErrText )
return
end if
end if
SetPointer( Arrow! )
```

The first task that we perform in this script is to get confirmation from the user that they want to apply the changes to the data. If they give a positive reply, we call the **Update()** function and commit the changes, otherwise we **RollBack**. While we are saving information to the database, we change the mouse pointer to an hourglass to show that some operation is taking place.

You should always keep your user informed of what is going on in an application. If there are some lengthy processes taking place, you should give them some kind of indication, otherwise the unknowledgeable user may think that things have gone wrong. The following table illustrates some of the general guidelines for lengthy operations:

Duration	Action
<= 4 seconds	Optional hourglass cursor.
5 - 15 seconds	Display the hourglass cursor.
15+ seconds	Display a message box and preferably an indicator of progress for the operation.

The Query CommandButton

When the user clicks on the Query button, we want to hide the first DataWindow control and display the second one which displays the dw_item_master_free_format_for_query DataWindow object. This object has been designed to allow us to type in our own criteria for the search to be based upon. The code is as follows:

```
// Object: cb_query for w_item_master
// Event: clicked

dwc_1.hide()
dwc_2.show()
dwc_2.dwmodify('datawindow.querymode = yes')
```

This simply hides the first DataWindow control, displays the second and then calls the **dwmodify()** function, setting the querymode ready to accept the criteria:

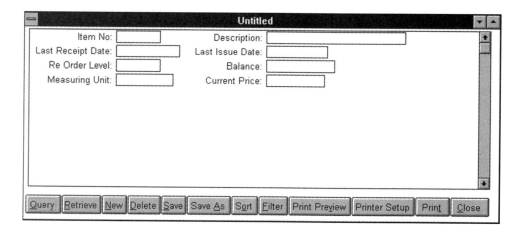

For example, if we specify a criteria of '>2' for the Balance and then click the Retrieve button, the DataWindow will only display the rows which have a Balance of 3 or greater:

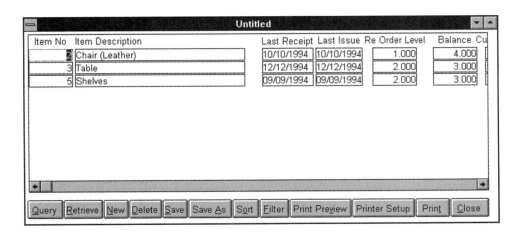

Item No	Item Description	Last Receipt	Last Issue	Re Order Level	Balance Cu
2	Chair (Leather)	10/10/1994	10/10/1994	1.000	4.000
3	Table	12/12/1994	12/12/1994	2.000	3.000
5	Shelves	09/09/1994	09/09/1994	2.000	3.000

Query Retrieve New Delete Save Save As Sort Filter Print Preview Printer Setup Print Close

Adding the Finishing Touches

We'll now look at some of the final pieces of script which we need for the w_item_master window, so completing the first version of our application. We won't write scripts for the Save As, Sort and Filter CommandButtons, as these require some extra window painting and a deeper understanding of PowerScript.

We'll see in Chapter 13 how to convert our application to present an MDI and we'll add the extra button functionality for this second version of our application. The final scripts that we need to cover for the first version of our application are all concerned with printing options.

DataWindow Printing

There are three buttons on our window which relate to printing the DataWindow:

- Print Preview
- Printer Setup
- Print

Let's look at each of these in turn to see how we add this useful functionality to our application.

Print Preview CommandButton

If the entire DataWindow won't fit on the screen, either horizontally or vertically, it may be better to allow the user to see a Print Preview before it is actually sent to the printer. This button works in toggle mode, so the first thing we do is check what state the DataWindow control is in:

```
// Object: cb_Print_Preview in w_item_master
// Event: Clicked

if dwc_1.DwDescribe("datawindow.Print.Preview") = "yes" then
dwc_1.DwModify("datawindow.Print.Preview = no")
else
dwc_1.DwModify("datawindow.Print.Preview = yes")
end if
```

The **DwDescribe()** function returns the state of the control and we use the **DwModify()** function to change it. This has the effect of turning the reorganization of the DataWindow on or off in preparation for printing, illustrated by the blue border line which encloses the area that will be printed:

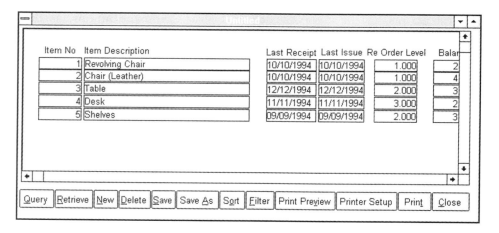

Printer Setup CommandButton

We'll allow our users to specify their printer options by clicking on this button. The script is a single function call:

```
// Object: cb_printer_setup of w_item_master
// Event: Clicked

PrintSetup()
```

This brings up the standard Windows printer select dialog box:

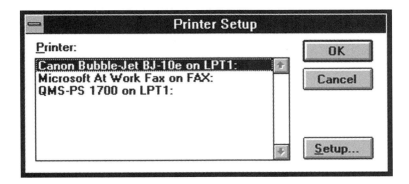

Print CommandButton

Again, this is a single line of script:

```
// Object: cb_print in w_item_master
// Event: Clicked

dwc_1.print( TRUE )
```

The parameter **TRUE** displays the printing status dialog box with a Cancel CommandButton to allow the user to stop the print job at any time:

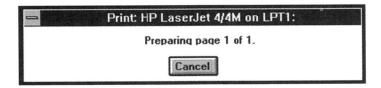

The Close CommandButton

The final button on the window is the Close button. This simply closes the window when it is clicked:

```
Close ( Parent )
```

Summary

You now have a fully functional application which allows you to retrieve data from a database, query the data on specific criteria and add or delete rows in the database. You also have the ability to print any of that data to any of the printers connected to your network.

However, there are still some limitations to the application and we haven't used all the Windows, DataWindows, Tables and Menus which we've painted in previous chapters. All of these objects have been designed for the second version of our application, a luxury you don't always have!

In the next chapter, we'll look at what you can do to track down problems in your code and then we'll move on to introduce you to the object-oriented features of PowerBuilder, in preparation for the conversion of our single window application to an MDI version.

Debugging Applications

Sometimes applications don't work as you expect them to. You may come across unexpected loops, or MessageBoxes that don't appear or simply refuse to display the correct message.

As you write scripts for events, you will probably be able to follow most of the execution flow as you would in a traditional program. However, there will be cases when you lose the thread, especially when you are using inheritance or multiple instances of your objects. As object-oriented programs get more complex, using more and more of the advanced language features, debugging gets exponentially more complicated. When your programs get to this level of complexity, it becomes imperative to see how PowerBuilder is executing the script.

This chapter explains how to debug programs in PowerBuilder and some of the common situations when you see 'remarkable' behavior whilst running or debugging an application.

In this chapter, we will cover:

- The debugging environment
- Some common debugging problems
- Some advanced debugging techniques

Running Your Applications

While it is still under development, PowerBuilder allows you to run your application in one of two modes: Run and Debug. When using Run mode, PowerBuilder displays your application in full glory, running scripts when appropriate and displaying dialog boxes under the appropriate conditions, so allowing you to review the overall effect.

In Debug mode, you can add break points at a particular line in the script or function which, when the application is run, causes PowerBuilder to temporarily halt the execution at that point. As the program executes, you can see how a particular variable changes at these key points throughout its lifetime.

Before you attempt to debug your application, it is advisable to save all the currently opened objects. This ensures that the Debug is working against the most up-to-date objects in your libraries and allows you to close down any painters you have been working with.

> If there are any painters open holding information about any of the objects that the debug operation may be using, PowerBuilder won't allow you to open the Debug Painter.

If things appear to be going wrong in your application or it doesn't appear to be running smoothly, it is time to close down all the painters, save the objects and kick in the Debug Painter.

Invoking the Debug Painter 🐞

The Debug Painter is one of the most flexible tools that PowerBuilder has to offer, combining the ability to debug the code attached to any event or function with the ability to dynamically interrogate the variables that the code affects as the application runs.

When you initiate the Debug Painter, PowerBuilder starts a debugging session for the currently opened application - as defined in the Application Preferences under AppLib:

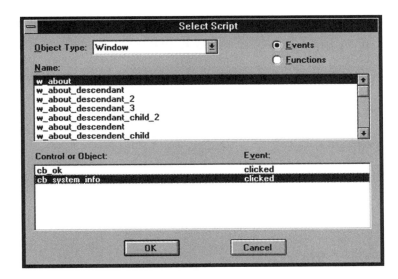

When you call up the Debug Painter, you must be prepared to supply the following information:

1 The type of object that the buggy code is associated with.

2 Whether the code is resident in an event or a function.

3 The specific name of the object that you are interested in.

4 The combination of the related control or object with the appropriate event or the name of the function.

If you want to debug a global function, you should select the Function option in the Object Type: listbox. If you want to select an object level function, select the appropriate object type and make sure that the Functions radio button is selected.

This information is enough to allow the Debug Painter to accurately identify the code that you wish to test, allowing the painter to create the main debug session:

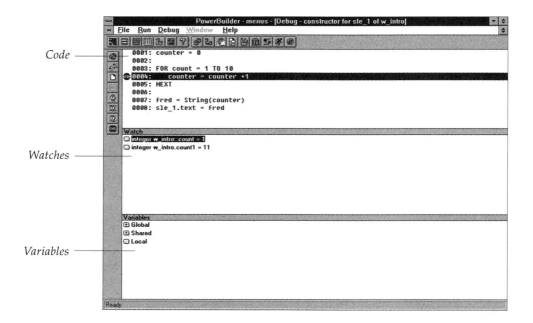

Code

Watches

Variables

The main debug window is broken into three major sections: the variable lists, any active watches and the code.

The Variable Lists

This part of the main debug window is used in conjunction with the active watches to provide you with valuable information about the performance of the program as it is running.

As we saw in Chapter 9, PowerBuilder combines the ideas of scope and variables. This provides the developer with the flexibility that is required when programming with an object-oriented language such as PowerScript. The variables are broken up into the three main subsets: Global, Shared and Local.

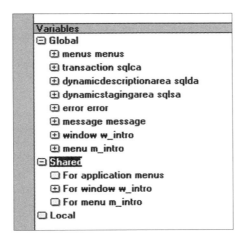

As you double click on each of these variable groups, PowerBuilder presents you with different lists of available choices. As you descend the depths, each list takes you closer and closer to the property of the control or the value of the variable that you're interested in. This ability to focus in on any property of any control or any variable of any program allows you to maintain control over the most complex of applications.

The Watches

As you can see by moving amongst the variable listings as the program runs, PowerBuilder displays the changing values of each variable or control. This feature allows you to track the progress of the application, letting you examine the cogs of the machine rather than the results that it produces.

However, you can immediately see a problem - what if you want to track two variables at the same time, which are located in different branches of the organization? PowerBuilder solves this problem by allowing you to set up a watch on a variable or property. This watch forgets about the other related variables and controls, and just spends its time focused on the one attribute.

```
Watch
☐ integer w_intro::count = 1
☐ integer w_intro.count1 = 11
☐ string m_intro.m_file.microhelp = ""
```

By setting watches against the key elements of your application, you'll be able to track the progress in one simple and easy-to-understand place - the Watch section of the main debug window.

The Code

This part of the main debug window allows you to view, but not alter, the code which is under review. It's in this part of the debug session that you can inform PowerBuilder of the key stages of the code, the stages that you wish the program to stop at while it is running in Debug mode.

When you identify a problem, you must close down the debug session before you can change the code. Re-open the appropriate script and make the necessary changes, before running a new debug session as a check on the changes.

Now we have completed a brief tour of the main debug window, let's take a look at the final preparations that are required before you can begin the debugging process.

Stop Points

There are two ways to run through a program in Debug mode: Stepping and Continuous. Stepping allows you to move from one command to the next, temporarily pausing until you force the computer to move onto the next entry. This can be very time-consuming and it may not provide you with the information about the part of the program that you are interested in. The other method, Continuous, allows you to run one command after another, a task that the computer will continue to perform until it reaches the end of the listing, or until it encounters a **Stop Point**.

A Stop Point is a flag that you can set against any line of a program that PowerBuilder recognizes, as a request to temporarily halt the program until you ask it to move on. This allows you to quickly move through the running application to the part of the program that you have identified as troublesome. At this point, you can change to Stepping through the program in an attempt to slowly work through each line of code to further narrow down the location of the problem.

Using Stop Points

When you open a debug session, PowerBuilder might throw up the Edit Stops dialog box. This dialog box displays all the Stop Points you set in the previous debug session for the current application.

> This dialog box displays all the Stop Points that you have set for any code associated with this application, not just the particular slice of code that you have requested to interrogate.

When you are ready to run the debug session, select Start, and as soon as PowerBuilder encounters the first Stop Point, it displays the main debug window. The Stop Point, and therefore the 'code of interest', appears in the Code section, while the watches display the current values of the variables and properties of interest - you are debugging!

Flow in the Debug Window

There are several options from the Debug PainterBar which allow you to control the flow of execution and what is visible in the Debug window:

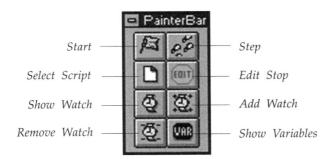

If you want to see the execution of the script line-by-line, click on the Step icon. PowerBuilder will move through the script, one line at a time, taking no notice of any Stop Points that you have set. After a while, you might decide to jump to your first Stop Point.

If you hit the Continue icon, PowerBuilder runs the application as normal. The only way to tell that you are in Debug mode, is when you run some script that has a Stop Point associated to one of its lines - you are automatically thrown into the debug window when PowerBuilder hits that Stop Point.

> Note that the **Continue** icon replaces the **Start** icon on the PainterBar when PowerBuilder is running in Debug mode.

Suppose you wrote some script for the `clicked` event of a CommandButton, that called a function and triggered a certain event. If you set a stop for the CommandButton's `clicked` event, you can see the execution of the function and the triggered event step-by-step in the debug window. If the function in this script is calling another, this second function is also displayed in the debug window.

> *If there is a **PostEvent** function in the script which you are debugging, the event called through the PostEvent function won't be displayed in the debug window, unless you set a Stop Point in the **Posted** event.*

Before we look at some of the techniques and problems that you can encounter while debugging, let's complete the scene setting, ready for the debugger to do its stuff.

Adding Stop Points

When you first approach some code with the intent of using the debugger against it, you need to set up your Stop Points. If you haven't added any Stop Points to your application so far, when you have selected the code that you want to review, PowerBuilder throws you straight into the main debug window.

You can place Stop Points against any line of code simply by double clicking against the line number.

> Actually, there are some occasions in your code where you can't use Stop Points. These include any commented out lines, variable definitions and blank entries. In fact, you could say that you can only set Stop Points against lines that actually alter something, as opposed to lines that improve readability or do some preparatory work for the code to run successfully.

You can repeat this task as many times as you like, denoting each and every key point in your program as a point at which you would like to stop and review the progress:

```
STOP 0001:  counter = 0
     0002:
     0003:  FOR count = 1 TO 10
STOP 0004:       counter = counter +1
     0005:  NEXT
     0006:
STOP 0007:  fred = String(counter)
     0008:  sle_1.text = fred
```

Stop Points and Embedded SQL

Embedded SQL throws up its own restrictions. For the purpose of Stop Points, PowerBuilder reads all declaration statements as no-go areas. This means that an SQL declaration statement, which might include cursor and procedure declarations, is read in just the same way as an integer declaration - no Stop Points allowed.

PowerBuilder also has problems with embedded SQL statements that span multiple lines. Clearly, due to the way that SQL is structured, it doesn't make sense to stop a program half-way through an SQL statement. You either need to read all the SQL statement or none at all, and so PowerBuilder won't allow you to place a Stop Point between the first and last lines of a multi-line embedded SQL statement.

If you want to set such an SQL statement as a Stop Point, double click on the last line. For example, to set a Stop Point on the following SQL statement, you would double click on the line that contains the FROM clause:

```
SELECT "item_master"."item_no",
    "item_master"."balance"
    INTO : lItemNo,
    :lBalance
    FROM "item_master" ;
```

Editing Stop Points

When you have set some of the Stop Points that you require in your code, you might like to try out the Edit Stops dialog box:

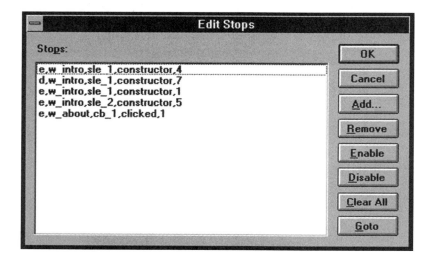

As you will see if you try to open a debug session on some code that already has some Stop Points associated with it, this dialog provides you with the ability to review and modify any or all of those Stop Points.

Enabling and Disabling

As you move through the process of debugging a program, you may set several Stop Points as you try to narrow the problem down. If you try to run the debug session with all these Stop Points in place, you might find it quite time-consuming to get to the 'interesting' part of the program.

To circumvent this problem, PowerBuilder allows you to temporarily disable the earlier Stop Points, removing the need to pass through them all. The debugger doesn't pick up on any disabled Stop Points, only the enabled ones.

PowerBuilder displays the status of each Stop Point in two different ways:

▲   The Stop Point symbol is grayed out for a disabled entry.

▲   The entry in the Edit Stop dialog is altered to reflect the new status of the Stop Point.

No matter how you like to review the status of the Stop Points, PowerBuilder only allows you to affect the status through the Edit Stops dialog box:

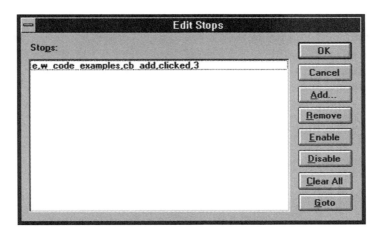

This dialog box also allows you to add and remove Stop Points, whilst also providing you with information about each one in turn.

The entries in the Edit Stops dialog box have the following syntax:

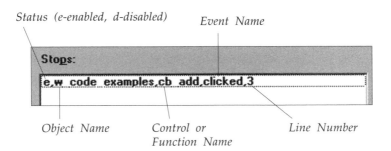

Changing Variable Values

If you are debugging a program that contains a lot of changing variables, you may want to modify the variables as you are debugging. For example, if you have a loop, you may want to increase the value of the counter in order to jump forward in the program; or if you have a menu selection window which gets input from the user, you may want to change the value input to test out all the options without having to run the full program every time.

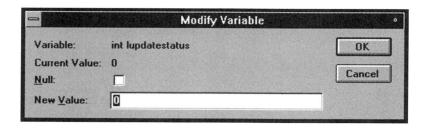

You can see that this displays the variable name and current value. You can enter a new value or set the value to Null.

Adding Watches

As we have already seen, PowerBuilder allows you to set watches against key variables, enabling you to track those values without the baggage of a variable's scope, or the organizational structure of the variables hampering your efforts.

By indicating the exact variable(s) that you wish to concentrate on, PowerBuilder is capable of setting up the appropriate watch, illustrating a unique 'path' to the variable/property and providing the current value of that item at any time before, during and after the debugging process is complete.

To add a variable to the watch window, simply highlight the variable in the list and click on the Add icon in the PainterBar. This causes PowerBuilder to initial a watch against that variable, the content of which is illustrated using the syntax given on the opposite page:

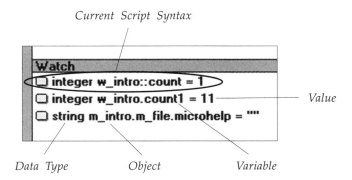

Current Script Syntax

Value

Data Type   *Object*   *Variable*

Debugging Inherited Objects

When debugging inherited objects, any scripts which have been written for ancestor objects won't be displayed in the debug window. If you want to see the ancestor script while you are debugging, you also need to set a break point in the ancestor script.

If there are several levels of ancestors and you set break points in the top level, you will be able to see all the descendant scripts executing in the debug window.

Solutions to Common Debugging Problems

In general, there are several occasions when the debugger won't help you to solve your program's problems. This section is dedicated to those problems and some of the solutions that we have found. We hope that the following information may help you to avoid these minefields, saving you from hours of fighting unexpected PowerBuilder behavior.

In this section, we cover:

- ▲ Using the **MessageBox()** function in the debugging process
- ▲ Problems with **KeyDown()** and **dwGetObjectAtPointer()** when debugging
- ▲ Message Objects

381

MessageBox()

Instead of using the step-by-step technique of debugging, you might decide to use the PowerBuilder **MessageBox()** function to indicate the passage of some code, together with pertinent information about the state of some variable or property.

Any problem surfaces when the variable you want to display is a NULL. In this case, PowerBuilder neglects to display the message box at all. In the debug window, you will see the **MessageBox()** being executed, but it never appears on screen.

This often happens when you are dealing with embedded SQL commands. If the column you are selecting isn't protected by a NOT NULL flag or a default value, you run the risk of acquiring a NULL and falling foul of this problem.

To further exacerbate the problem, PowerBuilder doesn't support an **IsNull** function to check whether the variable contains a NULL value, and you can't perform a check with an equality sign, as shown below:

```
If Variable = NULL then ...
```

Fortunately, SQL provides a mechanism that allows you to get around this problem:

```
SELECT "item_master1"."item_description"
   INTO :lItemDesc:lDescInd1
   FROM "item_master1"
   WHERE "item_master1"."item_no" = :lItemNo ;
```

In the above example, you can check **lDescInd1** for the presence of a NULL value. For more details on this, refer to Embedded SQL in Chapter 18.

KeyDown() or dwGetObjectAtPointer()

When you are using the **KeyDown()** and **dwGetObjectAtPointer()** functions, you will experience trouble when debugging, because while debugging, the debug window is the active window and is placed at the front. When you are executing step-by-step, the key you pressed is sent to the active window, which is the debug rather than the active window in the application.

The solution to this problem is to set Stop Points above and below the line containing the `KeyDown()` function, and once you reach the first Stop Point above the `KeyDown()` function, select the Continue icon instead of the step icon. This allows the pressed key to be passed to the active window in the application, and the execution stops at the next Stop Point after the `KeyDown()` function.

Follow the same technique with `dwGetObjectAtPointer()`.

Messages

To pass values between windows you may often use a message object. Like `KeyDown()`, this also works well in run-time. Typically, while you are debugging the script, you go through the code, step-by-step, watching the variables and trying to work out what is happening. Unfortunately, by using this method of debugging, you are allowing some time between execution of the lines, a result that can itself produce adverse effects.

Windows is a message-based operating system. This means every application working under Windows sends and receives messages. When there is time left before you execute the line that checks the message object value, there is a chance that other application messages may override your content. This leaves the script without the exact content of the message object.

At run-time, as there is no intervention in most cases, it works as you would want it to.

To overcome this problem, in the called event (triggered event) declare a local or instance variable and assign the message object value in the first statement of the event itself. For example:

```
// CommandButton cb_browse in WindowA
OpenWithParm( WindowB, "String Value" )
```

In the **Open** event of WindowB, you would then add the following line of code as the first line:

```
InstanceStringVariable = Message.StringParm
```

Closing the Debug Window

You should always wait until the execution of code has stopped before you exit the debugger. If you do try to close the debug window during a debug session, you will get the following warning:

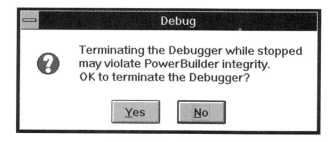

You can exit the debugger from here, but there is a possibility of your application crashing. To reduce the chance of this happening, you should go back into the debug session and wait until the execution stops.

Tracing PowerBuilder's Internal Execution

Up until now, we have described how you use the debugger interactively. If you are interested in the flow of an application's execution line by line, PowerBuilder provides a way to do this. With this facility you can log the flow of an application's execution line by line, but since PowerBuilder logs every line of execution, you will find that the application executes very slowly.

To do this, after creating the executable version of the application, supply PBDEBUG as the command line argument for the `.EXE` file in the Program Item Properties box:

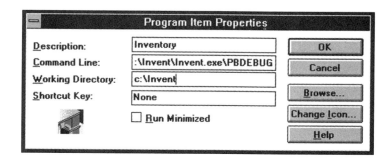

You have no control over the log file name. It is by default the `.EXE` file name with the `.DBG` file extension. This file will be created in the working directory you specify in the properties box.

PowerBuilder starts logging from the beginning of the application and continues logging until you exit the application. You have no control over specifying beginning and end points to log. A typical trace file looks like the one shown below:

```
Executing event script UE_RETRIEVE for class W_ITEM_MASTER, lib entry
    W_ITEM_MASTER
  Executing instruction at line 1
  Executing object function RETRIEVE for class DATAWINDOW, lib entry
      _TYPEDEF
    Executing event script SQLPREVIEW for class DWC_1, lib entry
      W_ITEM_MASTER
    Executing instruction at line 1
    Executing instruction at line 15
  End event script SQLPREVIEW for class DWC_1, lib entry W_ITEM_MASTER
  Executing event script ITEMFOCUSCHANGED for class DWC_1, lib entry
      W_ITEM_MASTER
    Executing instruction at line 2
    Executing object function GETCOLUMNNAME for class DATAWINDOW, lib
      entry _TYPEDEF
    End object function GETCOLUMNNAME for class DATAWINDOW, lib entry
      _TYPEDEF
    Executing instruction at line 3
    Executing system function TRIM
    Executing instruction at line 4
    Executing object function DWDESCRIBE for class DATAWINDOW, lib entry
      _TYPEDEF
    End object function DWDESCRIBE for class DATAWINDOW, lib entry
      _TYPEDEF
    Executing instruction at line 5
    Executing system function ISNULL
    Executing system function TRIM
    Executing system function TRIM
    Executing instruction at line 9
  End event script ITEMFOCUSCHANGED for class DWC_1, lib entry
    W_ITEM_MASTER
  Executing event script RETRIEVEEND for class DWC_1, lib entry
      W_ITEM_MASTER
    Executing instruction at line 1
    Executing object function ROWCOUNT for class DATAWINDOW, lib entry
      _TYPEDEF
    End object function ROWCOUNT for class DATAWINDOW, lib entry
      _TYPEDEF
```

Executing instruction at line 5
End event script RETRIEVEEND for class DWC_1, lib entry W_ITEM_MASTER
End object function RETRIEVE for class DATAWINDOW, lib entry _TYPEDEF
Executing instruction at line 1
End event script UE_RETRIEVE for class W_ITEM_MASTER, lib entry
W_ITEM_MASTER

You may find that lines appear for which you haven't written any code. The reason for this, is that as we have already explained in previous chapters, every PowerBuilder object is inherited from the base PowerClass object. There may be certain scripts in these base objects, which PowerBuilder executes behind the scenes and which we never see. When you use the logging feature, PowerBuilder displays these just like any other code which we've written ourselves. There is no way to find out exactly what the code does, or to open it up and change it.

Logging SQL Statement Execution

All the above procedures follow the flow of execution and display the content of variables as the program executes. However, this doesn't include what exactly is being sent to the connected database, the time it takes and so on. To display this information, you can add the word 'trace' before the DBMS name in your database profile:

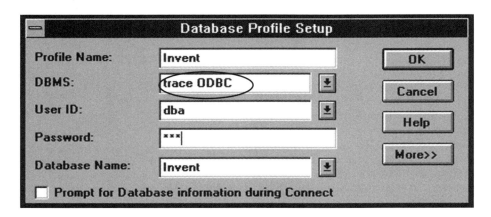

> You should remember to remove the 'trace' before distributing your application, as you will find logging all the database information will seriously affect the performance.

We can see how this works by logging onto our application as follows:

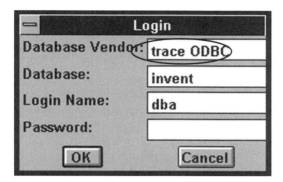

When you type in the password and click on the OK button, you'll get the following message box confirming that the log file has been created in your Windows directory:

If the log file already exists, new information will be appended, so it can get very big very quickly if you don't keep an eye on it.

The PowerBuilder log is used to relate three points of interest:

- Parameters that are used to connect to the database
- Any SQL statements executed against that database
- The time it took to connect to the database and execute that statement

The following log was created when we executed our Stock Control application with a trace flag:

387

```
LOGIN: (4723 MilliSeconds)
CONNECT TO trace ODBC:
USERID=dba
DATA=invent
DBPARM=Connectstring='DSN=invent_02' (0 MilliSeconds)
PREPARE: (0 MilliSeconds)
BEGIN TRANSACTION: (0 MilliSeconds)
```

Immediately after it connects to the database, it starts a transaction. The first time (while logging to the database), it logs an exact time, and from then onwards, the time is logged in 55 millisecond increments. So, for example, if an SQL statement execution takes over 55 milliseconds but less than 110 milliseconds, it will be logged as 55 milliseconds.

We retrieved the item master details into w_item_master window. When PowerBuilder encounters **Retrieve()** in the script, it sends the SQL statement defined in the DataWindow to the connected database for parsing:

```
PREPARE:
SELECT "item_master"."item_no" , "item_master"."item_description" ,
"item_master"."last_receipt_date" , "item_master"."last_issue_date" ,
"item_master"."balance" , "item_master"."re_order_level" , "item_master"."measuring_unit"
, "item_master"."current_price" FROM "item_master" (55 MilliSeconds)
```

Once the SQL statement is parsed, it gets the column descriptions, binds the data to the DataWindow columns and then asks the connected database to execute the statement:

```
DESCRIBE: (0 MilliSeconds)
name=item_no,len=40,type=DECIMAL,pbt4,dbt2,ct0,dec0
name=item_description,len=31,type=????,pbt2,dbt12,ct0,dec0
...
BIND SELECT OUTPUT BUFFER (DataWindow): (0 MilliSeconds)
name=item_no,len=40,type=DECIMAL,pbt4,dbt2,ct0,dec0
...
EXECUTE: (0 MilliSeconds)
```

It fetches data row by row, until it knows there are no more rows. The last line, **rc 100**, is an **SQLCA.SQLCODE**, which indicates that there are no more result rows for this command.

```
FETCH NEXT: (0 MilliSeconds)
   item_no=10    item_description=Optical Disk(1GB)    last_receipt_date=10-01-2012 -
1:00:00:000000    last_issue_date=09-12-1993 -1:00:00:000000
   ...
```

FETCH NEXT: (55 MilliSeconds)
 Error 1 (rc 100)

When we changed the description of item_no 2 from 'Chair(Leather)' to 'Computer Desk' and selected File/Save from the menu, the following was recorded in the log file:

PREPARE WITH BIND VARIABLES:
UPDATE "item_master" SET "item_description" = ? WHERE "item_no" = ? AND "item_description" = ? AND "last_receipt_date" = ? AND "last_issue_date" = ? AND "balance" = ? AND "re_order_level" = ? AND "measuring_unit" = ? AND "current_price" = ? (0 MilliSeconds)
 VCHAR Length14 ID:1 *Computer Desk*
 DECIMAL Length0 ID:2 *2*
 VCHAR Length17 ID:3 *Chair(Leather)*
 ???? Length0 ID:4
 ???? Length0 ID:5
 DECIMAL Length0 ID:6 *5.000*
 DECIMAL Length0 ID:7 *2.000*
 VCHAR Length1 ID:8 *U*
 DECIMAL Length0 ID:9 *2240.00* (0 MilliSeconds)
EXECUTE: (55 MilliSeconds)
 GET AFFECTED ROWS: (0 MilliSeconds)
 ^ 1 Rows Affected

This simply sends the **UPDATE** statement to the database and records the number of rows affected by the **UPDATE** statement.

Finally, exiting from the database and disconnecting from the database produces the following:

COMMIT: (275 MilliSeconds)
 GET AFFECTED ROWS: (0 MilliSeconds)
 ^ 0 Rows Affected
DISCONNECT: (495 MilliSeconds)
 SHUTDOWN DATABASE INTERFACE: (0 MilliSeconds)

Tracing ODBC Driver Manager Calls

It is also possible to get details about the ODBC driver's API calls. To do this, you need to set the PBTrace flag in the PBCONNECTOPTIONS section of the **PBODB040.INI** file, which is available in the directory in which PowerBuilder is installed:

```
[PBCONNECTOPTIONS]
PBTrace='ON'
PBTraceFile='FILE NAME WITH FULL PATH'
```

In the file, you will find all the ODBC API calls that are sent to the database. The following are some of the commands we were given when running through a similar procedure to the one above:

```
SQLDriverConnect()
SQLGetInfo();
SQLGetConnectOption();
SQLAllocStmt();
SQLGetTypeInfo();
SQLBindCol();
SQLFetch();
SQLFreeStmt();
SQLGetFunctions();
SQLPrepare()
SQLDescribeParam()
SQLSetParam()
SQLExecute();
SQLRowCount();
SQLExecDirect()
SQLNumResultCols(hstmt539F0000, pccol);
SQLDescribeCol();
SQLTransact()
SQLSetConnectOption()
SQLDisconnect()
SQLFreeConnect()
SQLFreeEnv()
SQLGetTypeInfo()
```

GPF Error Logging

The only tool PowerBuilder doesn't provide, is one to log details of when a GPF error occurs. If you are running PowerBuilder under Windows 3.11 or Windows NT, there is a tool available to do this, called Dr. Watson.

> Note that this program must be running in memory before the GPF occurs for it to have any effect. It is suggested that you create a Program Item for this software in your StartUp Group. This means that everytime you run PowerBuilder, this facility is available to record the errors without you needing to remember to start it manually.

We tried to create a DataWindow of Quick Select data source and clicked on the item_master table name from the list of tables, which resulted in a GPF. Dr Watson prompted us to write a little description about the problem:

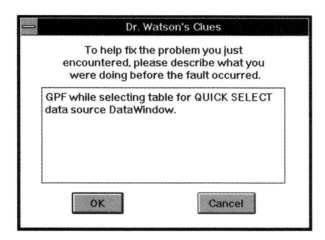

All the environment details are then recorded in the log. This file includes error details, CPU Registers dump, system information such as RAM, Storage, Free GDI and so on:

```
Start Dr. Watson 0.80 - Sun Dec 25 14:13:26 1994
************************************************
Dr. Watson 0.80 Failure Report - Sun Dec 25 14:14:49 1994
PB040 had a 'Null Selector (Read)' fault at PBDWE040 61:5964
$tag$PB040$Null Selector (Read)$PBDWE040 61:5964$repne scasb$Sun Dec 25
14:14:49 1995
```

You can then call PowerBuilder's technical support and give them this information to help solve the problem.

Debug Painter Preferences

All the following debug painter preferences will automatically be set as you change options in the Debug Painter:

Preference	Description
VariablesWindow	Display/Hide Variables window. 0 hides the window and 1 displays the window.
WatchWindow	Same as Variables window.
Stopn	This indicates the details for the nth Stop Point. The format is the same as we saw earlier in the Edit Stop Points topic.

Summary

We've shown how easy it is to navigate your way around the Debug Painter and to debug your scripts. We've also seen some of the other methods you can use to log the execution of your application and the database connections used by your application. You should now be able to find problems in your code simply and quickly.

In the next chapter, we'll look at how PowerBuilder implements object-oriented programming techniques in its objects and PowerScript language.

12

OOP and PowerBuilder Implementation

Object technology has become an area of intense focus in the computer industry and everywhere you look it is being discussed. Vendors of varied products, from application development tools to operating systems, frequently highlight their 'object-oriented' features and benefits to customers.

Object technology offers an approach to application design, development and database management that differs from traditional approaches. The object approach can provide greater flexibility and code reuse, as well as a better way to model 'real world' objects and business processes.

To grasp why object technology offers this potential requires an understanding of what the technology represents. This involves learning some basic concepts and terms. This can be a major stumbling block for many people with traditional programming and database backgrounds, because they find the new jargon almost incomprehensible, but an early understanding can be achieved by focusing on a few fundamental issues.

In this chapter, you will:

▲ Learn about the concepts and terminology of OOP

▲ See how these concepts are implemented in PowerBuilder

▲ Find out how to get the best results with inheritance

▲ Review a practical example of OOP making use of PowerBuilder's UserObjects

Introduction

If you consider a complex piece of machinery as a collection of cogs, then the cogs that make up the Object Orientation machine are objects, messages, methods, classes, instances and inheritance. For a system to earn the description of 'object-oriented', it should contain all of these essential mechanisms, although they may not be implemented (or named) in exactly the same way from one system to another. Before going into how PowerBuilder uses this technology, let's learn some OOP terminology.

Objects

A traditional program consists of procedures and data. An object-oriented program consists of a number of objects that contain both of these key programming elements. To put this in another way, objects are modules that contain the data that is associated with one particular task, together with the instructions that operate upon this data.

If you understand this delicate point, then it will immediately follow that within the objects in an OO program you still make use of the old conventional computing concepts such as numbers, arrays, strings and records, as well as functions, instructions and subroutines.

If we translate this idea into the language of OOP, we can understand that each of our objects are entities that have particular attributes (data) and ways of behaving (procedures). When an OOP system is in full swing, it is the manner in which the objects behave together and the attributes that are interrogated that give you the results that you are looking for.

Class

Many objects may act in similar ways, each performing a task, each of these tasks sharing some kind of relationship. To simplify the 'storage' of this family of similar objects, we create a **class**.

A class is a description of a set of nearly identical objects and it consists of methods and data that summarize the common characteristics shared by the objects. The ability to abstract common methods and data descriptions from a set of objects, together with the storage of them in a class, is central to the power of Object Orientation.

By defining classes, you are placing reusable code in a common repository, rather than having to repeatedly express it. In other words, classes contain the blueprints for creating objects - you simply take the common methods and data associated with the class, add your own custom features and create the object!

> **The definition of a class helps to clarify the definition of an object - an object is an instance of a class.**

Objects are created when a message requesting this action is received by the parent class. The new object takes its methods and data from its parent class. Essentially, all of the objects in a PowerBuilder application are derived from the granddaddy class of them all - the PowerClass. Each of the objects derived from the PowerClass can, in turn, be used as a class to derive more and more specialized objects.

In a typical development environment, you will encounter two 'different' types of class. The first is the classes that have already been derived from the PowerClass by PowerSoft - i.e. they come in the box with the software. The other type is the user-defined classes that the developers have derived to speed up their project development:

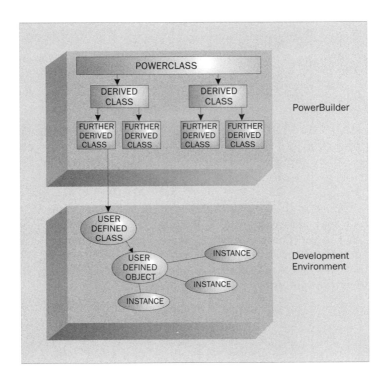

This diagram illustrates several interesting points, such as the organization of the PowerBuilder environment. Each of the classes that we, as developers, work with, follow the object-oriented concepts as they are derived from parent classes all the way back to the PowerClass. Another point is that you don't directly affect the contents of the PowerBuilder classes. You simply derive classes or objects from them to achieve your own custom effects.

Messages

Unlike the passive data items in traditional systems, objects have the ability to act. An action occurs when an object receives a message, that is, a request asking the object to behave in a certain way.

> **A message consists of the name of an operation plus any required arguments.**

When one object sends a message to another object, the sender is requesting that the receiver perform the named operation and (possibly) return some information. When the receiver receives the message, it performs the requested operation in any way that it knows. The request doesn't specify how an operation is to be performed - such information is always hidden from the sender.

In many ways this is similar to the Client/Server system model that we described in the opening chapter. Each object is defined as being able to perform certain operations and will only perform those operations. If a different operation is required, then a different object is used.

The set of messages to which an object can respond is known as the **behavior** of the object. However, not all the messages to which an object can respond to need to be part of its publicly accessible interface. An object can send private messages to itself to implement publicly accessible operations.

For example, suppose a drawing object has received a message to draw a pie chart. The object may internally call a method to calculate the percentage of each member in the pie chart. However, if you sent a message to the object asking it to calculate the percentages for each member, it would result in an error saying that this operation isn't available. Since it is private, it can only be called by another method from the same object.

Methods

When an object receives a message, it performs the requested operation by executing a method. A method is the step-by-step algorithm that is executed in response to a message whose name matches that of the method. A method is always part of the private representation of an object; it is never part of the public interface. For example, an object can send a message to the drawing object to draw a circle, but the sender object never says how to draw the circle.

Instances

Objects that behave in a manner specified by a class are called instances of the class; these instances are created when a creation message is received by the parent class. All objects are instances of one class or another.

Once an instance of a class is created, it behaves like all other instances of its class and is able to perform any operation for which it has methods. An application can have as many or as few instances of a particular class as required.

Subclass

A subclass is a class that inherits behavior from another class. A subclass inherits all the behavior of its parent class and then adds its own specific behavior to define its own unique kind of object.

Superclass

A superclass is a class from which specific behavior is inherited. A class might have only one superclass, or it might have several, combining behavior from several sources and adding only a little of its own to produce its own unique kind of object.

Persistence

Persistence refers to the performance of an object, that is, the amount of time for which it is allocated space and remains accessible in the computer's memory. In most of the object-oriented languages, instances of class are created as the program executes. Some of these instances are needed for only a brief amount of time, so when an object is no longer needed, it is destroyed and the memory space reclaimed.

After an OO program has been executed, the assembled objects are not normally stored away, that is, the objects are no longer persistent. An OO database maintains a distinction between objects created for the duration of execution and those intended for permanent storage.

> **Objects that are stored on a permanent basis are termed persistent.**

Inheritance

Inheritance is the most commonly used feature of an Object-oriented language. Inheritance is a mechanism which allows objects to share attributes and operations based on a predefined relationship; it allows you to define a hierarchy of objects. The inherited object is called a descendant object, while the object from which the descendant is inherited is called an ancestor.

For example, we can define a vehicle as having certain attributes such as height, weight, speed, maximum load and so on. All vehicles would share these common attributes, but not all vehicles are the same. We might have a car, a truck and an emergency vehicle, each with their own specific attributes:

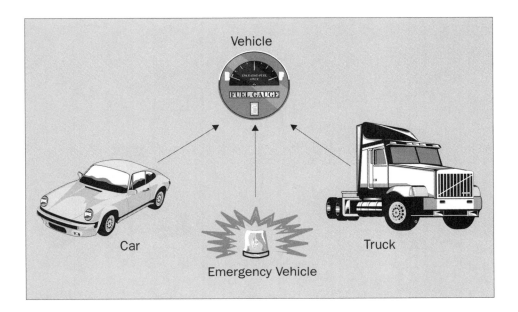

The first thing we have to do is define a class called Vehicle, which has general attributes for our vehicles. From there, you can derive other classes such as a Car class and a Truck class by inheriting from the Vehicle class. The Vehicle class is called the ancestor, the Car and Truck classes are called descendants.

Base Classes

In this example, the Vehicle class is called a **base** class. Base classes are not meant to be used directly, but they are used to define the general attributes that appear in your derived objects. As you descend the hierarchy, you define more specific attributes and functionality:

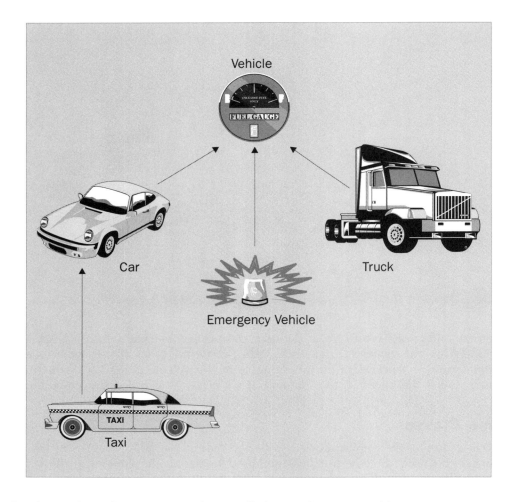

The descendant class, a Taxi, inherits all the attributes, variables, structures, functions and behavior from the ancestor, the Car class. An ancestor can have any number of descendant classes, and a descendant class may become an ancestor to other descendants. The attributes defined at the ancestor level are not copied into the descendant class, but are passed down to the descendant for reference.

If you change attributes at the ancestor level, the changes will reflect in descendant objects immediately. At the same time, changes done at the descendant level are not reflected at the ancestor level. In the above example, additional functionality defined at Car class is available to Taxi, but not to the Vehicle class. This allows you to localize changes and localize testing.

Multiple Inheritance

Multiple inheritance allows an object to inherit functionality from more than one object:

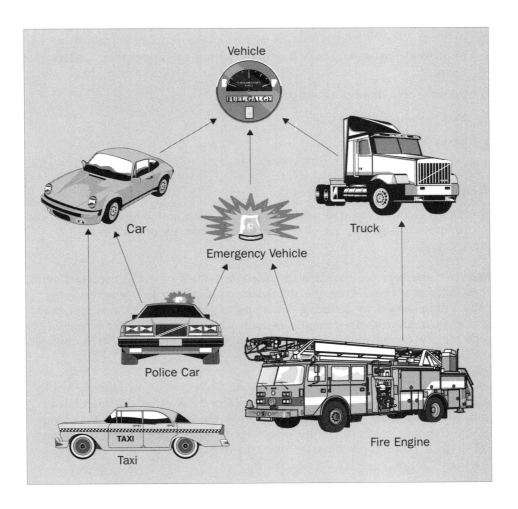

In the previous example, the Ambulance class not only inherits functionality from the Car, but also from the Emergency class. It therefore gets all the features of an Emergency vehicle, together with those on offer from the Car.

Benefits of Inheritance

There are several important benefits associated with inheritance:

- Allows reuse of code.
- Reduces development time.
- Improves consistency, both internally within the application and between them.
- Reduces the chances of error.
- Makes maintenance easier.
- Reduces space usage.

Encapsulation

Encapsulation is the technique used to combine data and methods into an object. It also attempts to separate an object's interface from its underlying implementation.

Methods are the services that are provided for other objects to interact with this one. Methods operate on the data defined at the object level and are typically implemented by defining functions at this level. Methods can take input and (sometimes) can generate output. This allows the details of the data and complexity of the method to be hidden from other objects. It is this result that is called encapsulation.

For example, return to our idea of a drawing object. As you already know, you can define attributes for the drawing object as well as the associated methods - in this case, these methods include the logic required to draw the object. By defining methods at the object level, an object can call a function **draw()** with a radius and a center point to draw a circle.

This is all part of the 'method hiding' philosophy that is part of the generic OOP languages - the calling object doesn't need to know how to draw the circle, it only needs to know the appropriate message to send to the receiver together with the required parameters.

One of the advantages of this 'method hiding' is the efficiency savings that can be gained when you are maintaining the logic. As long as you leave the message syntax alone, you can alter the contents of the method without needing to alter any of the references to the `draw()` function throughout your application.

Benefits of Encapsulation

The main benefits of encapsulation are:

- Shields complexity
- Less duplicate code
- Easier maintenance/enhancements

Polymorphism

Polymorphism is an OOP ability that allows an operation to behave differently depending on the particular class you are working with. It allows you to define the same function with different parameters and different data types. One example would be where you defined a base class for drawing objects and derived two classes for circle object and polygon object. By using polymorphism, you can create the same interface (the `draw()` function) to draw both objects.

In this example, you might notice that the parameters required for both of these geometric shapes are completely different. Fortunately, through a combination of inheritance and polymorphism, you can solve this problem. When you call the `draw()` function, the appropriate object is drawn depending on the parameters you supply.

The main advantage of polymorphism is its ability to call one function and have several different versions of code ready to run, depending on some predefined criteria.

The Benefits of Object-Oriented Design and Programming

In conclusion, we can sum up the benefits of OOP as:

- Stable design
- Reduced development time
- Reduced maintenance costs
- More consistency in applications
- Performance improvements

The following table illustrates the main differences between the object-oriented and the traditional procedural programming techniques:

Object-Oriented Techniques	Traditional Techniques
Methods	Procedures, functions, or subroutines
Instance Variables	Data
Messages	Procedure calls or function calls
Classes	Abstract data types
Inheritance	(No similar technique)
Calls under system's control	Calls under programmer's control

Now let's see how each of these object-oriented features is implemented in PowerBuilder.

PowerBuilder Implementation

We've explained some of the concepts to you, now let's begin to deal with how PowerBuilder implements each of them.

Object Components

An object contains three components: the class name, data (attributes) and methods (functions and so on). Some of the attributes that you might encounter include the window title, color, window dimensions and so on, while the variables include all those declared at the object level, that is, local, instance and shared variables. Examples of the methods that you might use could be the scripts for different events or references to the functions declared at the object level.

Since you derive new objects from the PowerBuilder PowerClass objects (i.e. the classes that ship with PowerBuilder), you can't add new attributes or remove existing ones, but you can change the attributes by specifying the values as you paint the object or at run-time using scripts.

For example, take the Window painter. You paint a window in the Window painter and specify certain attributes, such as type of window, color, title, associated menu and so on, at design time. However, you can change the title of the window at run-time using the following code:

```
Window_Name.Title = "New Title"
```

The methods associated with a window are the functions that are declared in the Window painter, together with the scripts you have written for any window events. For example, you can write code for the **clicked** event of a CommandButton on a window. The action of clicking on the CommandButton causes the event to be triggered. Functions declared while painting the window can be called from the event scripts and from other functions declared for the same object.

Scoping

As we saw in Chapter 9, there are four types of PowerBuilder variables, each of which is associated with a different level of scope. When considering object-oriented programming, it's important to keep track of which variables you have access to in all the different areas of your application. The following table summarizes these variable types:

Scope of Variable	Description
Local	These variables are only available in the declared script and cannot be accessed by any other script or function. They are destroyed when the script or function ends.
Instance	Each instance of an object has its own set of instance variables. They are available to all object level scripts and functions, but they are destroyed when the instance is destroyed.
Shared	These variables are available to all object level scripts and functions. They are shared among instances of an object and remain in memory even after the last instance of an object is destroyed.
Global	These are available to all scripts and functions in an application and are only destroyed when the application execution is over.

Access Levels

As we have seen, when you create instances from the generic classes, these objects acquire two types of variables: instance and shared variables. The instance variables are used to hold any information that is directly related to that instance of the object, while shared variables hold information that is applicable to all of the instances derived from their associated class.

This scoping of variables can be very useful, but in certain circumstances it becomes necessary to further refine the availability of these variables throughout your application. You must remember that even though an instance variable holds information directly related to the working of that instance, it is still available for interrogation and manipulation by any other object in your application.

To solve this problem, PowerBuilder provides **access levels**. Access levels define which objects can access the specified variable. You can specify three different access levels:

Access Level	Description
Public	Accessible by all objects in an application - this is the default access level for all of your user defined objects
Protected	Only accessible by that object and its descendant objects
Private	Only accessible by other functions and scripts declared for the same object

These user defined access levels only apply to shared and instance variables, because the other types of variables have access levels that you can't change.

To specify access level to variables declared at the object, specify the keyword **private** or **protected** before the data type. For example:

```
Private Int Variable1, Variable2
```

When you specify an access level, all the following variables will be assigned to that access level until another access level declaration is encountered. In the following example, all the variables will be Private until it encounters either Public or Protected. You can declare access levels for shared variables in the same way.

```
Private:
Int Variable1, Variable2
Long lNewRow
```

The same access levels also apply to functions. If you declare functions from the Function Painter, they are public by default and the access level can't be changed. However, if you declare functions at the object level, you can specify an access level for them.

Creating an Instance

To create and display an instance of an object on the screen only requires one line of code. The following scripts would create an instance of a window, sheet and UserObject respectively with and without parameters:

```
/* Create an instance of a window in memory and display the created window on
the screen */
Open()
OpenWithParm()

/* Functions to open a window as a sheet */
OpenSheet()
OpenSheetWithParm()

/* Functions to open a UserObject. */
OpenUserObject()
OpenUserObjectWithParm()
```

Any object you define through a PowerBuilder painter is declared as global. If you export the w_item_master window from the Library Painter and then have a look at the **.SRW** file you'll see the following:

```
$PBExportHeader$w_item_master.srw
forward
global type w_item_master from Window
end type
type dwc_1 from datawindow within w_item_master
end type
```

The parameter to this function may be either the name of a window or a variable that refers to an instance of a specific window. Either of the following is correct:

```
/* Method 1: Specifying the window name directly */
Open(w_item_master)
```

```
/* Method 2: Using a variable */
w_item_master Window1
Open(Window1)
```

The first method only allows you to define one instance of an object; this is due to the way that PowerBuilder allocates memory to the objects that you create. When you create an instance of this object, PowerBuilder allocates it some memory to that instance. If you try and call this function again, PowerBuilder simply returns you to this instance. This occurs because the instance has a global scope; this means that a reference to that instance is recognized throughout the application and can't be duplicated.

The second method allows you to open more than one instance of the window, because it is basing the instance of an object on a variable that can be given a scope. Imagine that you are opening this window from a menu option. If you declare it as an instance variable, the variable is created when the menu is created and is destroyed when you destroy the menu. This means that as long as the menu exists, the memory allocated for the menu is the same, which allows you to open only one instance of the window, no matter how many times you try to open the window.

To open more than one instance of the window, you would need to declare the window variable as local in the menu script. The local variable is created when the script starts executing and will be destroyed when the execution of the script compiles. That means that each time the script executes, a new variable is created and memory will be allocated to it. This makes it possible to open more than one instance of the window.

Unfortunately, there is one problem associated with this; the external reference to the window, other than that of the active window, is gone. Suppose you opened four instances of a window and with the third instance active, you want to disable a control in the first instance. Using the above method, you don't have the ability to reference the first instance specifically, so this wouldn't be possible.

The solution for this problem is to declare an instance window variable. For example:

```
// Declare these 2 variables as instance variables for the menu
w_item_master i_item_master[]
Int InstanceNo = 1

// Script for the menu item
OpenSheet(i_item_master[i], ParentWindow, 1, Cascaded!)
InstanceNo++
```

The **CREATE** statement is used to create an object in your script. This object is only created in memory, it isn't permanently saved in your library. The syntax is as follows:

CREATE <Object Name>

If you look at the exported version of the application, you can observe the `create` statements that PowerBuilder uses to create all the global objects internally:

```
on inventory_management_system.create
appname = "stock_control_system"
sqlca = create transaction
sqlda = create dynamicdescriptionarea
sqlsa = create dynamicstagingarea
error = create error
message = create message
end on
```

Destroying an Instance

There are two ways of destroying an instance of an object, the decision being based on the type of object you are using. If it is a visual object such as a window or UserObject, you should use the `Close()` function:

```
Close()            /* Clears an instance of a window from the screen and
                      clears from memory */
CloseUserObject() // Clears an instance of a UserObject
```

For a non-visual object, which is created using the `CREATE` statement (a transaction object, for example), you should use the `DESTROY` statement:

DESTROY <Object Name>   **// Removes any object from the memory**

You can only create and destroy one object at a time.

Inheritance

PowerBuilder supports inheritance from three objects:

- Menus
- Windows
- UserObjects

You can inherit an object in one of two ways:

1 By selecting Inherit from the Select dialog box which is brought up when you invoke one of these object painters.

2 By selecting File/Inherit... from the menu when you are in the relevant object painter.

When an object is inherited, everything in the ancestor object is passed to the descendant. If another object is created from the descendant, then that object also inherits everything from the first ancestor, as well as any new definitions that are defined in its immediate ancestor.

> *You may think that you could inherit an object, by selecting the* File/Save As *option from the menu when the ancestor object is open and giving it the new name. Unfortunately, this doesn't work as it simply makes a copy of the ancestor object and any subsequent changes to the ancestor object aren't reflected in the new copy.*

Inheritance works in approximately the same way for all three different types of objects, so we'll take an in-depth look at how it's used in Windows, highlighting any differences as we go.

Inheriting a Window

To inherit a window, you can use either of the methods outlined above, but you should note that if you use the second method, you should select File/Inherit when the window is blank, before you add any extra controls. If you add some controls and then decide to select File/Inherit, all of your controls will be lost.

In the descendant window, you can do any of the following:

- ▲ Override or extend the inherited scripts.
- ▲ Override and extend some events.
- ▲ Reference the ancestor's functions, events and structures, just as long as they aren't declared as private.
- ▲ Change attributes of controls and the content of variables.

413

These are things you can't do:

▲ Delete any controls in the descendant window if they are painted in the ancestor.

▲ Delete ancestor windows without deleting descendant windows.

▲ Change the name of the controls in descendant windows.

You can change the position of controls in the descendant window, but you should note that if you do this, further changes to the position of the control in the ancestor window won't be reflected in the descendant window. The same is true of changes made to any other attributes in the descendant window - this effectively severs the link with the attribute in the ancestor window, so inheritance doesn't take place.

> *As you can't delete controls from an ancestor window in a descendant, you can simply hide the control if you don't need it.*

Scripts

When you select a control in the Window Painter, the Script icon will change to display script lines if there is any script for any events associated with that control:

This will only work if there is script for any events associated with that particular window - the icon won't change to show scripts in the ancestor window. This can become a bit tedious when you are debugging an application because you have to go into the Script Painter to determine if there are any scripts that have been inherited from an ancestor window.

When you go into the Script Painter, there can be three versions of the standard icon displayed beside the event names:

Icon	Description
Full Color Script	Script only exists for the event in the ancestor window.
Black and White Script window.	Script only exists for the event in the descendant
Half Color/Half B & W Script	Script exists for the event in both the ancestor and descendant windows.

Viewing Ancestor Script

When you invoke the Script Painter for a descendant window, PowerBuilder doesn't display the ancestor script. For example, if you open a new window and inherit from our w_about window, you won't be able to see any script for the open event. However, you will see that there is a colored script icon beside the event indicating that there is a script in the ancestor window:

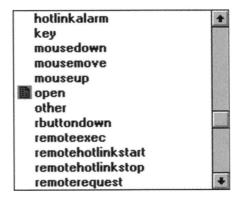

To see the script for the ancestor window, you have to select Compile/Display Ancestor Script...:

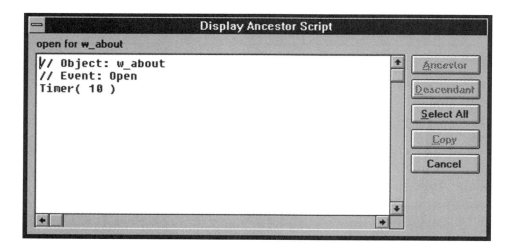

You are not allowed to edit an ancestor script from the descendant script, but you can copy and paste the script to and from the clipboard.

Overriding Ancestor Script

If you don't want to execute the ancestor script, you can select Compile/Override Ancestor Script. When selected, the ancestor level script isn't executed - any results you get from this object when this event occurs are related to the descendant level script. If you don't want to execute an ancestor level script and there is no script in the descendant window, after selecting Compile/Override Ancestor Script, simply add a comment in the descendant script. If you don't do this, PowerBuilder will assume that you still want the ancestor script to be executed and will ignore your menu selection:

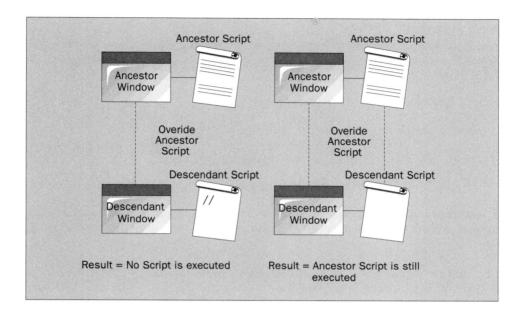

Extending Ancestor Script

If both the ancestor and descendant windows have scripts, then the script for the ancestor window will be executed first, followed by the descendant window script. This is PowerBuilder's default behavior and is specified by selecting Compile/Extend Ancestor Script from the menu in the Script Painter.

> *Note that the ancestor script is never displayed in the descendant script, even though it is executed. You could cut and paste the ancestor script into the descendant, but this would have the effect of executing the same script twice in succession.*

Calling Ancestor Scripts

Sometimes, you may want to execute a script for the descendant window before the ancestor script executes. To do this you have to follow these steps:

1 Select Compile/Override Ancestor Script

2 Write the required script for the descendant window

3 Call the ancestor script using the following syntax:

```
Call  Super::<Event  Name>
```

The **Super** pronoun refers to the same object in the ancestor. You can also execute an event of another control in the ancestor by using the following syntax:

```
Call  Super'<Control  Name>::<Event  name>
```

For example, if we wanted to execute the script for the OK CommandButton in our w_about window from the **close** event of a descendant window, we would use the following code:

```
Call Super'cb_ok::clicked
```

Grandparent-Parent-Child Hierarchy

PowerBuilder allows you to inherit objects from the results of an inheritance, a process that produces a Grandparent-Parent-Child hierarchy. You should also note that this extends to the nth level. Unfortunately, when you start to use this more complex setup, things can quickly get complicated.

Here are some things you should note about using more than one level of inheritance:

1 If you Extend Ancestor Script at both the child and parent levels, then the grandparent script will be executed at the child level:

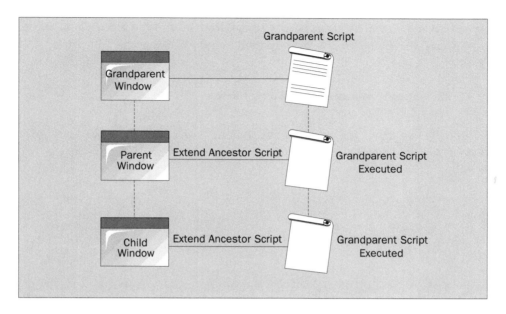

2 If you Override Ancestor Script at the parent level and Extend Ancestor Script at the child level, the child will inherit the parent script, not the grandparent script:

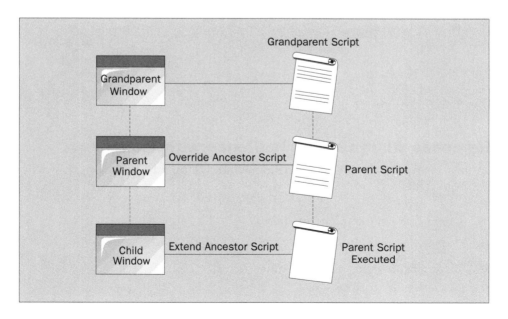

3 If you want to call a grandparent script from a child window, you have to specify the name of the grandparent window using the following syntax:

```
Call<Object  Name>::<Event  Name>
```

4 If you have scripts for grandparent, parent and child windows and you Extend Ancestor Scripts throughout, all three scripts will execute at the child level:

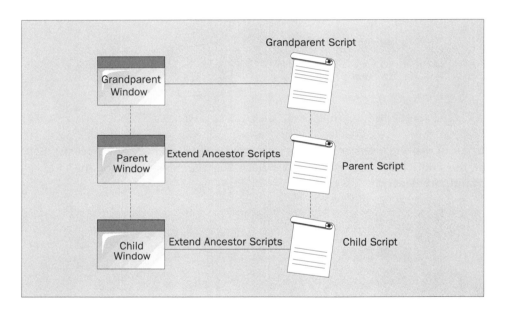

Differences when Using Inheritance with Menus

Inheriting menus is similar to inheriting windows but the following restrictions apply. You can't:

▲ Change the order of menu items

▲ Delete menu items

▲ Insert menu items between other items

Multiple Inheritance

PowerBuilder doesn't directly support multiple inheritance. For example, if you wanted a window to inherit properties and functionality from two other windows, you would need to use a workaround using UserObjects. Instead of building functionality in two windows, you divide the functionality and create a window and a UserObject. When you create your window, you need to inherit from the window and place the UserObject in the descendant window to get the required functionality.

We can use our vehicle analogy to show the difference between a traditional implementation of multiple inheritance and PowerBuilder's implementation:

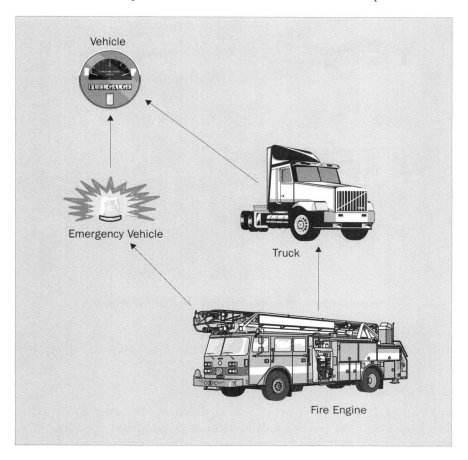

Traditional Implementation of Multiple Inheritance

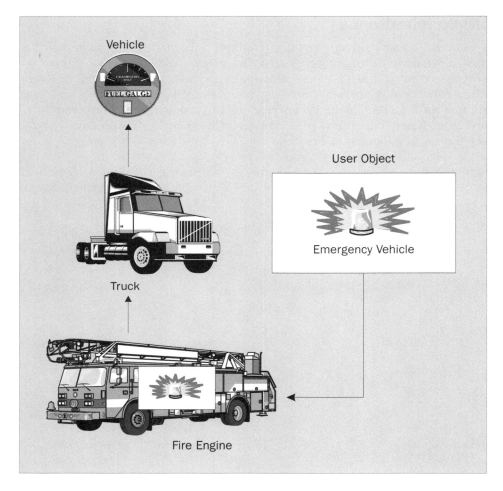

PowerBuilder's Implementation of Multiple Inheritance

The Emergency Vehicle UserObject is placed in the Fire Engine object to give it the functionality of both an Emergency Vehicle and a Truck.

Class Browser

Back in Chapter 2, we took a brief look at the Class Browser and it's worth returning to it now that we've explained the concepts behind classes. If you remember, you view the class hierarchy by selecting Utilities/Browse Class Hierarchy... in the Library Painter. If you look at the Window object hierarchy for our Stock Control system, you'll see something like this:

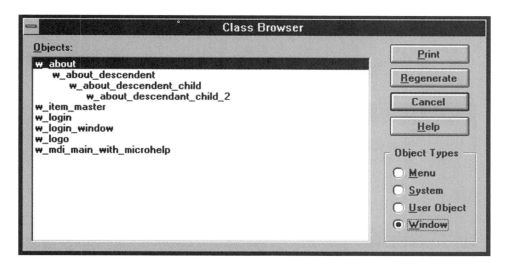

As an indent signifies a descendant object, you can see that we've created several levels of inheritance from the w_about window. If you have more than one library in your application's library list, then all the objects in these libraries will be displayed in the Class Browser.

> *You have to be careful if you have more than one library in the library list and you have objects inherited across libraries. If the library containing ancestor objects is removed from the library list, then you won't be able to open the descendants:*

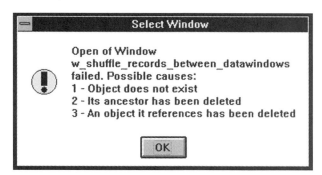

> *This doesn't follow if you are using DataWindows with inheritance. If you have a DataWindow control on a window and the associated DataWindow isn't in one of the libraries in the list, then a blank DataWindow will be displayed in the window at run-time. No error will be displayed.*

You can print out a copy of the class hierarchy and, as we said in Chapter 2, you can also regenerate objects from here.

Regenerating an Object

If you delete a control in an ancestor object and then try to open a descendant, an information message will be displayed telling you what has happened:

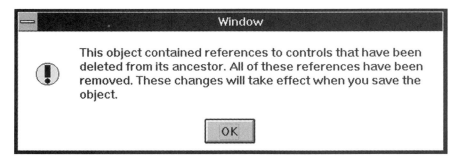

This can happen in the following circumstances:

- When an instance variable name is changed or deleted in the ancestor object.

- When a user-defined function is deleted from the ancestor and is being referenced in the dependent.

- When a control is renamed or deleted from the ancestor.

You won't see the message unless you open the descendant object, so, if you are making changes to ancestor objects, it's a good idea to regenerate all dependent objects as this will apply any changes that you've made to the ancestor object. This will save any problems that you might encounter later when creating an executable file.

Polymorphism

PowerBuilder allows you to implement polymorphism in two ways:

- Sending messages
- Function overloading

PowerBuilder itself implements both of these in the PowerClass. Let's look at each of these methods in turn.

Sending Messages

If you look at the PowerBuilder system class hierarchy, you'll see that the PictureButton control is inherited from the CommandButton control. This makes sense as both of these perform the same function:

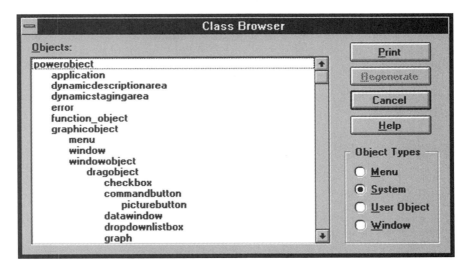

Whenever you click on a CommandButton, the script for the clicked event is executed; the same is true for a PictureButton. Since both of these are in the same polymorphic family, there is no need to call different event names for each of them. They can have the same event, but execute different scripts. This is polymorphism in practice - the same event is called in both cases, but the script which is executed is passed like a parameter to the executing function depending on which control is clicked.

Function Overloading

Function overloading allows you to use the same function name to get different sets of results from your script. PowerBuilder allows this flexibility by responding to the various parameters that are sent with the function call.

As an example of how function overloading works, let's look at PowerBuilder's
MessageBox() function. This function allows you to output to the screen, via a
dialog box, a string, a numeric or a boolean value. Usually, you would need to
develop three nearly identical scripts to handle this functionality, but by using
function overloading you can achieve the same results with only a little more
effort.

The compiler understands which version of the function to use based upon one
of the parameters that you must pass to it, which in this case is the **text**
parameter. This allows you to use a much smaller function set which has a
much greater range of functionality. The disadvantage to this methodology is
that each function call is more complicated, involving more and more
parameters.

In PowerBuilder, function overloading can be done in two ways: inheritance or
external functions.

Function Overloading Using Inheritance

If you want to use inheritance to allow function overloading, you must
complete two basic tasks:

1 Define a base class that contains the basic definition of the function.

2 Inherit a class from this original, altering the definition of the function to
reflect the overloading that you require.

By performing these two steps, you produce two similarly named functions
that share a relationship, organized into a predefined structure that
PowerBuilder understands and can use when a call to this function name is
received.

PowerBuilder looks for the appropriate function in your entire object hierarchy,
starting from the current level and working towards the top, until it finds the
first appropriate version of the function.

For example, suppose you have three objects A, B and C in the same
hierarchy, where A is at the top and B is inherited from it. If you declared a
function in A that prints a message to the printer, then B inherits it. By

modifying this function, you can set up your overloaded function to, say, print out a message in Times New Roman, rather than the default font.

If you now call this function from C, the function declared at B will be executed, causing the specified message to appear at your printer in Times New Roman, rather than the default font that the function defined at A would have used:

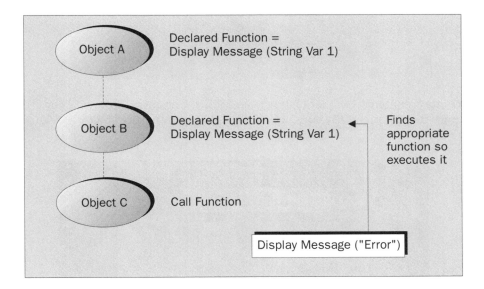

Function Overloading Using External Functions

If you have a DLL that has these functions, you can use the functions in PowerBuilder. Declare each version of the function in PowerBuilder supplying the function name and name of the DLL, and PowerBuilder will find the appropriate function and execute it.

A Practical Example of OOP

Now that we've explained the concepts of object-oriented programming and how PowerBuilder implements these concepts, we'll show you how they can be used in practice. In the **EXAMPLES.PBL** file on the CD-ROM, there is a window called w_chapter_oop. Open this window and run it using the *Ctrl+Shift+W* keys:

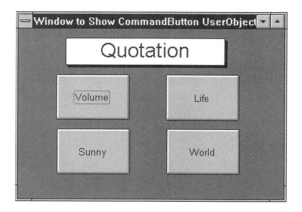

The window contains a StaticText box and four CommandButtons. If you click on one of the CommandButtons a message box will pop up with a relevant quotation:

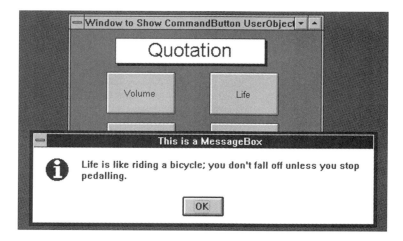

The script for the **clicked** event of the CommandButtons simply displays a message box with a quote, depending on which button is clicked. However, the script was only written once, not four times as you might think. We performed this task using a UserObject (a user defined object created through inheritance) based on PowerBuilder's CommandButton class.

You can create various types of UserObjects, both visual and non-visual. In Chapter 15, we'll take a detailed look at how to use the UserObject Painter to create UserObjects, especially those we are going to use in our Stock Control System.

We created the CommandButton UserObject at the size we require and typed in the following script for its **clicked** event:

```
// Event: clicked
// Object: CommandButton UserObject
MessageBox ("This is a Message Box",This.Tag)
```

This code still uses the **MessageBox()** function, but it now displays the tag value of the current object. If you remember from Chapter 5, every control on a window has a tag value which can be used for displaying microhelp.

The keyword in this line of code is **This**. We don't hard code the name of the control we want to display, we simply tell it to display the tag value of whichever control is running the script. We then saved the script, created a new window and added our UserObject four times. We labeled the four CommandButtons and gave them the relevant tag values:

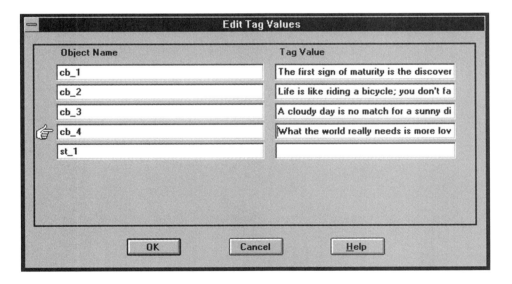

Now, whenever a CommandButton is clicked, PowerBuilder determines which CommandButton it is and runs the script, displaying the relevant tag value.

This is a simple example, but it saved us development time, as we only had to specify the properties and script for one CommandButton. In a full-blown application with lots of windows and controls, you can imagine how much time this could save.

Summary

We've covered a lot of theory in this chapter and explained a lot of the terminology and jargon which is used in object-oriented programming. It is probably useful to return to this chapter throughout the rest of the book as we are going to use more and more object-oriented methods to improve our Stock Control application.

In the next chapter, we'll look at how to convert our Stock Control System into a Multiple Document Interface application and after that we'll look in more depth at UserObjects and see how they can be used to add functionality to our application.

13

MDI Applications

Multiple Document Interfaces are everywhere. You and your users probably use them all the time and don't even realize it. The PowerBuilder environment is an MDI application, as are most Windows packages.

Basically, using an MDI application means that you can open several windows at the same time, and more than one copy of the same window. You can move, resize, minimize, maximize, tile and cascade any or all these windows, allowing you to see exactly the information you require, when you need it.

Due to all this added functionality and the demands of today's users, you are now 'forced' to produce this type of application, reproducing all the options that every other Windows application has to offer.

In this chapter, we will cover:

▲ The concepts behind MDI applications

▲ A brief tour around MDI

▲ How objects communicate in an MDI environment

▲ How to convert our Stock Control System into an MDI application

Introduction

The Stock Control application that we've been developing until now has been based around one single window. Whilst this works well, it would be useful for the user to be able to see information about another item while entering new data. As it stands, the user would have to cancel the new item number, query on the item_no, switch to data entry mode and begin to enter afresh the new item number along with its associated information.

This is all because the user can't open the same window more than once in the same application. If you try to open a window that is already open, PowerBuilder simply activates the opened window - it won't open another instance of the window. To solve this problem, we need to convert our application to use a Multiple Document Interface.

MDI Concepts

A Multiple Document Interface is an application style that allows users to open multiple windows (called **sheets**) in a single window (MDI Frame) and to move freely among them. PowerBuilder supports a Multiple Document Interface as you can open several painters at once and swap between them as required:

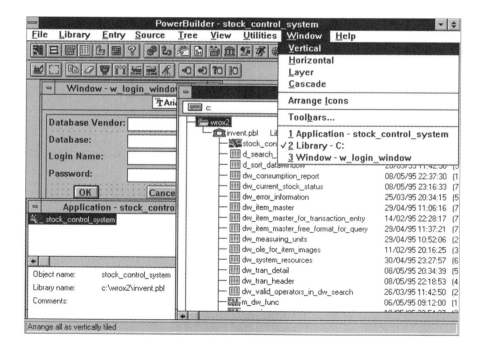

Here we have the Application, Library and Window Painters open and you can see from the Window menu in what order the painters have been opened and which is currently selected. You can move between the windows simply by clicking on the window you want or by selecting the appropriate entry from this Window menu. When you move the focus from one window to another, the menu bar and toolbar will change to reflect the options available for your choice.

MDI Basics

In an MDI application, there is a main window, not to be confused with the PowerBuilder Main type of window, and other windows or sheets are opened within it. This main window can have one of two PowerBuilder window styles: MDI Frame or MDI Frame with Microhelp.

> *Typically, PowerBuilder Main windows are opened in the MDI Frame as sheets.*

Generally, an MDI main window has a status bar for displaying Microhelp, and a menu bar. This menu bar is displayed until you open a sheet in the window, when it changes depending on the menu associated with the active sheet. When a sheet is active, the rest of the sheets are deactivated and the title bars of these sheets are grayed out. If there isn't a menu attached to a sheet, the menu associated with the MDI frame remains displayed and active for that sheet.

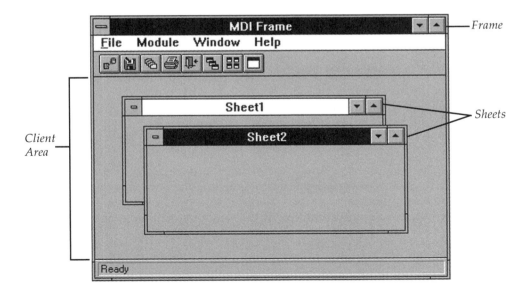

The MDI frame window has three parts:

- Frame
- Client area
- Sheets

Frame

The **Frame Area** consists of a menu bar, a window title and a status bar to display Microhelp. If you paint anything on an MDI Frame window, other than new sheets, that area will also be included in the frame area.

> The toolbar attached to the menu is also part of the frame area.

Client Area

The area between an MDI Frame title bar and the Microhelp status bar is called the **Client Area** and it is here that sheets are opened. The Client area is automatically resized to take account of any menus, toolbars and help status bars that are attached to any of the sheets.

However, if you paint any objects in the Frame window, this automatic resizing is canceled and you will have to resize the client area programmatically.

Sheets

The `OpenSheet()` and `OpenSheetWithParm()` are the two functions provided by PowerBuilder to open sheets in the Client area. Any type of PowerBuilder window can be opened as a sheet in an MDI Frame window except, of course, another MDI Frame window. In other words, you can't embed MDI Frames within each other.

The standard sizing, minimizing and maximizing features of windows are automatically defined by PowerBuilder when you use the `OpenSheet()` or `OpenSheetWithParm()` functions. As an example, suppose you have defined a window of type Main without a control menu, without maximize and minimize icons and as non-resizable. When you open this window with `Open()`, all the properties you defined are retained. However, when you open the same window with `OpenSheet()` or `OpenSheetWithParm()`, it is opened with the standard features of an MDI sheet, which include the control menu, maximize and minimize icons and resizable properties.

> **When you close an MDI Frame, PowerBuilder first closes all the sheets that are opened within that window and then closes the MDI Frame itself.**

MDI_1 Control

Whenever an MDI Frame is painted and saved, PowerBuilder automatically creates a control called MDI_1 which refers to the Client area. You can then use this name in your scripts to refer specifically to the Client area, but you should note that unlike other controls, MDI_1 has no events associated with it.

> *Note that* **MDI_1** *is not a reserved word so there is nothing to stop you calling a control* **MDI_1**. *However, this isn't recommended as it will obviously cause confusion in your scripts.*

If you add an object to an MDI frame, the size of the client area will be affected. You will have to take care of the resizing of the client area by writing script for the MDI Frame `resize` event.

> **If you don't resize the client area in your script, users will be able to open sheets, but they won't be visible.**

When resizing the client area, you will have to take the space occupied by toolbars, objects and the status bar into account. The `WorkspaceWidth()` and `WorkspaceHeight()` functions will help in determining the exact size of an MDI Frame.

Moving Sheets

Sheets opened in an MDI Frame are not visible if they are moved outside of the Frame area; the area of the sheet outside a Frame is clipped from view. You can, however, set vertical and horizontal scrollbars for an MDI Frame and these allow the user to see any sheet area that is by default outside of the MDI Frame. If scrollbars are not set, the user has to move the sheet by clicking and dragging it.

Converting to an MDI Application

The first and most obvious thing to remember when converting from a single window application to an MDI version is that you have to create an MDI Frame window. Invoke the Window Painter and create a new window. Select Design/Window Style... from the menu and fill in the following details:

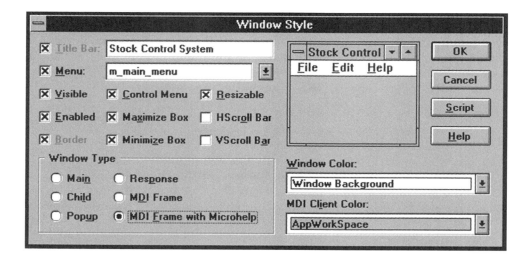

You can see that we've attached the m_main_menu that we painted in Chapter 4 and we've specified the window type as MDI Frame with Microhelp. Click OK and save the window as w_mdi_main_with_microhelp:

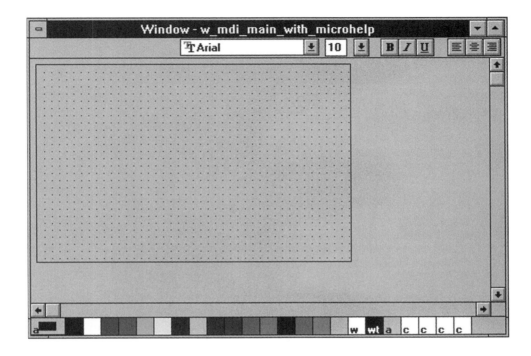

We could paint some objects on the window, but as we said above, if you do this you have to write script for the **resize** event. For now, let's continue with a standard MDI Frame.

After logging into our application, we now want to open the MDI window rather than w_item_master. We also want to allow the user to open w_item_master as a sheet within the MDI Frame when he selects the Module/Item Master option from our main menu. Switch to the Application Painter, go to the Script Painter and for the **open** event, change the script to:

```
open ( w_mdi_main_with_microhelp )
```

Now run the application and you will see an empty window along with a menu and a toolbar:

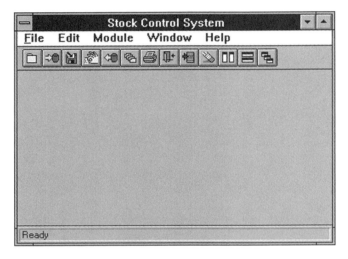

Clicking the right mouse button on the toolbar will display the right-click menu allowing you to position the toolbar, close it or show the associated text on it:

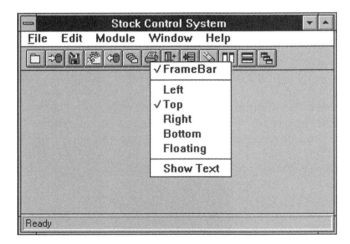

This menu is exactly the same as the one displayed in the development environment which allows you to re-position the PainterBars. PowerBuilder provides this default behavior without requiring you to write any additional code.

Since you have not coded anything to the menu option events, you can't open the w_item_master window from the menu at this point. Double-click the control menu to close the application.

Opening an Instance of a Window

To open an instance of a window as a sheet, we use the **OpenSheet()** function and a local variable declaration. If we open more than one instance of a window, the data in every instance is independent.

We want to allow the user to open an instance of w_item_master whenever he selects the option Item Master from the Module menu, so we will have to write some script for this menu item. If you look at the events that can occur for a menu item, you'll see that there are two: **clicked** and **selected**.

The **selected** event occurs whenever a user scrolls through the menu options using the arrow keys or the mouse pointer. The **clicked** event occurs when the user clicks on the option or presses the Enter key when the option is highlighted. This is the event for which we want to write code, so open the m_main_menu menu and type in the following script for the Module/Item Master **clicked** event:

```
// Event: Clicked
// Object: m_itemmaster of m_module
w_item_master isheet1
OpenSheet( isheet1, ParentWindow, 4, Cascaded! )
```

The first line declares **isheet1** as a local variable based on **w_item_master**. The second line calls the **OpenSheet()** function with the following parameters:

isheet1   The name of the window which is to be opened.

ParentWindow   The name of the MDI Frame in which the window is to be opened. When you code this script for a menu item, the value of this parameter is always **ParentWindow.** You could hard code the name into the script, but by using **ParentWindow,** you reduce the amount of maintenance required if you change the name of the MDI Frame window. This also allows the menu to be attached to any MDI Frame window.

4   The menu option under which you want the list of opened sheets to be displayed. The number 4 means that the list of open sheets will be displayed in the fourth menu item from the left, which in our case is the Window menu item. This is the standard place to list the open sheets for Windows applications, while the standard place to have the Window menu item on a menu bar is second from the right. PowerBuilder allows you to specify this as the default by using zero, so for our menu, four and zero have the same effect.

Cascaded!   Indicates how the opened sheets will be arranged in the frame. PowerBuilder supports the three basic formats: Cascaded!, Layered! and Tile!

> We declared **w_item_master** as a local variable and then used this in the **OpenSheet()** function as it allows us to open more than one instance of the **w_item_master** window. If we simply use the following code:
>
> ```
> OpenSheet( w_item_master, ParentWindow, 4, Cascaded! )
> ```
>
> then trying to open another instance of the window would have simply activated the sheet.

Try running the application now to see how the menu option allows you to open multiple instances of w_item_master:

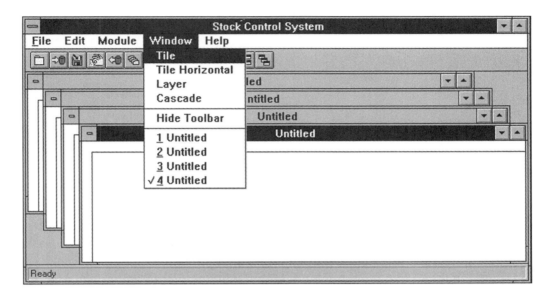

You can see from the Window menu that we have opened four instances of the same window and the sheets are displayed in a cascaded fashion.

Closing an Instance of a Window

To close an instance of a window, you could use the following code:

```
Close(GetActiveSheet(ParentWindow))
```

However, on some occasions you might want to perform some pre-processing before the window is closed, say, saving any information held in that window to the database. On these occasions, it is worth using your own user defined event, rather than the PowerBuilder provided event.

Creating a User Event

The user defined event to close the window has to be defined at the window level, so open up the w_item_master window and select Declare/User Events...:

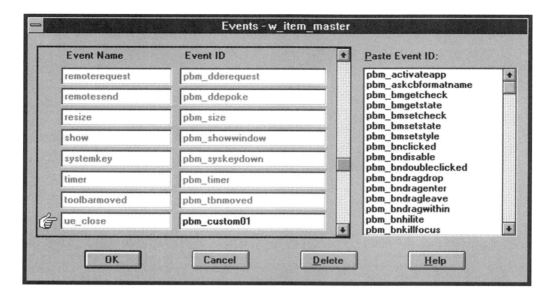

Note that you must declare the user defined event at the correct window level. If you declare the event at the **w_mdi_frame_with_microhelp** level, it will not be available to the **w_item_master** window!

Supply the event name ue_close, select the Event ID pbm_custom01 and click OK. Now if you look at the events list for the window, you'll see that ue_close is now available:

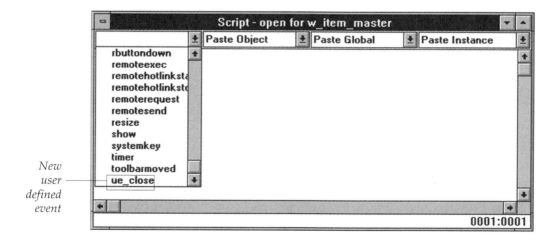

New user defined event

In our application we don't have any processing to do - we simply want to close the window - so the code is simple:

```
// Event: ue_close
// Object: w_item_master
Close (This)
```

Note that we used the keyword **This**. This is because we will always want to close the current window, so in an attempt to make our code reusable, we don't specify the window name. Now the final thing to do is add the code to the **clicked** event of the Close menu option:

```
// Event: Clicked
// Object: m_close of m_file
Window iSheet1
iSheet1 = ParentWindow.GetActiveSheet()
If IsValid( iSheet1 ) then PostEvent( iSheet1, "ue_close" )
```

The **IsValid** function is used to check whether the object that is supplied as an argument is valid or not. If you don't add this check to the code, when you attempt to close down a sheet when none exist, PowerBuilder will generate a 'Null reference error' and will abruptly halt your application.

After checking for a window, the script calls the **ue_close** event using the **PostEvent()** function. We'll look in more depth at events and what the **PostEvent()** function does a little later in the chapter.

Arranging Sheets

PowerBuilder allows you to arrange sheets in four different ways: cascade, tile, horizontal tile or layer. The script to do this is just one single line, so enter the following scripts into the **clicked** event for each of the options under the Window menu item:

```
// Event: Clicked
// Object: m_tile of m_window
ParentWindow.ArrangeSheets ( Tile! )
```

```
// Event: Clicked
// Object: m_tilehorizontal of m_window
ParentWindow.ArrangeSheets ( TileHorizontal! )
```

```
// Event: Clicked
// Object: m_layer of m_window
ParentWindow.ArrangeSheets ( Layer! )
```

```
// Event: Clicked
// Object: m_cascade of m_window
ParentWindow.ArrangeSheets ( Cascade! )
```

*Notice that the argument for the ArrangeSheet() function is **Cascade!**, but in the **OpenSheet()** function it is **Cascaded!**. The same is true for **Layer!**, **Layered!** for **OpenSheet()**. This can be somewhat confusing!*

All four of these parameters only affect the sheets that are currently open and active. If you wanted to arrange minimized icons, you could add a new menu item, say 'Arrange Icons', and use the same code with the argument **Icons!**.

We've now seen how to open and close instances of the item_master window and how to arrange the sheets in the MDI frame. In the next section we'll look in more depth at events and add the scripts to more of our remaining menu options.

Events

Windows is a message-based system. This means that if an action occurs, all the currently active applications are informed by a message generated by the operating system. The applications can also generate these messages, allowing them to hold two-way conversations with both the operating system and other active applications.

Broadly speaking, there are three types of messages available to the PowerBuilder developer:

1 Standard messages which have a pre-defined functionality.

2 VBX messages which are mapped for Visual Basic control messages.

3 Other messages which must be meaningfully coded by the programmer.

In PowerBuilder, every event has an **Event ID** and there are three types which correspond to the three types of messages. In PowerBuilder script we don't refer to Event IDs directly, but rather to the event name. We've already seen how we map a user-defined event to a PowerBuilder Event ID:

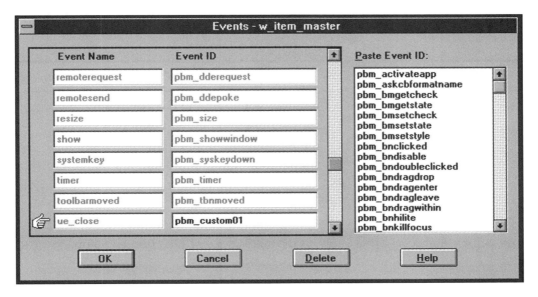

Other standard PowerBuilder events are mapped the same way. For example, you can see that the timer event is mapped to the pbm_timer Event ID. Every object in PowerBuilder has a number of pre-defined events which are mapped to Event IDs. We can't change these mappings.

> Note that only some Event IDs are mapped at each object level depending on the requirement of the object. For example, the **pbm_ddepoke** Event ID is mapped to the **RemoteSend** event at the window level but is unmapped at the DataWindow level. This means that at that level, this Event ID could be mapped to a custom user event.

Event IDs like pbm_vbxevent26 are mapped to Visual Basic control messages and custom Event IDs such as pbm_custom23 are available to be mapped to user-defined events.

User Events

We've already seen how to create the ue_close user event. We also need to create several other user events which we can trigger from some of our other menu selections. The following table contains the list of user events which should be created at the w_item_master window level and the menu options to which they refer:

User Event	Event ID	Related Menu Option
ue_retrieve	pbm_custom02	File/Retrieve
ue_query	pbm_custom03	File/Query
ue_new	pbm_custom04	Edit/New
ue_delete	pbm_custom05	Edit/Delete
ue_print	pbm_custom06	File/Print
ue_print_preview	pbm_custom07	File/Print Preview
ue_printer_setup	pbm_custom08	File/Printer Setup
ue_save_as	pbm_custom09	File/Save As
ue_sort	pbm_custom10	File/Save
ue_filter	pbm_custom11	File/Filter
ue_save	pbm_custom12	File/Sort

Now, for each of the menu options, write the following code:

```
Window iSheet1
iSheet1 = ParentWindow.GetActiveSheet()
If IsValid( iSheet1 ) then PostEvent( iSheet1, "***" )
```

The code for each of the menu options is exactly the same. You can simply replace the asterisks in the last line with the relevant user event name.

The final step is to add the code for each of the user events. We've already added code to most of the CommandButtons on the w_item_master window, so it's a simple matter of copying the following scripts to the relevant user event:

Copy clicked event script from	To user event
cb_retrieve	ue_retrieve
cb_query	ue_query
cb_new	ue_new
cb_delete	ue_delete
cb_print	ue_print
cb_print_preview	ue_print_preview
cb_printer_setup	ue_printer_setup

Once you have copied the scripts to the user events, delete all the CommandButtons in the w_item_master window, leaving the DataWindow controls dwc_1 and dwc_2 as the only controls in the window.

We can make the w_item_master window more useful, simply by resizing the DataWindow controls whenever the user resizes the window. To do this, we have to add some code to the resize event of w_item_master:

```
// Object: w_item_master
// Event: Resize

dwc_1.x = 10
dwc_1.y = 10
dwc_1.Width = WorkSpaceWidth() - 20
dwc_1.Height = WorkSpaceHeight() - 20

dwc_2.x = dwc_1.x
dwc_2.y = dwc_1.y
dwc_2.Width = dwc_1.Width
dwc_2.Height = dwc_1.Height
```

We are using the **WorkSpaceWidth()** and **WorkSpaceHeight()** functions to determine the width and height of the workspace and then to resize the controls, leaving a border of 10 units around the DataWindow controls.

449

Triggering Events

When you use user events, they must be manually triggered. There are two functions which PowerBuilder provides to accomplish this: `TriggerEvent()` and `PostEvent()`. For both of these functions, you must supply the object name and the event name as arguments. For example:

```
TriggerEvent( ParentWindow, "ue_close" )
PostEvent( ParentWindow, "ue_close" )
```

> You can also trigger standard pre-defined events by using the following syntax:

```
TriggerEvent ( ParentWindow, Close! )
```

It is important to note that neither of these functions actually causes the event to occur - they simply call the relevant script.

TriggerEvent() Versus PostEvent()

There is a subtle but important difference between the `TriggerEvent()` and the `PostEvent()` functions. The `TriggerEvent()` function executes the script for a specified event that occurs to a specified object. The next statement after the `TriggerEvent()` is executed only after the script specified in the `TriggerEvent()` is executed. This is called synchronous execution. If you want to execute a script after the execution of the current script, then you would call the `PostEvent()`.

Communication Between Objects

When you have lots of objects in your application, you will probably want them to communicate, share variables and pass values between themselves. In a procedural programming language, this isn't too much of a problem; you either have one long program or a main routine with several subroutines where you pass variables as parameters in the subroutine calls.

When using an event-driven language, the process of communicating between objects is made more complex by the fact that you don't always know what the user is going to do next. PowerBuilder provides several different ways to communicate between its objects and we'll look at each of these in turn, highlighting some of the pros and cons for each method.

Global Variables

As we've already discussed in a previous chapter, global variables can be accessed by any object in an application. This is the easiest way to pass values between objects, but as we've said before, they should be used sparingly.

Unless you adhere to a set of strict naming conventions, global variables can cause problems when integrating modules developed by more than one development team. Another disadvantage is that they can be changed from anywhere in an application and since they exist throughout the duration of an application, you may not be using your memory as efficiently as possible.

Directly Referencing Window Variables

Instance variables are declared at the object level and as such are considered as attributes of the appropriate object. You can therefore refer to instance variables as you would any other attribute of an object:

```
w_item_master.visible = TRUE        // Standard window attribute
w_item_master.iChangeTable = FALSE   // Instance variable attribute
```

As we discussed before, instance variables can be declared with different access levels. To be able to refer to an instance variable from another object, it must be declared as **Public** access. This is the default access level, so you only have to worry about it if you change the access level. It is a good idea to restrict access to these instance variables by providing methods which act on them and only allowing other objects to access them through these methods.

Opening a Window with a Parameter

With windows, sheets and UserObjects, you can pass parameters by using these functions:

- OpenWithParm()
- OpenSheetWithParm()
- OpenUserObjectWithParm()

rather than the standard opening functions. If you are working with PowerBuilder windows, you can also return values by using the

`CloseWithReturn()` function instead of the `Close()` function. The syntax for these functions is as follows:

`OpenWithParm (<window name>, <parameter>)`

The only disadvantage to this method is that you can only pass one parameter. We can get round this though by using structures.

Structures

Structures are basically collections of variables which you define in the Structure Painter:

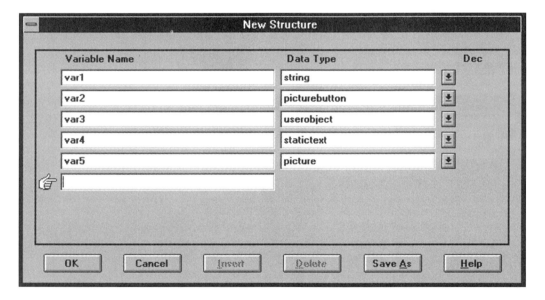

When you save a structure, you give it a name and you can then use this name as the parameter in one of the above functions to transfer lots of information in one go.

The Message Object

When you use one of these functions, the parameter value is stored in a Message Object. The Message Object is a global, pre-declared object that can be used as a carrier for the parameter, distributing the parameter value as and where it is required.

Once the parameter value has been allocated to a Message Object, you can refer to that value through references to that object from any other object in your application. Typically, you can send one of the following data types through the Message Object:

Data Type	Stored In
String	Message.StringParm
Numeric	Message.DoubleParm
PowerBuilder Object	Message.PowerObjectParm

The parameter is stored in the relevant Message Object attribute, depending on the data type of the parameter. You can then refer to the parameter in the calling object using the **Message.** notation. For example:

```
idw_2_save = Message.PowerObjectParm
```

One possible problem that is associated with Message Objects is that all currently running applications can generate messages, so there is a chance that the Message Object can get overwritten.

The solution to this problem is to declare an instance or local variable in the called object and then assign this variable to the Message Object attribute in the object's **open** event. We'll see this in action in Chapter 15.

Calling Functions

You can call functions declared in another object by using the following syntax:

```
<Object Name>.<Function Name> ( Parameter1, Parameter2, ...)
```

Keep in mind that, like instance variables, functions declared at the object level have an access level, so they must be declared as **Public** to be available to other objects.

Triggering or Posting Events

Calling the **TriggerEvent()** or **PostEvent()** functions is a convenient way to execute the scripts of other windows or window control events. These functions allow you to write a script in one place and execute it any number of times from other objects.

We've already used some of these methods of communication earlier in the chapter and throughout the rest of the chapter, together with the next couple of chapters, you'll see examples of all of them. We can't recommend any single method as each has its own merits and can be used in many diverse circumstances. The best advice we can give is to try all the various methods and you'll will find which ones you are comfortable with.

Adding Some Nice Touches

For the rest of this chapter, we'll show you various ways of improving the look of your application and making it easier to use.

Displaying a Background Logo

This might seem like quite a simple thing to do, but it does require some thought. You might think that to display a background logo, you could paint the logo in the MDI Frame window itself. However, as we've already discussed, this would disable PowerBuilder's automatic resizing of the client area and mean that you had to write script to take care of it. When you take into account the fact that a logo is typically centered on the screen, you might not be left with much room to resize your sheets.

Instead, you could paint the company logo in a window, opening this window before opening the login window. However, this doesn't solve the problem, because the `Open()` function makes the window independent and when you come to open another sheet, this window will go out of the MDI frame window area. If you open the logo window with `OpenSheet()`, PowerBuilder displays a title bar, as well as the minimize and maximize icons. In other words, the window is given functionality that draws attention to it, rather than fading it into the background.

A Response window wouldn't work either, because the user can't work with the application under the window that has been closed.

This only leaves a Child window or a Popup window. Only in these two types of window can you disable all the attributes in the Design/Window Style dialog box in the Window Painter. If you open a window with the `OpenSheet()` function, the window name will be displayed under one of the menu bar items, which allows it to be selected by the user. We don't want to do this, so we'll have to use the `Open()` function.

To open a new window and paint a logo on it, select Design/Window Style..., turn off all its attributes except the visible attribute and make it into a Child window.

Save the window as w_logo and in the **open** event script of the w_mdi_main_with_microhelp window call this logo window with the **open()** function. Try running the application now and you'll see that this does work:

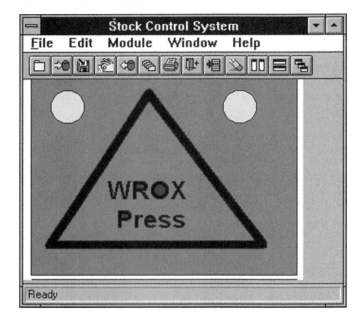

However, there are still a couple of problems. Whenever the MDI Frame is resized, the w_logo window and the logo within it are not resized accordingly. Also, if you open any sheets in the MDI Frame, they won't be visible because the child window will always be on top of any opened windows.

We can solve the first problem by writing script for the **resize** event of the MDI Frame, but this won't solve the second. The best solution is to display the logo when we open the MDI main window and then turn its visible property off when we open a sheet. We can then check if there are any sheets open after we have run the File/Close menu option script and if not, turn the visible property back on. We would also need to add the following line to the start of the script for the Module/Item Master menu option:

```
w_logo.visible = FALSE
```

We can then create a new user event **ue_check_for_active_sheets** at the MDI window level and assign it a custom Event ID. We then write the following code for this event:

```
Window lSheet1
lSheet1 = GetActiveSheet( This )
If not IsValid( lSheet1 ) Then w_logo.visible = True
```

and call this event from the File/Close menu script using:

```
PostEvent ( ParentWindow, "ue_check_for_active_sheets")
```

About Window

One of the options available from the Help menu is About. When selected, the following window should be displayed:

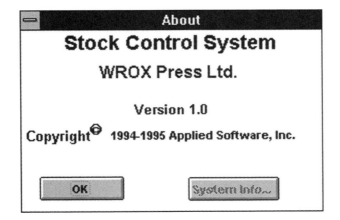

Paint the window and behind the OK button **clicked** event, put the following script:

```
Close ( Parent )
```

This will allow the user to close the window. We can also cause the window to close down automatically after ten seconds if it hasn't already been closed by the user. To do this, we'll have to write two scripts: one for the **open** event and one for the **timer** event:

```
// Object: w_about
// Event: Open
Timer( 10 )
```

```
// Object: w_about
// Event: Timer
Close( This )
```

The first one simply passes the parameter 10 to the **timer** event when the window is opened, while the **timer** event closes the window after the time has elapsed. The final stage is to open the window from the Help/About menu option. Put the following script in the **clicked** event for the menu option:

```
// Object: m_about in m_main_menu
// Event: Clicked
Open( w_about )
```

Now when you run the application, you can select Help/About to bring up the w_about window and if you don't click the OK button, it will close automatically after ten seconds:

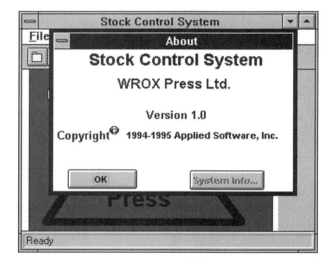

The script for the System Info... CommandButton on the w_about window is covered in the Chapter 14.

Minimizing the Application When Idle

Sometimes users may leave an application without logging out. If the application contains confidential information, there is a possibility that the data could be seen by someone who shouldn't see it. You could rely on a Windows screen saver, but it is best to handle this security from within your application.

Your goal might be to disconnect from the server and minimize the application if it is idle for more than five minutes. In a multi-user environment, it is better to disconnect from the server whenever it is not needed for an extended period of time.

Add the following line to the **open** event of the application:

```
Open ( w_login_window )
Idle( 300 ) // Write this line after Open( w_login_window )
```

This calls the **idle** event if 300 seconds or 5 minutes elapse with nothing happening. In the **idle** event for the application, put the following script:

```
// Object: Application
// Event: Idle
Disconnect using SQLCA ;
w_mdi_main_with_MicroHelp.WindowState = Minimized!
```

Disabling Non-applicable Menu Options

When there are no sheets, it makes sense to remove some of the menu options from the user's palette. This helps to reinforce the overall functionality of your application by disabling the menu options that no longer offer any useful actions.

Create a user event called **ue_chk_is_there_any_active_sheet** in the w_mdi_main_with_microhelp window and write the following code in the script for the event:

```
// Object: w_mdi_main_with_microhelp
// Event: ue_chk_is_there_any_active_sheet

Int i = 1
Boolean lEnableMenuItem = FALSE
Window lSheet

lSheet = GetActiveSheet( This )
If IsValid( lSheet ) Then
   lEnableMenuItem = True
Else
```

```
      lEnableMenuItem = False
   End If

   For i = 1 to 13
      This.Menuid.item[1].item[i].enabled = lEnableMenuItem
   Next

   For i = 1 to 2
      This.Menuid.item[2].item[i].enabled = lEnableMenuItem
   Next

   For i = 1 to 4
      This.Menuid.item[4].item[i].enabled = lEnableMenuItem
   Next
```

Now add the following code to the **open** event of the window:

```
PostEvent( This, "ue_chk_is_there_any_active_sheet")
```

and add the following line to the **ue_close** event for w_item_master:

```
PostEvent( w_mdi_main_with_microhelp,"ue_chk_is_there_any_active_sheet")
```

Unfortunately, there is one disadvantage to using this code: it will enable all the menu options for any particular instance of a sheet. If you wanted to disable some menu options for a particular instance of a sheet, you would have to take care of this in your code.

Customizing Toolbars

When you click on any toolbar icon with the right mouse button, PowerBuilder displays a pop-up menu and allows you to change the toolbar position, show/hide the toolbar text and even the toolbar itself:

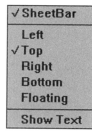

If you hide the toolbar by deselecting the SheetBar option, there is no default method that allows you to display the toolbar again; you need to provide a menu option to display the toolbar. This is the purpose of the menu option Window/Toolbar in the m_main_menu. Add the following code to the Window/Toolbar menu option:

```
// Object: m_toolbar
// Event: Clicked

If ParentWindow.Toolbarvisible = true Then
    ParentWindow.Toolbarvisible = False
    This.Text = "Show Toolbar"
Else
    ParentWindow.Toolbarvisible = True
    This.Text = "Hide Toolbar"
end if
```

This simply checks if the toolbar is visible and toggles it on or off, changing the text that is displayed in the menu option at the same time.

Naturally, even this code has its disadvantages. If you show/hide the toolbar by selecting this option, it works fine. However, if you hide the toolbar by selecting from the pop-up menu, the menu item text will not be changed accordingly. To solve this problem, add this code to the m_window menu option:

```
// Object: m_window
// Event: Clicked

If ParentWindow.Toolbarvisible = true Then
    Parent.m_window.m_toolbar.Text = "Hide Toolbar"
Else
    Parent.m_window.m_toolbar.Text = "Show Toolbar"
end if
```

To select the Toolbar option from the menu, the user has to click on the Window menu option. At this point, just change the text so that the user always sees the correct menu option.

You also have to provide for the possibility that the user presses the *Alt* key to activate the menu, rather than clicking on it. This is simply one line of code in the **selected** event of the menu bar item:

```
// Object: m_window
// Event: Selected

TriggerEvent( This, Clicked! )
```

Summary

This chapter explained the concepts of Multiple Document Interfaces and started the process of converting our Stock Control application to an MDI version. We finished off by considering some nice touches that can be added to our application related to the toolbars and menu options.

In the next chapter we'll add more functionality to our application and cover some more advanced scripting techniques.

14

Advanced Scripting

In Chapter 9, we introduced PowerScript and provided some stand-alone examples to illustrate the basics of the language. We then went on to add some code to our application, adding functionality to CommandButtons and providing error handling capabilities.

However, we didn't cover all of the CommandButtons. As our application was still running around a Single Document Interface, not all of the CommandButtons and menu items that we designed were applicable.

In the previous chapter, we converted our application to run on an MDI footing, so we can now implement that extra functionality. This is the main focus of this chapter, but we have also covered some interesting information on some of the other uses that PowerScript can endow upon your application.

We'll take you through the design of some reusable objects, and by the end of the chapter you'll have a complete class library of reusable objects which you can use for any application.

In this chapter, we will cover:

- Adding more functionality to our application
- Mail enabling your application using MAPI
- Creating class libraries

Introduction

In Chapter 13, we converted our application to an MDI application and added some scripts to various menu options. We also created user events to handle the scripts for the other menu options, but we haven't yet added the code to these.

The particular menu options we're interested in are:

▲ File/Save As

▲ File/Sort

▲ File/Print Preview

Let's take a look at the extra functionality that we can add to these options.

Saving a DataWindow in Other Formats

You can save the data contained in a DataWindow in most of the popular file formats, including `.XLS`, `.DBF`, tab delimited text and so on. The logic by which you save the object in a different format is very simple.

> *With the introduction of v4.0, PowerBuilder now supports two new formats, Windows Meta File (WMF) and PowerBuilder Report (PSR). The following code doesn't make use of these, but it would be simple to add them.*

First, we have to paint a Popup window, as shown below:

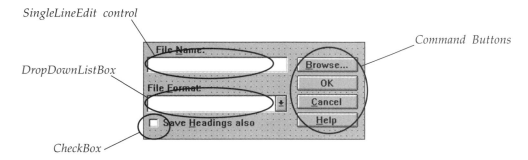

SingleLineEdit control

DropDownListBox

CheckBox

Command Buttons

Disable the maximize, minimize and resize options and supply the following item names for the DropDownListBox:

- Excel (XLS)
- SQL Syntax (SQL)
- Tab Separated Text (TXT)
- Comma Separated Values (CSV)
- Microsoft Multiplan (SLV)
- Lotus 1-2-3 (WKS)
- Data Interchange (DIF)
- dBase III (DBF)

Save the window as w_save_as and declare an instance variable called idw_to_save as a DataWindow:

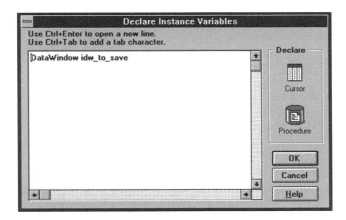

Now we have to add some code to the **open** event of this window:

```
If IsValid( Message.PowerObjectParm ) Then
   idw_to_save = Message.PowerObjectParm
Else
   Close ( This )
End If
SetFocus( ddlb_file_format )
Return
```

This assigns the parameter in Message Object to the instance variable - this is discussed in depth in Chapter 12 - and sets the focus to the DropDownListBox.

We then have to write the following code for the **clicked** event of the cb_file_name CommandButton:

```
/*
This script makes sure that user selects one of the file types and
if selected, invokes a dialog box to accept the file name
All the if conditions below simply display the selected type
of files in the Select File dialog box.
*/

string lFileTypes, lFileExt, lFileName, lTitle1
int lRetValue

If Trim(ddlb_file_format.text) <> "" Then
   lFileName = Right(ddlb_file_format.text,5)
Else
   MessageBox( "Info", "First select one of the above file type" )
   Return
End If

If lFileName= "(CSV)" then
   lFileTypes = "Comma separated files (*.CSV),*.CSV"
   lFileExt = "CSV"
elseif lFileName= "(DBF)" then
   lFileTypes = "Dbase files (*.DBF),*.DBF"
   lFileExt = "DBF"
elseif lFileName= "(DIF)" then
   lFileTypes = "DIF files (*.DIF),*.DIF"
   lFileExt = "DIF"
elseif lFileName= "(XLS)" then
   lFileTypes = "Excel files (*.XLS),*.XLS"
   lFileExt = "XLS"
elseif lFileName= "(WKS)" then
   lFileTypes = "Lotus 1-2-3 files (*.WKS),*.WKS"
   lFileExt = "WKS"
elseif lFileName= "(SLV)" then
   lFileTypes = "Multiplan files (*.SLV),*.SLV"
   lFileExt = "SLV"
elseif lFileName= "(SQL)" then
   lFileTypes = "SQL files (*.SQL),*.SQL"
   lFileExt = "SQL"
elseif lFileName= "(TXT)" then
   lFileTypes = "Text files (*.TXT),*.TXT"
   lFileExt = "TXT"
end if
```

```
lRetValue = GetFileSaveName("Save file as", sle_1.text, lTitle1, &
      lFileExt, lFileTypes)
If lRetValue = 1 then cb_ok.enabled = TRUE
```

We simply check which file type the user selects from the DropDownListBox and call the `GetFileSaveName()` function. This function invokes a standard dialog box, to allow the user to select or supply a file. It takes the following five parameters:

1 Heading to the dialog box

2 Variable to store the user selected file name with full path in the dialog box

3 Variable to store the file name returned

4 Type of files to display

5 Default file extension to add to the file if the user neglects to provide this

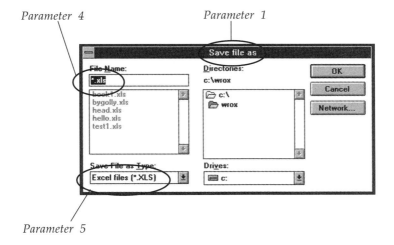

Parameter 4   *Parameter 1*

Parameter 5

If the user supplies a valid filename, we enable the OK CommandButton. The code for this control's `clicked` event is as follows:

```
/*
Basically, this script uses the SaveAs() function. Depending on the format
type user selects, the appropriate Enumerated file type is supplied to the
function. You cannot use macro like in dBase/FoxPro. That's why the
script looks very big for a simple thing.
*/

boolean lSaveHeadings
Int lUserAnswer
String lFileName, lFileExt

lFileName = Trim(sle_1.Text)
lFileExt = Upper(right(ddlb_file_format.text,5))

If lFileName <> "" then
    If FileExists( lFileName ) then
        lUserAnswer = MessageBox( "Warning!", lFileName + &
                " already exists." + "~r" + &
                "Do you want to override the existing file? ", &
                StopSign!, YesNo!, 2)
        If lUserAnswer = 2 Then Return
    End If

    If cbx_headings.checked then lSaveHeadings = TRUE
    else lSaveHeadings = FALSE

    If lFileExt = "(CSV)" then
        idw_to_save.SaveAs( lFileName, CSV!, lSaveHeadings )
    elseif lFileExt= "(DBF)" then
        idw_to_save.SaveAs( lFileName, dBASE3!, lSaveHeadings )
    elseif lFileExt= "(DIF)" then
        idw_to_save.SaveAs( lFileName, DIF!, lSaveHeadings )
    elseif lFileExt= "(XLS)" then
        idw_to_save.SaveAs( lFileName, Excel!, lSaveHeadings )
    elseif lFileExt= "(WKS)" then
        idw_to_save.SaveAs( lFileName, WKS!, lSaveHeadings )
    elseif lFileExt= "(SLK)" then
        idw_to_save.SaveAs( lFileName, SYLK!, lSaveHeadings )
    elseif lFileExt= "(SQL)" then
        idw_to_save.SaveAs( lFileName, SQLInsert!, lSaveHeadings )
    elseif lFileExt= "(TXT)" then
        idw_to_save.SaveAs( lFileName, Text!, lSaveHeadings )
    end if
    Close ( Parent )
end if
```

This script makes use of the **SaveAs()** DataWindow function. Depending on
the selected file format, it calls the **SaveAs()** with appropriate enumerated data
type. If the user has selected the Save Headings also checkbox, we also set

lSaveHeadings to **TRUE**. This causes the function to include the headings with the main data.

The Close button simply closes the window:

```
// Object: cb_close
// Event: Clicked

close( Parent )
```

To see this feature working, you have to add code to the File/Save As menu option, which sets **idw_to_save** to the DataWindow control and then opens the w_save_as window.

If you run the application and try selecting this menu option, you'll be able to save the DataWindow control in any of the formats. For example, if you save it as an Excel spreadsheet, you'll get the following result:

DataWindow Sort Utility

Let's now create a window that allows you to sort the data held in a specific DataWindow. We could supply this functionality by displaying all the columns and asking the user to select from the available list.

However, we already have the columns displayed in the DataWindow control, so we can make use of them by getting the user to select the columns to sort on by physically clicking on them. To achieve this, we'll have to write a little more code than in previous examples.

First, we need to paint the following DataWindow:

471

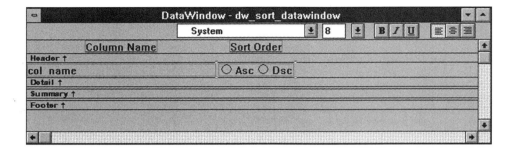

This is a tabular style DataWindow operating with an external data source. The result set for the DataWindow is defined as follows:

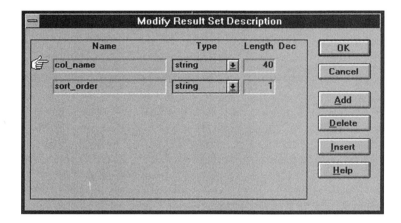

Save this as dw_sort and paint a new window as follows, associating the DataWindow control to the DataWindow object we've just created:

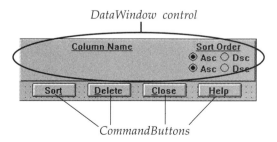

To complete this part of the creation process, we need to declare two instance variables: **iWindow** as a Window, and **iDw** as a DataWindow.

The purpose of **iDw** is to store the DataWindow that the user wants to sort on, while **iWindow** stores the window. Actually, storing the window isn't necessary, but if we do, it allows the sort window to be more flexible. For example, suppose that two sheets are open and the user invoked the sort window from Sheet2. As you know, we are allowing the user to select the column by clicking on the appropriate sheet, so if the user clicks on a column from Sheet1, we won't be able to find the column name.

Sending both the Window and the DataWindow overcomes this problem. Save the window as w_sort_datawindow.

Activating the Window

We could activate this window from the File/Sort menu, but one problem with this method is that you can have more than one DataWindow in a window. We need a way of determining which DataWindow the user wants to sort.

The simplest option is to add a Sort option to the Popup menu associated with that part of the window, thereby drawing the name of the DataWindow into the code. We trigger the user-defined **ue_sort** event from this menu option and so run the following code:

```
Open( w_sort_datawindow)
w_sort_datawindow.wf_initialize( this, dwc_1)
```

This opens the w_sort_datawindow window and calls an initialization function. The **wf_initialize()** function determines the existing sort order and displays it in the w_sort_datawindow:

```
// Object: w_sort_datawindow
// Function: wf_initialize
// Access: public
// Returns: (none)
// Arguments: p_window window value
// p_dw datawindow value
String lSortOrderStr, lSortOrderStr1, lColName, lSortOrder
Int lEndPos = 0, lSpacePos
Long lNewRow
```

```
iWindow = p_window
idw = p_dw

lSortOrderStr = idw.dwDescribe( "datawindow.Table.Sort" )

If lSortOrderStr <> "!" and lSortOrderStr <> "?" Then
   dwc_sort.Reset()
   Do While Len(Trim(lSortOrderStr)) <> 0
      lEndPos = Pos(lSortOrderStr, ",")
      If lEndPos = 0 Then lEndPos = len(lSortOrderStr)
      lSortOrderStr1 = Left( lSortOrderStr, lEndPos -1 )
      lSortOrderStr = trim(Mid ( lSortOrderStr, lEndPos+1 ))
      lSpacePos = Pos(lSortOrderStr1, " ")
      lColName = Left(lSortOrderStr1, lSpacePos)
      lSortOrder = Trim(Mid(lSortOrderStr1, lSpacePos))
      lNewRow = dwc_sort.InsertRow(0)
      dwc_sort.SetItem( lNewRow,1, lColName )
      dwc_sort.SetItem( lNewRow,2, lSortOrder )
   Loop

End If

If dwc_sort.RowCOunt() = 0 Then
   cb_sort.enabled = False
   cb_delete.enabled = False
Else
   cb_sort.enabled = TRUE
   cb_delete.enabled = TRUE
End If

Return
```

This function assigns the Window and DataWindow to instance variables and determines the existing sort order by calling **dwDescribe()**. If there is any problem, **dwDescribe()** will return either '!' or '?'. The following loop parses the sort order string returned by **dwDescribe()** and inserts each column name and sort order in the dw_sort DataWindow.

Column Selection

Now we have to allow the user to select a column by clicking on it. The following code has to be written for the **clicked** event for the DataWindow control on w_item_master:

```
// Object: Dwc_1
// Event: Clicked
```

```
If Handle( w_sort_datawindow ) > 0 Then
   w_sort_datawindow.wf_add_to_sort_cols( Parent, This)
   Return
End If
```

This code checks whether or not the w_sort_window is open using the **Handle()** function. If the return value is greater than zero, the window is open and we call another function to add the column. The function to add the column is as follows:

```
// Object: w_sort_datawindow
// Event: wf_add_to_sort_cols
// Access: Public
// Returns: (none)
// Arguments: p_window window value
// p_dw datawindow value

Int lClickedColNo
String lArg1, lClickedColName
Long lNewRow

If IsValid( p_dw ) Then
   If p_dw <> idw Then
      idw = p_dw
      dwc_sort.Reset()
   End If
Else
   Return
End If

If IsValid( p_Window ) Then
   If p_Window <> iWindow Then iWindow = p_Window
Else
   Return
End If

lclickedcolNo = idw.GetClickedColumn()

lArg1 = "#" + trim(string(lClickedColNo)) + ".Name"
lClickedColName = idw.dwDescribe( lArg1 )

lNewRow = dwc_sort.InsertRow(0)
dwc_sort.SetItem( lNewRow, "col_name", lClickedColName )
idw.AcceptText()
cb_sort.enabled = TRUE
cb_delete.enabled = TRUE

Return
```

This function checks that the DataWindow and Window are valid and then retrieves the clicked column by calling `GetClickedColumn()`. We add the column name to the dwc_sort DataWindow control and enable the Sort and Delete buttons.

Applying the Sort Criteria

The final thing to do is to apply the sort when the user clicks on the Sort button. The code for the **clicked** event of the Sort button is as follows:

```
Long lTotRows, i ; String lSortStr

dwc_sort.AcceptText()

lTotRows = dwc_sort.RowCount()
If lTotRows > 0 Then
   lSortStr = dwc_sort.GetItemString(1,1) + " " + &
         dwc_sort.GetItemString(1,2)
End If

If lTotRows > 1 Then
   For i = 2 to lTotRows Step 1
      lSortStr = lSortStr + ", " + dwc_sort.GetItemString(i,1) + &
            " " + dwc_sort.GetItemString(i,2)
   Next
End If

idw.SetSort( lSortStr )
SetPointer( HourGlass! )
idw.Sort()
SetPointer( Arrow! )
```

This sets the values from each row in the dwc_sort DataWindow control and prepares the sort strings with a loop. Before we actually sort the DataWindow, we call **SetSort()** with the new sort criteria. We then change the pointer to an hourglass, and call the **Sort()** function, before changing the pointer back.

> To display PowerBuilder's own **Sort Criteria** dialog box, set
> **lSortStr** to NULL by calling **SetNull()**.

As a final touch, we've allowed the user to delete a sort criteria by clicking on the Delete button:

```
// Object: cb_delete
// Event: Clicked

Long lCurRow
lCurRow = dwc_sort.GetRow()
If lCurRow > 0 Then dwc_sort.DeleteRow( lCurRow )
If dwc_sort.RowCount() = 0 Then
   This.enabled = FALSE
   cb_sort.enabled = FALSE
End If
```

Trying Out the Sort Function

When you try this out, you'll be presented with the sort window:

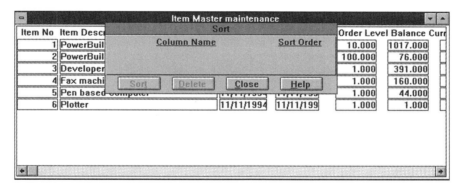

If you click on the item_description and re_order_level columns, and select Asc for ascending, when you click on the Sort button, the DataWindow will be sorted based on the values in these columns:

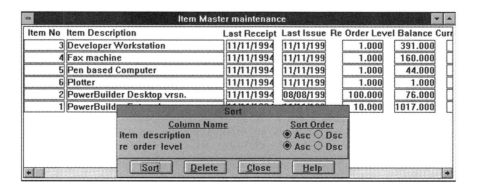

477

Print Preview - Zoom Utility

We've already added some code to implement the Print Preview function, but as you will remember, it wasn't very useful - all it did was format the object ready for printing; no other functionality was provided.

We can improve on this by allowing the user to zoom in or out on the object when they Print Preview. As our user interface is now becoming much more graphically based, let's use a scrollbar to implement this extra feature.

Painting the Window

First, we need a child window painted as follows, disabling the control menu and the resize, maximize and minimize buttons:

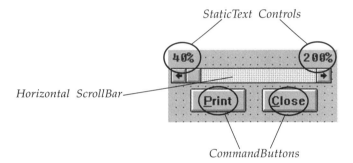

Create an instance variable called **iDw** of type DataWindow and save the window as w_print_preview. This window will be opened when you select File/ Print Preview from the menu. We'll trigger the user-defined **ue_print_preview** event from there, causing the following script to run:

```
OpenWithParm( w_print_preview, dwc_1 )
```

Now, in the **open** event of the w_print_preview window, we can write the following script:

```
/*
This script sets the minimum and maximum values for the horizontal
scroll bar, takes the print preview zoom percentage of the datawindow
through DwDescribe function and sets the position of the scroll bar to
the same position.
*/
```

```
Integer lDwZoom
iDw = Message.PowerObjectParm
iDw.dwModify( "datawindow.print.preview=yes" )
lDwZoom = Integer( iDw.DwDescribe( "datawindow.print.Preview.Zoom"))

hsb_1.MinPosition = 40
hsb_1.MaxPosition = 200
hsb_1.Position = lDwZoom

iDw.DwModify("datawindow.Print.Preview.Rulers=yes")
```

The comments in the code explain exactly what this does.

> *The final line turns on the rulers for print preview.*

The Scrollbar Scripts

There are five specific events associated with a scrollbar, as depicted in the following figure:

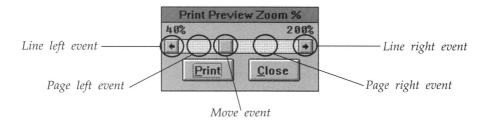

These events are executed depending on what the user does or where he clicks:

Event	When It Occurs
lineleft	Occurs when the user clicks on the left arrow
pageleft	Occurs when the user clicks between the current position and the left arrow
move	Occurs whenever the user drags the current position indicator
pageright	Occurs when the user clicks between the current position and the right arrow
lineright	Occurs when the user clicks on the right arrow

The code for each of these is fairly simple. First, the `lineleft` event:

```
/*
This event occurs when you click on the left arrow of the scrollbar. You need
to set the position of the scrollbar and take care when the position goes
below the minimum position and change datawindow print preview zoom
percentage accordingly
*/

String lArg1
This.Position = This.Position - 1
If This.Position < This.MinPosition then This.Position = This.MinPosition
lArg1 = "datawindow.Print.Preview.Zoom=" + String( This.Position)
iDw.DwModify( lArg1 )
```

We decrease the current position of the scrollbar by one unit and use `DwModify()` to alter the print preview zoom value.

> Note that both the `lineleft` and `pageleft` events use code to make
> sure that the zoom value doesn't exceed the minimum value.

The code for the `pageleft` event is exactly the same, except that we move the current position by five units, as opposed to one:

```
String lArg1
This.Position = This.Position - 5
If This.Position < This.MinPosition then This.Position = This.MinPosition
lArg1 = "datawindow.Print.Preview.Zoom=" + String( This.Position)
iDw.DwModify( lArg1 )
```

> The amount by which you move the current position is entirely optional.

The scripts for `lineright` and `pageright` are exactly the same, except that they increase the current position and check that we don't go over the maximum value.

The code for the `moved` event is slightly different, but simpler than its cousins:

```
/* Sets the print preview zoom percentage to the position of the horizontal
scroll bar */
String lArg1
lArg1 = "datawindow.Print.Preview.Zoom=" + String( This.Position)
iDw.DwModify( lArg1 )
```

This code simply sets the print preview zoom property to the value of the current position of the scrollbar.

Finally, we want to actually be able to print the DataWindow once we've previewed it, so we add the following code to the Print button:

```
// Object: cb_print
// Event: Clicked

idw.DwModify( "datawindow.Print.Prompt=yes")
idw.Print( TRUE )
```

Print Preview in Action

When you select File/Print Preview, you'll be presented with the following:

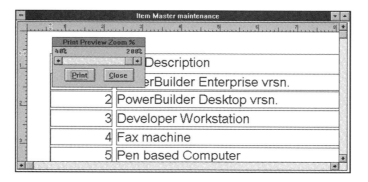

You can zoom in and out and the DataWindow display will change almost instantaneously:

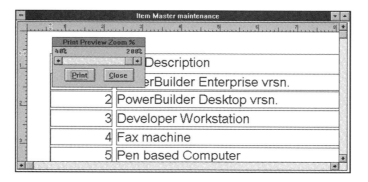

Drag and Drop

Drag and drop is an advanced user interface technique that makes handling objects on the screen much, much simpler. The user selects an object (called the source object) by clicking with the left mouse button and, by holding the button down, drags the object and drops it (by releasing the mouse button) onto another object (called the target object). When an object is dropped onto another object, certain events occur. By writing scripts for these events, we can provide additional user-friendly, graphically based functionality.

Drag and Drop Events

There are four drag and drop events that can occur for a window control:

Events	When It Occurs
dragdrop	This occurs when an object is dropped on to a target object.
dragenter	This occurs when a dragged object enters the borders of a target object.
dragleave	This occurs when a dragged object leaves a target object.
dragwithin	This occurs whenever a dragged is moving within the borders of a target object.

Each of these events are generated at the target object and can have script run against them.

> *Note that drawing controls, like line and rectangle, can't be dragged and dropped, so they don't have drag and drop events.*

Specifying a Drag Icon

For each object which can be dragged and dropped you can specify a drag icon, which will be displayed when the object is moving. To do this, right-click on the object and select Drag and Drop/Drag Icon...:

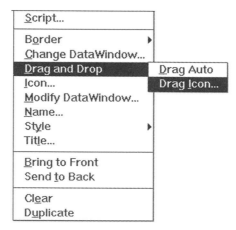

This will take you to an icon selection dialog box, allowing you to select any of the stock icons which ship with PowerBuilder, or you can supply one of your own:

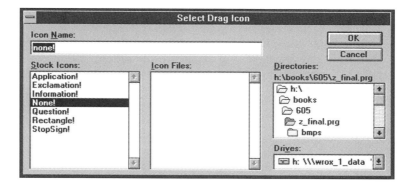

By using these events, you can also dynamically change the icon while an object is moving across a window. We'll take a closer look at how to perform this task in the next chapter.

> *The code for this uses the DragIcon property of objects. For example,*
> **`this.DragIcon = "c:\icon.ico"`**

The other option that is available from the pop-up menu is Drag Auto. When this is turned on, drag mode will be automatically activated whenever a user clicks on an object. This activation occurs instead of the **clicked** event. If Drag Auto is turned off, you will have to take care of manually activating drag mode in your script.

Drag and Drop Functions

There are two drag and drop functions which you can use in your scripts: **Drag()** and **DraggedObject()**. The **Drag()** function starts or ends the dragging of an object and has the following syntax:

```
<control>.Drag  (Dragmode)
```

Dragmode can have three values:

Value	Description
Begin!	This puts a control into drag mode.
Cancel!	This stops the dragging of a control but doesn't trigger a **dragdrop** event.
End!	This stops the dragging of a control, and if it is over a target object, it will trigger a **dragdrop** event.

The **DraggedObject()** function returns the type of object being dragged. This has to be used in conjunction with the **TypeOf()** function, which returns an enumerated data type corresponding to the type of object. You can also determine the name of the object being dragged using the **ClassName()** function.

Multiple Table DataWindow Update

One limitation of the DataWindow is that you can only update one table at a time. When you paint a DataWindow based on a single table, PowerBuilder automatically makes that table updatable. You can see this happen if you observe the DataWindow update characteristics in the DataWindow Painter.

However, if the DataWindow consists of more than one table, PowerBuilder doesn't automatically set these attributes for you - you can't even programmatically set these attributes for multiple tables simultaneously.

Fortunately, this doesn't mean that you can't update a multiple table DataWindow. You always have the ultimate function, `dwModify()`, especially for tasks such as this. For example, let's take the simple join between item_master and transaction_table, as shown below:

```
SELECT "transaction_table"."transaction_no",
    "transaction_table"."item_no",
    "item_master"."item_description", "transaction_table"."quantity",
    "item_master"."balance"
FROM "item_master", "transaction_table"
WHERE ( "item_master"."item_no" = "transaction_table"."item_no" )
```

We can set the transaction_table as updatable, as shown below:

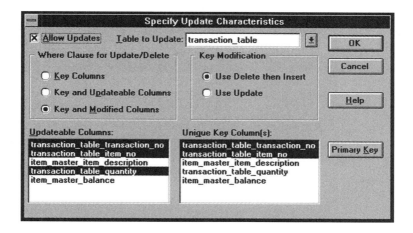

In the script, if you update the DataWindow by calling `dwc_1.Update()`, it will update transaction_table. So how would we go about updating item_master?

The `Update()` function takes two parameters: the first is whether or not to call the `AcceptText()` function internally, while the second determines whether or not to set the update flag. Calling `AcceptText()` performs the necessary validations on the last column in the DataWindow and copies data from the DataWindow Edit buffer to the Primary buffer. When the update flag is reset, PowerBuilder resets all the row status to `NotModified!`.

> *You can see this in action if you issue an **Update()** call again. Since all the rows currently hold a **NotModified!** status, PowerBuilder doesn't generate any SQL statements.*

If you call **Update(True,False)** or **Update(False,False)**, the flag isn't reset, and it wouldn't be changed until another **Update()** function is called, resetting the flag. We can take advantage of this behavior by updating two or more tables while the flag is unset:

```
int lUpdateStatus

lUpdateStatus = dwc_1.Update(true,false)

If lUpdateStatus = 1 Then
   dwc_1.dwModify("transaction_table_transaction_no.Update = No")
   dwc_1.dwModify("transaction_table_item_no.Update = No")
   dwc_1.dwModify("transaction_table_quantity.Update = No")
   dwc_1.dwModify("transaction_table_transaction_no.Key = No")
   dwc_1.dwModify("transaction_table_item_no.Key = No")

   dwc_1.dwdwModify("DataWindow.Table.UpdateTable = ~"item_master~"")

   dwc_1.dwModify("item_master_item_description.Update = No")
   dwc_1.dwModify("item_master_item_description.Update = Yes")
   dwc_1.dwModify("item_master_balance.Update = Yes")
   dwc_1.dwModify("item_master_item_no.Key = Yes")

   lUpdateStatus = dwc_1.Update()
   If lUpdateStatus = 1 Then
      Commit;
   Else
      RollBack ;
      MessageBox("Update", "Error: " + SQLCA.SQLErrorText + &
            "~r" + "No changes made to database" )
   End If

   dwc_1.dwdwModify("DataWindow.Table.UpdateTable = &
         ~"transaction_table~"")

   dwc_1.dwModify("transaction_table_transaction_no.Update = Yes")
   dwc_1.dwModify("transaction_table_item_no.Update = Yes")
   dwc_1.dwModify("transaction_table_quantity.Update = Yes")

   dwc_1.dwModify("transaction_table_transaction_no.Key = Yes")
   dwc_1.dwModify("transaction_table_item_no.Key = Yes")

   dwc_1.dwModify("item_master_item_description.Update = No")
   dwc_1.dwModify("item_master_item_description.Update = No")
   dwc_1.dwModify("item_master_balance.Update = No")
   dwc_1.dwModify("item_master_item_no.Key = No")
```

```
Else
   MessageBox("Update", "Error: " + SQLCA.SQLErrorText + &
      "~r" + "No changes made to database" )
   RollBack ;
End If
```

First, we call **Update(True,False)**, which will update the table and won't reset the flag. Then we make all the columns in the transaction_table not updatable and also let PowerBuilder know not to use the primary key of transaction_table for future updates.

Now we set all the columns in the item_master table as updatable and also let PowerBuilder know which key it has to use for an update. When this stage is complete, we can call **Update()**, still without a flag, which will reset the row status for all columns after a successful update.

If you have more than two tables, you can call **Update(True,False)** for all tables except the last table, which should set the flag and cause all the tables to be updated.

DropDownDataWindows

A column in a DataWindow can be one of six different types. We've looked at most of these and seen situations where each style has its advantages, but one that we haven't looked at in detail is the **DropDownDataWindow**. When you use the other styles, the information you supply is contained in the PowerBuilder library. This is fine for static data, but if you want to use dynamic data, the best solution is to use a DropDownDataWindow.

As an example, when adding a new item to our item_master table, the measuring_unit should exist in the measuring_unit table. We can use a DropDownDataWindow to display the information already contained in the measuring_unit table and allow the user to select from the available options, rather than checking the existence of the measuring_unit by issuing an SQL statement.

To do this, we would need to create a DataWindow for the measuring_units table, based upon a SQL Select data source with tabular presentation style:

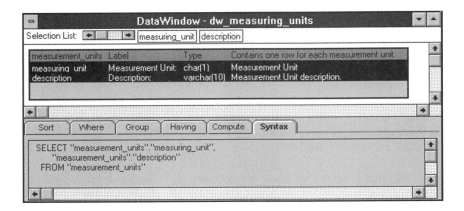

Now, we have to change the edit style of the measuring_unit column in the dw_item_master DataWindow by right-clicking on the column and selecting EditStyles/DropDownDataWindow...:

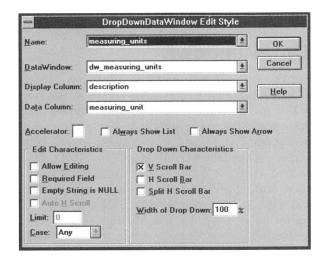

We select the DataWindow we just painted from the DataWindow prompt and fill in the rest of the details as shown. Selecting the Always Show Arrow option will display an arrow at the right side of the column in the DataWindow.

Now, if we preview the dw_item_master DataWindow, you'll see that for the measuring_unit column we have a DropDownDataWindow containing the details from the measuring_units table:

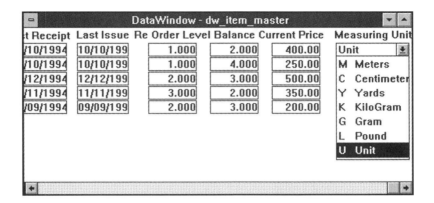

DDDW Dynamic Modification

All the attributes that you set in the DropDownDataWindow Edit Style dialog box can also be modified using **dwModify()**. The important attributes that you can modify using this method include:

▲ name

▲ datacolumn

▲ displaycolumn

For example, if you wanted to make measuring_unit the display column for the above DropDown DataWindow, you would use the following code:

```
datawindowchild dwc1

dwc_1.dwModify( "measuring_unit.dddw.displaycolumn=~"measuring_unit~"")

dwc1.Settransobject( sqlca )
dwc1.retrieve( lParameter1 )
```

All the other attributes can be set in a similar way.

Windows SDK Function Calls

No development software is capable of doing everything you need, and PowerBuilder is no exception. Sometimes, you may be able to get more control over your application by exploring the operating system facilities. PowerBuilder allows you to address the underlying operating system's capabilities by making calls to Windows SDK functions. The following topic covers how to use the Windows APIs in your PowerBuilder applications.

You can access Windows API calls from DLLs or EXEs. Before using these functions, you need to declare them as either global or local external functions. This lets PowerBuilder know where these functions are, what parameters they take and the return values they offer.

Select Declare from the menu and either of the Global External or Local External function menu options. In the resulting dialog box, you need to declare the function or the subroutine using one of the following:

```
[ Access ] FUNCTION ReturnDataType FunctionName &
( [REF] [DataType1 Arg1, ..., ] ) LIBRARY LibName
```
or
```
[ Access ] SUBROUTINE SubroutineName &
( [REF] [DataType1 Arg1, ...,] ) LIBRARY LibName
```

We've used a Windows SDK call in our application to look at the system resources. This is the w_system_info window, which is opened by the System Info... button on the w_about window:

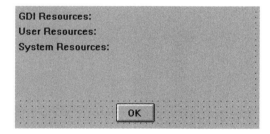

This contains a DataWindow control, which is defined in the **open** event of the window:

```
Timer( 10 )

dwc_1.SetTransObject( SQLCA )
dwc_1.InsertRow( 0 )

dwc_1.setitem(1,"system"," " + string( GetFreeSystemResources(0) ) + &
    " % ")
dwc_1.setitem(1,"gdi"," " + string( GetFreeSystemResources(1) ) + " % ")
dwc_1.setitem(1,"user"," " + string( GetFreeSystemResources(2) ) + " % ")
```

This simply calls the **GetFreeSystemResources()** function and assigns the returned values to the DataWindow control. The function is defined as a local external function, as follows:

FUNCTION uint **GetFreeSystemResources** (unit resource) **LIBRARY** "user.exe"

When you look at this window, you'll see the following:

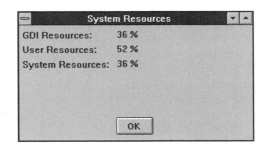

Multimedia and PowerBuilder

Windows provides a variety of multimedia services through the **Media Control Interface** (MCI). MCI provides applications with device independent capabilities for controlling audio and visual peripherals. PowerBuilder applications can use MCI to control any of the supported multimedia devices.

*The important DLL for MCI communication is **MMSYSTEM.DLL**.*

The MCI includes two interfaces:

▲ **Low-Level Interface** (Command Message Interface): Consists of C constants and structures.

▲ **High-Level Interface** (Command String Interface): Textual version of Low-Level Interfaces that are in an easy-to-read format.

Windows converts **Command Strings** into **Command Messages** before sending them to the MCI Driver for processing. Windows scans both the **WIN.INI** and the **SYSTEM.INI**, loading the appropriate drivers into memory. It then processes the commands sent by the application and sends them to the appropriate driver for execution.

491

The [MCI EXTENSIONS] section in **WIN.INI** contains all the required file extensions and related physical devices names.

```
[mci extensions]
wav=waveaudio
mid=sequencer
rmi=sequencer
avi=AVIVideo
cmv=CorelMOVE
mwf=CorelMOVE
```

After examining this **.INI** file, the **MMSYSTEM.DLL** reads the [MCI] section in the **SYSTEM.INI** to discover the appropriate driver and loads it. For example, the physical device for MDI extension is a sequencer. The driver that plays the sequencer is **MCISEQ.DRV**, which is listed in the [MCI] section in **SYSTEM.INI**.

```
[mci]
WaveAudio=mciwave.drv
Sequencer=mciseq.drv
CDAudio=mcicda.drv
AVIVideo=mciavi.drv
CorelMOVE=C:\COREL40\PROGRAMS\mcicmv40.drv
```

Windows comes with the following drivers:

Device Name	Driver Name
sequencer	**MCISEQ.DRV**
waveaudio	**MCIWAVE.DRV**

There are a few others which come with the SDK, and if you need more you can buy them from third-party vendors. There are two important functions available in the high-level interface, which are enough for any PowerBuilder application. These are **mciSendString()** and **mciGetErrorString()**.

We can declare these as external functions as we did above, and then use them in our PowerBuilder applications. For example, we could declare **mciSendString()** as follows:

```
Function Long mciSendString(String lpstrCommand, Long lpstrReturnString, &
     Int uReturnLength, Int hWindCallBack) Library "MMSystem"
```

The first parameter is the most used parameter and is the command string to execute, for example, **"Play c:\windows\ringin.wav"**.

The following list illustrates the most common commands used as the first parameter of **mciSendString()**:

```
Open  <Device ID>  [Parameters]  [Notify]  [Wait]
Play  <Device ID>  [Parameters]  [Notify]  [Wait]
Close <Device ID>  [Notify]  [Wait]
```

The **Open** command loads the driver into memory (if it isn't already loaded) and assigns a **Device ID** that you can use to identify the device in subsequent commands. If you don't include a **Wait** parameter, the application immediately gets control after issuing the command to the driver, instead of waiting until the operation is complete.

The **Play** command has a lot of parameters depending on the type of device. For example, you can specify the first and last track numbers to play from a CD, such as 'Play CDAUDIO from 6 to 10'. If it is a video device, you can specify it to play fast, slow, reverse and so on.

Finally, you need to close the device.

Some other useful basic commands are **Record**, **Pause**, **Resume**, **Stop** and **Seek**. To see how use to multimedia in a PowerBuilder application, you should look at the u_external_function_win32 UserObject in the **PBEXAMUO.PBL** library, which comes with PowerBuilder.

MAPI

With the emergence of powerful enterprise-wide workgroup applications for scheduling, forms routing, order processing, project management and more, the need for such a communications backbone has never been greater. Unfortunately, today's messaging systems and applications have vastly different user interfaces, and development tools are largely incompatible with one another.

The advantage of having a messaging subsystem is that messaging applications don't have to rely on the particular code of each vendor's messaging product. Instead, developers can create applications that will work reliably and consistently for all customers who are using the operating system, regardless of the underlying messaging services or network system.

Under Windows, Microsoft provides a standard interface, 'Messaging Application Programming Interface (MAPI)', to ensure complete system independence for messaging applications.

Developers can rely on the common user interface and the message functions available on every user's computer (via the messaging subsystem of the operating system). Consequently, the developer of a PowerBuilder program who wants to add Send Mail as a menu option is assured that this command will always look and work the same way for every user, regardless of which messaging or network system is running in the background.

The MAPI messaging subsystem works just like the Print subsystem in the Windows operating system. All Windows applications share common dialog boxes to prompt the user for printing their documents and selecting printers. Different print drivers, which work with the Windows operating system, rather than directly with each application, allow applications to work with a variety of printers. The Print Manager and Spooler let a wordprocessor print to a network laser printer, for example, while a spreadsheet is printing to a local dot-matrix printer. MAPI's messaging subsystem works in the same way - different messaging applications communicate to a variety of messaging services.

If you have Windows for Workgroups, you can make use of MAPI functions. We'll show you a simple example of how to call these functions from within your PowerBuilder applications. Run the mapi_demo_sending_mail application in the **MAPI.PBL** library:

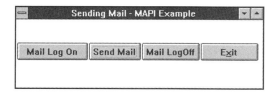

This is a simple window which lets you log on, send mail and log off.

Logging on to the Mail System

When you click on the Mail Log On button, you'll be prompted to sign in to a mail session:

If you don't already have mailboxes and passwords set up, you'll have to read the documentation which comes with Windows for Workgroups to see how to do this.

The code which brings up this window is as follows:

```
iMailSession = CREATE MailSession
iMailRetCode = iMailSession.MailLogOn( MailNewSession! )
```

We simply declare a variable of type MailSession and create an instance of it. You have to declare two instance variables in all:

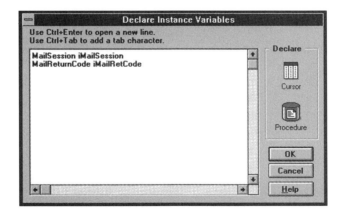

Once you've signed in, you'll come back to our PowerBuilder window. In the background, you'll be able to see that the MS Mail Spooler is running:

Specifying Address Details

Now that you've signed on, you can send mail by clicking on the Send Mail button. This will bring up an address window to allow you to select who you want to send a message to:

This is the code behind the Send Mail button:

```
MailMessage lMailMessage
MailReturnCode lMailRetCode
MailFileDescription lmFileDetails

lmFileDetails.FileName = "Letter2.Doc"
lmFileDetails.PathName = "C:\wrox\"
lmFileDetails.FileType = MailAttach!
lmFileDetails.Position = -1

lMailMessage.Subject = "Last JAD session details."
lMailMessage.NoteText = "See attached file."
lMailMessage.AttachmentFile[1] = lmFileDetails
```

```
iMailSession.MailAddress( lMailMessage )

iMailSession.MailSend( lMailMessage )
```

This declares **lMailMessage** as a **MailMessage,** and **lmFileDetails** as a **MailFileDescription**. **lMailMessage** is the message that we want to send, and **lmFileDetails** contains the details of any file that we wish to attach to the message.

We set up various attributes for these variables, including the name of the file we want to send, the text for our message and any files we wish to attach to the message. The final line sends the message. You should see the message and attached file appear at the recipient's machine.

The full list of attributes for a **MailMessage** are as follows:

Attribute	Data type
ReceiptRequested	Boolean
MessageSent	Boolean
Unread	Boolean
Subject	String
NoteText	String
MessageType	String
DateReceived	String
ConversationID	String
Recipient[ ]	mailRecipient array
AttachmentFile[ ]	mailFileDescription array

Sending a Message

If you want to allow the user to fill in the address details and create a message from scratch, rather than assigning all the attributes of the **MailMessage** and **MailFileDescription**, you can simply call:

```
lMailSession.MailSend( lMailMessage )
```

This function sends the message to the specified user if details are supplied as the parameter. If not, it will prompt the user to supply the details:

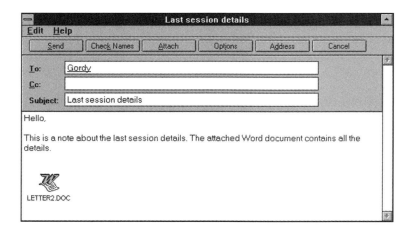

For more information on using MAPI, check in PowerBuilder's on-line help and the documentation that comes with Windows for Workgroups.

The final bit of code behind the Mail Log Off button closes down the mail session and destroys it:

```
iMailSession.MailLogOff()
DESTROY iMailSession
```

Summary

We've covered a lot of interesting things in this chapter, from adding extra functionality to our application, to showing you a stand-alone example of using MAPI. If you look at the completed version of our application, you'll see that we've implemented a lot of the interesting things, as well as some extras that we didn't go into detail about - a DataWindow search facility, for instance.

> *The code to achieve this is similar to other code which we've already discussed.*

In the final version of our application we've implemented a lot of this functionality by creating a class library of generic functions and windows which can be reused in other applications. As such, you may find that some of the code we've shown you doesn't exactly match to what you'll find in the final version of our application. However, we have tried to show you the code as generic as possible. To use the class library, we simply ensure that the class library 'pibble' is in our application's library list. This cements the links and enables our application to call any object which exists in the class library.

In the next chapter, we'll discuss UserObjects. This is probably the most useful object-oriented feature available to PowerBuilder and allows you to write generic code, which can be reused again and again.

UserObjects

We've already looked at the theory and some of the benefits of using object-oriented programming techniques. In this chapter we'll look in greater detail at one of the major object-oriented features of PowerBuilder - UserObjects.

We'll look at the various types of UserObject which you can create, both visual and non-visual, and we'll see exactly how these can be used to speed up the application development process.

In this chapter, we will cover:

▲ The various types of UserObjects

▲ How to implement context sensitive help

▲ The use of external objects

▲ Tips for programming with UserObjects

Chapter 15

Introduction

One of the main features of object-oriented programming is reusability. In an application, you will normally have a selection of controls or objects scattered throughout your design that essentially perform the same task. Two good examples of this are the Print CommandButtons which allow users to receive hard copies of what they see on screen, and the related Printer CommandButtons that allow users to specify printer parameters, and so on.

If you have a large number of windows, you might want to allow your users to print from every one, a feature that would usually mean rewriting the same piece of code many times. UserObjects provide a way round this problem by allowing you to reuse one object or a piece of code many times throughout your application.

UserObjects allow you to customize PowerBuilder's standard controls, to make use of third party controls, and to create your own. You can reuse these objects and so simplify standardization of the functionality in your applications. As an example of this, you could use the same Print CommandButton UserObject throughout your application and never need to worry about, or spend time checking, the functionality being the same in each instance.

UserObjects can be broadly divided into two categories:

▲ Visual

▲ Class (non-visual)

Let's take a look at each of these categories in turn.

Visual UserObjects

A visual UserObject is a control or a set of controls with a certain functionality. Our Print CommandButton is an example of a visual UserObject. There are four types of visual UserObjects:

▲ Standard

▲ Custom

▲ External

▲ VBX

Class (Non-Visual UserObjects)

This type of UserObject doesn't have a visual component - it only has functionality. For example, you could write a function `DisplayErrorMessage()` and then call this function whenever you need it in your application.

Non-Visual UserObjects allow you to write business rules and to perform other processing which can then be reused as many times as required. There are three types of non-visual UserObjects:

- Standard
- Custom
- C++

Creating a UserObject

To create a UserObject, click on the UserObject icon and select the New button:

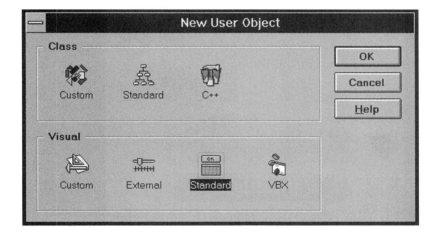

Note that the C++ option will only be available if you have the Enterprise version of PowerBuilder or have installed the Advanced Developer's Kit.

From here, you have to specify which type of UserObject you want to create. Let's look at how we created our example from Chapter 12 which displayed various quotes when different CommandButtons were clicked.

Select the Standard icon in the Visual group, click OK and select commandbutton from the list of standard visual objects:

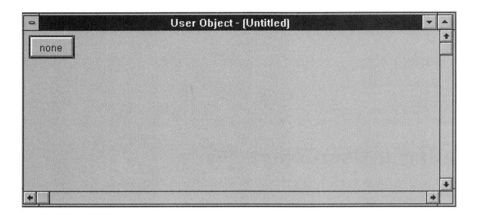

The UserObject development environment is similar to that found in the Window Painter and a CommandButton should be ready and waiting for you.

> If you remember back to our discussion of inheritance, we have just created our own class, crossing the boundary from PowerBuilder to User Defined Classes. When we have added our own functionality to this CommandButton, we will be able to create instances of it for use in our application.

Creating a CommandButton UserObject

All the events that are available to a standard CommandButton control are available to this UserObject. In order to customize our UserObject, PowerBuilder offers us the chance to declare variables, structures, functions and our own user events.

To complete our CommandButton UserObject, we need to add the functionality that will allow it to display a message when it is clicked. To begin with, we have to define the properties of the UserObject. First, change the size of the CommandButton to reflect the size that we had in our example and then right-click on it and select Pointer...:

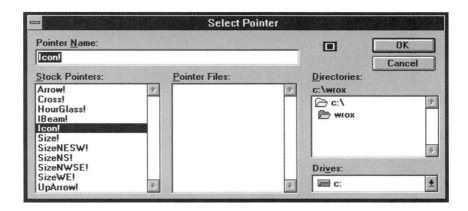

This allows you to define the pointer shape that will be displayed when the mouse moves over the object. Select Icon! from the list of stock pointers and click OK. Now, go into the Script Painter and type in the following script for the **clicked** event:

```
// Event: clicked
// Object: CommandButton UserObject
MessageBox("This is a MessageBox",This.Tag)
```

We've already explained this code in Chapter 12, so you should know that it displays a message box with the message related to the tag value of the current object.

> When creating a UserObject, you should try to avoid hard coding anything into the scripts. By hard coding your scripts, you are reducing the flexibility of the UserObject, the cornerstone of their usefulness. In this case, we've used the This keyword so that the displayed message depends on the object that is clicked.

Save the UserObject as uo_commandbutton and create a new window. Now instead of adding CommandButtons to the window, add our new UserObject. To mimic our previous example, you need to add four copies of our UserObject to the window and label them Volume, Life, Sunny and World.

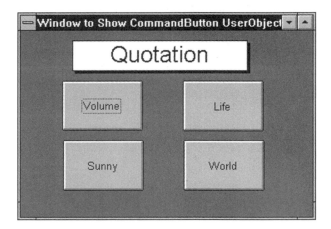

Now you need to type in and assign the tag values by selecting Edit/Tag List..., so that when you run the window, clicking on any of the CommandButtons will bring up the relevant quotation. Also note that moving the mouse over any of the CommandButtons will display the different cursor:

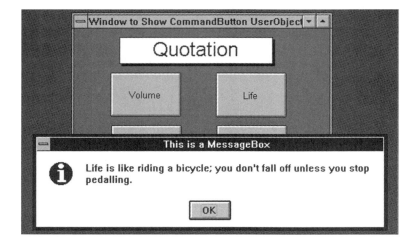

The code written for the UserObject class is available to each UserObject instance that you have placed in the window and if we change that code in the UserObject class, the changes will be reflected in each instance of the object. This provides you with more reusability, easier maintenance and less time consuming development.

Let's now go on to create a more complex standard UserObject that we can use in our Stock Control application.

Creating a DataWindow UserObject

By default, you can't select multiple rows, either continuously or randomly, in a DataWindow; you are restricted to one row at a time. This can be quite restrictive, so let's look at how to create a DataWindow UserObject which does have this functionality.

> Note that this kind of functionality is already supported by programs such as File Manager. It has been commonly accepted that the users needs to use the *Ctrl* and *Shift* keys in conjunction with a mouse click to select random or continuous items respectively, and so it would make sense to copy this standard.

Invoke the UserObject Painter and this time create a Standard DataWindow object:

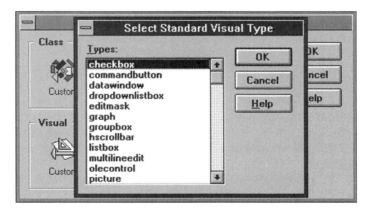

Chapter 5

The logic for this UserObject is quite simple. We will store the selected row in an instance variable and if the user then uses the *Shift* key when selecting a new row, we will select all the rows in a loop between the previously selected and the current row. If they use the *Ctrl* key, we simply add the current row to the list of selected rows.

We could write the entire code in the object's `clicked` event, but splitting the logic between two events, one standard and one custom, would be better. Therefore, let's create a user defined event called ue_shiftclicked and assign the pbm_custom75 event ID to it:

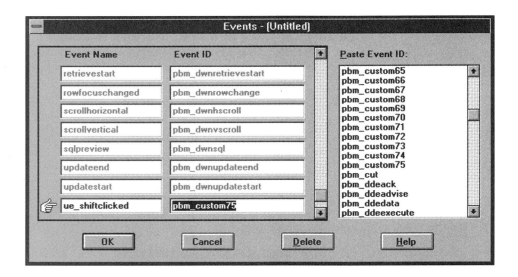

Next, we have to declare an instance variable to hold the selected rows, so select Declare/Instance Variables... and declare the following variable:

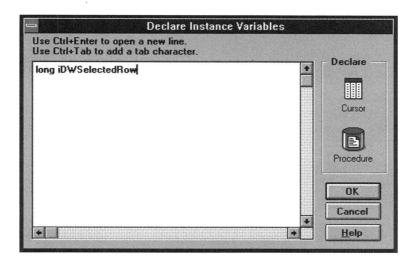

Now put the following code in the **clicked** event for the UserObject:

```
// Object: DataWindow control UserObject
// Event: Clicked

int lRowNo
lRowNo = this.getclickedrow()

if lRowNo > 0 then
   if KeyDown(KeyControl!) then
      this.selectrow(lRowNo,true)
   else
      this.selectrow(0,false)
      this.selectrow(lRowNo,true)
   end if
   if KeyDown(KeyShift!) then
      this.TriggerEvent ("ue_ShiftClicked")
      return
   end if
end if
```

```
iDWSelectedRow = lRowNo
this.SetRow(lRowNo)
```

The **KeyDown()** function is used to establish which key the user has pressed. If the user clicked with the left mouse button without using any key combination, we select the clicked row, deselecting any others. If the *Ctrl* key combination is used, we add the highlighted row to our current selection and if the *Shift* key combination is used we trigger the user event.

> The parameter for the **KeyDown()** is an enumerated data type. PowerBuilder's on-line help contains a full list of all the keys that can be used as parameters for the **KeyDown()** function.

If you look at the list of events that are possible for the UserObject, you'll see that our new user event ue_shiftclicked is now available. We need to put the following code into this event:

```
// Object: DataWindow Control UserObject
// Event: ue_shiftclicked

int lOldRow, lNewRow, lStartRow, lEndRow, lRowCounter
lOldRow = iDWSelectedRow
lNewRow = this.getclickedrow()

if lOldRow > lNewRow then
   lStartRow = lNewRow
   lEndRow = lOldRow
else
   lStartRow = lOldRow
   lEndRow = lNewRow
end if

for lRowCounter = lStartRow to lEndRow Step 1
   this.SelectRow( lRowCounter, true )
next

this.SetRow( lNewRow )
this.SetColumn( 1 )
```

You should be aware that the currently selected row may be either greater or less than the previously clicked row. For example, if you click on row 10 and click on row 16 with a *Shift* combination, the **lStartRow** is 10 and **lEndRow** is 16, but you might click on another row with a *Shift* combination that is less than 10, say 5. In this case, **lStartRow** will be 5 and **lEndRow** will be 10.

These endpoints are organized into sensible start and final variables by the **if** statement.

The **for** loop is used by the **SelectRow()** function to select all the rows from **lStartRow** to **lEndRow**. The second argument to the **SelectRow** decides whether to select (**true**) or deselect (**false**) the specified row. After this we store the currently selected row in the **iDWSelectedRow** variable.

Save this UserObject as uo_dw_multiple_row_select and to use it:

▲ Open up the w_item_master window and delete the dwc_1 DataWindow control.

▲ Add our new UserObject control and resize it to cover dwc_2.

▲ Rename it as dwc_1 and link it to the dw_item_master DataWindow.

We've effectively replaced dwc_1 with our UserObject. To gain the full functionality of dwc_1, you'll also have to copy the scripts that were written for its various events.

If you run the window as it is, you'll be able to see the effect of our new functionality:

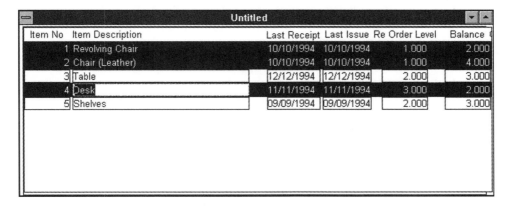

As you can see, we can now select multiple rows on the DataWindow.

Context Sensitive Help for DataWindow Controls

Like any other control in a window, you can specify tag values for the DataWindow control and then use them to display context sensitive help. However this is restricted to the DataWindow as a whole. If you want to display different textual help messages for each column in the DataWindow control, you will encounter some problems.

To solve this problem, we need to find out which column the user is currently focused upon and then supply an appropriate message. For the first part of the problem, we can make use of the **itemfocuschanged** event. When a user presses the *Tab* key or clicks on another column, either the **itemchanged**, **itemerror** or **itemfocuschanged** events will be triggered depending on whether or not the data has been changed, and if it has changed whether the new entry passes any predefined validation rules.

By using the **GetColumnName()** function in the **itemchanged** event, we can get PowerBuilder to return the current column and by using the same command in the **itemfocuschanged** event, we can get the next column name in the tab order.

For example, if the user presses *Tab* when the focus is on item_no in the w_item_master window, the **GetColumnName()** function in the **itemchanged** event would return item_no, while the same function in the **itemfocuschanged** event would return item_description.

The following code gets the column name, uses the **dwDescribe()** function to obtain the tag values and sets the Microhelp. Put this script in the **itemfocuschanged** event for the DataWindow Control UserObject that we have just created.

```
// Object: DataWindow Control UserObject
// Event: ItemFocusChanged

string lColumnName, lTagValue, lArgument
lColumnName = GetColumnName()
lArgument = trim( lColumnName ) + ".Tag"
lTagValue = dwDescribe( lArgument )
```

```
if lTagValue = "" or isnull( lTagValue ) or trim( lTagValue ) = "?" &
     or trim( lTagValue ) = "!" then
   lTagValue = "Ready"
end if

w_mdi_main_with_microhelp.setmicrohelp( lTagValue )
```

The **dwDescribe()** function returns an exclamation mark (!) when an argument is bad and returns a question mark (?) when the specified attribute has no value. We can use these returns in a test, setting **lTagValue** to 'Ready'. This is the default value that will appear in the status bar if anything goes wrong.

If you run the w_mdi_main_with_microhelp window and tab between the columns, you'll see the Microhelp in the status bar change to reflect the column name:

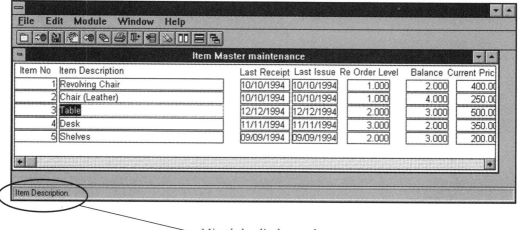

Microhelp displays column name

Custom UserObjects

A custom UserObject is created by grouping more than one control together. For example, in the first version of our w_item_master window we had a series of CommandButtons and a DataWindow control, but by using a custom UserObject, we could group all of these controls together.

PowerBuilder allows you to place UserObjects in custom versions and you can inherit them from other custom UserObjects. This allows us to create any type of UserObject that we can think of, using any of the objects offered by PowerBuilder, or any of the objects that we have customized or inherited from the PowerBuilder parents.

One way of using UserObjects is to solve the multiple selection problem. We've already discussed how we can allow a user to use the standard *Shift* and *Ctrl* keys to select more than one item from a list. However, if you want to improve the user-friendliness of your application, you can provide them with a shuffle box. These are becoming ever more popular in a wide variety of software packages. The following example is from Microsoft's Access database package:

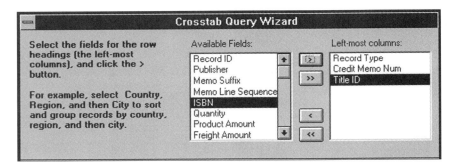

It is based on a very simple idea. The user simply highlights the entries that he is interested in and passes them over to the right hand side of the window. The user can also remove previous selections or pass all of the options from one side to the other at a click of a button. This is very useful because it allows you to include functionality that acts upon the order that the entries appear in the list.

These types of window are useful for multi-stage selections such as when you are defining the fields for a query or the sort order that the query is supposed to use.

shuffle_rows_between_dws

This is the shuffle_rows_between_dws application in the **SHUFFLE.PBL** library. If you run this application, you'll get the standard login window:

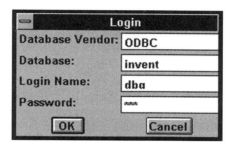

Login as usual to the **INVENT.DB** supplying the usual parameters and you'll see the shuffle window:

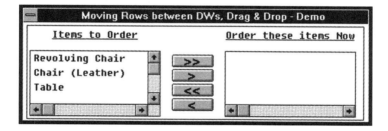

You can see that this window contains two DataWindow controls, one of which contains the item_descriptions from the item_master table. We'll see later how you can control the data which appears here, allowing you to customize this UserObject for reuse in your own applications.

The four buttons are what you would expect on this type of dialog box:

>>   This allows you to move all the entries from left to right.

>   This allows you to move a single highlighted entry from left to right.

<<   This allows you to move all the entries from right to left.

<   This allows you to move a single highlighted entry from right to left.

Try clicking on the top button to see what happens:

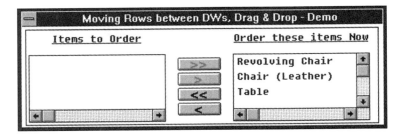

All the entries move to the right hand DataWindow control and the 'move to the right' buttons are disabled as there is nothing else in the left hand control.

Note that we've also implemented the *Shift* and *Ctrl* key functionality that we created in the previous example. To see this working, try clicking on the entry Revolving Chair and then hold down the *Ctrl* key and click on the entry Table:

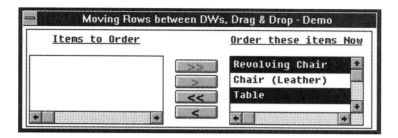

The two entries are highlighted simultaneously and if you now click on the single 'move to the left' button, you'll see that both of the selected entries are moved across:

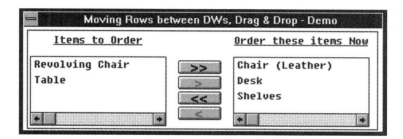

The *Shift* key works in the same way, allowing you to select a range of entries to move from one side to the other.

Drag and Drop

We've also implemented drag and drop features which allow you to drag an entry from one control and drop it into the other. To see this working, select one of the entries, hold the mouse button down and drag it to the other side:

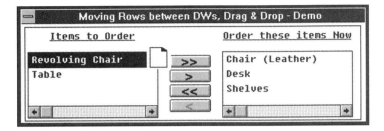

When you start dragging, PowerBuilder automatically changes the mouse pointer to the Drag icon. As you drag the item across the window, the icon changes:

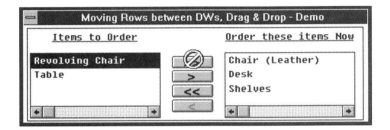

This is similar to the standard Stop icon used in commercial applications to indicate that the item can't be dropped here. As you move into the other control the icon changes again:

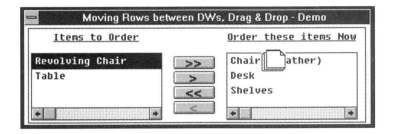

This icon indicates that the item can be dropped here, so if you release the mouse button the item will be copied across:

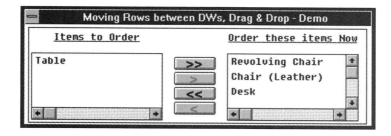

This will work in either direction, but it won't let you drag and drop multiple items even if you try to use it in conjunction with the *Ctrl* or *Shift* keys.

How Does It Work?

There are several important components to this application. The following figure illustrates the whole process:

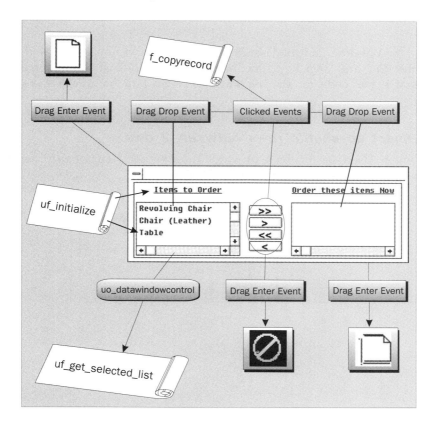

519

As you can see it is quite complex so we'll look at each of them in turn, highlighting the areas where you can customize the components for reuse in your own applications.

The UserObject uo_datawindowcontrol

Invoke the UserObject Painter and open this UserObject:

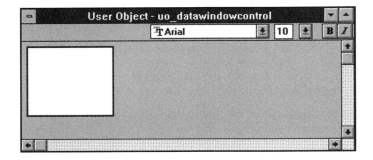

This is the DataWindow control UserObject which we've already created to implement the *Ctrl* and *Shift* key functionality. If you look at the event list, you'll see that it has code for the **ue_shiftclicked** and **ue_ctrlclicked** user events.

The UserObject uo_shuffle_rows_between_2_dws

This is the main UserObject which provides most of the functionality for the shuffle window:

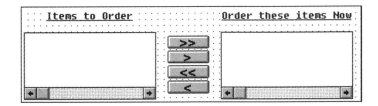

The two DataWindow controls are inherited from our DataWindow control UserObject. You can see this if you click on the Script icon and look at the list of events:

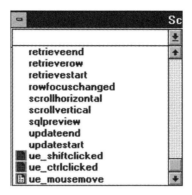

You can see that the **ue_shiftclicked** and **ue_ctrlclicked** events are ancestor scripts of the DataWindow controls. This is object-oriented design working in practice; when we inherited the DataWindow controls, we gained all the functionality of the previously defined UserObject. This means we don't have to write the same code over and over again.

Functions

A function is basically a collection of PowerScript statements which perform some processing. If you have a series of statements which you will use several times in your application, then it makes sense to create a function and simply call the function each time you want to execute the statements.

Functions consist of two distinct components: a function declaration and the actual code. The function declaration defines the arguments that the function uses as variables in the code. The code manipulates the arguments to achieve the required functionality.

> For an analogy to traditional programming languages, you can
> think of functions as subroutines. For the desk-top applications,
> this analogy could be re-directed to that of a macro.

We use several functions in this example:

1 `f_copyrecord`:   This is used to copy the records
between the controls.

2 `uf_initialize`:   This is used to initialize the left and
right DataWindow Controls and headings.

3 `uf_get_selected_list`:   This is used to send all the selected
row values back.

We'll look briefly at each of these functions for our example.

f_copyrecord

As with all functions, this function is defined in the Function Painter. Invoke
the painter and open the function:

```
String lColType
int lTotCol, lColCounter
Long lCurRow
lCurRow = pm_destination_dw.InsertRow(0)
lTotCol = integer( pm_source_dw.dwDescribe( "datawindow.column.count"))

for lColCounter = 1 to lTotCol
   lColType = pm_source_dw.dwDescribe("#" + String( lColCounter ) + &
        ".ColType")
   choose case upper( left( lColType,5))
   case "CHAR("pm_destination_dw.SetItem( lCurRow, lColCounter, &
        pm_source_dw.GetItemString( pm_row, lColCounter ))
      case "NUMBE","DECIM"
         pm_destination_dw.SetItem( lCurRow, lColCounter, &
            pm_source_dw.GetItemNumber( pm_row, lColCounter ))
      case "DATE"
         pm_destination_dw.SetItem( lCurRow, lColCounter, &
            pm_source_dw.GetItemDate( pm_row, lColCounter ))
      case "DATET"
         pm_destination_dw.SetItem( lCurRow, lColCounter, &
```

```
                pm_source_dw.GetItemDateTime( pm_row, lColCounter ))
        case "TIME"
            pm_destination_dw.SetItem( lCurRow, lColCounter, &
                pm_source_dw.GetItemTime( pm_row, lColCounter ))
    end choose
next

return lCurRow
```

This inserts a row made up from all the columns within the source DataWindow into the destination DataWindow. The arguments for the **dwDescribe()** function return the total number of columns to the source DataWindow, while the **for** loop determines the data type of the columns. The **case** statement simply calls the appropriate function, depending on the data type, to get the column value and then copies the value into the destination DataWindow.

> *We use the first five characters of the data type to decide which case statement to execute as this is the minimum number required to give unique values. If we used less than five, we wouldn't be able to distinguish between **DATE** and **DATETIME**.*

To see the function declaration, select Edit/Function Declaration...:

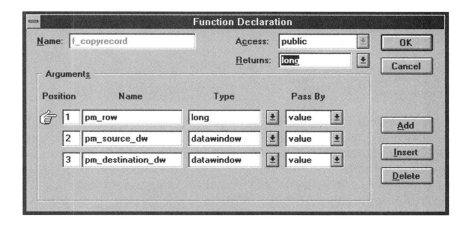

We declare the access level as Public so that the function is available to all objects in the application. We don't need to return anything from this function, but we do need to pass three parameters to it, each by value.

You can send any number of parameters to a function, but you have to specify how they are passed: either by value or by reference:

1 By Value: When a parameter is passed by value, the function gets a copy of the parameter so that any changes done in the function are kept within the scope of the function. When the function completes execution the parameter retains its previous value.

2 By Reference: When a parameter is passed by reference, the address of the parameter is passed to the function so that any changes made in the function are retained when the function completes execution.

This completes the definition of the **f_copyrecord** function.

uf_initialize

This is declared at the UserObject level. Select Declare/User Object Functions... to see the code:

```
st_left.text = heading_left
st_right.text = heading_right
dwc_left.dataobject = dw1
dwc_right.dataobject = dw1
dwc_left.SetTransObject( tranobject)
dwc_right.SetTransObject( tranobject)
dwc_left.retrieve()
```

Since this is a reusable object, we neither specified any text for the StaticText controls nor assigned any DataWindow objects to the dwc_left and dwc_right DataWindow controls. In order to do this, we write an initialization function which sets these controls. The function passes a transaction object as a parameter which makes it more flexible if you are using more than one transaction in an application.

The function declaration is as follows:

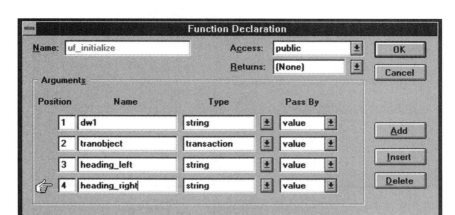

Again, we declare the function as public, we don't return anything from it, but we pass the function arguments by value.

uf_get_selected_list

This function is also declared at the UserObject level:

```
Integer lTotRows, i
lTotRows = dwc_right.RowCount()
If lTotRows > 0 Then
    p_selected_list = dwc_right.GetItemString(1,1)
    For i = 2 to lTotRows Step 1
        p_selected_list = p_selected_list + "~t" + dwc_right.GetItemString(i,1)
    Next
End If
    Return
```

This sends all of the selected row values back using the `GetItemString()` function. The declaration for this is as follows:

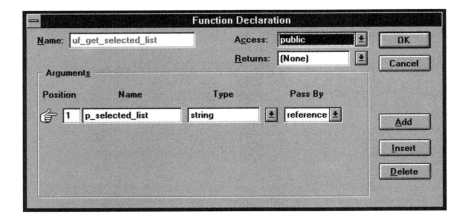

As you can see, there is only one argument, and it is passed by reference.

This completes the definition of the various functions. The final scripts are for the DataWindow controls and CommandButtons on the UserObject.

The DataWindow Control Scripts

The following code is in the **clicked** event of the dwc_left control:

```
if this.GetClickedRow() > 0 then
   cb_transfer_to_right.Enabled = TRUE
else
   cb_transfer_to_right.Enabled = FALSE
end if
```

This simply checks if any rows are selected in the control and enables or disables the cb_transfer_to_right CommandButton accordingly. The logic for the other DataWindow control is exactly the same.

> *Because the script for both these DataWindows is almost identical, we could implement the script in another function and then call the same function from both DataWindow events, passing the relevant parameters to distinguish between them.*

The CommandButtons Code

The code for all the CommandButtons is very similar, so we'll just look at one of them - the cb_transfer_to_right button. This is the **clicked** event code:

```
/* Copy all the selected rows to the right side DataWindow and
   delete each row when copied. Then sort both the DataWindows
   on the first column */

Long lSelectedRow = 0
string lColName
lSelectedRow = dwc_left.GetSelectedRow( lSelectedRow )
if lSelectedRow = 0 then return

do while lSelectedRow <> 0
   f_CopyRecord( lSelectedRow, dwc_left, dwc_right )
   dwc_left.DeleteRow( lSelectedRow )
   lSelectedRow = lSelectedRow - 1
   lSelectedRow = dwc_left.GetSelectedRow( lSelectedRow )
loop

lColName = dwc_left.dwdescribe("#1.Name")
dwc_left.setsort( lColName + " A" )
dwc_left.Sort()

lColName = dwc_right.dwdescribe("#1.Name")
dwc_right.setsort( lColName + " A" )
dwc_right.Sort()

this.Enabled = FALSE
if dwc_left.rowcount() = 0 then cb_select_all.enabled = false
if dwc_right.rowcount() > 0 then cb_unselect_all.enabled = true
```

In our design, we have allowed the user to select more than one row using the *Ctrl* and *Shift* keys, so we have to take care to transfer all the selected rows. **GetSelectedRow()** gives the next highlighted row after the argument row number and once we know the selected row, we call the **f_copy_record** function to copy the specified row from the source DataWindow to the destination DataWindow.

Once the row has been copied over, we delete it from the source DataWindow and sort the destination DataWindow on the first column of the DataWindow. The arguments passed to the **dwDescribe()** function return the name of the first column in the DataWindow and we use the **SetSort()** function to specify the sort criteria, before performing the sort using **Sort()**.

*Note that if you don't specify a sort criteria using **SetSort()** and you haven't set it before, PowerBuilder will prompt for a sort criteria.*

Implementing the Drag and Drop Functionality

There are several little scripts that we've written for various drag and drop events in the UserObject. We won't go through all of these, but we'll explain what events we use and what they do:

Object	Event	Function
dwc_left	dragdrop	Triggers the 'Copy to the left' CommandButton
	dragenter	Sets the drag icon
CommandButtons	dragenter	Sets the drag icon
dwc_right	dragdrop	Triggers the 'Copy to the right' CommandButton
	dragenter	Sets the drag icon

We've supplied three icons, one for the left control, one for the right and one for when the mouse is over the CommandButtons. We simply specify each of these icons in the relevant **dragenter** events. So, for each of the CommandButtons the code is:

```
this.dragicon = "c:\wrox\stop01.ico"
```

The **dragdrop** events for each DataWindow control simply trigger the relevant CommandButton **clicked** event. So, the **dragdrop** event for the right hand control triggers the cb_transfer_to_right CommandButton:

```
triggerevent( cb_transfer_to_right,Clicked! )
if draggedobject() = dwc_left then
   dwc_left.dragicon = "c:\wrox\drag01.ico"
end if
```

The final part of the application is the window which displays the UserObject. There is a single script for this window - in the **open** event - which assigns the DataWindow controls to the dw_item_master_for_demo DataWindow and retrieves the data from the database.

This has been a fairly complex example, but you can see that we've made the most of PowerBuilder's object-oriented features to cut down as much as possible on the amount of code we have to write. We've also tried to make the example as generic as possible so that you should easily be able to manipulate them for your own applications. You would simply have to change the database which you log on to and change the DataWindow assignment statements to match the new database.

We'll run through the remaining types of UserObjects fairly quickly, giving you a brief overview of what they are and how they would be used. The **EXAMPLES** directory which ships with PowerBuilder contains some of these, so we'll refer you to these in the relevant places.

External UserObjects

External UserObjects are created from underlying Windows DLLs. By defining a custom DLL as an external UserObjects, you can use the functionality that it has to offer in your application. For example, in PowerBuilder there is no control to display the progress of a process. The **CPALETTE.DLL** in the **EXAMPLES** directory does have a control to do this, allowing you to solve the problem.

What this ultimately means is that this type of UserObject lets you use third party controls. When using controls derived from DLLs, you should be able to find out which events are declared for that control, how it responds and the limitations of the control in general. The events declared for the control are not displayed in the UserObject Painter, so for these and the other information you will have to go through the documentation provided with the DLL.

In the UserObject Painter you can still declare user events, functions, structures and variables, thus allowing you to both access to a control written in another language and to extend the functionality of the UserObject, even if you aren't that familiar with that language.

Invoke the UserObject Painter, create a new object and select External from the Visual group. When PowerBuilder prompts for the name of a DLL, supply **CPALETTE.DLL**:

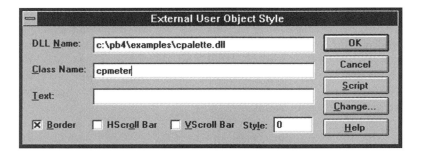

You need to specify the class name that is declared for the control in the DLL, in this case this is cpmeter. The value you supply in the Text prompt will appear on top of the control, if the control supports the property, otherwise any entry you make is ignored. You can turn on horizontal and vertical scrollbars, choose to have a border, and select from the different available styles by typing a number in the Style box.

For example, Style 4 is a raised effect. When you click the OK button, you should see the UserObject as follows:

You can see how this can be used by looking at the y_3d_meter in **PBEXAMUO.PBL** and w_progress_meter in **PBEXAMW2.PBL**.

VBX UserObjects

PowerBuilder allows you to use Visual Basic v1.0 compatible controls to create UserObjects. Support for Visual Basic controls gives the user more flexibility, but you need to have access to the documentation, otherwise you may end up hanging applications at run-time.

For example, we have a VBX called **MCIWNDX.VBX** in our Windows directory. We can create a new UserObject and specify this file:

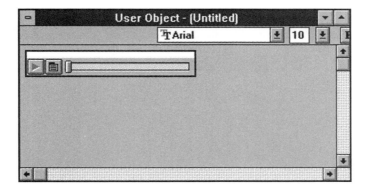

Once you select the control, it reads all the VBX attributes, and unlike external UserObjects, you can view and change these attributes in PowerBuilder by selecting Design/UserObject Style...:

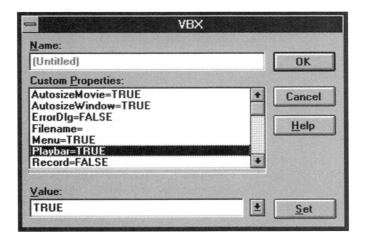

You can also set these attributes dynamically using PowerBuilder's dot notation. When you create a VBX UserObject, you automatically acquire the use of the VB events that are associated with the control, but you won't be able to see the actual code associated with them. This makes sense as the code isn't PowerScript:

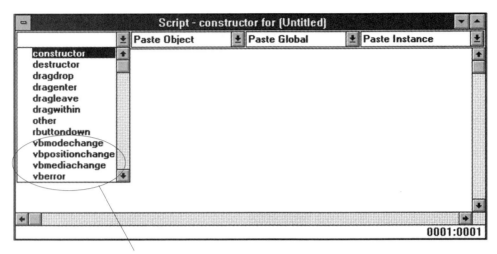

These are the VBX events for this control

The attributes that you can set for the UserObject can be accessed from the Script Painter by clicking on the Browse Object icon. If you want to see a VBX UserObject at work, you can look at the UserObject uo_1 in the **PBEXAMW3.PBL** file.

Standard Class

Non-visual UserObjects are just like any other object you define in PowerBuilder except they have no visual or GUI component. They act just like classes in C++. These objects can have variables, events and functions associated with them and they allow you to implement encapsulation. You can create classes, such as transaction, error and so on, from the standard ones:

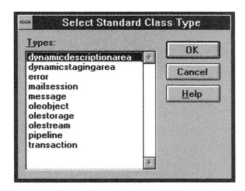

Once you create a new class, you can use this instead of the standard types. For example, you could create a class called **uo_transaction** inherited from Transaction. If you needed to create another transaction object in your application, you would simply declare it as:

```
uo_transaction TranObj1 // instead of Transaction TranObj1.
```

In the Application Painter, you would select Edit/Default Global Variables... and replace 'Transaction' with 'uo_transaction' for the SQLCA prompt:

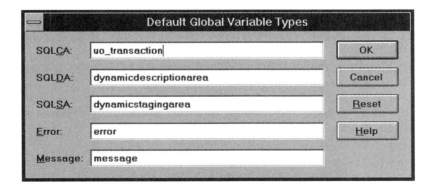

In the application, you would still use SQLCA, but now PowerBuilder internally declares the uo_transaction SQLCA instead of the standard Transaction SQLCA. This effectively provides an extra layer to which you can add functionality:

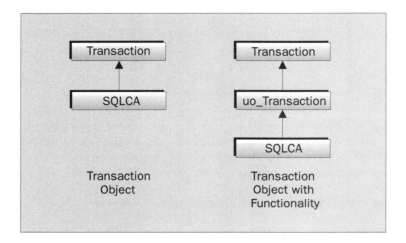

Custom Class

These are non-visual objects. Typically, they are used to encapsulate business rules and extra functionality. You can add attributes (instance variables) and declare events and functions (methods). Whenever you want to manipulate the attributes, you simply call the methods.

You should declare the instance variables as either protected or private, otherwise any object can set the values without going through the methods declared at the object.

For example, you could create an external function UserObject to access 16-bit Windows API calls. Methods (functions) are then defined to get information from Windows by using these external functions.

C++ **Class**

With v4.0, you are allowed to create a C++ DLL from within PowerBuilder. Powersoft provides a selection of tools to create DLLs as part of 'Watcom Integrated Development Environment (IDE)', shipped with the Enterprise edition of PowerBuilder. With this facility, you can create UserObjects and declare functions that are coded in C++.

Typically this is useful when we want to do arithmetic intensive functions such as complex calculations, because C++ offers better performance than PowerScript.

Each DLL you create for Windows 3.x requires three main components:

1 Entry: PowerBuilder takes care of providing 'LibMain' as C++ source code when you build a C++ user object

2 Main: Watcom C++ provides a DLL Entry function 'LibEntry' in its linker libraries

3 WEP : WEP is optional for Windows (Windows Exit Point) version 3.1

We've created an application contained in the **CPLS_PLS.PBL** library which uses a C++ UserObject. When you run this application, you'll be prompted to enter a number and the function will return the factorial value of the number:

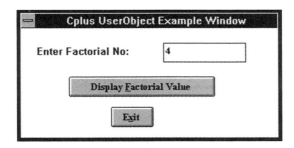

When you click the Display Factorial Value button, a message box will pop-up displaying the factorial value:

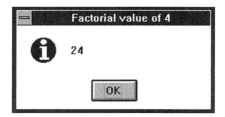

When you create a C++ UserObject, PowerBuilder automatically invokes the Watcom IDE and creates various templates to allow you to type in and compile your C++ code:

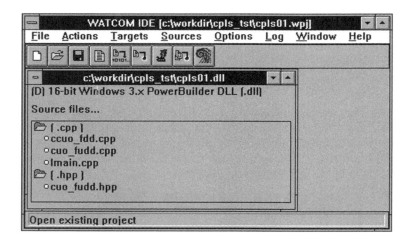

The .HPP Files

These are header files which contain functions and data member definitions. We refer to these files in **.CPP** files with the **#INCLUDE** directive, so that we can use their functions in our code. PowerBuilder automatically generates this file for us by declaring the functions we provided in the UserObject Painter.

The .CPP Files

These files contain the actual C++ source code. PowerBuilder generates three files for us:

1 `lmain.cpp`, which contains LibMain and WEP functions that are required for the DLL.

2 A file that contains the PowerBuilder interface. PowerBuilder doesn't make calls to the functions directly, but uses this file instead. Typically this file name is prefixed with 'c'. Don't change anything in this file.

3 The third file is the one in which we write the actual function logic for the objects we declared in the UserObject Painter.

We've provided all these files for you on the CD-ROM, so you can browse through them to see exactly what they contain.

UserObject Programming: Tips & Techniques

This section contains some useful hints and tips for using the UserObjects that you have created.

UserObjects on Windows

You can use UserObjects in a window in two ways:

▲ By placing the UserObject in a window.

▲ By opening the UserObject dynamically from script.

When you place a UserObject in the window, you must give it a name just as you would for any other type of control. You can then refer to the UserObject in your script using this name.

Resizing UserObjects

When a UserObject is resized, the controls inside don't resize accordingly. If you want to allow the user to move the UserObject at execution time, you need to write code to do this.

Time Related Existence

There may be some situations where you only need the UserObject to exist in the window for a certain amount of time. You can do this in one of two ways:

1 You can place the UserObject in the window and toggle its visible property so that it is displayed only when you need it. In this case, it will take up the same amount of memory no matter whether it is hidden or visible.

2 You can open the UserObject dynamically whenever it is required and close it down when no longer needed. The function to open the UserObject is **OpenUserObject()**. If you need to send a certain parameter to the UserObject you can use **OpenUserObjectWithParm()**. For both of these functions, you can specify the x and y co-ordinates of the UserObject in the window.

Placing Non-Visual UserObjects

You can't place a custom class (Non-Visual UserObject) on the surface of a window. What you need to do is declare a variable and create an instance of the class and access that instance. For example, if you had a custom class cc_1, and wanted to call **uf_close()**, the typical code would be:

```
cc_1 l_nvo_1
l_nvo_1 = CREATE cc_1
l_nvo_1.uf_Close()
```

Whenever you are finished with the class you can destroy it:

```
DESTROY l_nvo_1
```

Parent and This

If you create a standard UserObject, you can use reserved words **Parent** and **This** in the same way as a standard control. For example, if you write **Close(Parent)** for the **clicked** event of a CommandButton type UserObject, clicking on the CommandButton will close the window. This will happen even if you open the UserObject dynamically with **OpenUserObject()** or **OpenUserObjectWithParm()**.

UserObject Events

You can't trigger any UserObject events that are declared in the UserObject Painter. For example, suppose you have a user event **ue_1** and you placed a UserObject uoc_1 in a window w_1 and named the UserObject as uo_1.

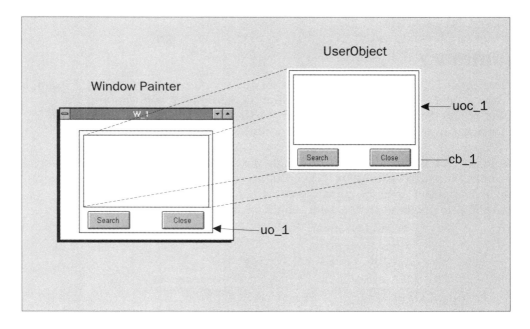

If you call **TriggerEvent(uo_1, "ue_1")** from any of the window's events, it won't be executed, even though no compiler errors were generated. You can only trigger any of the custom UserObject's events if you declare the events in the Window Painter.

In the above example, you can't declare **ue_1** for uoc_1, because **ue_1** is already declared in the UserObject Painter. The only solution is to define functions in the UserObject Painter.

Suppose that you declare **uf_close_parent()** in the UserObject Painter and call **uf_close_parent()** from the cb_1 **clicked** event - it will close the window that contains this UserObject.

Unlike custom UserObjects, if you write script for External type UserObjects events in the UserObject Painter, you can trigger these events from the window.

Summary

We've looked at quite a lot of theory in this chapter and seen several examples of how you can use UserObjects in your PowerBuilder applications. The object-oriented approach provides a higher level of abstraction than the approach supported by traditional procedures and data.

We hope that we've illustrated, through the use of UserObjects, how powerful the object-oriented features of PowerBuilder can be. If you put some thought into the application development process before you begin, you can save yourself a lot of time in the later stages of a project.

CHAPTER 16

Dynamic Data Exchange

This chapter is the first of two concerned with how you can use PowerBuilder to communicate with other software packages. If PowerBuilder can't perform a task, you can ship the data to another package, let it use its functionality to perform the task and wait for the polished results to return.

For example, suppose you wanted to spell check the textual information held in your database. As Powersoft did not build a spell checker into PowerBuilder, this is a task that normally you wouldn't be able to perform. However, by using some form of communication between packages, you could use a wordprocessor to perform the check for you.

The form of communication that we are going to investigate here is called Dynamic Data Exchange (DDE), one of the first really Client/Server ways of exchanging data.

In this chapter, we will cover:

▲ The concepts of DDE

▲ DDE related events in PowerBuilder

▲ Communicating with Excel using DDE

▲ Mail Merge Using Word and DDE

Introduction

Windows allows you to run more than one application at a time, and as such it is possible to communicate between two applications running on your own computer. DDE allows you to do this by setting up a conversation between two applications. When you start to think about it, the benefits of this are obvious.

Each different software package has been designed for some clear, specific purpose. Wordprocessors are designed to manipulate text, spreadsheets for number crunching and databases for handling large amounts of information. But what happens if you want an application to retrieve numerical information from a database, perform some summary statistics upon it, graph the results and print out a textual report based on the information revealed by the statistics and the graphs?

Without the use of some communication technology between these packages, the design of the software would defeat you. However, with the introduction of DDE, a light appeared at the end of the MIS tunnel. Okay, DDE can't write the report for you, but it can move all the data around to achieve the results you need!

Concepts

When you want to use DDE, the process demands that at least two applications are involved. The application that requests data or sends executable commands is called the **Client**, while the application that executes the requested command or returns the requested data is called the **Server**.

> *In many ways, this is similar to the Client/Server model which we looked at in the opening chapter.*

Depending on how DDE is implemented in a package, the finished application may be able to act as both a client and a server. PowerBuilder has been developed to support DDE as both.

The Registration Database

All applications that wish to participate in DDE must be registered in a database called **REGEDIT.DAT**. This is one of the elements of all the operating systems that make up the Windows family. In this database, the operating system stores, in a binary format, all the information it requires to organize the conversations. Generally, this registration is done automatically when you install a product, but if you encounter problems, you can edit the application's DDE properties in **REGEDIT.DAT**.

To do this, select File/Run from Program Manager and type in REGEDIT. This runs **REGEDIT.EXE**, bringing up the Registration Info Editor dialog box:

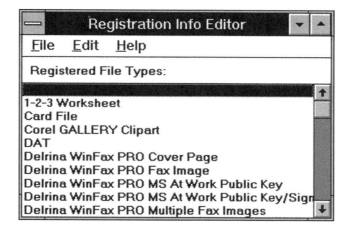

In this window, you are given a list of all the applications that your operating system currently has registered. You can also add, delete and copy entries by selecting the appropriate actions from the Edit menu, although this isn't advisable as, unless you understand exactly how the registry works, you can cause your system to lose functionality. To modify an entry, double-click on the name of the application. This brings up the Modify File Type dialog box:

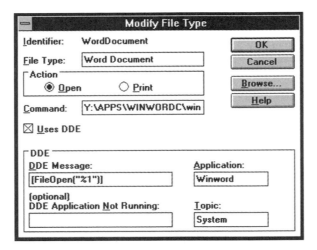

The top half of the window deals with the running of the actual application itself. As you can see, this dialog refers to a Word Document. The File Type: is Word Document and the command to run the application is provided and is editable in the Command: box.

The lower half of the window is the part that most interests us, as it deals with DDE. The Application and Topic options are used to reference the application you want to communicate with. Let's take a look at each of these entries in more detail, while also introducing **Item**, a subdivision of Topic.

Application

The **Application** is the name under which the server software has been registered to Windows. Typically, it is the name of the executable file without the `.EXE` extension, but it may be a different name.

Topic

The nature of the **Topic** depends on the server. For Word, a Topic may be a document name; for Excel, it may be a name of a spreadsheet. There is also a special Topic called 'System', which is supplied by most applications that support DDE.

The System Topic is used when there may be several Topics available - for example, when you are accessing data from multiple spreadsheets. The System Topic is also used to perform certain tasks at the application level.

Item

Under a Topic, you may want to access more than one location. For example, Word could use an Item Name to reference a bookmark, while Excel could use an Item Name to access a range of rows and cells.

For a DDE conversation to begin, the client application requests a conversation channel on which to communicate. This message is broadcast throughout the Windows environment and if the server application is running, a channel, identified by a numerical return, is assigned and the conversation can begin.

If the server application isn't running, Windows takes control and sends a message to the client letting it know that the server isn't running.

> **The server application must be running before a DDE conversation can begin. Some applications (when acting as a client) automatically load the server if it isn't already running, but PowerBuilder doesn't support this feature.**

You can specify a period of time for the client to wait for a channel by specifying a value of the **DDETimeout** parameter.

Links

There are two types of DDE links: Hot Links and Cold Links. The distinction is made based on when data will be sent to the client from the server.

Hot Link

When operating a Hot Link DDE conversation, as soon as any data changes in the server application, it is automatically sent to the client. It is only necessary for the client to request data once: when it initially establishes a link to the server.

A Hot Link is used when you want constantly updated information from the server application. The following PowerBuilder functions are related to a Hot Link:

- StartHotLink (location, appl_name, topic)

- GetDataDDEOrigin (which_appl, what_topic, what_loc)

- GetDataDDE (string)

- RespondRemote (Boolean)

- StopHotLink (location, appl_name, topic)

Cold Link

In a Cold Link conversation, data is sent from the server to the client when the client requests it, rather than whenever data is changed. This is useful when the client doesn't need to be aware of changed data immediately. However, it is more processor intensive than a Hot Link, because the client must request data from the server each time it wants it. The following PowerBuilder functions are related to a cold link:

- ExecRemote (command, appl_name, topic)

- GetRemote (location, target, appl_name, topic)

- SetRemote (location, value, appl_name, topic)

DDE-Related Events in PowerBuilder

The table on the next page lists all the PowerBuilder events related to DDE. All of these events are, by default, declared at the window level. This makes sense because we can think of a window as a DDE Topic and the data or controls on the window as DDE Items.

The table shows all the events together with their corresponding Client actions and the command used to get the required results:

Client Action	Event	Commands Used
Client initiates a Hot Link	RemoteHotLinkStart	
Client sends a command to the server	RemoteExec	GetCommandDDEOrigin() GetCommandDDE()
Client sends data to the server	Remote send	GetDataDDEOrigin() GetDataDDE()
Client requests data from the server	RemoteRequest	GetDataDDEOrigin() SetDataDDE() RespondRemote()
Client terminates a Hot Link	RemoteHotLinkStop	StopServerDDE()

Using DDE with PowerBuilder

Now that we've explained some of the concepts behind DDE, let's look at some examples of using the technique with PowerBuilder working as both a client and a server. The examples make use of two windows which are to be found in the **DDE.PBL** library on the CD-ROM. The first of these is the w_dde_demonstration window:

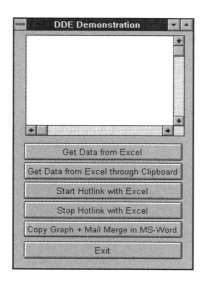

The top control is a DataWindow which we'll use to display information. This is created by selecting three columns from a dummy database which contains no data. We then assign data to the DataWindow depending on which CommandButton is pressed.

> Note that for all the Excel examples, we must have Excel running in the background with the required spreadsheet open. You can open Excel from PowerBuilder using the Run command, but you may experience problems when doing this. It's worth experimenting, but for guaranteed success, we'd recommend you always have Excel running.

DDE with Excel

Our first example imports data from an Excel spreadsheet and displays it in the DataWindow. We've provided the Excel 5 spreadsheet called **TEST1.XLS** on the CD-ROM. If you open it up, you'll see that it contains four rows of data:

	A	B	C	D	E	F
1						
2		12	15	20		
3		21	18	35		
4		45	26	25		
5		32	42	16		
6						
7						

TEST1.XLS — Sheet1 / Sheet2 / Sheet3

We've left the first row and column blank as these would normally contain headings and labels. To see this working, leave the spreadsheet open, run the PowerBuilder window and click on the Get Data from Excel button:

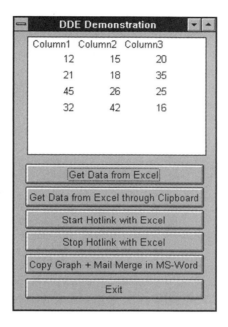

The code which achieves this importation is in the `clicked` event associated with the CommandButton:

```
// Object: cb_1 in window w_dde_demonstration
// Event:  Clicked

integer i, j, lExcelChannelNumber, lDDEGetRetVal
string lRetValFromExcel
long lNewRowNo

dwc_1.DataObject = "dw_dde_example"
dwc_1.SetTransObject( Sqlca )

lExcelChannelNumber = OpenChannel( "Excel","test1.xls")

For i = 2 to 5
   lNewRowNo = dwc_1.InsertRow(0)
   For j = 2 to 4
      lDDEGetRetVal = GetRemote( "R" + string(i) + "C" + string(j), &
            lRetValFromExcel, lExcelChannelNumber )
      dwc_1.setitem( lNewRowNo, (j - 1), integer( lRetValFromExcel ))
   next
next

ExecRemote( '[File.Close()]', lExcelChannelNumber )
```

As the same DataWindow control can be related to any DataWindow object, our first task is to reassign **dwc_1** to the DataWindow **dw_dde_example** object and then set up the default Transaction Object ready for the data exchange.

After the Transaction Object is set, a channel must be opened between PowerBuilder and Excel - remember that in order for a DDE conversation to take place, a DDE channel must already have been allocated as a carrier. The **OpenChannel()** function accepts two parameters; the name of the application with which we want to converse and the specific Topic that contains the data that we are interested in. In our case, the Application is Excel and the Topic is the name of the appropriate spreadsheet, **TEST1.XLS**.

> *In a full, commercial application, you would need to add an error handling routine to check that a positive number channel was returned, and if not, notify the user that there was some problem.*

We then use the **GetRemote()** function, passing the specific cell references of the data that we are interested in retrieving. For example, 'R1C1' would refer to row one and column one. Once the required data has been retrieved, we close the **TEST1.XLS** file by sending the **Close()** function.

> *Note that the formula used to locate the data in the server application's current Topic may differ from server to server. The 'R1C1' formula is specific to Excel. If you are using any other type of spreadsheet, or indeed any other type of DDE server, you should refer to the documentation for that software for more information.*

Importing a Spreadsheet through the Clipboard

This example uses the same spreadsheet as the previous one and basically achieves the same result. The difference between the examples is the way in which the data is transferred. In the first example, the data was pulled straight into the DataWindow from the DDE server, but this example uses the Windows clipboard as a temporary storage point.

> **One advantage of using this method of data transfer is that once the data has been copied to the clipboard on the orders of one client, any number of clients can then access the data. No more server calls are required.**

To achieve this functionality, we use an Excel macro. Open up the Excel spreadsheet and select the Macro 1 sheet to see the steps:

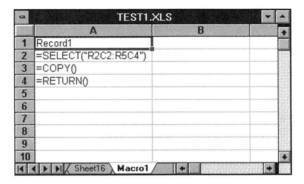

This is an Excel 4.0 macro. If you are familiar with Excel 5, you might be more familiar with macros written in Visual Basic for Applications. The VBA version of this shortcut is as follows:

```
'
'   Record1 Macro
'   Macro recorded 10/07/95 by Gateway 2000 Licensed User.
'
'
Sub Record1()
    Range("B2:D5").Select
    Selection.Copy
End Sub
```

Both versions of this macro simply select the required range of cells and copy them to the clipboard. If you run the PowerBuilder window again and click on the second button, you will see exactly the same result as before.

The code for this CommandButton is:

```
// Object: cb_2 in window w_dde_demonstration
// Event: Clicked

integer lExcelChannelNumber

dwc_1.DataObject = "dw_dde_example"
dwc_1.SetTransObject( Sqlca )

lExcelChannelNumber = OpenChannel( "Excel","test1.xls")

ExecRemote('[Run("Record1")]', lExcelChannelNumber )
dwc_1.ImportClipboard()

ExecRemote( '[File.Close()]', lExcelChannelNumber )
```

As you can see, the first few lines are similar to the previous example - we specify the DataWindow, set the Transaction Object and open a channel. We then issue an **ExecRemote** command specifying the name of the macro, followed by a call to the **ImportClipboard()** function to import the data into the DataWindow control. The final line closes the spreadsheet.

This example produces a considerable performance improvement over the previous method as copying cell by cell involves sending a request to the server for each cell, which requires both a lot of time and resources. You probably wouldn't notice the difference with such a small amount of data, but in a full blown application, it would be considerably quicker.

> *This DDE-based technique is very useful if you want to save spreadsheet data into a Sybase database.*

The **FileClose()** function closes the currently active spreadsheet or macro sheet. However, if you make changes to a file and then attempt to close it, Excel will prompt you as to whether to save the changes or not. This requires user intervention, and therefore will halt the flow of our application. To prevent this, you could use the following code before the final line:

```
ExecRemote('[Run("Record1")]', lExcelChannelNumber )
dwc_1.ImportClipboard()

ExecRemote( '[ERROR(FALSE)]', lExcelChannelNumber )
ExecRemote( '[File.Close()]', lExcelChannelNumber )
```

This automatically answers 'no' to Excel's Save Changes prompt. By replacing the word **FALSE** with **TRUE**, you would be asking Excel to save the changes, rather than throwing them away with **FALSE**.

Using Excel Names

As with all user-friendly applications, there are several ways to perform the same task. Instead of referring to the cell references explicitly, you can name the range that you are interested in and then use this name in the macro.

There are three steps to defining a name in Excel:

1 Select the range of cells

2 Select Insert/Name/Define...

3 Supply a name and click OK

We've set up a name in our spreadsheet called importdata. You can change the first line of the Record1 macro so that it reads:

=SELECT("importdata")

Now if you run the DDE Demonstration window and click on the second CommandButton, you'll get exactly the same data in the DataWindow control.

You may wonder what benefit we have gained by using names - our next example will show you. Open the **TEST1.XLS** spreadsheet again and go to sheet1 which contains the data. Now, insert a row before the fifth row and add some extra data:

	A	B	C	D	E	F
1						
2		12	15	20		
3		21	18	35		
4		12	56	34		
5		45	26	25		
6		32	42	16		
7						

Sheet1 / Sheet2 / Sheet3 / She

If you now open the DDE Demonstration window and import the data again, you'll see that all the data is inserted in the DataWindow control, including the extra row:

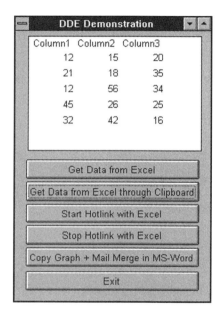

This is an example of how we can take advantage of Excel's relative addressing. When you insert a row, it notices that the new information has been inserted inside the boundaries of a predefined data set (that denoted by the name criteria) and alters the cell range of the Name to take it into account.

You can see this by selecting Insert/Name/Define... and reviewing importdata:

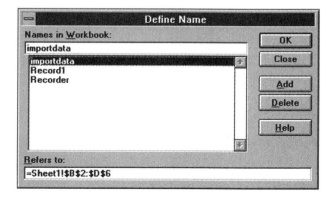

You can see that the cell range has changed to reflect the inserted row.

Unfortunately, things won't run as smoothly as you would expect if you use our code as it stands at the moment. You may notice that Excel's title bar starts flashing in the background when the data is retrieved. This indicates that Excel is waiting for a response. If you use the *Alt+Tab* keys to switch to Excel, you'll see what the problem is:

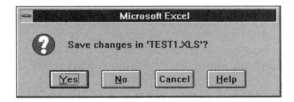

We've added data to the spreadsheet so, of course, Excel prompts us as to whether to save the changes to **TEST1.XLS** or not. As we said, the way to solve this problem is to add the **[ERROR()]** command to our script with the parameter, depending on what we wish to do with the changes.

Hot Link with Excel

The examples we've looked at so far have used Cold Links. That means that the client only obtains a new set of data when it asks for it. In the case of a Hot Link, whenever data changes in the server, the client application is automatically informed. To organize this type of connection, the client must establish a link to each cell it wants to track, but you don't have to worry about opening or using a channel.

The command to start a Hot Link is **StartHotLink()**. This function accepts three parameters: location of data, Application and Topic. As an example of how to use this type of data transfer, we'll use the same spreadsheet as in the previous examples.

First, we have to set up the necessary Hot Links. This is the code in the Start Hot Link with Excel CommandButton:

```
// Object: cb_3 in window w_dde_demonstration
// Event: Clicked
```

```
string lRetValFromExcel

StartHotLink( "R2C2","Excel","test1.xls" )
StartHotLink( "R3C2","Excel","test1.xls" )
StartHotLink( "R4C2","Excel","test1.xls" )
StartHotLink( "R5C2","Excel","test1.xls" )
StartHotLink( "R2C3","Excel","test1.xls" )
StartHotLink( "R3C3","Excel","test1.xls" )
StartHotLink( "R4C3","Excel","test1.xls" )
StartHotLink( "R5C3","Excel","test1.xls" )
```

The function to stop a Hot Link is **StopHotLink()**; its arguments are the same as **StartHotLink()**. You need to call **StopHotLink()** for each cell for which a Hot Link exists. To optimize your application, you should only start Hot Links when they are required, stopping them as soon as possible.

This is the code in the Stop Hot Link with Excel CommandButton:

```
// Object: cb_4 in window w_dde_demonstration
// Event:  Clicked

StopHotLink( "R2C2","Excel","test1.xls" )
StopHotLink( "R3C2","Excel","test1.xls" )
StopHotLink( "R4C2","Excel","test1.xls" )
StopHotLink( "R5C2","Excel","test1.xls" )
StopHotLink( "R2C3","Excel","test1.xls" )
StopHotLink( "R3C3","Excel","test1.xls" )
StopHotLink( "R4C3","Excel","test1.xls" )
StopHotLink( "R5C3","Excel","test1.xls" )
```

When a DDE conversation is running as a Hot Link, whenever data changes, the server informs the client. It is the client's responsibility whether or not to accept the data, and how to process it.

Whenever the server talks to the client during a Hot Link, a **hotlinkalarm** event occurs at the window level. Thus, any code that you produce with respect to how the client should react to a Hot Link broadcast should be assigned to this event. One important function that can be very useful for this event is **GetDataDDEOrigin()**. This function informs the client of the Application, Topic and location of data from the server:

```
// Object: w_dde_demonstration
// Event:  HotLinkAlarm

int lRowNumber, lColumnNumber, lPosition1
string lApplication, lTopic, lLocation, lDDEDataValue
long lInsertedRow

GetDataDDEOrigin( lApplication, lTopic, lLocation )
lPosition1 = Pos( lLocation, "C")
lRowNumber = integer( mid( lLocation, 2, (lPosition1 - 2)))
lColumnNumber = integer( mid( lLocation, (lPosition1 + 1)))
lInsertedRow = dwc_1.InsertRow(0)
GetDataDDE( lDDEDataValue )
RespondRemote( TRUE )
dwc_1.SetItem( (lRowNumber - 1), (lColumnNumber - 1), &
        integer( lDDEDataValue ))
```

In order to find the row number and column number, insert a row in the DataWindow and set the values based on row and column number obtained from the server. Since the spreadsheet used in this example has row 1 and column 1 blank, you must subtract 1 from the Row and Column number we received.

Whereas **GetDDEDataOrigin()** doesn't return the actual value received from the client, **GetDataDDE()** does, and it is used here to pass the value into a local variable defined in your PowerBuilder script.

Run the DDE Demonstration window again and open up the **TEST1.XLS** spreadsheet in Excel. Size the windows so that you can see what is happening in both Excel and the PowerBuilder application. Get the data from Excel by clicking on the first or second CommandButtons:

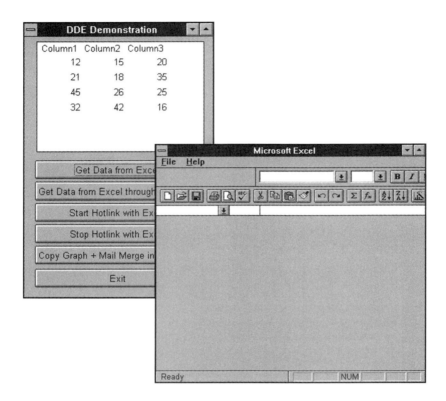

The data is retrieved from Excel as before and the spreadsheet is closed down. Now to see the Hot Link in action we'll have to open up the spreadsheet again. Do this and then click on the Start Hotlink with Excel button. You won't see anything happen, but in the background the Hot Link has been set up.

To see it work, go into the spreadsheet and change one of the values. When you hit the Enter key, the same value will change in the DataWindow control:

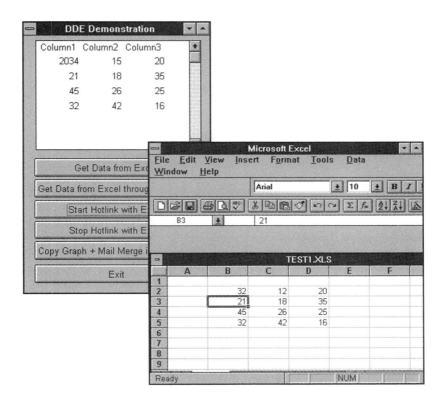

We set up the Hot Links to watch the first and second columns, so you can change any of the values in columns B and C of the spreadsheet and the changes will be seen in the DataWindow control. To close the Hot Links, click on the Stop Hotlink with Excel button.

Mail Merge

Very often you need to send the same letter or memo to more than one person. This can be done using Mail Merge to fill in all the personal information into a standard letter, the personal information being drawn from your database or from your PowerScript.

> *Note that you could hard code extra information into your PowerScript,*
> *but this would be very inflexible. However, you could throw up a dialog*
> *box for the user to add any extra information to specific letters.*

When you start to consider the problem using the 'rules of software' that we illustrated in a previous section, this task automatically falls under the realms of DDE. By default, the personal information will be held in a database, but the standard letter has probably been prepared using a wordprocessor. Moving the personal information from database to wordprocessor is simple if you use DDE.

> *Mail Merge is a common business requirement. In the increasingly*
> *common Client/Server environment, it is typical for data to be stored in*
> *different applications.*

In this example, we will use PowerBuilder to send data from a DataWindow to a text file that our wordprocessor, Word 6.0, can read, before using a Word macro to import the data and merge it with an existing document. The logic for this can be seen in the following figure:

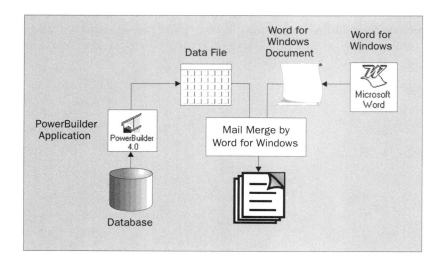

We'll also copy a DataWindow Graph object to the clipboard and paste this into the merged document using the same Word macro.

Setup for Mail Merge

There are several components to this example. The following figure shows the execution flow in more detail:

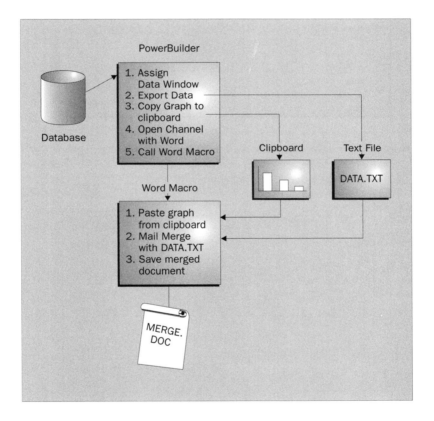

Let's look at each of these steps in turn. First, let's take a look at the Word side of the example.

ITRBDY1.doc

This is a mail merge document which contains the main body of text, the macro which merges the data and all the links required to carry out the actual process of mail merging:

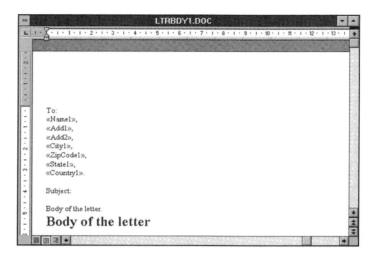

The text between the angle brackets are field names and correspond to the relevant fields which contain the data we're interested in. You can see how these were set up by selecting Tools/Mail Merge...:

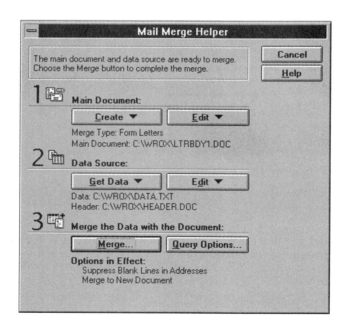

In the Data Source section, you can see that there are two files specified:

1 `C:\WROX\DATA.TXT`: This is the text file from which Word will import the data

2 `C:\WROX\HEADER.DOC` This is a Word document which contains the header information for the fields

We'll look at these files in a moment, but first let's take a look at the macro which is contained in this document. Select Tools/Macro... and Edit the InsertGraphAndMailMerge macro:

```
Sub MAIN
    EditGoTo .Destination = "GraphHolder"
    EditPaste
    MailMergeToDoc
    FileSaveAs .Name = "C:\wrox\merge.doc", .Format = 0, .LockAnnot = 0,
.Password = ""
    DocClose
    EditGoTo .Destination = "GraphHolder"
    CharRight 2, 1
    EditClear
    FileSave
    DocClose
    FileExit
End Sub
```

This macro moves to a bookmark called GraphHolder, which we've defined in the document, and pastes the graph at that position and then merges the data in **DATA.TXT** into the document. It then saves the new merged document as **C:\WROX\MERGE.DOC**. Finally it tidies up the existing document by deleting the graph and clearing all the merged text ready for the next time it is used.

There are quite a few steps involved in creating this document, but the Word Mail Merge Helper makes the process fairly painless.

HEADER.doc

This contains header information which relates the data copied into the text file to the field names in the main document:

You can see that there are seven fields containing name and address data. The data from PowerBuilder should match these fields.

DATA.txt

We use this file to contain the data that we copy from PowerBuilder, before it is merged with the main Word document. You can open it in Notepad:

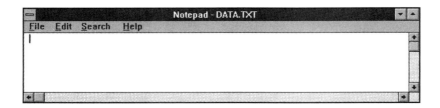

As you can see, it is completely empty. This is because we simply use it as a temporary store for the data. Each time you run the example, you should open this file and delete the information, ready for the next test run.

This completes the set up of the Word side. Now let's look at the PowerBuilder side.

The clicked Event Code

Open the w_dde_demonstration window and look at the code behind the clicked event of the Copy Graph + Mail Merge in MS Word button:

```
// Object:     cb_Copy_Graph_and_MailMerge in window w_for_dde_demo
// Event:    Clicked

integer lChannelNumber
string lExeFile, lDocFile

dwc_1.DataObject = "dw_for_addresses_export"
```

```
dwc_1.SetTransObject( Sqlca )
dwc_1.SaveAs( "c:\wrox\data.txt", Text!, False )

dwc_1.DataObject = "dw_graph_for_dde"
dwc_1.SetTransObject( Sqlca )
dwc_1.grClipboard( "gr_1" )

lExeFile = "c:\msoffice\winword\winword.exe"
// Replace with actual path in your computer
lDocFile = "c:\wrox\LtrBdy1.doc"

if GetModuleHandle( lExeFile ) < 1 then
   Run( lExeFile + " " + lDocFile )
   lChannelNumber = OpenChannel( "winword", lDocFile )
else
   lChannelNumber = OpenChannel( "winword", "System" )
   ExecRemote( & '[FileOpen.Name=~"c:\wrox\ltrbdy1.doc~"]', & lChannelNumber)

lChannelNumber = OpenChannel( "winword", "c:\wrox\ltrbdy1.doc" )
end if

ExecRemote( '[ToolsMacro.name=~"InsertGraphAndMailMerge~",.run]',
lChannelNumber )
CloseChannel( lChannelNumber )
ExecRemote( '[FileExit,.no]', lChannelNumber )
```

The first thing we do is retrieve the data from the dw_for_addresses DataWindow and save it as **C:\WROX\DATA.TXT**. The parameters of the **SaveAs()** function specify that it should appear as tab-delimited text without headers.

Next, we get the Graph object from dw_graph_for_dde and copy it to the clipboard. The next few lines simply set up the directory for Word and the name of the document to open.

> Note that if you have Word installed in a directory other than **C:\MSOFFICE\WINWORD** you will have to alter this line accordingly. You can delete this path reference altogether if the correct reference appears in your DOS path.

The **GetModuleHandle** function is a Windows SDK function which returns the handle of the specified application. If the handle is zero, this means the application isn't running, and so we need to run Word, open the document and open a channel to it.

If Word is already running, i.e. the handle isn't zero, then we open a channel to the System Topic, so enabling us to send the appropriate commands to open the document and a channel.

> This might sound confusing, but it does makes sense. Remember you can't start a DDE conversation until you have opened a channel. This means that we can't send a `FileOpen` command until we start a conversation - in this case with the System Topic. If Word isn't already running, we can open the document straight away using the `Run` command and allocate a channel to it, all in one go.

The command to run the macro is slightly different from the commands sent to Excel in the previous examples simply because of the differences between Excel and Word macros.

The dw_for_addresses_export DataWindow

This is the DataWindow which contains the name and address information which we want to export. If you preview it, you'll see the information it contains:

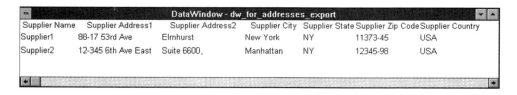

DataWindow - dw_for_addresses_export						
Supplier Name	Supplier Address1	Supplier Address2	Supplier City	Supplier State	Supplier Zip Code	Supplier Country
Supplier1	88-17 53rd Ave	Elmhurst	New York	NY	11373-45	USA
Supplier2	12-345 6th Ave East	Suite 6600,	Manhattan	NY	12345-98	USA

You can see that the order of the fields matches the order we set up in the header document. To keep our example simple, we've specified that the DataWindow should retrieve this data on save, so that we don't actually have to retrieve the information from a database before saving it as a text file:

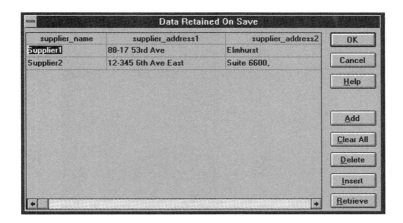

You could easily change the code, so that it calls the **Retrieve()** function before assigning the data to the DataWindow.

The dw_graph_for_dde DataWindow

This contains the graph which we copy to the clipboard, before pasting it into the Word document:

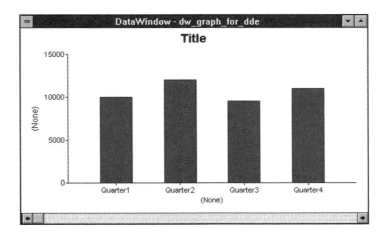

If you look at the data source for the graph, you'll see that it simply contains two fields: one is a string and the other, a number:

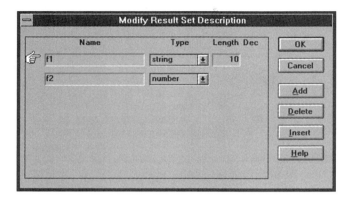

Again we've made our example simple, but you could change the code so that it retrieves data from a database before creating the graph and copying it to the clipboard.

The GetModuleHandle() Function

This is the final thing we have to look at before we can run the example. As we said above, this is an external Windows function, so in order to use it, we have to declare as such to our application at the window level:

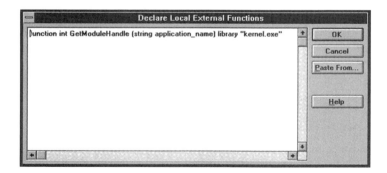

This completes the setup for this example. Let's see it in action.

Running the Example

Run our demonstration window, clicking on the Copy Graph + Mail Merge button. Note that you don't have to have Word running in the background for this example:

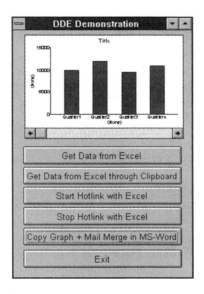

You'll see the data briefly flash up in the DataWindow control and then the graph will appear. Word opens in the background and you'll see data coming in and windows being opened and closed as the macro does its stuff.

You can see the final result by opening the **MERGE.DOC** document which should be in your **C:\WROX** directory:

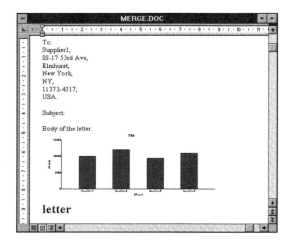

You can see that we have all the details of the first record and the graph inserted in the correct place. If you scroll down the document, you'll see that the next page contains the data for the second record.

Our example, although quite complex to set up, was fairly easy to execute. As we said before, you could very easily alter the code to give more functionality.

PowerBuilder as a DDE Server

The previous examples have used PowerBuilder as a client in the DDE conversation. Our final example shows how we can use PowerBuilder as the server and call information from it with Word.

We'll use a different window for this example and another Word macro to initiate the conversation. There is quite a bit of setting up in this example, so once again, we'll go through each of the various components in turn.

The Word Macro

Open up the **PBSERVER.DOC** which you should have copied from the CD-ROM into your **C:\WROX** directory and select Tools/Macro... to see the list of available macros. Select the TalkToPBServer macro and hit the Edit button to view it:

```
Sub MAIN
channel = DDEInitiate("PBApp", "BookModule")
```

```
DDEPoke channel, "1874416605", "Testing data,(DDE from Word)"
a$ = DDERequest$(channel, "Isbn,Title,Author")
Insert a$
DDETerminate channel
End Sub
```

There are four DDE specific commands here:

1 The **DDEInitiate** command takes two parameters: the Application and the Topic, and initiates the conversation.

2 The **DDEPoke** command sends values to the application.

3 **DDERequest$** gets information from the application.

4 **DDETerminate** stops the conversation.

The **Insert** command simply inserts the retrieved data into the Word document. The data that we're using for this example relates to book information, so we want to retrieve the ISBN, title and author fields from the database.

The PowerBuilder Window

The window which we use for this example is the w_dde_server window:

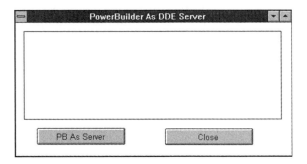

Like the previous example, we use a DataWindow control to display the data and we have a CommandButton to initialize PowerBuilder as a server.

573

DataWindow - dw_books_for_dde		
Isbn	Title	Author
1874416397	Rev Access	Stephen Wynkoop
1874416605	Rev PowerBuilder	Prasad Bodepudi
1874416192	Beginner's Visual Basic	Peter Wright
1874416575	Instant Delphi	Dave Jewell
1874416400	Rev Foxpro	Will Phelps / Jeanne Rimpo

The PB As Server CommandButton

Before we can use PowerBuilder as a DDE server, we have to set up an Application and Topic. The code in the **clicked** event does exactly this:

```
integer lRetVal
dw_1.DataObject = "dw_books_for_dde"
dw_1.SetTransObject( Sqlca )

lRetVal = StartServerDDE( "PBApp", "BookModule")
If lRetVal <> 1 then
   MessageBox( "Starting server Error", lRetVal )
end if
```

We set the DataWindow control to the DataWindow dw_books_for_dde and then use the **StartServerDDE()** function to set up the Application and Topic.

Again we've made the example simple by using a DataWindow which has been set up with data saved on retrieve. If you preview dw_books_for_dde, you'll see the kind of information that it contains:

When PowerBuilder acts as a server, it is necessary to check the commands sent by the client and trigger events explicitly. To do this we have to write code for three window level events:

1 RemoteExec

2 RemoteSend

3 RemoteRequest

Let's look at what each of these does and see the code for each of them.

The RemoteExec Event

When PowerBuilder receives a request from a client, a **remoteexec** event occurs. We use this event to determine which client has sent the commands:

```
String lApplication
int lRetVal

lRetVal = GetCommandDDEOrigin( lApplication )
If lRetVal = 1 then
   RespondRemote( TRUE )
End if
```

The **GetCommandDDEOrigin()** function determines the client, and if it is successful, we set **RespondRemote** to TRUE.

The RemoteSend Event

This event occurs whenever a client sends data to PowerBuilder. If you remember, in the Word macro, we use a **DDEPoke** command, so we have to add code here to handle this occurrence:

```
String lCommand, lApplication, lTopic, lItem, lData, lDWArg
int lRetVal
Long lRowNoFound

lRetVal = GetDataDDEOrigin( lApplication, lTopic, lItem )
If lRetVal = 1 then
   GetDataDDE( lData )
   lDWArg = "isbn = " + lItem
   lRowNoFound = dw_1.DwFind( lDWArg, 0, dw_1.RowCount())
   If lRowNoFound > 0 then
       dw_1.SetItem( lRowNoFound, "title", lData )
       RespondRemote( TRUE )
   Else
       RespondRemote( FALSE )
   End if
End if
```

Just to remind you, the **DDEPoke** command was:

```
DDEPoke channel, "1874416605", "Testing data, (DDE from Word)"
```

This second parameter is the Item we are interested in and the third parameter is the data we want to send. Translating this command, we would say 'Find the item with ISBN 1874416605 and replace the Title with 'Testing data, (DDE from Word)''.

The **GetDataDDE()** function strips out the value of the third parameter and places it into a local variable, ready for when we have successfully located the Item. We then simply replace the current Title with the data in the local variable.

The RemoteRequest Event

This event occurs whenever a client requests data from PowerBuilder. As PowerBuilder doesn't have easily referenced data locations, such as the cells in a spreadsheet, we have to customize the data that is requested in the **DDERequest** command from the client:

```
string lApplication, ltopic, litem, lDataToclient
long lTotRows, i
int lRetVal

lRetVal = GetDataDDEOrigin( lApplication, lTopic, lItem )

lItem = Upper( lItem )
lTotRows = dw_1.RowCount()
For i = 1 to lTotRows
   If Pos( lItem, "ISBN" ) > 0 then
      if i = 1 then
         lDataToclient = lDataToclient + string( &
               dw_1.GetItemNumber(i,"isbn"))
      else
         lDataToclient = lDataToclient + char (13) + &
               string( dw_1.GetItemNumber(i,"isbn"))
      End if
   End if
   If Pos( lItem, "TITLE" ) > 0 then
      lDataToclient = lDataToclient + "~t" + &
            dw_1.GetItemString(i,"title")
   End if
   If Pos( lItem, "AUTHOR" ) > 0 then
      lDataToclient = lDataToclient + "~t" + &
            dw_1.GetItemString(i,"author")
   End if

Next
SetDataDDE( lDataToclient )
RespondRemote( TRUE )
```

We simply loop through all the data in the DataWindow control using the **GetItemNumber()** or **GetItemString()** functions to retrieve the required data, and add it to **lDataToClient**.

The ~**t** is a special character that is used to place a tab between each of these entries - this is the way to manually create a tab-delimited list. When we've gone through all the data, we send **lDataToClient** to the client using the **SetDataDDE** command.

Running the Example

To see the example running, open up the w_dde_server window and click on the PB As Server button:

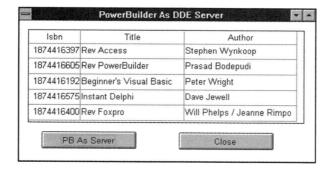

This fills the DataWindow control and sets up PowerBuilder as a server. Now open up the **PBSERVER.DOC** document and run the TalkToPBServer macro. You should get the following information inserted into the Word document:

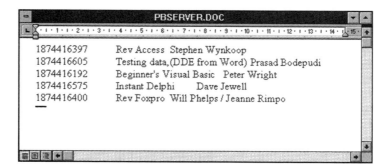

You can see that the Title of ISBN 1874416605 has been changed to display the test message, but has it been changed in PowerBuilder? Switch back to the w_dde_server window and you'll see that the value in the DataWindow control has also been changed:

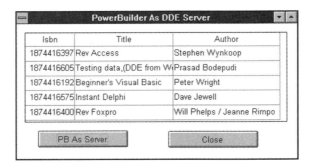

The actual value in the DataWindow object hasn't been changed, just the display in the DataWindow control. However, just as in the last example, it would be very easy to extend the code to retrieve and update actual information in a database.

> DDE can be temperamental so if you do experience problems getting any of the examples to work, try experimenting with different commands or use some of the logic used in other examples. The first step in finding problems is to check the references to file names used in the code and macros, ensuring that they correspond to your set up.
>
> If you have Microsoft Office installed on your C drive and you copy all the examples into a `C:\WROX` directory, you shouldn't have any problems running these examples as they stand.

Summary

In this chapter, we've seen the theory and concepts behind DDE and we've looked at a few examples which illustrate how PowerBuilder can be used as both a DDE Client and DDE Server.

Whilst DDE is a useful technology, it can be quite complex as you will have seen in some of the examples. In the next chapter we'll look at another method of inter-process communication - Object Linking and Embedding (OLE). We'll look at the concepts behind this fairly new technology and again provide you with some examples which illustrate just how easy it is to use OLE compared to the older standard of DDE.

Object Linking and Embedding

The new communication standard that everyone is interested in is called Object Linking and Embedding. By using OLE, you are working at the object level to share data by either physically embedding it into a working document or simply by providing the working document with the appropriate links to the source file.

This methodology transcends software boundaries, allowing you to pass information between different applications without the need for a third party file format that both the source and the target understand.

In this chapter, we will cover:

- The concepts behind OLE
- The differences between linking and embedding
- OLE Control attributes
- OLE Server menus
- OLE Automation

Introduction

The theory behind OLE is based upon one application using the functionality provided by another. Objects are linked to or embedded in your application and when activated, the application that originally created the alien object is used to handle any interactions that the user wishes to perform.

The application that has the object embedded or linked into it is called the **OLE Client** or **OLE Container Object**, while the application that created the embedded object is called **OLE Server**.

> *An application can be either an OLE Container or an OLE Server, or indeed both.*

Let's now move on to look at the benefits of using OLE.

Object Linking

By implementing object linking, applications can be linked to data objects within other applications. For example, a spreadsheet table can be linked to multiple custom business reports, and as changes are made to this table within the spreadsheet application, all report documents are automatically updated.

This is particularly useful for objects which may change over time or that are accessed by other people. You don't have to worry about checking if something has changed on your linked spreadsheet, because any changes done outside of your reports will automatically be reflected in the reports.

OLE Visual Editing

Visual Editing allows your users to easily create rich, compound documents, incorporating graphics, sound, video and other diverse object types. Instead of switching between applications to create parts of the compound document, users can work within the context of their document.

As the user begins to edit an object that originated in another application, such as a spreadsheet or graphics package, the menus and toolbars of the container application automatically change to the menu and toolbars of that object's native (server) application. The user can then edit the object in the context of the document, without worrying about activating and switching to another application.

Object Conversion

Objects can be converted to different types so that different applications can be used with the same object. For example, an object created with one type of wordprocessor can be converted so that it can be interpreted by a different wordprocessor.

Optimized Object Storage

Objects remain on disk until needed and are not loaded into memory each time the container application is opened. OLE also supports a transaction type storage system, providing the user with the ability to commit or rollback any changes that they make to the object. This ensures that data integrity is maintained as objects are stored in the file system.

Inserting Objects

All applications that can act as OLE Clients have a menu option called Insert Object. When this option is selected, all the installed OLE object classes for which supporting servers have been installed are displayed in a dialog box.

You can see this list if you open a new PowerBuilder window and select OLE 2.0 from the Controls menu. When you add the OLE object to the window, you'll get the following dialog box prompting for the type of OLE object to insert:

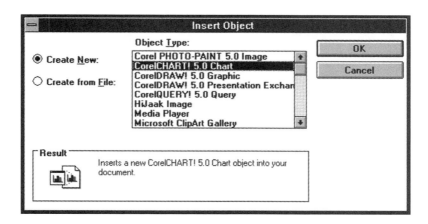

You can see that you have the choice of creating a new object or selecting from existing files. If you click the Create from File option, you'll be prompted for the filename and the option of linking or embedding:

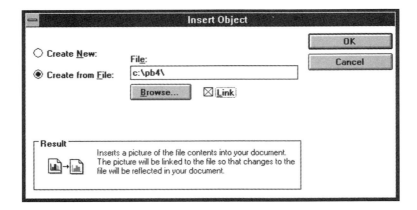

Whether you choose to link or embed an object, create a new object or select from existing files, the server application will be started up. So, if we select a .BMP file, Paintbrush will be opened, allowing us to edit the object:

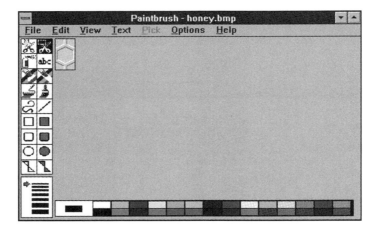

Linking or Embedding

There are several things to consider when deciding between linking or embedding an object:

- ▲ Will anyone else have access to data contained in objects outside of your application?

- ▲ Is the data contained in your objects of a static nature?

- ▲ Is the size of your application important?

- ▲ Is there a chance of someone moving files containing objects?

- ▲ Is speed important?

The following table highlights some of the differences between linking and embedding when considering these questions:

Linking	Embedding
If objects are changed outside your application, then the object in your application will be updated automatically.	An embedded object can only be edited from within your application.
Using linked objects will keep the size of your application down, as the objects are not stored within your application.	Embedded objects are stored within your application, so the file size is bigger.
When you use linked objects, your application contains the reference to the linked file, so if the file is moved, the link will be severed.	This isn't a problem with embedded objects.

Linking	Embedding
Linked objects are only loaded into your application when they are required, so start-up speed should be quicker. However, working with a linked object reduces the speed of your application, because the container has to link to the file.	Start-up speed will be slower because the file is bigger, but work with the embedded objects is quicker because the object already exists in your application.

A Practical Example

You can see the differences between linking and embedding in practical terms by running the w_link_embed window in the **OLE.PBL** library:

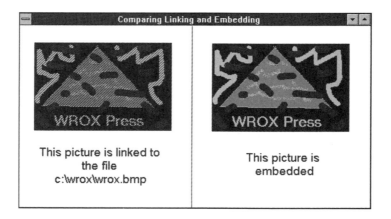

This contains two OLE objects which are exactly identical, except that one is linked and the other is embedded. You can edit either picture by double-clicking on it.

Linking

If you double-click on the linked picture and make changes to the picture in Paintbrush, you'll see that the changes immediately appear in the PowerBuilder window:

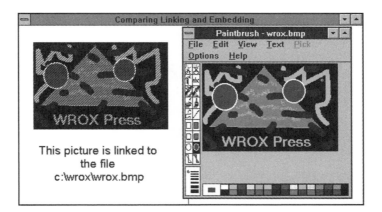

This is like the DDE Hotlink that we looked at in the previous chapter. If you close down Paintbrush, you'll be prompted to save the changes to file:

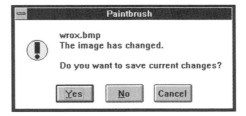

Even if you answer 'No' to this prompt, the changes you've made will still appear in the PowerBuilder window, but if you double-click on the image again, Paintbrush will open up with the unaltered image. The links to PowerBuilder are then updated, so the picture in the PowerBuilder window will change back to the original image:

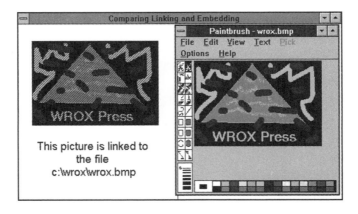

The same thing happens if you close the window and then run it again. PowerBuilder will update the links to the bitmap file:

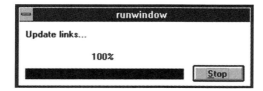

One of the main reasons for linking files is that you don't have to open PowerBuilder to get at the file. This is more important for multi-user applications, where many people have access to the same information. For example, you might have a spreadsheet containing sales information to which several departments in a company need access.

Linking allows you to hold the information in a single file and dynamically pull it to all the departments' applications. Whenever the sales information changes, you could update all the links, so that everybody sees the new information.

You can also implement a level of security with linked objects by restricting who can open them. For example, we might allow all the departments to view the sales figures, but only allow the Sales Department to change them. We'll see how you would do this later in the chapter when we look at OLE control properties.

If you open up the **WROX.BMP** file in Paintbrush and make some changes, when you run the PowerBuilder window without closing Paintbrush, you'll see the updated picture. If you then close the PowerBuilder window and return to the development environment, the changes will not be visible. In fact there are only four occasions when a linked document will be updated:

▲ When the window is first opened in the development environment.

▲ Whenever the window is actually run.

▲ When the changes that you make to the linked object are saved to disk.

▲ When you open the linked object from the development environment.

One potential problem that you might encounter when with using linked objects is that if the file containing the object is renamed or moved, PowerBuilder will not be able to find it. You can see what happens by renaming the **WROX.BMP** file and running the window again:

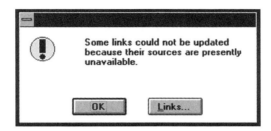

PowerBuilder informs us that some links couldn't be updated, and if you click on the Links... button it will display more information:

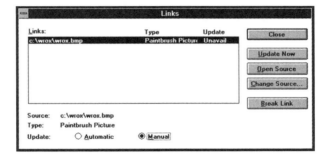

This allows you to break the link completely, force an update of the link or change the source of the object. If you change the source, you'll be prompted to supply the new name of the object:

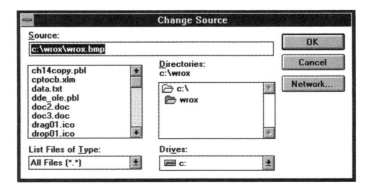

589

If you can't find the object, you can still open the PowerBuilder window and it will display the last saved version of the picture, but you won't be able to edit it.

Embedding

If you double-click on the embedded picture to activate Paintbrush and make some changes, you'll see that the image in the PowerBuilder window is not immediately updated:

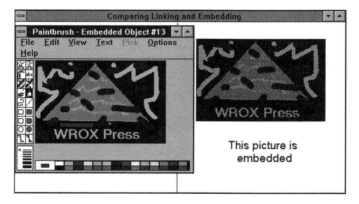

You can update the PowerBuilder window by selecting File/Update from Paintbrush or by closing Paintbrush, when you will be prompted to update the embedded picture:

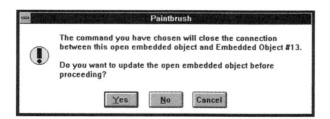

Answering 'No' to this will lose all the changes.

> Although embedded objects can only be activated from within PowerBuilder you can save them to a file simply by selecting **File**/ **Save As...** from the menu in the server application. However, this doesn't create any kind of link - to do this, you will have to start from scratch using linking rather than embedding.

OLE Control Attributes

To see an OLE control's attributes, double-click on it in the development environment:

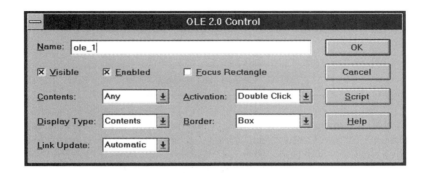

These options allow you to control how the OLE object behaves and how the user interacts with it at run-time. Let's take a look at the interesting ones.

Contents

This attribute defines the content of the OLE control. This attribute only applies to circumstances where the content is dynamically allocated at run-time using the **InsertObject()** function. There are three possibilities:

Option	Description
Any:	Allows linked or embedded objects to be inserted
Embedded:	Allows only embedded objects to be inserted
Linked:	Allows only linked objects to be inserted

You can see how this works by running the w_dynamic_ole window in the **OLE.PBL** library:

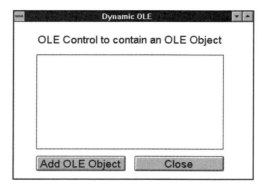

This allows you to assign an OLE object to the OLE control by clicking on the Add OLE Object button. Doing this brings up the standard Insert Object dialog box, allowing you to select the type of object you want to add:

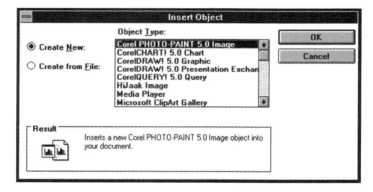

If you select the Create from File option, you'll get the usual screen except that the link option isn't available:

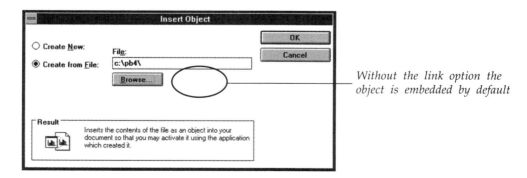

Without the link option the object is embedded by default

This is because we've specified that the contents should be embedded. If you close the window, change the Contents attribute of the OLE control to linked and run the window again. Clicking on the Add OLE Object button will then launch the select file dialog with the Link option already selected:

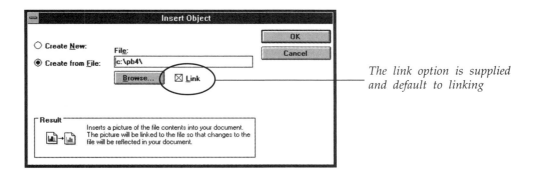

The link option is supplied and default to linking

> The **Contents** attribute is generally used to specify a default behavior as it can still be overwritten at run-time.

Display Type

This is used to specify whether you want to see the actual contents of the OLE object or an icon representing the server application. In our w_dynamic_ole window we've specified the display type to be icon. If you add a Paintbrush picture and specify an existing bitmap file, you'll see the following:

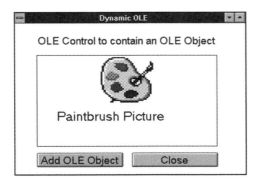

When you double-click on the control, the server application is invoked as usual and the bitmap file is displayed.

Note that you can only specify an icon when you add an object from an existing file.

In the Insert Object dialog box you have the option of changing the icon that is displayed for the server application. For example, if you insert an Excel spreadsheet you have the following options:

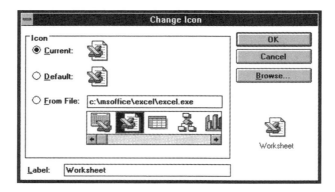

Activation

This allows you to specify how the OLE Server application is activated. The default method is Double Click, but you can change it to Get Focus or Manual. If you specify Manual, then you have to take care of activating the server programmatically. This is how you would implement the level of security which we talked about earlier. We've provided an example of this in the **OLE.PBL** library. Run the w_ole_security window:

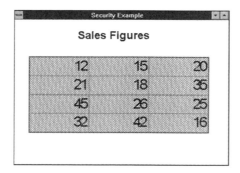

The OLE object that we have used for this example is the `TEST1.XLS` spreadsheet that we used in the previous DDE example.

> *It is a linked object, so if you've put this file in a different directory, you'll have to change the link information.*

We've specified the Activation to be Manual, so double-clicking on the OLE object won't activate the OLE Server. Instead, we've written some code in the `doubleclicked` event of the control to display a text box and SingleLineEdit control to accept a password to access it:

Please enter Password [|]

If you type in the wrong password, we display a message box telling you that the password is wrong:

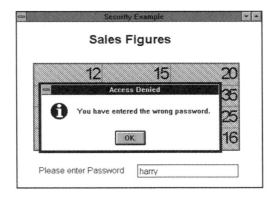

If you type in the correct password, 'fred', then we activate the OLE Server using the following line of code:

```
result = ole_1.Activate(Offsite!)
```

The `Offsite!` enumerated variable opens the server in its own window.

> *When using OLE, you can choose to have the server open in its own window or in the same window as your PowerBuilder application. We'll see in the next section how this works.*

595

Excel will open up, displaying the **TEST1.XLS** spreadsheet ready for us to edit:

This is a very simple example with only a few lines of code, but you can see how powerful it can be.

OLE Server Menus

In the example above, we opened Excel in its own window. You can also open a server in the same window as your PowerBuilder application, which is, in fact, the default behaviour. When an OLE Server is opened in-place, the PowerBuilder application's menu bar will be occupied by the Server application's version.

How this occupation is implemented depends on the options you set in the PowerBuilder application's menu:

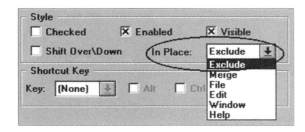

The In Place attribute is set only for menu bar items, not menu items. Some useful options are:

Option	Description
Exclude:	When the menu bar item is set to Exclude, it will not be displayed in the resulting menu.
Merge:	The menu bar item will be merged with the server application menu.
File:	This will display the menu bar item in the place occupied by the File menu option, that is, the first option on the menu.
Window:	This will display the menu bar item in the place usually occupied by the Window menu option, that is, the second option from the right.

To see this working, we've included several windows in the `OLEMENU.PBL` library which contain an OLE 2.0 control containing an embedded Word 6.0 document. All the windows have the same basic menu attached to them:

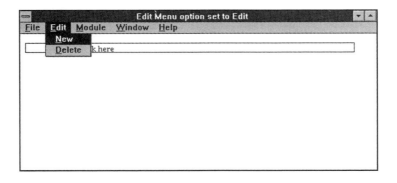

The In Place options have been set for the Edit menu bar item.

w_edit_menu_option_set_to_exclude

In this window, all the menu bar items have been set to Exclude, so when you double-click on the OLE control, none of the PowerBuilder application's menu options will be visible:

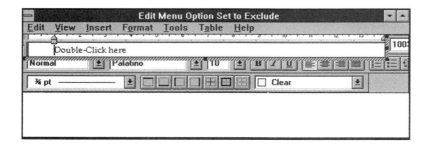

Note that this is exactly the same as a standard Word 6.0 menu.

> *Note that the **File** menu isn't available. This is because the OLE object is embedded rather than linked.*

w_edit_menu_option_set_to_merge

In this window the Edit menu bar item has been set to Merge, so when you activate the OLE object, you'll see two Edit menu options:

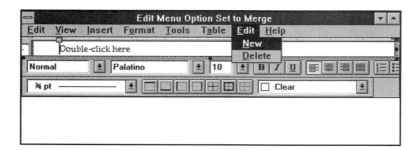

You can see that the second Edit menu option is our PowerBuilder application's menu option.

w_edit_menu_option_set_to_file

This window has the Edit menu bar item set to File. When you run this window and open the server application, our Edit menu appears where the File menu would normally be:

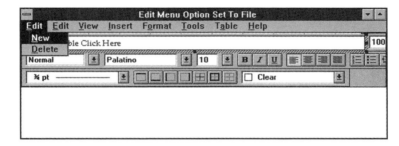

w_edit_menu_option_set_to_window

Our final example has the Edit menu bar item set to Window. Opening the server application from this window gives the following:

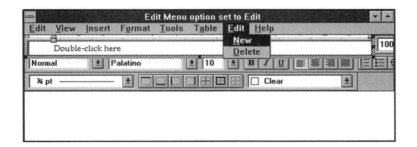

You can see that our Edit menu option appears second from the right, the position normally occupied by the Window menu option.

OLE 2.0 Automation

Up until now, you have been learning about the activation of an OLE 2.0 server from a PowerBuilder application and how the user can interact with the server application. However, OLE 2.0 allows you to do much more than simply activate the server application.

OLE Automation is a Windows protocol intended to replace DDE. As with DDE, an application can use OLE Automation to share data or control another application. Once the server is active, you can use a command set provided by the server to manipulate the object, a task that you can perform behind the scenes, out of the user's sight.

This technology is especially useful if you need to use features of one application in another. With OLE Automation, you can integrate features from both applications in a single procedure. For example, a PowerBuilder application can use Microsoft Excel as a financial calculation engine.

Whenever the PowerBuilder application needs to have a financial calculation performed, it can simply call one of Excel's functions, passing the data to be calculated as parameters. Excel performs the calculation and returns the results to the PowerBuilder application. In this way, applications can greatly extend their capabilities by transparently using the functions of other applications.

In the DDE section, we did a mail merge in Microsoft Word by sending data from our PowerBuilder application. In the following example, we'll do something similar using OLE Automation.

Mail Merge with OLE 2.0

In the case of DDE, the server application (Word) is visible to the user. The same is true when you place an OLE 2.0 control in a window and invoke the server application. However, you don't need to place an OLE control on a window to manipulate an OLE object in your script. If you think that user interaction isn't necessary, you can create an OLE object independent of an OLE control, connect to the server application, calling functions and setting attributes as you wish for that object.

The following example uses the same DataWindow containing address details that we used in the DDE example and another Word document to act as the form letter. The following figure illustrates the process involved:

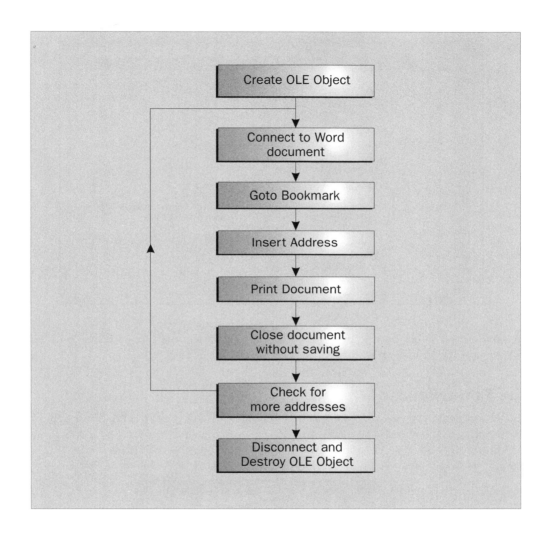

LETTER2.DOC

If you open up **LETTER2.DOC**, you'll see that it contains some text and a blank heading ready for the address:

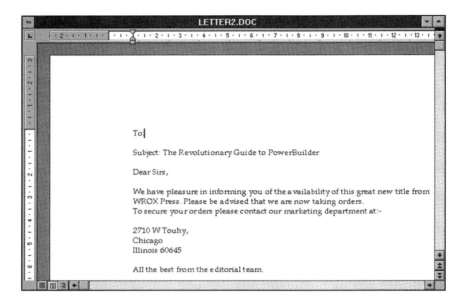

We've defined a bookmark called 'Address' after the word To: and we will use this to specify where the address should go.

The PowerBuilder Window

This example is the w_ole20_mail_merge window in the **OLE20.PBL** library. If you open up the window, you'll see that it contains a DataWindow control containing the address information and just two CommandButtons:

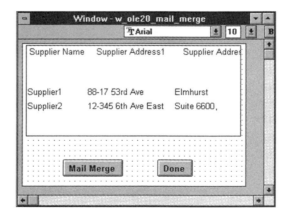

The code for the **clicked** event of the Mail Merge button is as follows:

```
Int lResult
Long lTotRows,i,j
String lAddress

// Declare and create ole object.
OLEObject OLEMailMerge
OLEMailMerge = CREATE OLEObject

lResult = OLEMailMerge.ConnectToNewObject( "word.basic" )

If lResult <> 0 Then
   DESTROY OLEMailMerge
   MessageBox( "Error in connecting to Word for Windows", &
         "Error Code: " + String( lResult ) )
   Return
End If

lTotRows = dwc_1.Rowcount()
For i = 1 to lTotRows Step 1
   lAddress = dwc_1.GetItemString(i,1)

   For j = 2 to 6 Step 1
      lAddress = lAddress + "~r~n" + dwc_1.GetItemString(i,j)
   Next

   ClipBoard( lAddress )
   lResult = OLEMailMerge.FileOpen( "C:\wrox\Letter2.Doc" )

   If lResult <> 0 Then
      DESTROY OLEMailMerge
      MessageBox( "Error in connecting to Word for Windows", &
            "Error Code: " + String( lResult ) )
      Return
   End If

// These are the important commands:

   OLEMailMerge.editgoto( "Address" )
   OLEMailMerge.insert( lAddress )
   OLEMailMerge.FilePrint()
   OLEMailMerge.FileClose( 2 )

Next

lResult = OLEMailMerge.DisConnectObject()
DESTROY OLEMailMerge
```

We define **OLEMailMerge** as an OLE object, connect to the Word document and then send the various server commands. The important lines are:

Code	Description
OLEMailMerge.editgo("Address"):	This sends the command to go to the bookmark.
OLEMailMerge.insert(lAddress):	This inserts the address.
OLEMailMerge.FilePrint():	This prints the document.
OLEMailMerge.FileClose(2):	This closes the document without saving it.

We close the document without saving it, so that when we loop around for the next address, we can reopen the document as a clean copy.

> **Any attribute, function or parameter used against this object is referred to the server. So PowerBuilder doesn't need to know whether they are valid or not, and will not check them. If the functions or attributes are invalid, you will get an error at run-time.**

When you run this window and click on the Mail Merge button, you won't see much happening, but assuming your computer is connected to a printer, you should get two printed copies of our form letter, one for each of the addresses in our DataWindow:

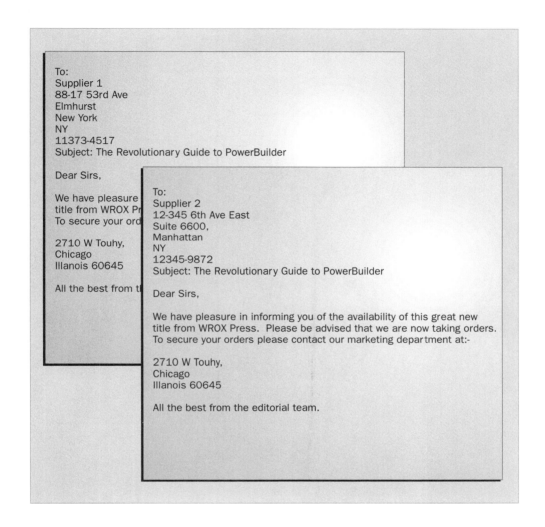

To:
Supplier 1
88-17 53rd Ave
Elmhurst
New York
NY
11373-4517
Subject: The Revolutionary Guide to PowerBuilder

Dear Sirs,

We have pleasure
title from WROX Pr
To secure your ord

2710 W Touhy,
Chicago
Illanois 60645

All the best from t

To:
Supplier 2
12-345 6th Ave East
Suite 6600,
Manhattan
NY
12345-9872
Subject: The Revolutionary Guide to PowerBuilder

Dear Sirs,

We have pleasure in informing you of the availability of this great new
title from WROX Press. Please be advised that we are now taking orders.
To secure your orders please contact our marketing department at:-

2710 W Touhy,
Chicago
Illanois 60645

All the best from the editorial team.

Summary

We've looked at the theory behind OLE technology and shown you how it can be implemented in your PowerBuilder applications. The Mail Merge example should have shown you how easy it is to use OLE Automation and highlighted the differences between OLE and DDE.

Embedded SQL and Dynamic DataWindows

Up to this point, you have learned how to use the **SELECT** statement in a DataWindow. You also know that when you issue the **Update()** function, PowerBuilder automatically generates **INSERT**, **DELETE** and **UPDATE** statements, depending on the row status, effectively saving your information back to the database.

Now we are going to extend our coverage of SQL to take into account two particular subsets: embedded SQL and dynamic SQL. We'll also take a look at Dynamic DataWindows, Cursors and Stored Procedures.

In this chapter, we will cover:

▲ PowerBuilder specific SQL statements

▲ Using Cursors and Stored Procedures

▲ Dynamic SQL formats

▲ Using the DW Syntax tool

Embedded SQL

The Structured Query Language is the most popular and commonly known database query language, so it makes sense that when you want to query a database, you should use SQL.

Providing support for embedded SQL ensures that a language has the means to query most database engines for information. When you use this particular type of SQL, the statements are directly embedded into your code, introduced by keywords particular to the language that you are using.

These statements are put through a pre-compilation which translates them into the equivalent functions or statements in the host language. For example, you can use embedded SQL in a C program as follows:

```
EXEC SQL INCLUDE SQLCA ;

EXEC SQL BEGIN DECLARE SECTION ;
    DBCHAR mDescription[32] ;
    DBINT mItemNumber ;
EXEC SQL END DECLARE SECTION ;
...
EXEC SQL SELECT DESCRIPTION
    INTO :mDescription
    FROM ITEM_MASTER
    WHERE ITEM_NO = :mItemNumber ;
...
printf( "Item No: %d, Description: %s", mItemNumber, mDescription) ;
```

EXEC SQL are the keywords that C uses to identify SQL statements. Otherwise, the SQL statements are exactly the same as you would find in a database administrator's handbook.

Writing embedded SQL is very easy in PowerBuilder as it automatically detects SQL keywords, making special keywords redundant. The only thing you need to do is terminate the SQL statements with a semicolon (;).

> SQL statements can span multiple lines without the need for the line continuation character.

PowerBuilder Implementation

SQL, and indeed the whole theory of relational databases, is based on sets. The subject of database theory is a whole book on its own, so we won't try to teach you everything here, but we can look at some of PowerBuilder's implementations.

The simplest way of using SQL in your PowerScript code is to use the Paste SQL option on the Script PainterBar. When you click on this icon, PowerBuilder presents you with the following options:

This allows you to select the type of SQL statement you want to insert, after which PowerBuilder launches the usual query selection dialog boxes designed to speed up the creation of the statement:

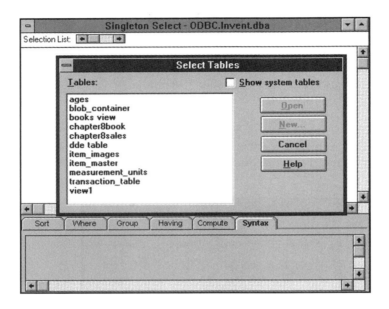

PowerBuilder now allows you to select the tables to be displayed for your reference. Before we can take a look at the various SQL structures that we can use at this stage, we must take a look at the concept of **Host Variables**.

Using Host Variables

SQL statements in PowerBuilder can make use of existing variables by prefixing the variable name with a colon (:). For example, in the following code we make reference to the **lItemNo** variable in the SQL statement:

```
Int lItemNo

lItemNo = Integer( sle_itemno.Text )

SELECT "item_master1"."item_description"
   INTO :lItemDesc
   FROM "item_master1"
   WHERE "item_master1"."item_no" = :lItemNo ;
```

Host variables are most commonly in the following areas:

▲ **WHERE** clause

▲ **HAVING** clause

▲ **INTO** variables

▲ **VALUES** clause in **INSERT** statements

▲ In place of values in **SET** clauses in **UPDATE** statements

▲ As parameter values for Stored Procedures

SELECT INTO

When the SQL statement returns a single row, you can use the **SELECT INTO** statement to pass the results into host variables. For example:

```
String lItemDesc
Int lItemNo

lItemNo = Integer( sle_itemno.Text )

SELECT "item_master1"."item_description"
    INTO :lItemDesc
    FROM "item_master1"
    WHERE "item_master1"."item_no" = :lItemNo ;

If SQLCA.SQLCODE <> 0 then
    // ....
End if
```

This stores the result of the **SELECT** statement in the host variable **lItemDesc**, earlier initialized as a string. **SQLCA** contains the result of the last executed SQL statement, so we can use it to check that the operation was successful. The **SQLCODE** attribute can have three possible values:

Value	Result
0	Success
-1	Error
10	No results returned

As we saw in a previous chapter, you can check the other attributes of **SQLCA** to see more information. For example, any error messages are contained in **SQLCA.SqlErrText**, while the database error number is in **SQLCA.SQLDbCode**.

There are times when the result column may return a NULL value. Even though PowerBuilder doesn't provide you with a method for checking for this value in normal SQL, there is a way to check for it in embedded SQL. This method is to suffix the host column variable name with an indicator, separated by a colon.

> Note that the indicator should be declared as an integer.

The following example assumes that the description column in item_master allows NULL values:

```
String lItemDesc
Int lItemNo, lDescInd1

lItemNo = Integer( sle_itemno.Text )

SELECT "item_master1"."item_description"
    INTO :lItemDesc:lDescInd1
    FROM "item_master1"
    WHERE "item_master1"."item_no" = :lItemNo;

If SQLCA.SQLCODE <> 0 then
    // ....
End if
```

lDescInd1 is the indicator we have used in this example and it can have one of the following values:

Value	Result
0	Valid, not a NULL
-1	NULL
-2	Conversion error

The UPDATE Statement

You can explicitly execute an **UPDATE** statement through embedded SQL. For example, in the w_transactions window in our application, for each receipt, you have to update the balance in the master file. Calling the **Update()** function updates the transaction file, but since you're not making any changes in the w_item_master DataWindow, you can't call it. The only way to do this is to update through embedded SQL, as shown in the following example:

```
UPDATE "item_master"
    SET "last_receipt_date" = :lRcptDt,
        "balance" = balance + :lQuantity,
        "current_price" = :lPrice
        WHERE item_no = :lItemNo ;

If SQLCA.SQLNRows Then
    RollBack Using SQLCA ;
    MessageBox( "Error while Updating Balance", "Error No:" + &
        SQLCA.SQLDbCode" + "~r" + &
        "Error Message: " + SQLCA.SQLErrText )
    Return
End If
```

To find the number of rows affected by the **UPDATE** statement, we can check **SQLCA.SqlNRows** after the **UPDATE** command has been successfully executed.

The INSERT Statement

You can execute two forms of the **INSERT** statement. The following format inserts a row into the **item_master1** table.

```
INSERT INTO guest.item_master1
    ( item_no,
    item_description,
    last_receipt_date,
    last_issue_date,
    balance,
    re_order_level,
    measuring_unit,
    current_price )
VALUES ( :lItemNo,
    :lDesc,
    :lRcptDt,
    :lIssDt,
    :lBal,
    :lROrdLvl,
    :lMsUnt,
    :lUntPrc ) ;
```

The second format inserts more than one row with a single statement. Suppose you wanted to insert all the records from the **item_master** table into a history table **item_master1**. You could use the following code:

```
INSERT INTO item_master1
   ( <column list> )
   SELECT < column list >
   FROM item_master ;
```

where you replace **<column list>** with the list of all the columns in the table. If you have a table with a lot of columns, this can turn into a very big SQL statement. However, PowerBuilder does support the asterisk wildcard character (*), which allows you to select all the columns at once:

```
INSERT INTO item_master1
   SELECT *
   FROM item_master ;
```

This may not work with all databases, so you will have to check with your specific database vendor's documentation.

The DELETE Statement

The **DELETE** statement can be used to delete selected entries from a database table. It can be used as follows:

```
Int iDelYears
iDelYears = Integer( em_DelYears.Text )

DELETE FROM item_master
   WHERE datediff( Year, GetDate(), last_receipt_date ) > :iDelYears ;
```

This uses the **datediff()** function to check the difference, in years, between the current date and the **last_receipt_date** column in the table. It deletes any record where the difference is greater than the value in the **iDelYears** variable entered by the user. Here, we could also check **SQLNRows** to determine how many rows were affected.

Cursors

Cursors are a useful way of retrieving more than one result row, and also allow you to process one row at a time. Like a cursor on the computer screen, a result set cursor indicates the current position in the result set. The cursor points to a single row of data and can only scroll forward one row at a time. In other words, an application can only retrieve one single row, or move through the result set, one row at a time.

Declaring and Executing a Cursor

To use a cursor in an application, you first need to define it using the **DECLARE** statement. This allows you to define both the cursor name and the associated SQL statement you want to execute. Unfortunately, simply defining the cursor with the DECLARE statement doesn't automatically execute the specified SQL statement - it's merely a declarative statement.

Creating a Cursor

When you paste a cursor declaration into your PowerScript, PowerBuilder lets you select a table and then creates a template for you:

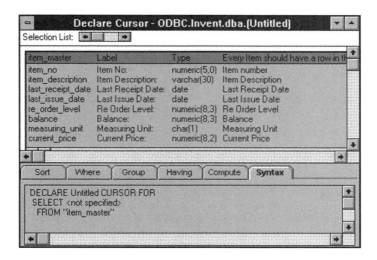

When you have created the SQL statement, PowerBuilder prompts for the cursor name and then pastes the statement into your script:

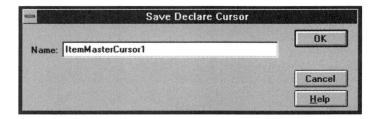

For example, to retrieve all the item numbers and descriptions from item_master, you could declare as follows:

```
DECLARE ItemMasterCursor1 CURSOR FOR
   SELECT item_no,
       item_description
   FROM item_master ;
```

ItemMasterCursor1 is the name of the cursor to which we will refer in the script.

Executing the Cursor

An **OPEN** statement actually executes the cursor:

```
OPEN ItemMasterCursor1 ;

If SQLCA.SQLCODE <> 0 then
       //
End If
```

Again, we can use **SQLCODE** to provide some error handling.

Isolation Level

Watcom supports **isolation levels** with the **OPEN   <cursor   name>** statement, but PowerBuilder doesn't support this. The isolation level specifies the kinds of actions which are not permitted while the current transactions execute. The ANSI standard defines three levels of isolation for SQL transactions:

▲ Level 1 prevents **dirty reads**

▲ Level 2 also prevents **non-repeatable reads**

▲ Level 3 prevents both types of reads and **phantoms**.

Dirty Reads

A dirty read occurs when one transaction modifies a row and a second reads it before the first has been able to commit the change. If the first transaction rolls back the change, the information read by the second transaction becomes invalid.

For example, Tran1 reads the row for **item_no** 10, which has a balance of 120, and then updates it to 100. Tran2 then reads the same row and gets the balance as 100. Now Tran1 issues a **RollBack**, which sets the balance to the previous value of 120. At this moment, Tran2 thinks the balance is 100, when in fact it is really 120:

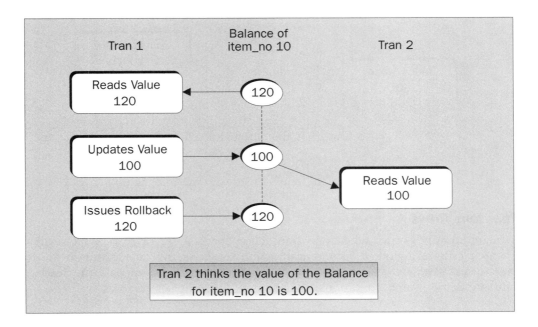

Non-Repeatable Reads

A non-repeatable read occurs when one transaction reads a row, and then a second transaction modifies that row. If the second transaction commits its change, subsequent reads by the first transaction yield different results from the original.

For example, Tran1 reads the row for **item_no** 10 and sets the balance to 120. Now Tran2 reads the same row, updates it to 80 and commits. If Tran1 then reads the same row again, it will get 80, instead of 120:

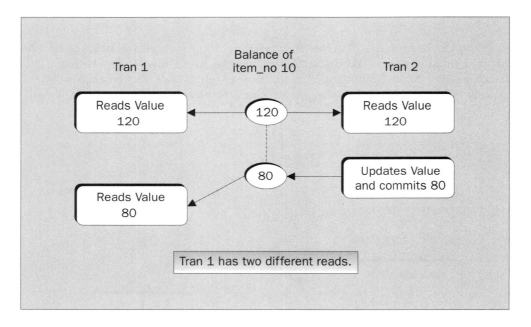

Phantom Rows

A phantom row occurs when one transaction reads a set of rows which satisfy a search criteria, before a second transaction modifies the data (through an **INSERT**, **DELETE**, **UPDATE** and so on). If the first transaction repeats the read with the same search conditions, it obtains a different set of rows.

Suppose Tran1 issues the following **SELECT** statement:

```
SELECT item_no FROM item_master WHERE balance < re_order_level
```

and gets 75 rows. If Tran2 then does some processing, which makes the balance of another 10 items fall below the `re_order_level`, when Tran1 issues the same statement again, it will get 85 rows instead of 75.

The FETCH Statement

To retrieve each row in a cursor and load it into host variables, you can use a **FETCH** statement. This statement allows you to fetch one row at a time, moving through the result set after each **FETCH**. You need to check **SQLCA.SQLCODE** to find the end of the result set. Have a look at the following example:

```
FETCH ItemMasterCursor1 INTO :lItemNo, :lItemDesc ;

Do While SQLCA.SQLCODE <> 100
    // Do While SQLCA.SQLCODE = 100
    // Some processing such as loading into a ListBox, etc.
    FETCH ItemMasterCursor1 INTO :lItemNo, :lItemDesc ;
Loop

CLOSE ItemMasterCursor1 ;
```

Once all the rows have been returned, we close the cursor with the **CLOSE** command.

Cursors and Transaction Objects

The **DECLARE** statement uses an **SQLCA** Transaction Object. If you need to use a different Transaction Object, you have to add a **USING   TransactObject_Name>** clause at the end of the **SELECT** part of the **DECLARE** statement. For example:

```
DECLARE ItemMasterCursor1 CURSOR FOR
    SELECT item_no,
        item_description
    FROM item_master
    USING TranObjForSQLServer ;
```

You can only specify a Transaction Object name in the **DECLARE** statement. There is no need to specify it in the **OPEN**, **FETCH** and **CLOSE** statements.

Scrollable Cursors

You can also make a cursor scrollable. It can move forwards or backwards through the result set, or move to an absolute or relative position in the result set. In other words, an application can retrieve the next or previous row of data, retrieve a specific row of data, or retrieve a row of data at a specified distance from the current row.

Even though PowerBuilder supports scrollable cursors, being able to use them depends on the back-end support. You can use the following commands while using scrollable cursors:

- FETCH PRIOR
- FETCH FIRST
- FETCH NEXT
- FETCH LAST

If you don't specify any clause after the **FETCH**, it is **NEXT** by default. Sybase System 10 doesn't support scrollable cursors, but Watcom supports scrolling to an absolute position or relative position in the cursor result set.

Updating Through a Cursor

An application can update or delete the row in the result set to which the cursor currently points using **CURRENT**. For example:

```
UPDATE "item_master"
   SET "balance" = balance + 100
   WHERE CURRENT OF ItemMasterCursor1 ;
```

In this example, instead of using a **WHERE** clause, we give the name of the cursor. This updates the row at the current cursor position - suppose you fetch four items and issue this command, the fourth row is the one that gets updated. Updating a cursor doesn't change the row position in the result set. There are a few points to bear in mind when updating through a cursor:

1 A fetch, update or delete will return an error if any of the columns have been changed since they were last read, even if the column is not included in the **SELECT** list. If any of the rows in the results' set been deleted, it will create a hole in the cursor result set, and if you try to fetch the same row, it will result in an error.

You can get round this by using a Dynamic Scroll cursor. The Watcom syntax for declaring a cursor is:

```
DECLARE <cursor-name> [ SCROLL | NO SCROLL | DYNAMIC SCROLL ]
CURSOR FOR <statement> [ FOR UPDATE | FOR READ ONLY ]
```

You simply specify whether you want scrolling, no scrolling or dynamic scrolling. A dynamic cursor won't return an error, but will skip the changed row and fetch the next row. The final clause of the declaration statement specifies whether you want to allow updates or if it is to be read-only.

2 If you use any aggregate functions, **DISTINCT** options, **GROUP BY** clauses, **ORDER BY** clauses or **UNION** operators, the cursor is not updatable. Also, when you specify **FOR UPDATE**, the table should have at least one unique index, otherwise it will result in an error.

3 You can't paint this **UPDATE** statement with a **WHERE CURRENT OF** clause from the Edit/Paste SQL menu option, if you have declared a cursor in the script. Only when you declare a cursor as a shared, instance or global cursor can you paste the SQL by selecting Declare from the menu option.

Deleting Through a Cursor

To delete the current row in a cursor result set, the procedure is similar to updating:

```
DELETE FROM "item_master"
   WHERE CURRENT OF ItemMasterCursor1 ;
```

As with updating through a cursor, deleting a row is not allowed if the **SELECT** list contains aggregate functions or uses a **GROUP BY** clause.

Stored Procedures

Stored procedures are collections of SQL statements which are stored at the database level. When a stored procedure is first run, an execution plan is prepared, which makes any subsequent execution of the procedure very fast. Also, since the stored procedure is stored in the database, the client application only needs to send the stored procedure name and parameters, if any, for the procedure to run. This reduces network traffic and makes the execution faster.

If the database back-end supports stored procedures, you can execute them from a PowerBuilder application's script. Both WATCOM v4.0 and SQL Server support stored procedures.

> *Versions of Watcom SQL prior to v4.0 don't support stored procedures.*

Let's look at the syntax involved in each of these.

Watcom Stored Procedures

A simple example of a procedure is shown below:

```
CREATE PROCEDURE sp_list_item_balance(IN pBalance integer)
RESULT(item_no integer, description char(32), balance integer)
   BEGIN
      SELECT item_no, item_description, balance
      FROM item_master
      WHERE balance > pBalance
   END ;
```

Note that we place any required parameters into the brackets following the procedure name. The keyword **IN** specifies the purpose of the parameter, and can be either **IN**, **OUT** or **INOUT**, and is followed by the name of the parameter and its data type.

In the result parentheses, you need to declare all the columns that are returned by the **SELECT** statement. We then declare the **SELECT** statement between the **BEGIN** and **END** keywords.

> *The names in the result declaration can be same as the column names.*

We could execute this procedure from the Database Administration Painter using the following syntax:

```
EXECUTE sp_list_item_balance( 1000 )
```

There are lots of limitations to Watcom stored procedures, such as that without conditional statements, you can't have more than one SQL statement and you can't specify a default value to be used as the parameter.

SQL Server Stored Procedures

On the other hand, SQL Server stored procedures are both powerful and flexible. Only for those parameters where you want a value returned do you need to specify the **OUTPUT** keyword. You can specify default values and have as many SQL statements as you want. The syntax is as follows:

```
CREATE PROCEDURE Proc2 @TimeInYears int, @affected_count int =NULL OUTPUT as
    SELECT item_no, item_description, balance
    FROM item_master
    WHERE datediff(Year, last_receipt_date, GetDate() ) >= @TimeInYears

SELECT @affected_count = @@rowcount

SELECT @affected_count

return (0)
```

Note that in SQL Server, there is no need to declare the result set.

To execute an SQL Server stored procedure in the Database Administration Painter, we would use the following:

```
Execute proc2 2 ;
```

> *Note that there is no need to use parentheses for the parameter.*

Using a Stored Procedure in PowerScript

As we've already seen, you can execute a stored procedure by specifying it as a data source to a DataWindow. To execute a stored procedure through PowerScript, you can either use embedded SQL or dynamic SQL.

There are four steps involved in using a stored procedure through embedded SQL:

1 Declaration

2 Execution

3 Retrieving rows

4 Closing

623

Declaring a Stored Procedure

To declare a stored procedure, you simply select the icon in the Paste SQL dialog box. This brings up a list of the currently available procedures:

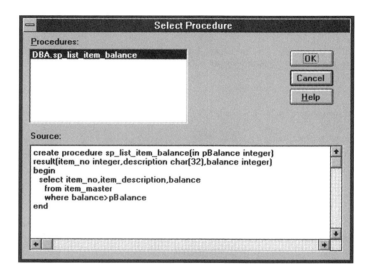

When you select the procedure you want, you'll be prompted to supply any parameters that are required:

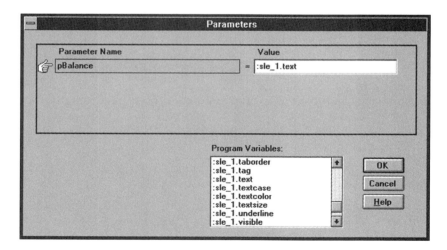

This allows you to select from a predefined list of available program variables, so for example, if you have a SingleLineEdit control on your window, you can supply a **text** attribute as the parameter, so that a user could type in a value at run-time.

Once you supply the parameter values, you'll be prompted for a name for the procedure:

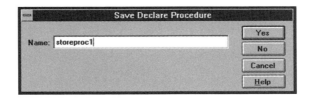

The declaration statement will then be pasted into your script:

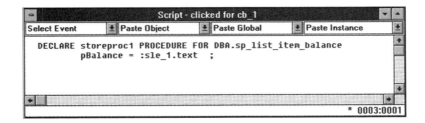

Executing a Stored Procedure

To execute a stored procedure, you simply use the **EXECUTE** command in your PowerScript:

```
EXECUTE storeproc1;
```

This is similar to the cursor's **OPEN** command, so it won't surprise you to know that we can also use the **FETCH** commands to retrieve all the data.

Executing a Remote Stored Procedure

When connected to SQL Server, you can execute a stored procedure based upon a different server to the one you are working on. To do this, you qualify the stored procedure name with the appropriate server and database names.

For example, if the SQL Server stored procedure we saw above is residing on Server2 and our application is connected to Server1, we could execute the stored procedure by declaring it as follows:

```
DECLARE lProc_0001 PROCEDURE FOR Server2.DB1.dbo.Proc2
   @TimeInYears = :lTimeInYears,
   @affected_count = :laffected_count OUTPUT ;
```

> *A remote stored procedure has a different meaning when connected to a DB2 database via the MDI Database Gateway for DB2. Here, a Remote Stored Procedure (RSP) is a customer-written CICS program which can be initiated by a client application, such as PowerBuilder. The CICS program can be written in COBOL II, Assembler, PL/1 or C. RSPs are unique to the MDI Database Gateway for DB2 or MVS solution.*

Retrieving Multiple Result Sets

When a stored procedure has more than one result set, you can only retrieve one set at a time. When the script fetches the first result set, **SQLCODE** is populated with the **100** result code. From then onwards, the values of the second result set are available to the script.

> Note that a stored procedure can contain multiple SQL **SELECT** statements.

For example, the following script would execute an **sp_help** stored procedure. If you supply a table name as parameter, it would give five result sets. The script listed below fetches the first two result sets:

```
// This script assumes there are 2 DataWindow controls in the window with
appropriate columns and data types.

String lObjectName, lOwner, lObjectType, lDataSegment
Long lNewRow
DateTime lCreationTime

lObjectName = "sysobjects"

DECLARE sp_help_proc PROCEDURE FOR dbo.sp_help
     @objname = :lObjectName ;

EXECUTE sp_help_proc ;
If SQLCA.SQLcode <> 0 Then
```

```
      MessageBox( "Error", SQLCA.SQLErrorText )
      Close sp_help_proc ;
      Return
End If

dwc_1.Title = "Result Set: #1"
Do While True
   Fetch sp_help_proc
      INTO :lObjectName, :lOwner, :lObjectType ;
   If SQLCA.SQLcode = 100 Then Exit
   lNewRow = dwc_1.InsertRow(0)
   dwc_1.SetItem( lNewRow, 1, lObjectName )
   dwc_1.SetItem( lNewRow, 2, lOwner )
   dwc_1.SetItem( lNewRow, 3, lObjectType )
Loop

dwc_2.Title = "Result Set: #2"
Do While True
   FETCH sp_help_proc
      INTO :lDataSegment, :lCreationTime ;
   If SQLCA.SQLCOde = 100 or SQLCA.SQLCode = -1 Then Exit
   lNewRow = dwc_2.InsertRow(0)
   dwc_2.SetItem( lNewRow, 1, lDataSegment )
   dwc_2.SetItem( lNewRow, 2, lCreationTime )
Loop

Close sp_help_proc ;
```

Dynamic SQL

Dynamic SQL consists of a set of embedded SQL facilities that are specially provided for the construction of generalized, on-line (and possibly interactive) applications. PowerBuilder doesn't support certain SQL statements either through a DataWindow or embedded SQL. These include:

- ▲ Data Definition Language (DDL), for example, **CREATE TABLE**
- ▲ Certain forms of **SELECT** statements, for example, **SELECT * from #Temp1**, which selects from a temporary table - a table that doesn't exist at compile time
- ▲ **SET** commands, for example, **SET ROWCOUNT 100**
- ▲ The commands to **GRANT** and **REVOKE** privileges, for example, **GRANT SELECT on item_master to public**

You can get round these problems by using dynamic SQL. Since PowerBuilder doesn't check for SQL syntax errors at compile time, it is up to the database to take care of the details.

We can broadly divide dynamic SQL statements into 4 categories:

1 Non-result set statements with no input parameters.

2 Non-result set statements with input parameters.

3 Result set statements in which the input parameters and result set columns are known at compile time.

4 Result set statements in which the input parameters, the result set columns or both are unknown at compile time.

You need to use slightly different formats in order to execute each of these statements. Dynamic SQL introduces two new terms, Dynamic Staging Area and Dynamic Description Area.

Dynamic Staging Area

Dynamic Staging Area is used internally by PowerBuilder and is the connection between the execution of a statement and a Transaction Object. You can't access the information in the Dynamic Staging Area. PowerBuilder provides a global-level Dynamic Staging Area named **SQLSA**. This contains the following information for use in subsequent statements:

- The SQL statement in your **PREPARE** statement
- The number of parameters
- The Transaction Object for use in subsequent statements

Dynamic Description Area

The Dynamic Description Area stores information about the input and output parameters and is used with the fourth format of dynamic SQL. PowerBuilder provides a global-level Dynamic Description Area named **SQLDA** that has the following structure:

Attributes	Meaning
SQLDA.NumInputs	Number of input parameters
SQLDA.InParmType	Array of input parameter types
SQLDA.NumOutputs	Number of output parameters
SQLDA.OutParmType	Array of output parameter types

The two principal statements of dynamic SQL are **PREPARE** and **EXECUTE**. The **PREPARE** statement takes the base SQL commands and places them in the **SQLSA** command buffer for execution. The **EXECUTE** statement passes these commands from the buffer to the back-end database and returns the feedback information to **SQLCA** as usual.

Format 1

If a series of SQL statements contains no **SELECT** statements and has no parameters, it can be executed without an explicit **PREPARE**. This is done with the **EXECUTE IMMEDIATE** statement which has the following form:

```
EXECUTE  IMMEDIATE  :
String_Variable_that_contains_SQL_Statement  ;
```

The following example creates a table called item_price_table:

```
String lSqlString
lSqlString = 'CREATE TABLE "dba"."item_price_table" ' + &
    ' ("item_no" numeric(5,0) NOT NULL, ' + &
    ' "effective_date" date NOT NULL, ' + &
    ' "price" numeric(8,3) NOT NULL ' + &
    ' , PRIMARY KEY (item_no, effective_date) ' + &
    ' , FOREIGN KEY item_master_foreignkey_to_item_price(' + &
    'item_no ) REFERENCES "dba"."item_master" )'

EXECUTE IMMEDIATE :lSqlString ;

if SQLCA.SQLCODE <> 0 then
   MessageBox( "ERROR", string( sqlca.sqlcode ) + SQLCA.SqlErrText )
end if
Return
```

This batch of SQL statements doesn't take any input from the user and doesn't generate any result set - it simply creates a new table.

Format 2

When you consider Format 2, you need to be prepared to handle user-defined parameters, although you still don't have to worry about the result set. Before executing the SQL statement, it has to be prepared using the **PREPARE** command. The syntax is as follows:

PREPARE command FROM :string ;

Here, **string** is an expression of the host language that yields the character string representation of an SQL statement, and **command** is the name of an SQL variable used to reference the prepared version of that SQL statement.

> *The statement to be prepared can be any interactive SQL statement.*

An example of a Format 2 dynamic SQL statement is shown below:

```
Int ItemNo ; Date PriceDate ; Decimal Price
ItemNo     = 10 ; PriceDate = Today() ; Price = 120.43

PREPARE SQLSA FROM 'INSERT INTO "dba"."item_price_table" VALUES (?,?,?)' ;

EXECUTE SQLSA USING :ItemNo, :PriceDate, :Price ;

if sqlca.sqlcode <> 0 then
   MessageBox( "ERROR", string( sqlca.sqlcode ) + SQLCA.SqlErrText )
end if
Return
```

Statements such as **DECLARE CURSOR**, **OPEN**, **FETCH**, **CLOSE** and so on can't be the subject of a **PREPARE**, and the source form of a statement must not include **UPDATE WHERE CURRENT OF**, **DELETE WHERE CURRENT OF** or a statement terminator.

> **The question marks in the INSERT statement are place holders. PowerBuilder replaces these with the values supplied in the EXECUTE SQLSA statement.**

Format 3

The methods of handling **SELECT** in dynamic SQL are different to those in other statements. This is because it returns data to the program; all the other statements simply return feedback information.

A program using **SELECT** needs to know something about the data values that should be retrieved, since it has to specify a set of target variables to receive those values. In other words, it needs to know how many values there will be in each result row, and also what the data types and lengths of those values will be.

```
String Item_Description ; Int Item_No

DECLARE Cursor1 DYNAMIC CURSOR FOR SQLSA ;
PREPARE SQLSA FROM "SELECT item_No, item_description from item_master" ;

OPEN DYNAMIC Cursor1 ;
FETCH Cursor1 INTO :Item_No, :Item_Description ;

if sqlca.sqlcode <> 0 then
   MessageBox( "ERROR", string(sqlca.sqlcode) + SQLCA.SqlErrText)
   Return
end if

DO WHILE Sqlca.Sqlcode = 0
   MessageBox( "Format 3 Results",String( Item_No) + " " &
         + Item_Description )
   FETCH Cursor1 INTO :Item_No, :Item_Description ;
LOOP
```

> At compilation time you know the result set, and that's why you can use the **FETCH** statement to return the results.

A typical use of this command is to select information from a temporary table, a table which doesn't exist at compile time. PowerBuilder doesn't check for the existence of the table, since it doesn't check the syntax of SQL statements and therefore doesn't generate any errors.

Format 4

This format is similar to Format 3, except that you don't know the result set, hence you can't issue a **FETCH** statement. Typically, this format is used to accept an SQL statement from, and execute and present the results to, the user. The following example uses a simple **SELECT** statement:

```
String lSQLStr
Integer lParm1

lSQLStr = "select item_description" + &
      " from item_master where balance > ?"
lParm1 = 10
```

```
PREPARE SQLSA from :lSQLStr ;
DESCRIBE SQLSA into SQLDA ;
DECLARE lCursor1 DYNAMIC CURSOR for SQLSA ;
SetDynamicParm( SQLDA, 1, lParm1 )

OPEN DYNAMIC lCursor1 USING descriptor SQLDA ;
FETCH lCursor1 USING descriptor SQLDA ;

DO while SQLCA.SQLCODE = 0
   lb_1.AddItem(GetDynamicString( SQLDA,1))
   FETCH lCursor1 USING descriptor SQLDA ;
LOOP
close lCursor1 ;
```

As described earlier, the **PREPARE** command formats the input SQL statement using the information specified in the **FROM** clause, and populates **SQLSA**, the object specified after the **PREPARE** command, with these statements.

Handling the Results

A similar process is required for handling the results. PowerBuilder needs to know where to populate the information about the results, so the **DESCRIBE** and **PREPARE** statements are used. Typically, this information storage container is **SQLDA**, unless you create another object of type **SQLDA** to connect to more sources.

Before the actual execution of an SQL statement, you need to call **SetDynamicParm()** to specify parameters. This command takes three parameters: Dynamic Staging Area, parameter number and the parameter itself. The **FETCH** command used here is different from the one you used in cursors and in Format 3. In this format, you don't specify the variables to store the result set, since you don't know the number of columns in the result set, the data type or the length of each column in the result set.

You can check both the **NumOutputs** attribute of **SQLDA**, to establish the number columns in the result set, and the **OutparmType** array. The data type can be any one of the following enumerated examples:

- ▲ TypeDate!
- ▲ TypeTime!
- ▲ TypeDateTime!

- TypeString!
- TypeDecimal!
- TypeDouble!
- TypeInteger!
- TypeLong!
- TypeReal!
- TypeBoolean!.

After checking for the data type, call one of the following corresponding functions to get the actual value:

- GetDynamicDate()
- GetDynamicTime()
- GetDynamicDateTime()
- GetDynamicString()
- GetDynamicNumber()

Dynamic DataWindows

This section discusses how you can change a DataWindow dynamically. This may only involve changing the SQL statement or the DataWindow attributes, but it might involve completely recreating the DataWindow dynamically.

Dynamic Assignments

We've already seen in Chapter 9 that we can dynamically assign DataWindow objects to a DataWindow control, using the **DataObject** attribute. Since all the events and scripts are associated with a DataWindow control, if the code is generic, it will operate on any DataWindow object that is assigned to the DataWindow control. For example:

```
dwc_1.DataObject = "dw_item_master_for_query"
dwc_1.SetTransObject( SQLCA )
dwc_1.Retrieve()
dwc_1.Print(TRUE)
```

633

After changing the **DataObject**, you need to set a Transaction Object by calling either **SetTransObject()** or **SetTrans()**, before performing any operation related to the database. This method is typically implemented to allow the user to select from a list of reports and then display the selected report in a single DataWindow control or a standard UserObject of this type.

If you are dynamically assigning any DataWindow objects, make sure you add a corresponding entry in the resource file. For example:

```
C:\WORKDIR\POWER\INVENT.PBL( DW_ITEM_MASTER_FOR_QUERY)
```

DwGetSqlPreview() and DwSetSqlPreview()

These statements allow you to change SQL statements dynamically at run-time. Executing **Retrieve()** triggers a **retrievestart** event, while executing **Update()** triggers an **updatestart** event. Both of these events then go on to trigger an **sqlpreview** event.

The actual SQL statements are only executed if the **sqlpreview** script is successfully completed. If you want to see the **UPDATE**, **INSERT** or **DELETE** statements generated by PowerBuilder, or the **SELECT** statement defined at painting time, we can call **DwSqlPreview()** from the **sqlpreview** event.

We can then use the **DwSetSqlPreview()** function to change the SQL statement. Typically, these commands are used to dynamically build **WHERE** and **HAVING** clauses. You can also change the list of columns, but it should match the number of columns and data types.

You can access all the statements such as **UPDATE**, **SELECT**, **INSERT** and **DELETE** by calling this command. For example, if 10 rows were modified and two rows were deleted, calling **MessageBox(" ", DwGetSqlPreview())** would display 12 times - 10 times displaying **UPDATE** statements and twice displaying **DELETE** statements.

If you change the table name in the **SELECT** statement, it won't change the **UPDATE** characteristics. For example, if you changed the table name from item_master to history_item_master, PowerBuilder would still generate the data manipulation commands pointing to item_master.

GetSQLSelect() and SetSQLSelect()

Unlike **DwGetSqlPreview()**, these statements can also be called from other events. When PowerBuilder validates the **SELECT** statement against the database, **SetSQLSelect()** is called - providing that the DataWindow is updatable.

If the select list doesn't match with the previously defined version, it will return an error and the new list of columns won't take effect. If the DataWindow is not updatable, PowerBuilder doesn't check for the validity of the **SELECT** statement.

If the **SELECT** statement contains computed columns, or if the **FROM** clause contains more than one table, PowerBuilder sets the DataWindow as not updatable, which makes the **Update()** call fail. If this happens, you need to change the **UPDATE** characteristics by calling **dwModify()**, which is explained next. Typically, these commands are called when a **WHERE** or **HAVING** clause has to be changed dynamically.

DwModify()

We've already seen how you can use **dwModify()** to change most of the attributes of a DataWindow and in the same way you can also use it to change SQL statements. The attribute you need to modify, in order to change the SQL statement, is **table.select**. For example:

```
String lArg1, lResult
lArg1 = "datawindow.table.select='select item_no, item_description," + &
    " balance from item_master where balance < re_order_leval'"
lResult = dwc_1.dwModify( lArg1)
If lResult = "" Then
   dwc_1.Retrieve()
Else
   MessageBox(Error in changing SQL statement", lResult )
   Return
End If
```

When **dwModify()** is used, it won't check the SQL statement against the database - this makes it faster, but obviously it is more prone to errors.

> *We would recommend that you thoroughly test any SQL statements associated with this function.*

The DW Syntax Tool

To help you create DataWindow statements, PowerBuilder ships with a syntax tool, which is, by default, installed in the same Program Group as PowerBuilder. When you run this application, you are presented with the following screen:

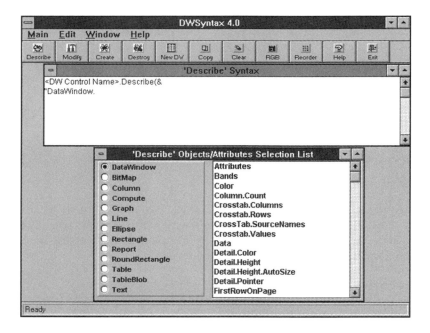

This helps you create the required DataWindow syntax for any purpose simply by making selections from the menu bar. You can then paste the syntax to the clipboard by selecting from the Edit menu and copy it into your PowerBuilder scripts.

This tool also offers an RGB calculator:

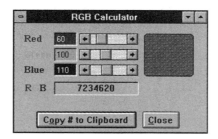

This allows you to create custom colors and then copy the RGB value to the clipboard, so that you can use it in your PowerBuilder application.

Creating DataWindows Dynamically

PowerBuilder allows you to create a DataWindow dynamically at execution time by using **dwCreate()**. You will need to create DataWindows dynamically if you want to allow the user to pick column names for the DataWindow. In such a case, you will not know anything about what the finished article will look like at painting time.

By having either a DataWindow or the custom UserObject control on your window, you need to complete three additional steps involved in the dynamic creation of a DataWindow in your script:

1 Dynamically build a **SELECT** statement and place it in a string variable

2 Create the DataWindow syntax by calling **DwSyntaxFromSQL()**

3 Create the DataWindow from this syntax by calling **dwCreate()**

You can then set the Transaction Object and retrieve the data as normal. The reason we have to call **DwSyntaxFromSQL()**, is that the syntax for a DataWindow is different from the **SELECT** statement - it also contains all the column attributes such as font details, colors and so on, as well as other attributes such as band details. A sample script for part of a DataWindow's syntax is shown on the following page.

release 4;
DataWindow(units=0 timer_interval=0 color=1073741824 processing=1
print.margin.bottom=97 print.margin.left=110 print.margin.right=110 print.margin.top=97)
table(column=(type=decimal(0) update=yes key=yes initial="0" name=item_no
dbname="item_master.item_no")

As an example, the following script creates a Grid style DataWindow and
retrieves data from item_master:

```
String lSQLStr, lErrorStr, ldwSyntax
Integer lResult

lSQLStr = "select item_no, item_description, balance " + &
" from item_master"

ldwSyntax = SQLCA.dwSyntaxFromSQL( lSQLStr, "style(type=grid)", &
    lErrorStr )
lResult = dwc_1.dwCreate( ldwSyntax, lErrorStr )

dwc_1.settransobject(sqlca)
dwc_1.retrieve()
```

DwSyntaxFromSQL() takes three parameters: a **SELECT** statement, a style and a
string variable to populate any error information. The style attribute is the
most complex parameter, using the following syntax:

```
"Style(Type=value  attribute=value  ...)  &
DataWindow(attribute=value  ...)  &
Column(attribute=value  ...)  &
Group(groupby_col1  groupby_col2  ...  attribute  ...)  &
Text(attribute=value  ...)  &
Title('titlestring')  "
```

Tabular DataWindow style is the default, and if you want to assume all of the
defaults you can simply specify an empty string as the parameter.

> Note that the **Composite** presentation style is not supported
> through this method.

Again, the simplest way to create this syntax is to use DW Syntax with the
Create option:

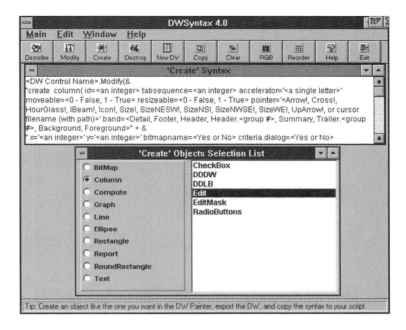

This results in the **CREATE** statement being pasted directly into your code.

Summary

We've covered a lot of material in this chapter and you should now be quite confident about using embedded and dynamic SQL in your applications. If you want a quick guide to SQL, then look out for the forthcoming Wrox title 'Instant SQL', written by Joe Celko.

Dynamic DataWindows are a complex subject and we could have spent much longer explaining them in greater detail. However, the best way to understand them is to try out the examples we've provided on the CD-ROM and play around with the DW Syntax tool.

19

Maintenance Free Security Layer

Controlling the access to your data is one of the most important considerations that you must take into account when designing applications for a Client/ Server environment. We have examined the security that the server has to offer, covering how to use this security at the application level in our login window, but once the user has gained access to the database, all the features of the application are at his beck and call.

In this chapter, we look at one method of restricting the user's functionality by removing some of the application's options, based on the user's access level - DBA, manager or data-entry clerk, for example.

In this chapter, we will cover:

▲ Some of the concepts behind database security.

▲ How to restrict access to window controls and menus.

▲ Suggestions for making your application easier to maintain.

Introduction

The security of your data can be protected at two levels: the database server and the front-end application. However, database level security is preferable for two main reasons:

- The actual data is stored in the database.
- It means that you can restrict access to data irrespective of the front-end tool used.

Unfortunately, if you are storing data in, for example, an xBase database, you don't have any built-in security features. This means that unless data access is restricted at the operating system level, a user must be restricted from fully accessing a database at the front-end application level.

Our solution to this problem is to disable the controls that the user shouldn't be able to access, based upon their login information. Unfortunately, this does throw up some awkward questions such as 'Where is this information held?', 'How does the application and the database security work in sync?' and 'What does the code that provides this functionality look like?'.

It is these and other questions that the rest of this chapter is devoted to answering.

Database Level Security

All popular RDBMSs store information about the users that are allowed to access their data. This information can include such details as:

- User name
- Password
- User group
- Last access date and time
- Password expiry date

Users are put into different groups based upon the type of operations they perform or the organization's management hierarchy.

Rather than demanding that the user logs in to yet another window, forcing the user to remember yet another set of User IDs and Passwords and requiring yet another set of tables to contain this information, we will use the information provided for the database login to set up the application level security.

To this end, it can be useful to understand exactly how the back-end database stores all the security information and what it uses it for.

The table names, database schema and procedure to maintain these tables may differ from one RDBMS to another. The SQL statements used in the following scripts are based on SQL Server. There may be some changes when you connect to other RDBMSs, but the front-end code should stand up unchanged.

SQL Server Security

When you are running a SQL Server database, all the login details are stored in the syslogins table. This table resides in the master database and is owned by the system administrator.

A single SQL Server can manage more than one database, so when a user wishes to access a database, he has to pass through two levels of security. The user needs to pass the first level to get access to the server and then the second level to gain access to the appropriate database.

> Password verification is done at the server level rather than at the database level.

This means that every user must have two IDs. The first is a server level user id (suid), and the second is the user id for the required database (uid). Each suid is unique in the server, while each uid is unique in the database.

Every database in the server maintains another system table called sysusers. Even though the user has access to the server, they don't automatically have access to the database unless they are specifically mentioned in this table.

Different User IDs

The user name stored in sysusers may be different from the server login name held in syslogins. This uid will be mapped to the suid in the syslogins table in the master database. User grouping is done at the database level, each group is unique in the database, and all these details are stored in the sysusers table.

The structure of the syslogins table is as follows:

Column Name	Type	Length	Nulls
suid	smallint	2	N
status	smallint	2	N
accdate	datetime	8	N
totcpu	int	4	N
totio	int	4	N
spacelimit	int	4	N
timelimit	int	4	N
resultlimit	int	4	N
dbname	sysname	30	Y
name	sysname	30	N
password	sysname	30	Y
language	varchar	30	Y

while the structure of the sysusers tables is as follows:

Column Name	Type	Length	Nulls
suid	smallint	2	N
uid	smallint	2	N
gid	smallint	2	N
name	sysname	30	N
environ	varchar	255	Y

Database administrators control the permissions for all objects by using the **GRANT** and **REVOKE** commands. All permissions altered through these commands are stored in the sysprotects system table.

Controlling the Front-end from the Database

Database administrators have no control over front-end menu options and other controls that appear in the front-end, which means that when objects such as CommandButtons, PictureButtons, Menu options and so on are enabled, the user can execute any of the scripts associated with these objects.

If you don't have permission to access tables referred to by the script, the database sends an error message back to the PowerBuilder application. For example, you could have the following script in the **clicked** event of a CommandButton:

```
DECLARE CURSOR lCursor1 FOR
    SELECT name, password from master.dbo.syslogins ;
```

If you attempt to execute this script, an error will be generated because, by default, the public group has no permissions for the password column. However, even though you don't have the appropriate permissions, there is nothing stopping you from attempting to execute the script, thus creating unnecessary network traffic in both the request and the return error.

> **If you have installed Audit Server (from Sybase), it will log any attempted access to unauthorized columns.**

This applies to any script that you have defined at the application level, but if you could disable objects at that level, you could reduce this effect. It also provides you with another level of security between the front-end application and the back-end database.

Take a look at the following diagram to get an understanding of how the maintenance-free security layer works with your application:

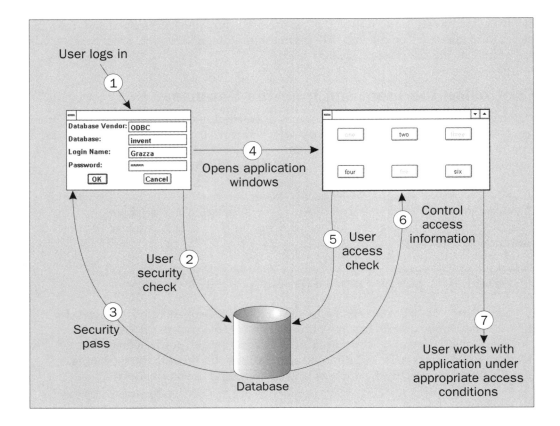

Database

Let's take a look at how to code this functionality, allowing us to provide the database administrator will the ability to control the front-end options from the database, without modifying the front-end code each time a new user joins or an old user leaves.

Front-end Applications

In a front-end application, you will encounter two basic types of control: those that allow the user to interact with the data and those that automatically trigger events depending on some given conditions.

Typically, the four objects that are used to trigger actions are:

▲   CommandButtons

▲   PictureButtons

▲   UserObjects containing CommandButtons or PictureButtons

▲   Menu Options

By enabling and disabling these objects appropriately, we can restrict access to the database. By doing this, we automatically restrict the data with which the user can interact in the other set of controls. Let's see how we can write some code that will take care of this, code that can easily be used in any application that needs access control.

CommandButtons and PictureButtons

Each window in your application has an attribute called `Control[]`. This attribute is an array that the window uses to register all of the controls, along with any relevant details about them.

By referencing this array, we can alter any control attribute. On any given window, each of the control names is unique. This allows PowerBuilder to create an array of these unique names and their details, an array that we can use to easily reference these controls without the need for hard coding. For example:

```
// Assuming control[1] is the CommandButton.
w_item_master.control[1].enabled = false
```

This means we can write a generic function to enable and disable CommandButtons and PictureButtons. By calling this function whenever the window activates, based on the user, we can provide the functionality that we are looking for.

UserObjects

PowerBuilder allows you to create UserObjects from selections of both CommandButtons and PictureButtons and if such a UserObject is placed upon our window, these buttons will be unaffected by the functions that we have just examined.

> Of course, a UserObject is just like any other control on a
> window, so we could use the generic control functions against it,
> but it would affect the whole object, not just the buttons held on
> it.

However, with a slight alteration in the syntax, we can delve to the depths of
these 'embedded' controls and affect them independently of the UserObject as
a whole. If we wanted to disable the first control in the UserObject, we could
use code like that shown below - note that this code assumes that the
UserObject is the second control on the window:

```
// Assuming that control[2] is the User Object
w_item_master.control[2].control[1].enabled = false
```

As you can see, controlling objects that are in a UserObject placed in a
window requires just a little extra code.

Menu Options

A menu can be attached to many different windows, so some of the options it
has to offer may not be applicable to all of them. For example, in our Stock
Control application, the Edit/New menu option is valid for a maintenance
window, but it wouldn't perform a useful task for a report window.

The security layer we are going to develop in this chapter keeps this in mind
and allows us to enable/disable menu options using a similar method to that
of a window's control array:

```
Disable(m_main_menu.item[1])
```

Designing Tables for Front-end Controls

In order to control the availability of controls at the front-end application level,
we need to know the permissions that each user has for each control. The
simplest way to code this information into our system is by hard coding the
data into the front-end script.

However, this is only really practical for a small number of users and doesn't
take into account the problems of maintenance when new users arrive or old
users wish to leave. To get around this problem, and dramatically increase the

flexibility of your system, we need to store all the user details and control permissions in the database.

Group names, login names and passwords are already available in the database in the syslogins and sysusers table, but these tables are not available as storage places for the control permissions. We need to create two extra tables to store these permissions.

New Database Tables

The first new table is used to store all the available controls in the front-end application:

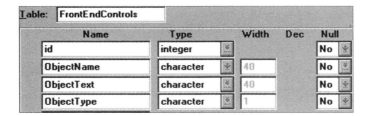

Name	Type	Width	Dec	Null
id	integer			No
ObjectName	character	40		No
ObjectText	character	40		No
ObjectType	character	1		No

Table: FrontEndControls

ObjectName is the name of the object which contains the control, so it will generally be a Window, Menu or UserObject. We'll use the initial letter to represent the object type and we'll store the control object text rather than its name.

> *Remember that the text associated with a control is that which will appear on the status bar. We store this name rather than the 'official' name of the control simply because it is more readable.*

The id field is simply to maintain a key and this field is used as a foreign key to the FrontEndSecurity table:

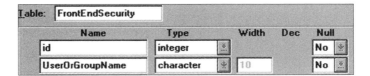

Name	Type	Width	Dec	Null
id	integer			No
UserOrGroupName	character	10		No

Table: FrontEndSecurity

The object id from FrontEndControls and the user login name are stored in this table. By default, all the controls in all the windows are enabled for every user, so we'll only include user names in this table if they don't have access to the control represented by the id.

After designing these tables, there are three things we need to consider:

▲ How to store the front-end objects' names in the database for the first time and whenever there are changes in programs.

▲ How the database administrator grants and revokes privileges to the front-end controls - this is basically the maintenance of the FrontEndControls and FrontEndSecurity tables.

▲ How to access these tables when a front-end application is active and how to disable/enable the front-end controls according to the permissions stored in the above tables.

Controlling Front-end Controls

Assuming that all the menu options, window control names and UserObject control names are stored in the FrontEndControls table and assuming that the FrontEndSecurity table holds all the information about who has permissions for the controls listed in the FrontEndControls table, we are ready to begin the interaction between the database and the front-end application.

If we develop a base window class, we can write the necessary code for this window and all the inherited windows will gain the same functionality. We'll need to write four functions and some script for the activate event of the window:

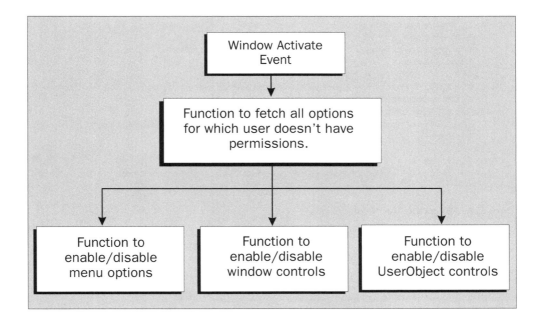

The following script retrieves all the controls for which the current user doesn't have permissions:

```
Function Name: f_set_access_to_menus_and_windowcontrols
Parameters: Parameter_Window Type: Window Pass By: Value
Access: Public   Return Value: [None]

String MenuOptionsArray[], WindowControlOptionsArray[]
String lWindowName, UserObjectControlsArray[]
String lObjectName = " ", lObjectText = " ", lObjectType = " "
Integer lWindowControlSubscript = 1, lMenuSubscript = 1
Integer lUserObjectSubscript  = 1

DECLARE GetControlsToDisable CURSOR FOR
    SELECT f.ObjectName, f.ObjectText, f.ObjectType
    FROM dbo.FrontEndControls f, dbo.FrontEndSecurity s
    WHERE f.id = s.id and f.ObjectName = :parameter_window.title and
        ( s.UserOrGroupName = :sqlca.logid or s.UserOrGroupName in
        ( SELECT a.name FROM sysusers a WHERE a.gid = a.uid and a.gid
        in ( SELECT c.gid FROM master.dbo.syslogins b, sysusers c
        WHERE b.suid = c.suid and b.name = :sqlca.logid )));

Open GetControlsToDisable ;
Fetch GetControlsToDisable into :lObjectName, :lObjectText, :lObjectType ;
```

```
do while sqlca.sqlcode = 0
   if lObjectType = "W" then
      MenuOptionsArray[ lMenuSubscript ] = lObjectText
      lMenuSubscript++
   elseif lObjectType = "M" then
      WindowControlOptionsArray[ lWindowControlSubscript ] = lObjectText
      lWindowControlSubscript++
   elseif lObjectType = "U" then
      UserObjectControlsArray[ lUserObjectSubscript] = lObjectText
      lUserObjectSubscript++
   end if
   lObjectText = " "
   Fetch GetControlsToDisable into :lObjectName, :lObjectText, :lObjectType ;
loop

Close GetControlsToDisable ;

If UpperBound( MenuOptionsArray[] ) > 0 then
   f_disable_selected_menu_options( parameter_window, &
         MenuOptionsArray[] )
end if

If UpperBound( WindowControlOptionsArray[] ) > 0 then
   f_disable_selected_window_controls( parameter_window, &
         WindowControlOptionsArray[] )
end if

If UpperBound( UserObjectControlsArray[] ) > 0 then
   f_disable_selected_window_uo_controls( parameter_window, &
         UserObjectControlsArray[] )
end if

return
```

Suppose the database administrator wants to enable a CommandButton for a certain user. In this case, the FrontEndSecurity table may contain information that disables the controls on either a user or a group level. This means that we need to check this table for two things:

▲ Has the current user already been given access to this control?

▲ Has the group to which the current user belongs already been given access to this control?

> *When you refer to the* FrontEndSecurity *table, the* UserOrGroupName *column contains the user or the group name for the controls that are not available.*

To find the group of the user name, we need to access the sysusers table in the connected database and syslogins in the master database. The declared cursor joins FrontEndSecurity and FrontEndControls and performs the required subqueries on the sysusers and syslogins tables:

```
DECLARE GetControlsToDisable CURSOR FOR
    SELECT f.ObjectName, f.ObjectText, f.ObjectType
    FROM dbo.FrontEndControls f, dbo.FrontEndSecurity s
    WHERE f.id = s.id  and f.ObjectName = :parameter_window.title and
      ( s.UserOrGroupName = :sqlca.logid or s.UserOrGroupName in
      ( SELECT a.name FROM sysusers a WHERE a.gid = a.uid and a.gid
      in ( SELECT c.gid FROM master.dbo.syslogins b, sysusers c
      WHERE b.suid = c.suid and b.name = :sqlca.logid )));
```

> *You could replace the cursor with a single DataWindow control, but we don't require a visual component and it would be better not to place a DataWindow control in the base window as it is an unneccessary waste of memory.*

We declared different boundless arrays at the beginning of the script for menu items, window controls and for controls in the user objects. Once the cursor execution is over, if an array contains at least one entry, you should call an appropriate function to disable the control that is specified in the array. We'll look at these individual functions next.

Controlling Menu Options

All the menu bar items are stored in the **item[]** attribute of menu. To access the items under a menu bar item, you need to refer to the **item[]** array for that item. For example, if you take m_main_menu as an example menu, this menu's **item[]** contains the following entries:

m_main_menu.item[1] = "File"
m_main_menu.item[2] = "Edit"
m_main_menu.item[3] = "Module"
m_main_menu.item[4] = "Window"
m_main_menu.item[5] = "Help"

To see the options available under the menu bar item, we use another level of dot notation. So, for example, we would refer to the menu items under the fourth menu bar item as follows:

m_main_menu.item[4].item[1] = "Cascade"
m_main_menu.item[4].item[1] = "Tile"
m_main_menu.item[4].item[1] = "Layer"
m_main_menu.item[4].item[1] = "Toolbar"

This layout is illustrated pictorially below:

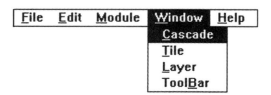

The function to disable the relevant menu options is as follows:

```
Function Name: f_disable_selected_menu_options
Parameters: Parameter_Window, Data Type: Window, Pass By: Value
Parameter: parameter_menu_options_text_array[], Data Type: String, Pass By:
Value
Access: Public  Return Value: [None]

int i, j, lTotalMenuBarItems, lTotalItems
int lTotalItemsToDisable, lCounter1

lTotalItemsToDisable = UpperBound( parameter_menu_options_text_array[] )
lTotalMenuBarItems = UpperBound( parameter_window.menuid.item )

For lCounter1 = 1 to lTotalItemsToDisable
   For i = 1 to lTotalMenuBarItems
      If Pos( Upper(parameter_window.menuid.item[i].text), &
            Upper( parameter_menu_options_text_array[ lCounter1 ])) > 0 &
                THEN
         Disable(parameter_window.menuid.item[i])
         Continue
      Else
         lTotalItems = UpperBound( parameter_window.menuid.item[i].item )
         For j = 1 to lTotalItems
            If Pos( Upper( parameter_window.menuid.item[i].item[j].text),&
                  Upper(parameter_menu_options_text_array[ lCounter1]))> &
                     0 THEN
               Disable(parameter_window.menuid.item[i].item[j])
            End if
         Next
      End if
```

```
    Next
  Next

  return
```

If one of the menu items under File contains a cascading menu, you need to refer to the specific item's **item[]** attribute. For example, you may be forced to use the following syntax:

m_main_menu.item[4].item[1].item[2] = ...

> *When sheets are opened in our application, the sheet names are appended to the Window Menu bar item, but they are not available in the* **item[]** *attribute of menu.*

Each window has an attribute called **menuid** with which you can refer to all the menu items in an attached menu. This script makes use of this attribute and checks for the existence of that item's text entry from those retrieved from the database - if it is found, you should disable that menu item.

The **UpperBound()** function returns the maximum number of elements in the array and can also be used to help you find out the number of menu bar items in the menu. Two loops can then be used:

- The first one for each option in the parameter array
- The second to find out the menu bar items

> Note that if an ampersand (&) is used to define an accelerator key in a menu option text, the same should also be stored in the database. For example, File should be stored as &File.

Function Limitations

When you disable a menu bar item, you can't access the menu items under it. However, if the menu has a toolbar, the toolbar still offers the functionality of the menu items to the user - in other words, the toolbar isn't affected when the associated menu items are disabled This is something that you need to take care of programmatically.

You should also be aware that if the parameter option text is available in any cascading menu, this remains unchecked by this function.

We will sort these problems out by the end of the chapter!

Controlling Window Controls

The general logic for this is similar to the above code for menus except that instead of looping through menu items, we loop through the window controls:

```
Function Name: f_disable_selected_window_controls
Parameters: Parameter_Window, Parameter Type: Window, Pass By: Value
Parameter: parameter_window_controls_text_array[], Parameter Type: String,
Pass By: Value
Access: Public   Return Value: [None]

integer lTotalControls, i, j, lNoOfControlsToDisable
CommandButton lCommandButtonToDisable

lTotalControls = UpperBound( parameter_window.control[] )
lNoOfControlsToDisable = UpperBound( &
     parameter_window_controls_text_array[] )

For i = 1 to lNoOfControlsToDisable step 1
   For j = 1 to lTotalControls step 1
      If TypeOf( parameter_window.control[j] ) = CommandButton! then
         lCommandButtonToDisable = parameter_window.control[j]
         If Pos( Upper( lCommandButtonToDisable.Text), &
               Upper( parameter_window_controls_text_array[i])) > 0 then
            lCommandButtonToDisable.enabled = false
            Continue
         End if
      End if
   Next
Next

return
```

One problem that you can encounter when working with controls is that not all the controls on a window are the same type, as they are with menus. This means that you can't just run through each menu item, checking to see if it should be available or not.

This problem arises because you can only reference the properties of a control when it is declared as local variable, and you can't declare a local variable with a generic type - you must declare it as a Window or a PictureButton and so on. Due to this limitation, it is necessary to check the type of the control before you attempt to assign it to the declared local variable.

> Note that our code only checks for CommandButtons. You will need to add in additional code for any extra control types that you wish to affect.

PowerBuilder provides the predefined **TypeOf()** function for this task. This function returns the type of the control and can be used as the test in a **For** loop. Once you have found the type of control that you are looking for, you can then move on to the next stage of checking to see whether the user should have access to it or not.

The rest of the logic is the same as the f_disable_selected_menu_options function.

Controlling Controls in the User Object

The logic for this function is exactly the same as before, except that we need to check one level deeper. In the first level we are checking for User Objects instead of CommandButtons.

Once a UserObject has been located, we use the same logic to check for CommandButtons on the UserObject rather than the window:

```
Function Name: f_disable_selected_window_uo_controls
Parameters: Parameter_Window, Parameter Type: Window, Pass By: Value
Parameter: parameter_uo_controls_text_array[], Type: String, Pass By: Value
Access: Public
Return Value: [None]

integer lTotalControls, i, j, k, lNoOfControlsToDisable
integer lNoOfControlsInUserObject
CommandButton lCommandButtonToDisable
User Object UoInWindow

lTotalControls      = UpperBound(parameter_window.control[])
lNoOfControlsToDisable = UpperBound( parameter_uo_controls_text_array[] )

For i = 1 to lNoOfControlsToDisable step 1
   For j = 1 to lTotalControls step 1
      If TypeOf( parameter_window.control[j] ) = User Object! then
```

```
            UoInWindow = parameter_window.control[j]
            lNoOfControlsInUserObject = UpperBound( oInWindow.control[] )
               For k = 1 to lNoOfControlsInUserObject step 1
                  If TypeOf( UoInWindow.control[k] ) = CommandButton! then
                     lCommandButtonToDisable = UoInWindow.control[k]
                     If Pos( Upper( lCommandButtonToDisable.text), &
                           Upper(parameter_uo_controls_text_array[i])) > 0 &
                              then
                        lCommandButtonToDisable.enabled = False
                     End if
                  End if
               Next
         End if
      Next
   Next

   return
```

There is an obvious problem if there are two user objects that both use a CommandButton with the same text and name - this is the limitation of this function. In the loop, it checks the first UserObject and when it is found, it is disabled and returned.

However, this situation will rarely occur, so you might be tempted to leave the function as it is - just as we did!

Storing the Objects and Options in the Database

If the database administrator is going to implement this system, he would have to manually add all the object names and their options to the FrontEndControls table. This isn't an ideal situation since every time a new window or menu is added to the application, the table would have to be updated.

The solution to this is to access the appropriate PowerBuilder libraries and store all the changed options dynamically in the database. We can access all the currently available windows and menus from the PowerBuilder library by using the **LibraryDirectory()** function. The syntax is as follows:

LibraryDirectory(<library name>, <object type>)

This function returns all the objects of the specified type, the date and time of their creation and any associated comments, all separated by tabs.

By calling this function, we can retrieve all the specified object names and store them in a DataWindow. Once the object names are in the DataWindow, we can open the object and note all the controls in it.

Here's the code that we would put in the **doubleclicked** event of the DataWindow which contains all the object names:

```
// Script for the double-clicked event of the DataWindow that has all the
window names.

Window lTempWindow
String lWindowName
lWindowName = dwGetItemString(1, "object_name" )

Open( lTempWindow, lWindowName, Parent)
```

Once you open the window using the above method, you need to retrieve all the controls in the window and check for their existence in the database. If a particular control doesn't exist for this window, add it to the table. This logic allows you to add front-end application objects to the database dynamically without hard-coding anything.

Remember, this only works for the current application. If you try to open any object that isn't in the application's library list, it will result in an error. So, you might consider adding a menu option that allows a database administrator to do administration tasks while the application is running, hiding this menu option if the logged-on user isn't the administrator.

Granting/Revoking Privileges on Controls

The final thing you might want to do is provide the database administrator with a nice user-friendly interface to enable him to grant and revoke permissions on front-end objects. You could implement drag and drop features or maybe the shuffle window which we looked at in the UserObjects chapter. This would save having to type in a lot of **GRANT** and **REVOKE** commands.

The practical way to do this would be to have two DataWindow - one listing all the users and group names and the other listing all the front-end objects - and implement some kind of drag and drop feature into another DataWindow which could then be used to update the FrontEndControls table.

Summary

This chapter explained how to add a layer of database security at the front-end application level. We looked at some of the concepts behind database security and gave you some suggestions for improving the quality of life of your database administrator!

In the next chapter, we will look at the ideas behind distributing your complete application to the world at large.

20

Distributing Your Applications

Once the development and the testing stages of your application are complete, you need to start thinking about how to deliver the finished product to your users. This chapter covers all the important issues concerning the distribution of your application.

It explains how to create dynamic linked libraries and executables, how to distribute the 'deliverables' to your users with the appropriate setup files and any other factors that are involved with the distribution of an application.

In this chapter, we will cover:

- The steps involved in putting together a help system.
- How to optimize your libraries.
- The creation of DLLs and executables.
- How to use the Project Painter.
- PowerBuilder's SETUP utility.

Introduction

Usually, the final two steps performed by a development team are the documentation of the application and the preparation of the software for full scale distribution.

> *The standard of the documentation provided by some of the software companies testifies to the fact that this is the one of the last stages in the process.*

Nowadays, software packages come with an on-line help system. Users have come to expect a help system with their applications, so that they don't have to hunt through reams of technically difficult reading to find the information they want.

Many software companies are moving towards the idea of on-line documentation in an attempt to reduce costs and streamline the products. Powersoft's Online Books are a good example of this, allowing the manuals in the box to be drastically reduced.

> *We have followed this trend, supplying a full hypertext version of the book on the accompanying CD-ROM.*

The improved multimedia capabilities of today's computers makes this a very good, and indeed cheap method of conveying information.

Creating a Help System for our Application

Before we go into the details of creating a help system, let's have a look at the tools you will need:

- ▲ A wordprocessor that supports rich text format (.RTF), such as Microsoft's Word 6.0.

- ▲ A help compiler, such as Microsoft's **HC.EXE** or **HC31.EXE.**

- ▲ A Hotspot Editor, such as the one that ships with Microsoft's Help Compilers, for adding context sensitive graphics.

- ▲ A multi-resolution graphics compiler, such as MRGC.EXE which also comes with Microsoft's Help Compiler, if you want to support a wide variety of screen formats.

The following figure illustrates the process involved:

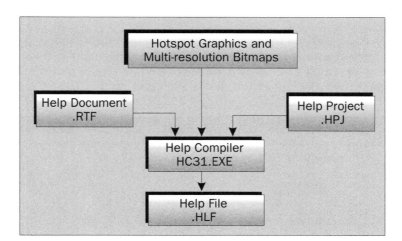

The logical steps involved in authoring a help system are listed below:

1 Create a document in rich text format.

2 Create a project file.

3 Create bitmaps and multi-resolution bitmaps.

4 Define Hotspot areas.

5 Compile with the help compiler.

6 Write script to access the help system from the application.

Before authoring the help system, it's important to plan the following areas:

▲ Topics - these are small related sections of descriptive text that cover one feature you want to explain.

▲ Links between topics, identifying topics that share some relationship. These links should be able to lead the interactive user through your help system, moving from one topic to another.

▲ The text that should appear in the compiler's version of MicroHelp.

Identifying keywords for each topic. Users can use these keywords when searching for appropriate topics.

Before we look at each of these tasks in detail, you might find it useful to look at the **.RTF** document, which will be used as the main body of the help system. We've provided you with a help system for our application, so open up the **GENERIC.RTF** document which we included on the CD-ROM:

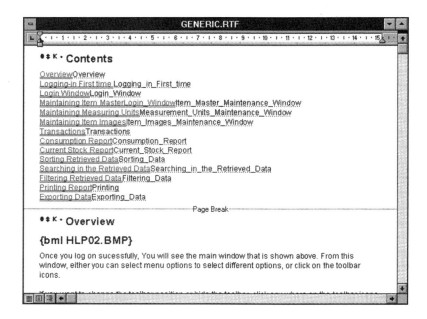

Topics

Any help document consists of one or more help **topics**. While authoring the help document, each topic is denoted by a hard page break - select Insert/ Break... from the menu in Word. A series of footnotes is inserted immediately after each page break - select View/Footnotes from the menu in Word. The contents of these footnotes and page breaks are invisible while viewing the help document; they are used by the help compiler as directives about how the document should be handled. Each character has a special meaning to the compiler.

Context Strings

The user also doesn't see the context string in the final help document. It is used as a reference for jumps from one topic to another, or to display pop-up help and so on. The hash character (#) indicates a context string that uniquely identifies the topic in the help system.

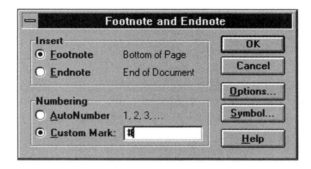

Context strings should be added to the footnote following each topic. Select Insert/Footnote...:

Spaces are not allowed in context strings, so you should use the underscore character (_) to represent any spaces in your context strings.

Keywords

For each topic you can specify one or more keywords that can be used to search through the topics. These keywords are defined in the footnotes along with the topic context strings, denoted by an upper case 'K' and are used to populate the Search window:

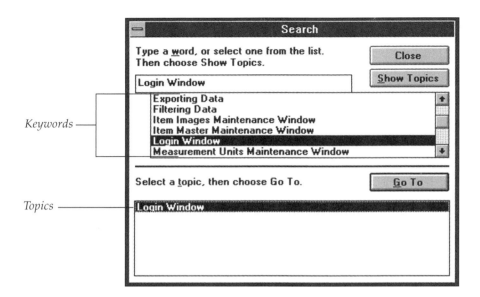

The spacing rules are the same as for context strings. If you want to specify multiple keywords, you can separate them with semi-colons. For example, you may have Item;Maintainence as the keywords for 'Item Master Maintenance'.

Title

The phrase you specify as a title is displayed in the bottom listbox in the Search window when a keyword is selected from above. The dollar sign is used to denote titles and is free format text, which means that spaces are allowed.

Jump Text

This text is used to jump to context strings. It is displayed in green with an underscore in the final compiled version of the help file. Moving the mouse over this text changes the pointer to a hand:

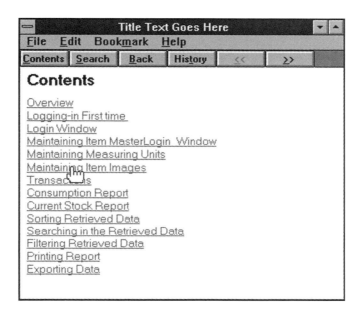

To define text as 'jump text', you need to change the text format to either Strikethrough or Double Underlined, by selecting Format/Font... from the menu. Once you complete the jump text, revert back to normal text, type in the context string name and change its format to 'Hidden'.

> **Don't leave any spaces between the context string and the jump text, and ensure that any carriage returns after the text of the context string are not in hidden format.**

Pop-up Text

This text is displayed in green with a dotted underline in the final compiled version of the help file and is used to supply more information about the specified term:

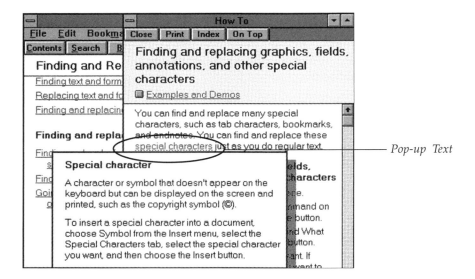

Pop-up Text

Pop-up text is defined in a similar way to jump text except that you use the Single Underlined text format rather than Strikethrough or Double Underlined.

Non-Scrolling Area

Typically, topic names are displayed at the top of the window below the buttons on a non-scrolling region of the window. This means that the viewer can always see which topic is being covered.

Defining the non-scrolling areas is simple. Highlight the text you want to show as a heading, select Format/Paragraph... and check the Keep with Next option:

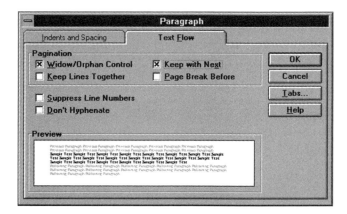

The other non-scrolling areas of the Help window are the menu options and the CommandButtons. These are set up by default with the buttons Contents, Search, Back and History and two others that allow you to scroll backwards and forwards through the topics.

> **If you need more functionality, you need to add more buttons and supply the macros to provide the appropriate functionality.**

Graphics

There are two ways of inserting a graphic into a help file. One is to insert the graph directly into the help document, but this will drastically increase the size of the help file and affect how you can amend the graphic.

The preferred method is to insert a reference to the required graphic file, so keeping the help file smaller and allowing you to change the graphic by simply updating the graphic file. Let's have a look at the main types of graphic formats.

Bitmaps

Bitmapped graphics are stored like sheets of graph paper. They are displayed as a grid of dots, each of which has its own color value. The storage space occupied by the bitmap is directly related to its dimensions and number of colors, regardless of the amount of information presented within it.

These files are stored with the `.BMP` extension and are supported by the Windows Help Viewer, unless you use 24-bit true color.

Icon Files and Cursor Files

Icon files are simply bitmap files which only use 16 colors and are stored with the `.ICO` file extension. All the icons that you see in Program Manager are icon files. Cursor files are similar except that they are monochrome.

The Microsoft Help Viewer doesn't allow icons and cursors to be placed directly in help files; they need to be converted to the `.BMP` format.

Metafiles

Metafile graphics store image information as a series of commands, which are interpreted and displayed as an image by the computer software. These files are stored with the **.WMF** extension and occupy less space than bitmap files.

Multi-Resolution Bitmaps

Bitmaps created under one resolution, such as 640 x 480, can't be displayed as effectively on a system that uses a different resolution, such as 800 x 600. To deal with this problem, Windows Help 3.1 introduced a file format called **multi-resolution bitmap**.

If you want to use these types of bitmap, you will need to create the same bitmap under different resolutions and compile them with the multi-resolution bitmap compiler, **MRBC.EXE**, which packs all these bitmaps into a single file. The Windows Help Viewer automatically takes care of which bitmap resolution to display.

Shed Hotspot Graphics

The Hotspot Editor that comes with the help compiler allows you to define hotspots on graphics and, in fact, more than one hotspot on a single graphic. If you want to use the source bitmap file or metafile for some other purpose, you will need to keep a backup copy of the file before you use it as a hotspot graphic. This is because the Hotspot Editor connects each hotspot to a certain action, and then saves the image as a hypergraphic file with a **.SHG** extension.

To define a hotspot on a graphic, run **SHED.EXE** and open the required graphics file. You then define the hotspot area by drawing a rectangle on it and set attributes against this hotspot area by selecting Edit/Attributes:

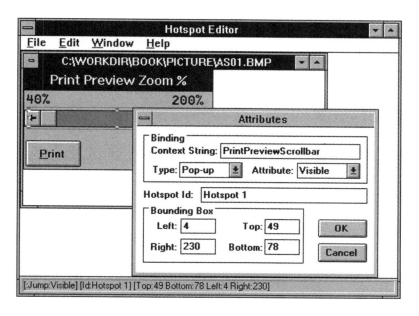

The Type dropdown list allows you to specify whether you want this area to be used as jump text or pop-up text, and you must also supply the context string name.

At run-time, whenever the user moves the mouse pointer over the area defined as a hotspot area, the pointer changes to a hand icon, as it does with jump text.

The Project File

The help project file contains several sections which specify which files are to be included in the final compiled help file: graphic files, the **.RTF** files, certain compiler directives, such as whether to compress the help file and so on.

The section names are enclosed within square brackets, with each entry taking up one line. Let's have a look at some important sections and entries.

The OPTIONS Section

The help compiler interprets the entries specified in this section and acts on them during compilation:

```
[OPTIONS]
; The optional ROOT= entry sets the working directory for the Help Compiler
; ROOT=C:\PROJECT

; The optional BMROOT= entry sets forth the directories which the
; help compiler will search for bitmaps used in the Help system.
;
;BMROOT=D:\ROBOHELP

; The CONTENTS= tells the help Engine which topic contains the contents
CONTENTS=IDH_CONTENTS

; Title is Displayed in the Title Bar of WINHELP.EXE
TITLE=Title Text Goes Here

; The BUILD= setting allows complex Help systems which require
; different versions to use the same source. This is similar to #ifdef's
; in the 'C' language. Everything to the right of the = sign in the
; BUILD= statement is an EXPRESSION. See the Help compiler
; documentation for more information about build expressions.
BUILD=WINDOWS

; The Warning Level is used by the Help Compiler (HC.EXE)
; WARNING=1 - Only the most severe warnings are reported
; WARNING=2 - Intermediate Level of warnings
; WARNING=3 - Most stringent error reporting
WARNING=3

; The Compress option is used by the Help Compiler to make
; smaller, faster loading .HLP files. However, using compression
; increases Compile times.
; COMPRESS=YES, ON, OFF, NO, TRUE or FALSE

COMPRESS=FALSE
OLDKEYPHRASE=FALSE
```

```
OPTCDROM=FALSE
REPORT=FALSE
ERRORLOG=D:\ROBOHELP\GENERIC.ERR
BMROOT=C:\WORKDIR\POWER,D:\ROBOHELP
```

For example, the **COMPRESS** option allows you to specify whether or not to compress the help file to save disk space. The **CONTENTS** = line tells the help engine which topic contains the contents of the file and is used when the user clicks on the Contents button, while the **TITLE** = line specifies the title bar text for the window.

The CONFIG Section

The **CONFIG** section allows you to define some macros and will be executed when the help system is first executed. For example, you can add buttons to the existing buttons in the help system:

```
[CONFIG]
; The config section allows you to define some macros which will be
; executed when the help system is first executed.
;
; The next line gives you browse buttons:
;
BrowseButtons()
;
; To create a glossary button which displays a list of defined terms
; in a secondary window, remove the semi colon at the start of the next
; line and do the same with the Glossary window in the [WINDOWS] section
;CreateButton("Glossary_Btn","&Glossary","JI(`bubble.hlp>Gloss',`IDH_Glossary')")
;
```

There are some built-in buttons which are not displayed by default - you need to call the macro to display them. For example, in the section above, **BrowseButtons()** causes the backward and forward buttons to be enabled.

You need to call **CreateButton()** to create a button of your own. For example, the following macro creates a Glossary button to display a list of helpful words in a secondary window:

```
CreateButton ("GlossaryBtn", "&Glossary", "JI('glossary.hlp>Gloss',
'IDH_Glossary')")
```

The Other Sections

There are three other important sections:

Section	Description
FILES	This is used to specify the required `.RTF` files.
BITMAPS	This is used to list the bitmaps which are referenced in the `.RTF` files.
WINDOWS	This is used to define any secondary windows required, for example, if you have defined any other buttons.

Once you are done with this, you need to compile it by calling `HC31.EXE` and specifying the project file as the command line argument.

Accessing Help from PowerBuilder

You can run your custom help system in conjunction with PowerBuilder's help system by setting a single variable in the `PB.INI` file. This is the line we're interested in:

`UserHelpFile=`

This is in the [PB] section of `PB.INI` and is used to specify the name of your help file. This specified file will then be displayed whenever the user clicks on the User button automatically displayed in the PowerBuilder help system. You should only specify the name of the file, not the full path, and ensure that the file is placed in your PowerBuilder directory.

> Note that if you name your help file as `PBUSR040.HLP` and place it in the PowerBuilder directory, clicking on the **User** button will automatically open this file without the need to edit the `PB.INI` file.

To learn more about integrating your help system with PowerBuilder's, click on the same User button in PowerBuilder's help!

Application Level Help

PowerBuilder provides a function called **ShowHelp()**, which enables you to provide help for an application at execution time.

ShowHelp() takes three parameters:

- ▲ A help file name with full path.
- ▲ An enumerated type which specifies the type of help.
- ▲ An optional parameter help command ID.

For example, to display the index in the help file, you would use the following code:

```
ShowHelp( "Invent.Hlp", Index!)
```

To allow the user to search on a keyword, you would use the following script:

```
ShowHelp( "Invent.Hlp", KeyWord! )
```

You can see these help features implemented in the final version of our Stock Control application.

Distributing Your Applications

Now that we've looked at the steps to creating a help system, we're ready to look at the steps involved in distributing your application. We've already looked at some of these when we looked at the Application and Library Painters in the early chapters, but now we'll show you how you bring everything together to produce a fully working production-ready application.

The figure on the following page illustrates everything that is required to distribute an application:

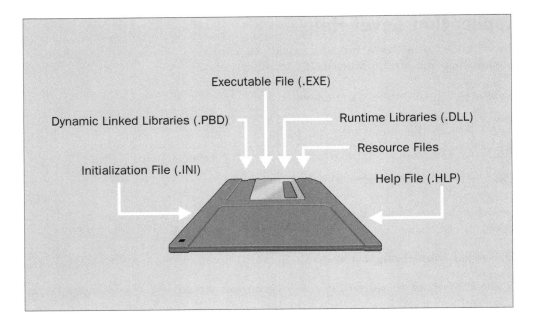

The following steps should be followed:

1 Remove test code from script.

2 Add icon to the application object.

3 Regenerate all objects.

4 Optimize library.

5 Create resource file.

6 Create dynamic linked libraries.

7 Create executable file.

Before you begin this process, it is a good idea to create a separate directory and make a copy of all of your work in it. This allows you to safely remove any code that you have implemented for the purposes of testing, without the fear of irretrievably deleting something important.

> **Indeed, as you are developing an application, it is a good idea to keep two copies of it, one as a working copy which you use to test out new and inventive sections of code, interesting new windows and so on, and the other as a clean copy to which you copy objects that have been thoroughly tested.**
>
> **By using this method, the job of removing test code should be much easier, and you have always got a backup set of objects if anything horrible happens to the working set.**

You might also want to consider your Application's library list. If you need to move your application to another directory or even to another machine, say for testing over a network, or from your developmental machine onto a network, PowerBuilder automatically removes all the library references from the library list. When the application library is settled into its new directory, you will have to recreate the library list based upon the new positions of the other libraries.

Regenerating Objects

Before you create an executable, it is advisable to regenerate your objects. Regenerating an object compiles the source code or displays any errors that the compilation generates. If you don't regenerate the object, these errors will be displayed at the time of linking, that is, while creating the executable.

We recommend that you regenerate any ancestor objects before you regenerate their descendant objects. As we saw in Chapter 2, selecting Utilities/Browse Class Hierarchy... from the menu in the Library Painter will provide you with the object hierarchy:

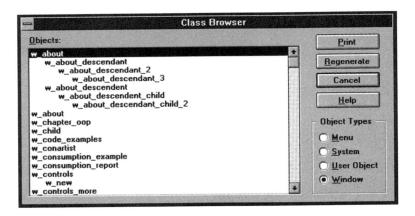

You can then select the various objects in your library and regenerate them from here.

Optimizing the Library

As we also discussed in Chapter 2, optimizing a PowerBuilder library removes unused space, so decreasing the size of your library. In the Library Painter, simply select Library/Optimize... and the name of the library that you wish to compress.

Creating Resource Files

If you are referring to external files such as bitmaps, icon files and so on, when you are preparing to create an executable, you need to create resource files for these others, together with any dynamic PowerBuilder objects. The resource file is a simple ASCII file with a **.PBR** extension, which contains the file names of all the external components that make up your application.

The resource file can contain any of the following items:

▲ Icon files (**.ICO** extension)

▲ Picture files (**.BMP**, **.RLE**, and **.WMF** extensions)

▲ Pointer files (**.CUR** extension)

▲ DataWindow objects

You need to list these items with their full path names:

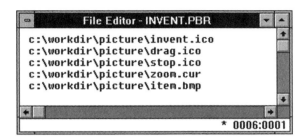

While listing DataWindow objects, you also need to include the PowerBuilder library name. For example:

c:\workdir\invent.pbl (dw_dynamic_datawindow1)

> *Make sure that there aren't any spaces between the parentheses and the DataWindow object name.*

This would be necessary if somewhere in your application you assigned this DataWindow object to a DataWindow control:

```
dwc_1.dataobject = "dw_dynamic_datawindow1"
```

For a small application, a single resource file will suffice, but if an application spans many libraries, you may consider creating separate resource files for each library. At execution time, when PowerBuilder encounters any external object reference, it first looks in the executable file, and if it doesn't find the reference it looks into the dynamic linked library in which the external object is referenced.

> *Note that when you create an executable, the resource files are compiled into PowerBuilder Dynamic Linked Libraries.*

If it still can't find it, it looks into other dynamic linked libraries and, as a final effort, through all the directories on your DOS path. If the resource is available in the primary PBD, PowerBuilder will not look into the others, so making execution faster and more efficient.

While developing an application, make sure to note down all external references and the referenced objects. When you have these details, you can easily identify which resource is referenced in the object, and this will make it easier to create separate resource files for each library.

Creating Dynamic Linked Libraries

When you reach this stage, you need to decide which of your libraries you want included in the executable and which you want to be held as **.PBD**s.

This decision is generally based on how often the objects in your libraries are used. If the objects are frequently called upon, you should consider including them as part of the executable - this makes the executable larger, but the recall time is greater reduced.

On the other hand, if you have provided objects for tasks that aren't performed so often, it makes sense to supply these libraries as **.PBD**s - this reduces the size of the executable but increases the recall time, as the **.PBD** must be loaded into memory before the objects it contains may be accessed.

You may also want to consider field maintenance and upgrading your application. We'll discuss these subjects in a moment.

For more information on creating a **.PBD**, you should refer to Chapter 2.

Creating Executables

The final step is to create an executable. To do this, you need to invoke the Application Painter. Select File/Create Executable... from the menu and when you supply a name for the executable file, PowerBuilder prompts for the names of any other **.PBL**s and resource files that are required:

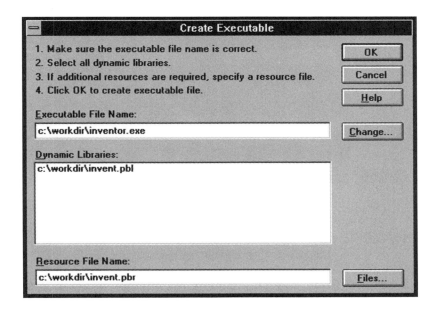

You should note that the decision on the location of your resource files in the compiled application is very similar to that of your PowerBuilder libraries. If resources are referred to on a regular basis, you should compile them directly into the executable, but for interesting yet under-used resources, you should associate them with the appropriate .PBD.

Project Object

With version 4.0, Powersoft has introduced the idea of Projects to the PowerBuilder vernacular. This makes creating executables much easier. Click on the Project icon to invoke this painter:

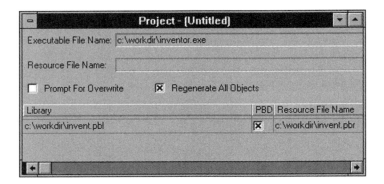

There is no need to switch between different painters, nor should you worry about which PowerBuilder library has a dynamic linked library. You can simply specify the executable file name, and PowerBuilder automatically lists all the library names in the application's library list under the Library column.

Select whether you want to add a dynamic linked library to the system, or whether you would rather add the library to the executable by checking/ unchecking the PBD checkbox. You must also specify any related resource files at this point.

If you check the Regenerate All Objects option, PowerBuilder regenerates all objects before it creates a dynamic linked library; it will even create one for those libraries where the PBD option is not checked. Selecting Options/Build Project from the menu creates the executable.

You can list all the objects that are part of the application and even sort on object name, object type and so on, by selecting Options/List Objects... from the menu:

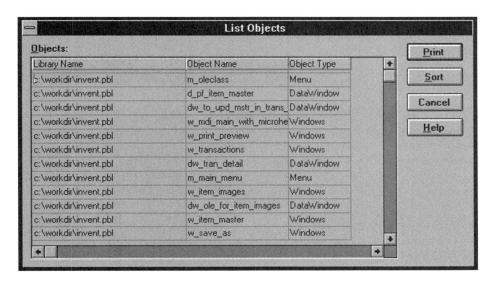

Another advantage of Projects is that you can create an executable from a previous version of a library, if you are using a version control package. When you are using such a package, whenever you create an executable, PowerBuilder stores the following information about the application in the Project object:

▲ PowerBuilder object names with `.PBL` name

▲ Archive names and revision numbers

▲ Version labels

When you restore the Project object from the archive and open it, PowerBuilder automatically retrieves all the objects to which it refers. This makes the task of creating executables from previous versions of your application much easier, a task that you might wish to perform for purposes of testing or comparison.

Distributing Applications

Creating executables completes the work you need to do at your workstation. Since PowerBuilder executes the application by interpreting the code, the executable that you create can't be run independently.

An executable created in C executes independently of any other code, because when you compile and link a C program, it creates the self-contained machine code. To make a PowerBuilder executable work, extra run-time DLLs are required.

These come as part of the Enterprise version of PowerBuilder, but if you are using PowerBuilder Desktop, you will need to purchase the 'PowerBuilder Team/ODBC' Deployment Kit.

The deployment kit installs the following files, which should be in the DOS path:

PBBGR040 DLL	PBITXT40 DLL
PBCMP040 DLL	PBLMI040 DLL
PBDBI040 DLL	PBOUI040 DLL
PBDBL040 DLL	PBPRT040 DLL
PBDEC040 DLL	PBRTE040 DLL
PBDWE040 DLL	PBRTF040 DLL
PBDWO040 DLL	PBSHR040 DLL
PBECT040 DLL	PBTYP040 DLL
PBIDBF40 DLL	PBVBX040 DLL

If you are using ODBC, the deployment kit also installs **PBODB040.DLL** and **PBODB040.INI** in the application directory, and **ODBCINST.INI** and **ODBC.INI** in the **WINDOWS** directory.

If you want to use native database drivers, the deployment kit also installs them for you. For example, if you select SQL Server, it installs **PBSYB040.DLL**, while Sybase SQL Server System 10 causes **PBSYC40.DLL** to be installed.

Let's look at how to provide a simple, easy setup rubric, similar to the one you encountered when you bought PowerBuilder and installed your software. What's good enough for you, should be good enough for your users!

SETUP Utility

Prior to version 4.0, providing setup programs wasn't that easy. You would probably have needed to write a C program or depend on a third party product. However, with v4.0, PowerBuilder now offers a setup utility of its own.

Note that this is another tool provided with the Enterprise version or via the PowerBuilder Team/ODBC Deployment Kit.

After creating an executable file, run this program and it will invoke the following window:

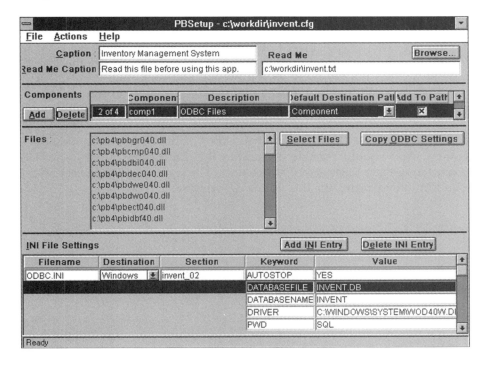

Before doing anything, you need to select a file name to store all the information specified in this window. Select File/New from the menu and specify a file with the **.CFG** extension.

You need to specify a caption in the Caption prompt, which will be displayed at the top of the screen while the user is installing this program. One use for this option is to provide the reader with extra, last-minute information about the product that they are installing.

You would normally call this file the standard **README.TXT,** which you see with most software packages, and indeed, which we have supplied on our CD-ROM. As the window displays the progress of installation, this file will be displayed in a separate window, so allowing the user to scroll through it.

Next, you need to specify the details of all the executable files and names of DLLs that you want to install in the Components DataWindow. These files can be installed in a user-specified directory, the **WINDOWS** directory or the **WINDOWS\SYSTEM** directory.

In a typical scenario, executables, PBDs, help files and maybe even Watcom run-time files will be installed in the user-specified directory. All the ODBC DLLs might go into the **WINDOWS** directory and any files related to ODBC settings, such as **ODBC.INI** and **ODBCINST.INI** files, might go into the **WINDOWS\SYSTEM** directory.

In the Default Destination Path DropDownListBox column, PowerBuilder provides four options. You should provide a value in the Description column and select Base from the Default Destination Path column. Click on the Select Files CommandButton to bring up the following window:

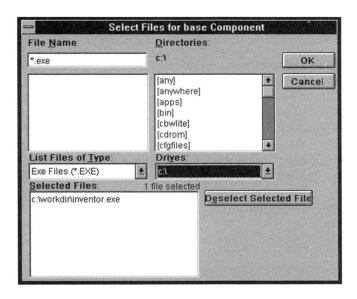

You should select the following files:

- Executable files that you created in the Project Painter
- Dynamic Linked Libraries for this application
- All the appropriate help files
- Any required PBDs

When this is done, you need to add another record in the Components DataWindow, selecting the ODBC DLLs and setting their destination path as Windows. Add another record and select the **ODBCINST.INI** and **ODBC.INI** files for the System destination path.

Setting Up .INI Files

You may need to specify other settings for the application in an `.INI` file. For example, to include **STOCK.INI**, you would click on the Copy QDBC Settings button and select the file. All the entries are copied into INI File Settings DataWindow. After copying, you can edit or delete entries as you wish.

You can allow this program to create a program group and program item in Program Manager, by selecting Actions/Define Program Group from the menu. Specify the program group title, the executable file name and program item name:

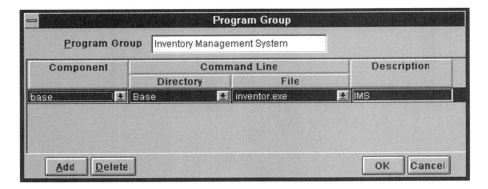

Creating Distribution Disks

To create a set of distribution disks for your application, select Actions/Create Diskette Images... from the menu. PowerBuilder estimates the number of disks required, depending on the disk size you select from the resulting prompt.

PowerBuilder then compresses the files, splits them if necessary, creating DISK1, DISK2 and so on, in the directory you specified, and then saves these images.

To copy the information directly onto the disks, select Actions/Create Diskettes from the menu and insert the floppy disks as required:

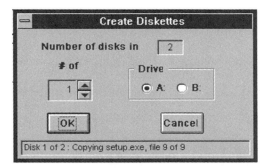

These floppy disks are now ready to distribute. At their site, the user simply needs to execute a simple command, A:\SETUP, assuming that the A: drive is being used for the installation. This opens the window below and allows the user to install your software with all the usual choices:

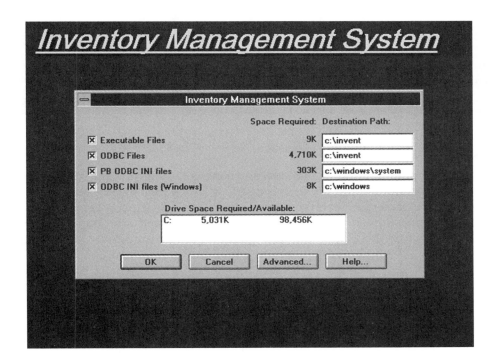

By selecting the Advanced... CommandButton, you can select whether or not the setup program should prompt before overwriting a file. This setup program automatically updates the **AUTOEXEC.BAT** file by default - although the user can select to save the proposed changes to their **AUTOEXEC.BAT** in a separate file.

The following figure shows a typical screen during installation at the user's site:

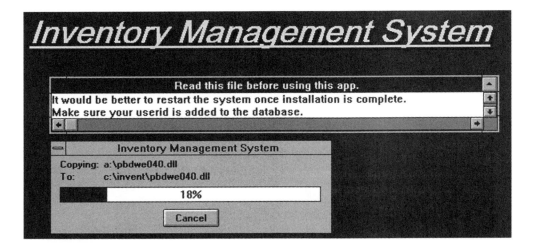

Debugging at Run-time

No software package is 100% bug-free and you will probably get complaints about anything, from the color of the interface to completely unexpected behavior. In such cases, where you can't perform a full experimental strip down of the uncompiled application, you may be interested to know that you can try to uncover the bug at the user's site while the executable is running.

You can do this by using the /PBDEBUG command line parameter or the **TRACE** parameter before the value in the DBMS prompt, as discussed in the chapter on Debugging.

Both of these options will result in a log file of all the actions that the application performs from start to finish. Hopefully, you should be able to interrogate this file, find the problem and begin to sort out a solution, without even returning to your developmental platform.

For more details on how to use both of these techniques, please refer to Chapter 11.

Maintenance Releases

You may want to improve the functionality or release updated versions of your application after releasing to the general populous. If you have laid the foundations, this should be no problem.

If you are using dynamic linked libraries (PBDs), you simply need to distribute those that have changed. This is one of the major advantages of PBDs, rather than the other option of including the resources in the main executable. If a problem occurs in one of these resources, you will need to replace the whole executable, a potentially costly experience.

If this application is to be a commercial product, you can place all the patches in a common directory, say in a CompuServe support forum or a Bulletin Board, to give all of your customers easy and regular access to any updates that you perform.

Summary

This chapter explained the steps in creating a help system for your users, as well as an overview of all the steps involved in creating a distributable version of your application. We illustrated how you can speed up this process using the Project Painter and then looked at using the SETUP utility to create a set of distribution disks and setup program, similar to that of PowerBuilder itself.

In the next chapter, we'll give you an overview of the application development process. We'll be looking at various developmental concepts, including the ideas of Class Libraries, Prototyping and advice on how to best develop your PowerBuilder applications.

CHAPTER

21

The Application Design Process

This chapter is intended to give you an overview of the design process involved in putting together a PowerBuilder application. A lot of what we'll discuss are generic concepts which would equally apply to any software development project.

In the first section, we'll discuss the concepts of prototyping as a design methodology and show you how PowerBuilder is particularly suited to this type of application development. The second section will then go into more detail and discuss the idea of building class libraries, showing you how you would do this in PowerBuilder, and some of the commonly required components in a PowerBuilder application.

In this chapter, we will cover:

- The advantages of prototyping over conventional methodologies.
- The prototyping tools available in PowerBuilder.
- The concepts of frameworks and components.
- Building PowerBuilder class libraries.
- Distributing a class library.

Prototyping

Software prototyping is the process of creating a working model of a new application before you start on the actual coding. Prototyping has long been used in engineering and other fields, but it is relatively new to software development. It is a highly effective method of clarifying an application's requirements to both developers and users, while enabling developers to build applications that do a better job of meeting users' needs, in a shorter time span and at a lower cost than conventional approaches allow.

A prototype is a preliminary version of an application which can be used as a demonstrative tool during meetings between developers and users. As such, it is a far more effective way of portraying the potential functionality than design documents or static visual models.

The prototyping process consists of creating and refining real, hands-on requirement models. A prototype should be made functional with a minimal amount of effort, and it need not be representative of the complete application. It should be easily modifiable and extensible, allowing the design to be finalized during development rather than before.

Formal Definitions

More formally, prototyping has been defined as 'a strategy for performing requirement definitions in which the user's needs are extracted, presented, and successively refined by building a working model, quickly and in context' - Bernard Boar, Application Prototyping: A Requirements Definition Strategy for the 80s, New York: John Wiley, 1983.

Another definition is 'a cost-effective means for discovering the true and complete set of functional requirements that will optimally satisfy the user's legitimate business needs.' - John L. Connell and Linda Brice Shafer, Structured Rapid Prototyping: An Evolutionary Approach to Software Development, Englewood Cliffs, New Jersey: Yourdon, 1989.

The primary difference between prototyping and other more conventional development methodologies is that it allows system analysts and users to develop applications together. The result is a set of specifications for a working system rather than a theoretical one. Providing users with tangible output enables them to inform developers about what is missing or incorrect, and this rapid feedback allows coders to develop new, more precise iterations much faster. If prototyping is done carefully, the end result can actually be a working system.

Prototyping is a very powerful approach that is being embraced by an increasingly wide spectrum of developers, even for large, complex applications. However, to be effective, prototyping must be a disciplined, structured methodology that encompasses the entire software life-cycle from project planning to post-delivery maintenance.

Prototyping Vs Traditional Development

In many software development projects, customers are asked to sign off specification requirements that they can't fully understand because there are no working models of that functionality. As a result, it is very common for users to receive a product that doesn't meet their true needs. The developers may believe the system is correct, but it may be completely unacceptable to the customer.

This may be true even when structured analysis techniques are used to create paper models of functionality. These models are an improvement over less well-defined methods for specifying design information, but they still leave too much room for misunderstanding. By producing a series of quick, inexpensive models to portray the look and feel of the proposed system, prototyping can produce a final application that is a whole order of magnitude more inviting to the customer.

Replacement or Complement

Prototype-developed software is much more likely to satisfy true user requirements, with more complete, accurate and meaningful functionality and documentation. Prototyping replaces traditional waterfall-based life cycle methodologies with an iterative, incremental, evolutionary approach that provides for a great deal more user input.

However, prototyping doesn't replace structured analysis, design and assessment methods; instead, it should be used in conjunction with the best elements of these techniques. Prototyping simplifies the initial analysis, enables developers to avoid decisions about things they are not sure of, and adds a dimension to structured analysis by developing a prototype in addition to paper specifications. Prototyping adds value to existing methodologies - it doesn't replace them.

Accommodating User Need Changes

Prototyping also allows developers to respond quickly when a user's needs change, as often happens over the course of a development cycle that can take months or even years. It provides enough flexibility that modifications can be made easily without locking developers into a specific solution. And in **evolutionary** prototyping, where the prototype is intended to be used as the basis for the deliverable application, software development time and costs are further reduced. The more of the prototype that survives into the delivered version, the easier modification work will be in the future. Prototyping makes it possible to do software maintenance work much earlier in the life cycle, and to do it faster and cheaper.

What Prototyping Isn't

There are a number of misconceptions about prototyping that should be addressed before presenting a detailed description of what prototyping actually is. First, prototyping isn't an unstructured methodology. Some people have the impression that it is nothing more than hacking together some quick and dirty code, then tweaking the code until it does what is required.

They also believe that requirement and design specifications may be bypassed altogether, or at least they aren't rigorous enough. This is most definitely not what prototyping is, and it will inevitably produce poor results. To deliver useful results, prototyping must be a disciplined, structured methodology.

Second, prototyping doesn't shrink development time by an order of magnitude. It doesn't compress the beginning of the life-cycle by reducing the time required for analysis. The reason for this is that most of the development portion of a life-cycle is spent preparing requirement specifications, design documents, test plans, user guides and a whole plethora of other documentation.

Prototyping doesn't eliminate any of these tasks; in fact it often makes them take somewhat longer, simply by increasing the amount of user involvement. Where prototyping saves time is in the maintenance phase of a project.

Applications Suitable for Prototyping

There is a common view that prototyping isn't suitable for performance-critical or algorithm-intensive applications. Although prototyping does have a higher payoff for some applications than others, the critical issue is whether the user interface is important to the system's success. Any application where there is a risk of building the user interface incorrectly is a strong candidate for prototyping.

This means that nearly all applications benefit from prototyping - particularly if you believe the user interface is the most significant part of an application. It is the main thing the customer pays for, but it is also usually the most poorly created component. Conventional software development techniques simply don't give users the chance to see or experiment with the interface until the end of a project - when it is most difficult to change. Prototyping is basically a highly effective means of discovering the right user interface. This is true for large or small systems, real-time or data processing.

If a large system is segmented, it may be possible to prototype some segments even if the entire system isn't prototyped. This approach works especially well with systems that are being redeveloped in phases.

Benefits of Prototyping

There are several major advantages in using prototyping. Let's look at a few of these in detail.

Prototyping is Iterative

If you are using this methodology, it is no longer necessary to 'get it right the first time'. Developers can admit that they will very probably get the application wrong the first time - while ensuring that the system they ultimately deliver is much closer to what is actually required. The first version of the application is intentionally imperfect, but it is very easy to modify.

It is well known that the cost to correct an error in a computer system increases by orders of magnitude as the system life-cycle progresses. A change made after delivery may cost ten or twenty times more than if it was made during the analysis phase. Using prototyping, many of these errors are eliminated long before the final version.

Prototyping is good at catching the most glaring errors and those that are most expensive to correct: those that deliver the wrong system to the user. Thus, although prototyping doesn't dramatically shorten development time, it does very substantially reduce total life-cycle costs.

Users Can Experiment

Prototyping allows users to experiment with the application from the beginning of the development process. It encourages changes, unlike the typical approach of freezing incorrect specifications. By examining options in various stages, users are often able to discover requirements that they would otherwise be totally unaware of until implementation. And by trying out changes, users obtain a much better idea of which enhancements they really want, and which they don't.

Prototyping Accommodates New User Requirements

Users are not always sure of what they want an application to do. They need to experiment interactively with different options to gain a clear idea. Often the opportunity to view a function in operation means users discover a need for additional or changed functionality.

Prototyping allows developers to accommodate these changes early in the life-cycle and at a very low cost. This results in a dramatic reduction in change activity during testing and post-implementation, and users who are encouraged to participate in development feel much better about the application when it is finally delivered.

Cost Savings in Maintenance

Most of the cost of current software systems isn't incurred during development, but in maintenance - bug fixing, enhancements and other modifications. Applications developed using prototyping tend to need fewer modifications after delivery, because the systems are much closer to what the users actually want. As a result, they have much lower maintenance costs. They are also much easier to modify because they are typically developed in an extremely modular way. The modules that survive into the delivered product remain as easy to modify as they were during development.

Using standard software development methodology, most of the mistakes that coders make are not discovered until the test phase, when there is an actual system to evaluate. Most of the work of testing and maintenance is simply correcting the mistakes that were made during analysis, design and coding - which means that most of the life-cycle is devoted to correcting mistakes rather than improving the whole.

Prototyping provides the opportunity to test right from the beginning of the life-cycle, and to test repeatedly.

Ease of Documentation

Prototyping makes it easier to write requirement and design specifications, since detailed specifications can be derived from a user-approved prototype. There will also be fewer surprises during testing because there is a fully integrated working system that incorporates real data.

User Satisfaction

Prototyping's 'what you see is what you get' approach eliminates most of the communication problems between developers and users, and allows errors to be corrected quickly. User participation gives them confidence in the application, because they see the errors being resolved quickly.

Risks of Prototyping

Although prototyping is primarily a risk-avoidance approach, it is possible for things to go wrong, usually because of misconceptions - by developers, users or management - about how prototyping should work. For example, users may try to evolve a prototype into a system that does everything for everybody, or developers may over-evolve the prototype, substituting elegance and efficiency for flexibility.

Without proper management, the process of prototype demonstration and revision can continue for too long. As users see their requirements being met, they may add new ones until the scope of the application far exceeds the feasibility study. A project plan must be prepared before anything else, and it must be continually refined. The project plan must communicate to the customer that as the number of deliverables increases or becomes more complex, the final delivery date gets later and the cost of the project increases.

Another problem can be budget, staff or schedule cuts that are imposed due to misconceptions about 'rapid' prototyping. Because a working model is available so quickly, users and managers can easily come to believe that the design, coding and testing phases should be equally fast. It is critical to remember that the menus and screens in a prototype are not backed up by a detailed design, and that performance issues may not have been addressed.

The critical issue in the evolution of a prototype to a final system is always performance - the response times of critical modules when executed in a production environment. Developers shouldn't be asked to deliver a prototype that has not been fully tested, tuned and documented.

Developing an Initial Prototype

The tasks involved in a prototyping project are somewhat different from those in a conventional software development project, and they are performed in a different sequence. The traditional life-cycle approach is sequential with occasional feedback loops, and it defines sharply separate development phases, milestones and deliverables. After the project planning phase, prototyping is iterative: analysis, design, development and testing are performed concurrently.

Prototyping isn't incompatible with the life-cycle model, however. Although it reduces the separation between development phases, it still uses milestones and deliverables at specific points in time. The milestones are almost the same as in a traditional project and they occur in the same sequence, but they occur at different points in time. For example, since the analysis and design phases involve different types of activities, they can take a different amount of time than in a traditional approach.

About 50% of the development effort in a prototyping project should be contributed by users. The prototyping team should consist of equal numbers of users and software developers. The users should be involved at all times during the project, from iterations to final approval of prototype functionality, and there should be frequent brainstorming sessions between the users and the developers. A prototype should be much more the users' product than the developers'.

Planning a Prototyping Project

The first step in a prototyping project, as in any project, is creating a project plan. Without a project plan, the people involved in development would be just as vulnerable to mismanagement as they would be in a traditional approach. There must be a well-understood agreement between the customer and the developers about the goals, scope, tools, responsibilities, timelines and deliverables. However, the project plan (and particularly the schedule) typically evolves over time.

Developing the project plan and performing the rapid analysis (see below) can consist of a two or three day intensive session similar to a joint application design (JAD) session. It is imperative that all users and developers be present during these phases.

Rapid Analysis

After an initial version of the project plan is completed, the next task is to perform some preliminary analysis work to get a better idea of what will be prototyped. Rapid analysis is the first active phase of a prototyping project. It consists of conducting brief user interviews to get an idea about the basic functionality required. This information is assumed to be incomplete and probably incorrect; the purpose is simply to sketch a model from which an initial prototype can be developed.

Rapid analysis should result in a prototyping concept, not a requirements specification. It should produce a model of how the system will work, without listing detailed or complete requirements. The model should consist of a preliminary data flow diagram (DFD), as a high-level design of prototype functionality; a preliminary entity-relationship diagram (ERD), as a suggestion for a database schema; and preliminary control flow graphs (CFGs), as an architecture for the prototype control structure.

Developing the Initial Prototype

Once all of the paper models have been completed, it is time to create a preliminary working prototype for the users to exercise. There are three objectives at this time:

- To get the model to the users quickly.

- To include user-familiar data so it will be easy for them to verify functionality and data requirements.

- To make sure the model and data storage structure are easy to modify.

The fastest and easiest way to create a working model is via the following steps:

1 Create a relational database.

2 Create tables within that database.

3 Copy existing, user-familiar data into the tables (or, if necessary, create test data).

4 Create the GUI screens.

5 Create the high-level functional modules to be called from the GUI.

Creating the relational database is usually a one-statement command naming the database. If the entity-relationship diagram (ERD) is good, creating the tables simply means creating one table for each entity on the diagram. You must assign attributes to each entity, and (now or later) normalize the database for efficiency. The attribute list for a prototype database table doesn't need to be complete or correct; only the critical attributes are required at first.

Once the preliminary database tables have been built, the next step is to copy any existing data into them. There will usually not be a one-to-one match between existing data elements and the newly-defined table attributes, but this is usually not a problem in a RDBMS. Typically, you simply name the target table, then list the attributes and their formats as they exist in the input file format.

You should also create a set of load-unload procedures for every table in the database at this time. When users begin experimenting with the prototype, you will have to restructure the tables quickly to make refinements such as correcting data types or lengths and adding and subtracting attributes. These utilities will speed up the process of unloading the 'good' test data, destroying the incorrect table, creating a new table, and reloading the data.

> The advantages of using existing data are that it has the idiosyncrasies of real data, it is familiar to the user, and it can be used for stress testing (if it exists in large enough volumes).

PowerBuilder's visual programming techniques allow you to improve the cosmetic appearance of screens iteratively, working with users. They also make it easy to arrive at data input specifications for required fields, display-only fields, highlighted fields, default values, retention of previous values ('sticky' fields) and data validation checks.

These specifications are very easy to modify, and because the screens are modular, there is no ripple effect to others. Once the screen design is finished, it is fairly simple to set up ways to capture data into the system, change data loaded in from existing automated files, display data on the screens and create test reports for printers.

At this stage in prototype development, the user can use the prototype to travel up and down screen hierarchies and view the functionality of the screens. Working in 'what you see is what you get' mode makes it quite easy to arrive at users' real requirements. Also, since developers are constantly exposed to the user interface, there will be few surprises during demonstrations of the prototype.

Most RDBMSs allow users to interactively add, modify and delete information in the database. Information can be retrieved on the basis of values entered in screen fields. The RDBMS commands used for data retrieval are typically menu-like choices. Thus the GUI screens include executable RDBMS commands that are transparent to the user.

The final step in prototype development is to create output functions which often make use of RDBMS views. A view is a temporary combination of information from multiple database tables. You can also create output functions with visual programming techniques, using default output screens generated by the RDBMS. The default screen can then be modified to give the desired appearance.

Prototype Iteration

After the initial prototype has been developed, you have a solid foundation for building the complete application. The initial prototype is a vehicle that can be used to dynamically discover further user requirements. It needs to be demonstrated to the user, and the user needs to be asked where it is inadequate. You can then deal with the inadequacies a few at a time, in a series of iterations. This process is repeated until the user is completely satisfied with the refined prototype. Only at this point will you know the user's true and complete functional requirements.

A prototype demonstration should last about one hour, which should provide enough change requests for one or two weeks of work by developers. The philosophy of prototype demonstrations is to find defects, not to fix them. This rapid turnaround to the next demonstration keeps the users involved in the project.

At a demonstration, the users experiment with the system. These experiments have the same objective as conventional requirements analysis: to determine what the users want the system to do and to provide a means for adding such functionality. Ideally, users should actually exercise the prototype, because they learn much more this way, uncover many more errors, and have more pride of ownership. Users should also receive samples of all reports and study them for errors, and should be given no more than two days to make this evaluation.

At each demonstration, the prototypers should ask the following questions:

▲ Which of the current functions are not correct?

▲ Have problems identified at the last demonstration been corrected?

▲ Have modifications resulted in any new problems? What additional functions would you like?

The answers to these questions should be published in a memo; this is a way to avoid excessive mind-changing, prototype iteration, and 'scope creep'. Deciding when to put an end to prototype iteration can be one of the most difficult problems in the prototype approach.

Most modifications to a prototype involve one or more of the three rapid analysis documents: DFD, CFG, and ERD. At early stages of the process, updating these documents is straightforward. However, when the prototype is close to the final system, recording the refinements to these documents is essential. For this reason, version control should be managed from the beginning, using a CASE tool.

The Functionally Approved Prototype

Once prototype iteration is completed (i.e. the user is satisfied with everything the prototype does), the prototype is functionally approved. It is important not to give in to the temptation to deliver the prototype as the final system. It still needs to be documented, stress tested and tuned for performance. Its response times will probably be slow when exposed to real volumes of data and users. It is important to make the differences between a prototype and the final product clear. A prototype is an experimental model; the final product has to be verified to be a long-term, usable system.

At this stage, you should have accurate versions of the functional requirements specification, detailed process specifications and a data dictionary (assuming they were kept up to date as you went through prototype iteration!). These should be published as final versions.

Performance Tuning

Once the final prototype has been functionally approved and documented, the last step is to determine the effects that increases in the volume of data or users will have on system performance. During development and iteration, you may have avoided specifying key attributes to be used as database table indices, normalizing tables, using real data in some database tables and/or testing with large user or data volumes.

These approaches are appropriate at these stages, when functionality is more important than performance. However, they inevitably build some performance traps into the system. These traps are likely to surface eventually, so they should be corrected before delivery of the final product.

The reason the prototyping approach addresses performance issues at this late stage is because it uses the philosophy of 'functionality first, performance as needed'. It can often be difficult to obtain reasonable performance criteria from users before they see the final version of an application, and it is far more common for projects to fail because of inadequate functionality than poor performance. It is generally more effective to address performance problems later rather than earlier.

You should perform stress testing, then thoroughly optimize the database structure, then perform unit stress testing a second time to see what performance gains have been achieved. Once stress testing is completed, the customer must provide explicit approval of system performance.

Delivering and Maintaining the Evolved Prototype

The final product must include a detailed functional requirements specification. This document will be a valuable learning tool for maintenance coders in the future. A team of potential maintenance personnel must also walk through the detailed design document and approve it. Maintenance personnel should become familiar enough with the design so that future maintenance will be conducted in a similar fashion to the prototype iteration.

Prototyping with PowerBuilder

The following list illustrates the specific features of PowerBuilder which enable the prototyping methodology to be used:

- Enhanced connectivity to many back-end databases
- Rapid screen generation through the Window Painter
- Rapid report generation and data capture using DataWindows
- Built-in Fourth Generation application programming language

▲ External language support for C++

▲ Completely open architecture

▲ Multi-user development support through check-in/check-out facilities

▲ Data migration facility using the Data Pipeline Painter

▲ Powerful SQL Painter allowing easy creation of SQL statements

▲ Sophisticated debugger

▲ Availability of third-party class libraries and tools

▲ Support for most object-oriented concepts

Creating a PowerBuilder Class Library

As a PowerBuilder application developer, there may be several situations where you find yourself putting similar functionality into various projects. If this is the case then it's time to start thinking about developing your own class library. This library would contain the most often used objects in your applications and any generic code which can be reused in several applications.

This section explains about the different types of class libraries, the approaches to creating a class library and explains in detail about the most often required reuseable objects for any PowerBuilder application.

Introduction

Encapsulation allows us to build entities that can be depended upon to behave in certain ways and to know certain information. Such entities can be reused in every application that can make use of this behavior and knowledge. With careful thought, it is possible to construct entities that will be useful in many situations.

Unfortunately, the use of object-oriented design tools isn't enough; it requires effort to design entities that are generically useful.

There are three types of software design tasks, distinguished by the result of the process:

▲ Components

▲ Frameworks

▲ Applications

You can reuse more software from each application if you spend time during the design phase identifying and designing components and frameworks. Components and frameworks are the results of abstracting reusability from your application while you build it.

Components

Components are entities that can be used in a number of different programs. For example, lists, arrays and strings are components of many different programs. More recently, radio buttons and checkboxes have become familiar user interface components.

The primary goal when designing components is to make them general, so they can be used as components in as many different applications as possible. To applications that make use of them, components are black boxes. Application developers that make use of components need not understand the implementation of those components. They are reusable code in its simplest form.

Components are typically 'discovered' when programmers find themselves repeatedly writing similar pieces of code. Although each piece has been written to accomplish specific tasks, the tasks themselves have enough in common that code written to accomplish them appears remarkably alike. When a programmer takes the time to abstract out the common elements from the disparate pieces into one, and create a uniform, generally useful interface to it, a component is born. Ultimately, programmers can aim for abstracting out common functionality as they design a piece of software, before they have coded similar pieces again and again.

Frameworks

Frameworks are skeletal structures of programs that must be fleshed out to build a complete application. For example, a windowing system or a simulation system can be viewed as a framework fleshed out by a windowed application or a simulation, respectively. The MacApp system developed by Apple Computer is another example of a framework, one for developing Macintosh applications. The use of this framework allows all applications developed using it to retain a similar look and feel while permitting programmers to concentrate on the details of their own applications.

The primary goal when designing frameworks is to make them refinable. The interface(s) to the rest of the application must be as clear and precise as possible. Frameworks are white boxes to those that make use of them. Application developers must be able to quickly understand the structure of a framework, and how to write code that will fit within it. Frameworks are reusable designs as well as reusable code.

Frameworks typically use unmodified components as well as framework-specific extensions of components. They also typically use code unique to the framework.

Applications

Applications are complete programs. A fully developed simulation, a word processing system, a spreadsheet, a calculator and an employee payroll system are all examples of applications.

The primary goal when designing applications is to make them maintainable. In this way, the behavior of the application can be kept appropriate and consistent during its lifetime.

Ideally, applications are built by fleshing out a framework with both components and application-specific entities. Applications may also extend certain components, or amplify a specific framework in ways unique to the application. This is where the domain-specific knowledge your design team has garnered becomes critical.

Application developers today must frequently make ingenious use of components and frameworks in order to fit existing systems. More and more, applications must be made compatible with existing software, files and peripherals, so as not to render a smoothly functioning system prematurely obsolete. This requirement makes the design of useful components and frameworks all the more pertinent. It also spells out a few requirements of its own for designers and builders of software.

If an application is successful, it will be maintained and extended in the future. Initial design choices can have a significant impact on how easy it is to make these changes. Application-specific entities should encapsulate implementation-specific details. They should also present an interface consistent with existing components and frameworks. If an application-specific object has potentially broader utility, one should seriously consider designing it as a component that can be reused by other applications.

PowerBuilder Frameworks

A good PowerBuilder class library supplies a template for all operations with the database such as retrieve/update, and re-usable objects for other operations such as sorting/filtering/printing a DataWindow. Depending on the percentage of code provided in the template, it can either be copied or inherited in the actual application. Whatever the method of inheritance, the developer needs to know the framework's implementation.

A typical application will be manipulating a database. It includes querying, adding new records, deleting existing records and changing the existing data. These operations may involve one or more tables with different relationships. The relationship can be divided into three categories, one-to-one relationship, one-to-many and many-to-many.

Let's examine the functionality and implementation of these tables.

Master Tables

A typical requirement for maintaining master tables will be add/delete/update rows, query, print preview, print, sort, filter, search in the retrieved results and scrolling to next/previous/beginning/end/specific rows.

The steps in adding a record would be inserting a row in the DataWindow and scrolling to the new row. Steps in deleting a row would include prompting the user as to whether he really wants to delete the record or not, and if yes, deleting the record.

The downside of using a framework in this situation is that, because you need to check for lot of things such as getting the column names, column data types, column values, and so on, there is a detrimental effect on performance.

Actual database manipulation details are unknown at the time of writing a class library. You can provide a template which can be either copied into the application library or inherited from it. The template may include generic logic to take care of database manipulation that consists of different relationship tables. This template has to be copied to your application or objects created in your application by inheriting from the class objects. For example, let us take a window that deals with master-detail relationship tables, say item master and transaction tables.

You could write the following generic functions to take care of certain operations:

- wf_Save_Detail
- wf_Apply_Detail_Deletes_in_Master
- wf_Apply_Detail_Updates_in_Master
- wf_Apply_Detail_Inserts_in_Master

In `wf_Save_Detail()`, you can call the next three functions before you update the detail table. You can also write code to update the detail table and error handling in `wf_Save_Detail()` itself.

In the actual application, the developer can create another window by inheriting from this window and can write actual code in the last three functions by declaring the same functions in the descendant window. Since PowerBuilder searches for functions from bottom to top, the function declared at the descendant object will execute.

PowerBuilder Components

As explained above, you can use components directly without writing any code except for one or two lines to handle opening, closing and so on. Typically, these components can be used anywhere without modification. If the developer wants to extend the functionality of these components, he can always build another object by inheriting from these objects, but the objects are themselves self-sufficient.

Most of the objects explained here can be implemented in two ways: the first is through UserObjects, and the second is by providing the same functionality in a window. The latter method would be easier to code in some cases and also efficient at run-time. For example, assume some functionality (say, sort/ filter/search/print preview) is required in 90% of the windows in your application.

If you create UserObjects to accomplish this functionality, you need to place these in every window that requires the functionality. That means, if the user opens five windows, five instances of each of the above objects are opened.

Instead, you should create a separate window (child or pop-up) and open it whenever it is required. The user can move the window easily anywhere in the parent window and closing the window frees-up memory.

There are several functions which are commonly required in many PowerBuilder applications and we've implemented many of these in our own class library. If you are developing a class library of your own, you should try to include as many of these as possible:

- Sorting a DataWindow
- Filtering a DataWindow
- Searching in a DataWindow
- Exporting a DataWindow
- Print Preview and Selective Printing
- Context Sensitive Help
- Error Handling

Functionality-Rich DataWindow

It is a good idea to provide a function-rich DataWindow which includes all the above functionality. You can also allow the selection of multiple rows, invoke a pop-up menu through the right mouse button, display SQL statements before sending them to the database when the executable is running in debug mode, validate the last column, inform the developer when the DataWindow takes more than a specified amount of memory and so on.

You can also provide a UserObject that lets the user select columns from any table in the connected database and retrieves data. You may also need to provide a separate object for each supported database, since the system tables and database schema is different for each database.

Menu for DataWindows

Create a menu that can be activated as a pop-up menu. Provide appropriate menu options which basically call all the components explained above such as sort, filter, find, export, print preview and print.

Functions and User Objects

You can provide lots of functions such as copying rows from a DataWindow to another DataWindow, financial functions, scientific functions and so on. Also, consider the availability of general functions such as difference in dates. File functions are available in the **Funcky DLL** that can be purchased separately from PowerBuilder.

With the introduction of the OLE 2.0 window control and C++ DLL support, you now have a lot more choice when it comes to developing a powerful PowerBuilder class library. You can provide some windows for mail merge, e-mail, e-mail that integrates with database manipulation activity such as insert, delete and update, DLLs for writing powerful functions and creating new controls, such as a dialog box to browse and select a file that also allows you to map network drives at the same time, and so on.

You can also consider providing a UserObject that converts from one graph style to another. Another useful UserObject is the combination of SingleLineEdit control and a PictureButton with a 'file open' picture placed side-by-side. The PictureButton lets the user select a file and automatically places the selected file name in the SingleLineEdit control.

Distributing a Class Library

If you want to give the source code, you can simply distribute `.PBL`s. Otherwise, you can ship the dynamic linked libraries. When you ship `.PBD`s, a developer can make use of these libraries simply by adding them to his application's library list.

> By default, the dialog box displays all `.PBLS`, but the developer can either type the `.PBD` name or select the `.PBD` by giving `*.PBD` as listing criteria in the dialog box.

Objects such as menu, window and user objects can be inherited as if they are using the `.PBL`, but they can't view the code in the ancestor object (objects in your class library) from the descendant.

Marketing

To successfully market a class library, you should consider the following:

- ▲ It should include all reusable objects that are applicable in all PowerBuilder applications.

- ▲ Provide the source code, don't make it a black box.

- ▲ Provide good documentation, with full examples of a variety of situations where the objects can be used. Consider providing a video-captured help.

- ▲ Develop frameworks for different sectors, Finance (mortgage, bonds, shares, etc.), manufacturing, banking, and so on. If the frameworks are not for a specific industry, the target market is bigger, but there is more competition.

- ▲ Enhance functionality beyond those that are available today.

- ▲ Provide more controls through DLLs, such as animated controls.

- ▲ Now you have C++ DLL support, think of using powerful and fast C++ functions.

Summary

We hope that this chapter has given you some ideas about how to make your applications more flexible, how to improve successive application designs through prototyping and how to speed your application coding through the use of class libraries, templates, frameworks and components.

As we discussed in the first chapter, it isn't the tools that you have available to you that produce a successful application, but rather the way in which you use them. Take time to develop a relationship with your customers, identifying their needs and selecting the appropriate tools for the job. Outside of direct contact with your customers, spend time developing class libraries of generic materials that you can pillage for future projects.

Most importantly, approach any task that you want to perform in a successful manner in as structured and documented fashion as possible. Lay out your thoughts on the process to your customers as soon as possible, giving them firm details on timing schedules, budgets or staffing levels. It will often be very detrimental to the finished product to cut corners in the developmental cycle. Keep the levels of communication between all sides as high as possible, and solve any problems that occur at that time, don't let them fester.

By following these common-sense guidelines and allowing for a little planning before the coders get to work, a project should be completed on time, within budget and satisfy all involved.

Application Development Guidelines

A complete and well-founded set of development standards will substantially reduce the development time of an application by preventing a lot of rework and confusion. The following guidelines should assist developers in applying standards for consistency between application objects and across independent applications.

It is important that your applications are constant in appearance and construction so that users know what to expect. Use of the application, on-going maintenance and development of enhancements are more efficient when consistent standards are followed. The look of the application shouldn't differ from other windows-based products used for word processing, spreadsheets, graphics and communications.

Keeping these points in mind, we would make the following recommendations for the various objects in your applications.

Windows

- Standard window resolution is 640 x 480 pixels, or 800 x 600 pixels using small fonts.
- Use MDI frame with help instead of MDI frame window type.
- Confirm closing the application in the MDI frame's `closequery` event.
- If any window that will be opened as a sheet has a menu, assign menus for all other windows.
- Provide a different menu for the MDI frame to display when no sheet is open.
- Define standard user events, such as `ue_initialize`, `ue_print`, `ue_print_preview`, `ue_query`, `ue_search`, `ue_security_check` and so on.

Window Controls

Place controls with primary functionality at the top left of a dialog box; other controls should appear in order of precedence.

CommandButtons

▲ In an MDI application, try to give the functionality of a CommandButton to a menu item and reduce the number of CommandButtons on a window surface.

▲ Use a consistent button order, grouping them by function. Groupings should be ordered from top to bottom along the right side of the window or from left to right at the bottom of the window. For example, the 'OK' and 'Cancel' buttons should always appear in the same place and in the same order.

▲ Gray out CommandButtons which are not applicable.

▲ Use a 'Close' CommandButton for all windows which don't have a system control menu.

▲ Actions behind similar buttons used in the same context should be consistent across windows. This assists in setting user expectations for window functionality. For example, Apply (rather than OK) updates the database and exits the window. Close (rather than Cancel) confirms a database update with the user and exits the window.

▲ A CommandButton should contain up to three words of text.

▲ Capitalize the first letter of each word, such as Print Letter. Don't capitalize small words (of, the, etc.).

▲ The same font and character size should be used on multiple CommandButtons within a window and across applications.

▲ The accelerator key should be the first letter of the command, except where duplication occurs. Alt + letter is the standard combination. The letter used should be consistent with the underlined letter on the window control.

▲ Use "..." on a text label when an additional window is called.

▲ Use ">>" on a text label that calls an expanding window. Gray out the button or make it unavailable once expansion occurs.

The following table lists some standard Windows CommandButtons which you'll see time and again, and the standard labels and accelerator keys which you should use for them:

Button Label	Definition	Accelerator Key
Query	Displays one or more blank records on the window and allows the user to specify query criteria.	Q
Search	Searches database for results based on user-defined criteria and returns the results to the window.	S
Find	Searches the DataWindow to match user-defined search criteria and scrolls to the first found row.	F
Add	Adds a blank record to the DataWindow, scrolls to the new row and displays initial values wherever applicable.	D
Delete	Deletes the selected record from the DataWindow, not from the database, upon user confirmation. Also deletes any records referencing the selected record.	T
Apply	Applies changes to the database, such as inserting new records, deleting records (deleted by pressing the *Delete* key) and updating.	A
Clear	Initializes all modifiable fields on the screen to initial values. No database updates are performed.	L
Cancel	Cancels any changes entered on the window and closes the current window.	*Esc*

Continued

Button Label	Definition	Accelerator Key
<u>C</u>lose	Closes the current active window and returns to the previous window. Before actually closing the window, it saves data to the database upon user confirmation. Used in addition to <u>A</u>pply.	C
OK	Accepts a user-defined condition. Doesn't infer any database modification. Used in addition to Cancel.	*Enter*
<	Moves an object to the left of its original location.	Left Arrow
>	Moves an object to the right of its original location.	Right arrow
^	Moves any selected record(s) from a lower location to an upper location.	Up arrow
v	Moves any selected record(s) from an upper location to a lower location.	Down arrow
>>	Moves all objects to the right.	
<<	Moves all objects to the left.	

CheckBoxes

▲ Use CheckBoxes for multiple binary selections from a small set of static data (up to four selections).

▲ When an On/Off choice is displayed, a CheckBox should be used instead of two radio buttons, reducing user navigation between objects.

▲ CheckBox text should be located to the right of the Checkbox and shouldn't change.

▲ CheckBoxes should be aligned vertically.

GroupBoxes

▲ Place the GroupBox label in the upper left corner of the GroupBox.

▲ 3D lowered style border is generally used.

RadioButtons

▲ Use when a single selection from a set of data is required - up to four values, displayed in a GroupBox. More than four values are more efficiently displayed in a DropDown ListBox.

▲ When RadioButtons are aligned horizontally, use minimum of five spaces between each RadioButton. This maintains a sense of cohesion without crowding the objects.

▲ RadioButton text shouldn't change. This avoids confusion for the user.

▲ Accelerator keys should be used with RadioButton text to allow for full keyboard capability.

▲ A default RadioButton should be displayed when a window containing RadioButtons is opened.

▲ Where applicable, provide a general choice such as 'None' as part of the selection values to allow the user an alternative.

DropDownDataWindows/DropDownListBoxes

▲ When a list of options will change over time, use a DropDownDataWindow.

▲ When a list of options remains static, use a DropDownListBox.

▲ Display a maximum of ten items in the list without the use of a scrollbar.

▲ Size the window or box to prevent entries from being truncated horizontally or vertically.

▲ In general, use a full description for options instead of codes.

▲ A default option should be displayed upon the opening of a window containing DropDownDataWindows or DropDownListBoxes.

723

▲ When multiple pages of data exist, check the Allow Editing option in DropDownDataWindow Edit Style. This allows the user to enter search criteria in the single line edit portion of the DropDown DataWindow.

▲ Check Always Show Arrow in DropDownDataWindow Edit Style. This tells the user that additional data display is a capability.

▲ Use vertical ScrollBars and avoid using horizontal ScrollBars. It is easier to comprehend lists in a vertical format.

▲ List items alphabetically or in the order of highest probability of selection. This avoids unnecessary scrolling.

DataWindow Columns and SingleLineEdits

▲ Capitalize all important words including the first word. No punctuation should be used with field labels.

▲ Length of border should correspond to the maximum length of data element to avoid the data display being truncated.

▲ 3D lowered style border is generally used.

▲ The vertical distance between 3D freeform DataWindow columns should be four units (counting from the position where the upper border of one column overlaps with the lower border of another column).

▲ The distance between the field label and the freeform DataWindow column should be one average character length. This distance applies to the longest field label when DataWindow columns are in tabular format.

▲ When focus moves to a data entry field displaying text, highlight the entire text in anticipation of the user's edit.

▲ The field label should be located to the left of a freeform DataWindow column. Field labels in a vertical grouping should be left-aligned with other field labels. Freeform DataWindow columns should also be left-aligned as a group.

▲ Date fields are automatically formatted as mm/dd/yy. Allow data entry into a date field without manually entering date slashes.

▲ Place the heading for the DataWindow in the Header band instead of DataWindow control title.

▲ Provide right mouse button support whenever it is applicable, by providing common options and context sensitive options.

▲ If you want to use the DataWindow for reporting purposes, make it read-only, which will use less buffers.

Spin Controls

▲ If possible, limit the number of spin control values to a maximum of ten values for good user comprehension.

▲ Because of scrolling and limited display of values, the user should know the upper and lower boundaries of the spin control.

▲ Values should not change and should be ordered.

▲ When the up arrow is clicked, a larger value displays; a smaller value displays for the down arrow.

▲ The first choice should display after the spin control comes to the end of the list, enhancing efficient user interaction.

UserObjects

▲ PowerBuilder suggests a limitation of twenty controls on a window. Each UserObject represents a set of controls - it isn't counted as one control. Keep this in mind when designing windows.

▲ UserObjects should be defined generically and placed in a public directory to allow for reuse and to simplify maintenance.

▲ Before creating a custom UserObject, make sure a standard PowerBuilder control doesn't exist that does nearly the same thing A custom UserObject that contains a CommandButton and a StaticText control directly below the button provides the same functionality as a PictureButton.

DataWindows

▲ If information can be scrolled horizontally, related headings will also scroll.

▲ Editable DataWindow columns should be set to auto selection.

▲ If an item is selected to be updated, and the DataWindow is on the same window as the detail information, the selected item remains highlighted while the detail information is being updated by the user.

▲ Double-clicking on a row de-selects any previously selected rows.

▲ When the cursor is on a field where additional detail is accessible, indicate this by changing the cursor to a magnifying glass.

▲ Whenever possible, replace groups of controls or custom UserObjects with a DataWindow control. Remember that a DataWindow control need not be tied to the database.

▲ Whenever possible, replace embedded SQL with a DataWindow control. Remember that a DataWindow control need not be visible or complex.

▲ Anything in the **retrieverow** event of a DataWindow (including comments) will cause a pause after each retrieve, which slows down retrieval significantly. Don't put code here unless it is unavoidable. Consider using **retrieveend** event instead, if possible.

▲ Use tabular style for non-freeform DataWindows displaying one column only. Use grid style for non-freeform DataWindows displaying more than one column.

▲ For tabular or grid style DataWindows, display text describing the DataWindow at the top left of the DataWindow frame rather than in a DataWindow title bar.

▲ Columns within a DataWindow should have headings which display headline-style capitalization.

▲ Tabular style DataWindows should display a 3D raised column header extending the width of the DataWindow.

▲ Headings for columns containing numeric data should be right justified.

▲ Headings for columns containing fixed length elements should be centered.

▲ Headings for columns containing variable length elements should be left justified.

▲ When rows are not available for selection, they should be grayed out.

Menus

▲ All applications should use a menu to navigate to the main functions.

▲ The most frequently used menu items should be in a top horizontal toolbar; less frequently used menu items should be in a far left vertical toolbar.

▲ A vertical toolbar item labeled Save should be provided as a means of updating the database within any window without having to exit the window.

▲ Display functions of windows should be included in the menu name Window on the menubar. For example, 'Tile', 'Layer', 'Cascade'.

▲ Display all opened sheets under the Window menubar item.

▲ Provide an About option under the Help menubar item, to display information about the application and copyright if any.

▲ Toolbar bitmaps should be unique. Investigate all available sources of bitmaps before selecting.

▲ Common functions across an application should use the same bitmap. This assists in setting user expectations for window functionality.

▲ PowerBuilder doesn't gray-out toolbar bitmaps that are disabled. You should paint the same bitmaps with gray effect and assign dynamically when the menu option is disabled.

▲ All menu items should have accelerator keys. Make sure that these keys will not conflict with the accelerator keys provided for window controls.

▲ If menu items on a pull-down are grouped by related function, the group should be separated with a horizontal bar (separator).

▲ "..." used after text on a menu item indicates a dialog box will be displayed when the menu item is selected.

Colors, Fonts & Extended Attributes

▲ The user should have some choice of window color. This supports the concept that the user has control of the application rather than the application having control of the user. Color settings in data-display window controls (DataWindows, single line edits, multi line edits, editable ListBoxes, etc.) should use the windows background color (w) for the background of editable window controls and the windows text color (wt) for the text in editable window controls.

▲ As a general rule, editable window controls and the text displayed in them should use colors set by the user in the Windows Control Panel. Non-editable window controls should be set to light gray.

▲ Window background color should be light gray. Field labels in a window should be set to black.

▲ A freeform DataWindow background color and non-editable columns on the DataWindow should be set to light gray. Editable columns should be set to the window's background color. Text in editable and non-editable columns should be set to the window's text color.

▲ Column headers in tabular DataWindows should be set to light gray.

▲ Use caution with color. Non-neutral colors (colors other than black, white, or gray) should be limited to icons and bitmaps.

▲ Only use coloured text to draw user's attention. Limitation of color usage allows for color sensitivity and reduces eye fatigue.

▲ When color is used, meanings attached to colors should be used consistently, for example you could use an icon displaying a yellow file folder throughout the application to save the DataWindow as a report.

▲ If you want to use other colors and fonts, decide on these first and apply them in the base window and other ancestor windows. Later if you want to change them, you'll only need to modify them in these limited windows.

▲ Use a consistent font and type size throughout the application.

Abbreviations and Symbols on Windows

▲ Interface text should be clear, unambiguous, and free of jargon. Consistent use of abbreviations and hyphens promotes user understanding and eases programming decisions and maintenance.

▲ GUI standards call for the use of the full spelling of words whenever possible. If you can't use the full spelling because of space limitations, use a standard abbreviation if one is listed.

Number Formats

▲ Use standard date format such as mm/dd/yy.

▲ Use standard time format such as 08:06AM.

▲ Dollar figures should be displayed in whole numbers, with cents rounded.

▲ All dollar figures should be capable of displaying $999,999,999,999 as the largest figure.

▲ Dollar figures may be positive or negative unless otherwise noted in the data dictionary. Display negative numbers in parentheses and in red.

▲ Percent change calculations should be rounded to the nearest hundredth of a percentage point, unless the requirements state otherwise. Display negative percentages in red and in parentheses.

▲ Calculated fields are not updatable. In order to change the calculated figure, the user must update one of the figures used in the calculation.

▲ Phone numbers should be formatted with parentheses around the area code and a dash between the phone number prefix and suffix.

▲ Zip codes should be displayed with a dash between the first five digits and the last four digits.

Feedback

Users should be given direct and intuitive methods to accomplish their tasks within the application. Ease of understanding, both visually and conceptually, should be objectives during construction of the application.

You should provide feedback for the user through the use of text and object attributes, such as focusing, blinking, changing color, becoming invisible etc.

The following are some ways of giving feedback.

Requiring Entry

▲ The user needs to know immediately what is required versus what is enterable on a window.

▲ Window controls requiring data entry and the text displayed in these window controls should use colors set by the user in the Windows Control Panel. Non-editable window controls should be set to light gray.

▲ If all required fields have not been entered, display an error message when the user clicks Apply, Save, or Close. For example: Field A, Field F, Field P are required.

Pointers

▲ The location and movement of the cursor on an individual window should depend on the procedure for which the window is designed.

▲ An arrow is the standard pointer for window navigation.

▲ Set the cursor on the first field that can be typed when the window is opened.

▲ Specify a function for *Enter* when the window is first opened. For example, what should happen if the users press *Enter* without doing anything on the window?

▲ When the pointer is on an editable field, the standard pointer should change to an I-beam.

▲ When the pointer is on a field that provides additional detail when double-clicked, you should change the standard pointer to a magnifying glass.

▲ While database access occurs, you should change the standard pointer to an hourglass.

▲ Paint and use an icon such as a spinning clock while database update is going on.

MicroHelp

▲ Use MicroHelp to indicate the status of the database within the application.

▲ The message should be brief and in context with the immediate task or location of the cursor. The objective is to provide relevant and timely feedback to the user.

▲ Date and time should be displayed in the far right corner of the message bar.

▲ Allow the user to cancel a lengthy retrieve at any time.

Message Boxes

▲ Keep messages simple. Avoid using negatives in message text. When applicable, include corrective action in text, such as invalid entry: balance should be positive.

▲ Message Boxes should contain a title bar which references the process encountering the error.

▲ Message Boxes should generally contain a user response button.

▲ To maintain uniformity, a message table may be used and accessed throughout the application.

Help

▲ Should be accessed either through the toolbar or the DropDown menubar.

▲ May also be accessed through dialog boxes.

▲ User communication describing ongoing maintenance and system enhancements should be included in the contents.

Error Messages

▲ Try to check for the most common errors and translate them into user-friendly messages instead of displaying the database message as it is.

▲ Allow the user to print, save the error details to a log file, resume and abort the application. You can write a common function and control it from the Application's System Error event and DataWindow **dberror** event.

Naming Conventions

If all developers on a project adhere to a standard set of naming conventions, it will be much easier for them to work with one anothers' code. A sound naming convention will substantially improve the longevity of an application by making it easier to support and modify.

Naming conventions should allow someone to determine the pertinent information about an object, variable, or function just by glancing at the code. The following naming conventions will provide a solid development standard that can be used as a basis for your own standards. Names should be short, but descriptive enough to be meaningful.

All PowerBuilder objects can be divided into two categories depending on the storage type. First, objects stored individually in a library, such as window, DataWindow, etc. The prefix for these object should be a single character in most cases. There are a few exceptions where duplication may occur, for example, we prefer to use the prefix 'dw' for DataWindows. The second category is objects that are stored as part of the first level objects, for example ListBox, CommandButton etc. These can have two or more characters as the prefix:

Object Type	Convention	Object Type	Convention
Project	p_	Data Pipeline	dp_
Application	a_	Query	q_
Window	w_	User Object	u_
Menu	m_	Function	f_
DataWindow	dw_	Structure	s_

Objects like functions and structures, which can be declared in another object, should be prefixed with the type of object in which they are declared. For example, the name of a function declared in a window would be `wf_check_errors`.

Window Controls	Convention	Window Controls	Convention
CheckBox	cbx_	Oval	oval_
CommandButton	cb_	OLE 2.0 control	ole_
DataWindowControl	dwc_	Picture	p_
DropDownListBox	ddlb_	PictureButton	pb_
GroupBox	gb_	RadioButton	rb_
HScrollBar	hsb_	Rectangle	r_
Line	ln_	RoundRectangle	rr_
ListBox	lb_	Static Text	st_
MultiLineEdit	mle_	VScrollBar	vsb_
SingleLineEdit	sle_	UserObject	uo_

Most of these are the standard PowerBuilder naming conventions for controls. PowerBuilder automatically names controls with the appropriate prefix followed by a number when they are placed on a window. Using these standard conventions can save you a lot of time otherwise spent typing in control names.

Variables and Data Types

The declaration of variables includes scope, data type, and the name. For example, an instance variable of type string: **i_s_StringVal1**. The following table lists suggested prefixes for variables:

Variable scope	Prefix
Global variable	g_
Shared variable	s_
Instance variable	i_
Shared variable, declared in ancestor	sa_
Instance variable, declared in ancestor	ia_
Local variables	l_

The next table lists the suggested prefixes for data types:

Data Type	Convention
Blob	blb_
Boolean	b_
Date	d_
DateTime	dt_
Decimal	c_
Double	db_
Graphic Object	go_
Integer	i_

Continued

Data Type	Convention
Long	l_
Real	r_
String	s_
Time	t_
Unsigned Int	ui_
Unsigned Long	ul_

Documentation

When documenting your applications, follow a standard methodology. Provide headers as comments with the following elements:

Events

▲ Name

▲ Description of process

Creation Section

▲ Creator Name

▲ Creation date

Modify Section

▲ Modifier Name

▲ Modification Date

Functions

▲ Name

▲ Description

▲ Parameters

▲ Allowable values

Creation Section

▲ Creator Name

▲ Creation date

Modify Section

▲ Modifier Name

▲ Modification Date

Environment

Create a development environment which organizes objects in a logical manner:

Directory	Used For
SAMPLE	Files for Test environment.
HELP	Contains the source and compiled versions of help files for the system.
LIB	Contains the compiled versions of the library (PBD).
SOURCE	Contains source code (PBL, INI, PBR).
BIN	Contains all production executable files.
SQL	Contains the scripts for creating the stored procedures and triggers.
DOCUMENT	All other document files other than help files.
RESOURCE	All resource files such as bitmaps, icon files and cursor files.

Error Files

An application should log pertinent messages to an error log file. The location and name of the file will be specified in the `.INI` file.

The format of the records should be:

▲ User name and terminal ID

▲ Date and Time, for example, 1/12/95 08:02:34

▲ Error Message

▲ Memory information such as GDI, USER, Free Memory %

▲ If the record is in error, write the full record to log for diagnostic purposes

Third-Party Products

There are a lot of third-party products currently available for PowerBuilder. Let's concentrate on one product from each of the key areas of application design and development. These areas include:

- CASE tools
- Help authoring tools
- Testing tools

We'll look at each of these areas and explain the features of each product as they relate to PowerBuilder applications.

The CASE Tool: ERwin

Logic Works provides a whole family of tools that help you incorporate process and data modeling. Two of these tools, BPwin and ERwin, have recently become very popular. BPwin uses the IDEF0 methodology for process modeling, while ERwin uses the IDEF1X methodology for the slightly different task of data modeling.

> Recently, the US Government decided to adopt the IDEF0 methodology as their standard for all process modeling.

ERwin comes in three different flavors, each designed for a specific segment of the database market:

- ERwin/SQL - for all popular RDBMS
- ERwin/DBF - for desktop databases
- ERwin/ERX - for both RDBMS and desktop databases, and includes reverse engineering tools.

The Facilities of ERwin

ERwin has many useful and time saving features that enable both the database developer and the front-end designer to model the problem they face and start down the road to creating a solution. Some of the facilities that ERwin boasts include:

- A bi-directional link with the supported software.
- Support for Subject Areas and Stored Displays.
- Automatic creation of the necessary SQL statements.
- Several tools designed to speed up the creation of SQL Server triggers.
- The generation of scripts at any time throughout the creation process.
- Support for FRE (Forward and Reverse Engineering).
- An in-built browser and report editor.

▲ Support for multiple data model formats.

▲ The ERwin Metamodel.

Supertypes and Subtypes

As you analyze the domain for your database, you will probably find that there are some entities that define a whole category of things of the same type. For example, you might be reviewing an employee entity, i.e. the part of a process concerned with employees. As part of this entity, you might be making the distinction between full-time and part-time employees, both of which have their own attributes, but are basically dependent on a range of common characteristics.

By using ERwin, you can depict these relationships in your overall data modeling diagram by creating both the entity that defines the category, together with each of the elements of the category. The software then goes on to connect all of these elements with a special type of relationship called the 'Subtype Relationship Connector'. The parent of the category is called the 'Supertype' and each of the children are called 'Subtypes'.

In our example, we can define 'employee' as the Supertype and both 'full-time employee' and 'part-time employee' as Subtypes. In other words, the basic attributes are held in the Supertype, while any more specific characteristics that we need for our modeling would be allocated to a Subtype, inheriting all the basic attributes from the associated Supertype.

Subject Areas

ERwin allows you to create different subject areas. A subject area is a named version of a data model that may include all the entities, relationships, Subtypes and text blocks connected with your database, or any subset of the objects in the complete data model.

Working with subject areas is especially useful when designing and maintaining a large complex data model. For example, you could create a subject area that focuses on some of the entities in our model, rather than on the whole model itself.

In our Stock Control system, we might want to display the smaller data model associated with the item_master table and all of its relationships, rather than blurring the picture by looking at the whole application.

Stored Displays

You can also define different stored displays. A stored display is an alternative presentation of a subject area that highlights a particular aspect of the total data structure. This feature allows you to define the data model in one way, building in all the detail required to fully describe it, and to view it on a multitude of different levels.

For example, you can define subject areas to cover the primary key, entity and physical data type levels to name but a few. Two examples of this feature are given below:

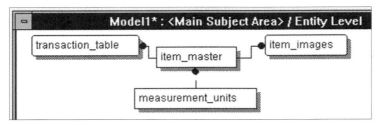

Stock Control System - Entity Level Data Model Diagram

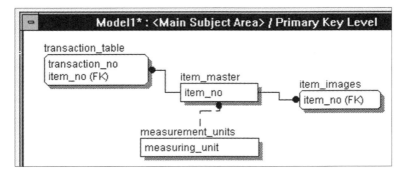

Stock Control System - Primary Key Level Data Model Diagram

Relationships

ERwin allows you to draw non-identifying recursive relationships. A non-identifying relationship is one where an instance of the child entity isn't directly identified through its association with a parent entity.

Automatic SQL Creation

By automating the creation of the SQL code, ERwin lets you take advantage of the two advanced features that are supported on several SQL servers: triggers and stored procedures.

Triggers and stored procedures are simply named blocks of SQL code that are pre-compiled and stored on the server in order to perform queries, data validation and other frequently requested functions at that level. As the triggers and stored procedures are pre-compiled, requests for information through these components are dealt with faster than normal queries.

Another advantage of these components is that the workload the network has to cope with is reduced. This is because you simply call the stored procedure with the necessary parameters rather than sending the whole query definition.

Triggers

ERwin provides a set of six default RI (Referential Integrity) triggers as templates that can be attached to events to tell the target server how to enforce referential integrity. These templates include:

- Child Insert
- Child Update
- Child Delete
- Parent Insert
- Parent Update
- Parent Delete

In special situations, you can override the default code that is generated by ERwin by customizing these RI trigger templates:

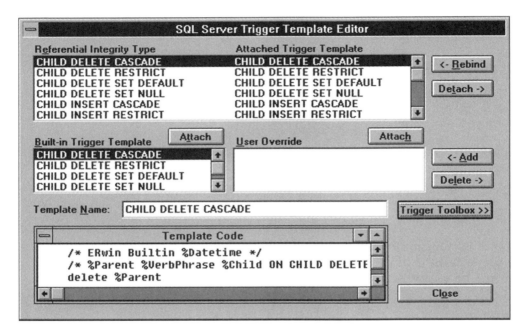

As you build your data model, ERwin automatically assigns a default RI trigger template to each entity in a relationship. The trigger template is assigned to the relationship and the SQL code that is generated is influenced by three criteria:

- ▲ The referential integrity rule that is applied to the relationship: **RESTRICT**, **CASCADE**, **SET NULL**, **SET DEFAULT** or **NONE**.

- ▲ The type of relationship to which it is attached: Identifying, Non-Identifying or Subtype.

- ▲ The entity's role in the relationship: Parent or Child.

Template Toolbox

ERwin provides the **Template Toolbox Editor** that can help you to customize the built-in trigger templates, create override RI trigger templates or write new SQL triggers or stored procedures:

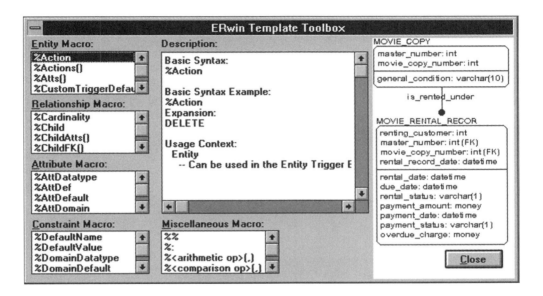

The predefined macros, which begin with the percent (%) symbol, produce pseudocode. This pseudocode is expanded into the specific SQL syntax supported by the target server when the physical schema is generated.

The Template Toolbox contains three sections: a set of five macro ListBoxes on the left, a window that displays a description about the selected macro in the center, and a static sample diagram on the right that illustrates the current entity diagram. Double-clicking on a macro name will insert the macro at the last position your cursor occupied in the code window.

Generation Scripts

ERwin allows you to generate both pre- and post-schema generation scripts. These are the SQL scripts that you want ERwin to execute immediately before or after the rest of the schema has been generated.

For example, when you forward engineer a database from an ERwin model, you can create a pre-schema generation script that drops the old database and creates a new one. The ground is now prepared for ERwin to begin generating the tables and indexes specified in the data model.

FRE: Forward and Reverse Engineering

ERwin supports FRE (forward and reverse engineering) in the same package. ERwin supports direct Catalog-based FRE on twelve target SQL DBMS:

- AS/400
- DB2
- Informix
- Ingress
- Netware SQL
- ORACLE
- Progress
- Rdb
- SQLBase
- SQL Server
- Sybase
- WATCOM SQL

ERwin desktop supports:

- FoxPro
- Access
- Clipper
- dBase III

▲ dBase IV

▲ Paradox

ERwin gives you two choices when generating a database schema:

▲ To connect ERwin directly to the system catalog in the target database and generate the schema in one step.

▲ To generate an ASCII DDL script, run as a separate step on the server.

You can also apply the concepts of reverse engineering in both of these ways.

Report Editor

ERwin provides both a built-in browser and a report editor to help you create your reports. Before you create a report, you can use the browser's features to view, sort or modify the entities, attributes and relationships that you are interested in.

> *You should also note that you can generate reports for a specific subject area.*

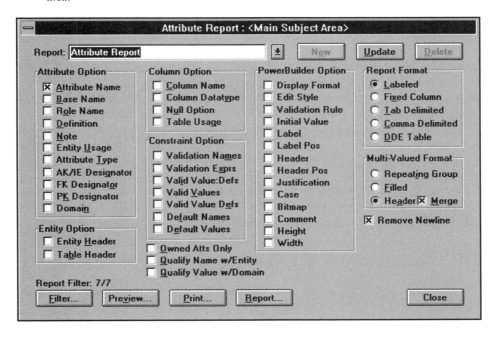

The report types include:

- ▲ Entity
- ▲ Attribute
- ▲ Relationship
- ▲ Physical Schema generation
- ▲ Domain
- ▲ Default

ERwin can also serve as a DDE client, sending data through the Report Module. It allows you to export any ERwin reports to a local wordprocessor or spreadsheet that can function as a DDE Server. Examples of such applications include Microsoft's Word and Excel.

To perform this task, all you have to do is select the DDE Table option from the Report Format section and the underlying code will automatically set up the conversation and build the required table, filling it with data as it becomes available.

Multiple Data Model Formats

When you save your data model, it is stored in a file with an .ER1 extension. In addition to generating SQL DDL scripts and creating DDL reports to send data to another Windows program, ERwin lets you create three special types of text files that you can use to transfer model information to other applications:

- ▲ **ERX format:** ERwin's native text format.
- ▲ **SML format:** SML (Structured Modeling Language) defines ERwin models in much the same way as SQL DDL (SQL Data Definition Language) defines databases. This is useful in that models can be stored and transferred between different tools that support the format. ERwin provides support for importing and exporting SML format files.

▲ **MPD ModelPro format:** another type of file that stores data model information in text format. ModelPro was introduced several years ago in a special version of ERwin. The current version (ERwin/ERX is currently on v2.0) includes support for the ModelPro format v3.5.

As long as you are always going to use ERwin for all of your data modeling needs, storing your models in the `.ER1` format is the better option. Other formats take more time to load, since they must be parsed - read in and interpreted line by line - as they are loaded into ERwin.

ERwin also provides support for the data model to be saved to the target server database. When you do this for the first time, you must complete two stages, the first of which is to create ERwin specific tables in the target server database. The second stage is the exporting of the data model itself to the target server database:

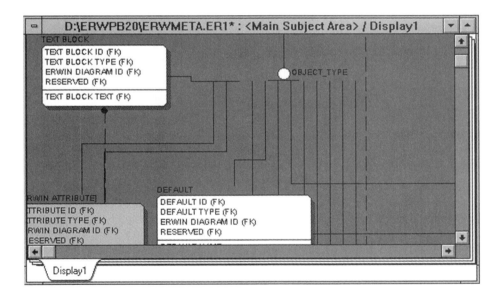

ERwin Metamodel

Along with the ERwin package, Logic Works have also shipped the **ERwin Dictionary Metamodel**. This component contains all the information that is required to generate a physical database on your selected target server:

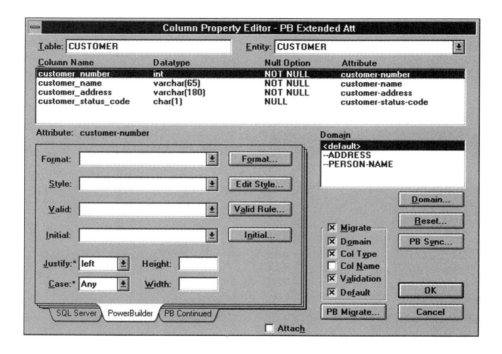

To create a physical database on your target database server, you need to generate a schema for the Metamodel. When this is complete, ERwin connects to the target server and creates all the tables required to store the data model. At this stage, all you need to do is open your data model and export information into the database.

ERwin/ERX for PowerBuilder lets you manage both client-oriented information such as PowerBuilder extended attributes and server-oriented information like triggers, stored procedures and physical storage objects from within ERwin.

By using ERwin, you are able to define all the attributes for the columns and tables in your database from one place. It allows you to assign all the required attributes such as fonts, colors, validation rules, initial values, edit styles and display styles from this screen, using a special editor. You can even synchronize any differences between ERwin and PowerBuilder column attributes:

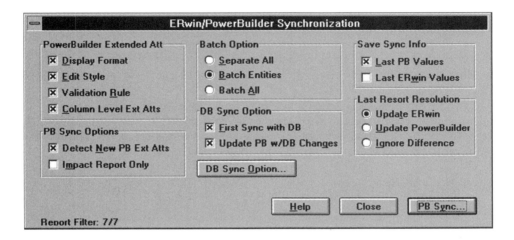

Close Links with PowerBuilder

ERwin/ERX for PowerBuilder lets you capture PowerBuilder's extended attributes in your database design with a bi-directional link to the PowerBuilder data dictionary. You can then make alterations inside the ERwin environment before updating the PowerBuilder side of the equation when you are satisfied with the results.

The ERwin environment also allows you to create any new extended attributes that you haven't touched on yet, passing them over into the PowerBuilder environment when the two systems are brought into line with one another. As a consequence of this feature, any of the options that are common to both the target database and your PowerBuilder application can be set in the ERwin environment and automatically transferred to both platforms.

Overview: ERwin

ERwin's schema and report generation is very fast. The hard copy documentation is very useful and easy to understand. A user with some experience of PowerBuilder can master this product in few days and a novice user can get data modeling concepts from the documentation.

The on-line documentation is also very good, except that the designers missed the chance of providing a context sensitive Help button for each dialog box. This means that a search for the meaning of a particular function may become quite time-consuming.

The technical support is free for forty-five days after registration, is of an excellent standard and has a quick response time. Even if you are unlucky enough to catch the tech support group during a busy period, by leaving a message you can expect a return call in under 5 minutes.

You can reach them at:

Logic Works, Inc.
1060 Route 206
Princeton, NJ 08540
Phone: (609) 252-1177
Fax: (609) 252-1175

The Windows Help Authoring Tool: RoboHelp

Windows Help has become a very popular way of presenting reference information to a Windows user. Windows users are notorious for abandoning the manuals as soon as they find the software in the box. They expect to find all the answers to their questions via on-line, context-sensitive help as they muddle through the application.

From the software developers point of view, Windows Help is a great idea as it reduces the cost of the initial purchase, any further updates and the distribution of both. It adds flexibility to the product development cycle, is faster to update than a manual and is instantly available to the user and offers the potential of almost unlimited color graphics and multimedia capability.

Due to this 'acceptance' from both sides of the fence, Windows Help is set to become the de facto method of support for any new software, and it is because of this evolution that any Windows applications that you provide will be more readily accepted by your users if it is provided 'in the box'.

Windows Help Viewer

Every copy of Windows comes with a Help viewer called `WINHELP.EXE`, but it is sadly lacking when it comes to a Help compiler for developers. The Help viewer can only use compiled Help files with a `.HLP` extension, so you need a compiler that can read formatted text and compile these `.HLP` extension files.

Due to this coding requirement meshing with the need for technical knowledge of the subject, the creation of a Windows Help system has traditionally required the efforts of both a technical writer for the actual subject matter and a programmer to handle the complexities of the `.RTF` file.

Writing the `.RTF` file format that is required by the help compiler is a real nightmare, especially when you start to take into consideration not only the formatting of the text received from the technical writer, but also the context-sensitive jumps and the browse order of the topics.

Using RoboHelp

RoboHelp, a help authoring tool from Blue Sky Software makes this process much easier. It automates all aspects of creating a Windows Help system, enabling the user to design, test and create comprehensive, context-sensitive Help systems for Windows and Windows NT.

RoboHelp draws a lot of its functionality from Word for Windows, working in a symbiotic relationship to produce the finished result. It automatically invokes Word, loading all the necessary macros and extends the existing menus to accommodate its own functionality.

753

RoboHelp requires Word 2.0 or 6.0 to be installed upon your system before it can successfully create an **.HLP** *file. RoboHelp handles the compilation side of the equation while Word is used as a text editor.*

You simply need to select the appropriate option and type in your text, leaving RoboHelp to take care of the necessary text formatting and any footnotes that are required. You can also get RoboHelp to automatically create the necessary project file if you select the correct combination of options.

Debugging the Script

From within the Word environment, you can compile the Help file and see any errors that have been uncovered. The Error Wizard can guide you to the exact location of a potential error before compiling, and provides a detailed explanation of what might be wrong with a possible solution.

In most cases, you will get no error messages when it comes to the actual process of compiling the **.HLP** file - the process of writing the file is that easy and coupled with the pre-compile debug you should never have any problems!

The Fully Integrated Environment

It is a fully integrated environment that gives you complete access to all the advanced features of the Windows Help Engine, such as macros, secondary windows and multiple hot spot graphics. With RoboHelp, you avoid the complexities of setting context strings, keywords, browse sequences and hypertext links as it creates the necessary `.H` `.HPJ` and `.RTF` files.

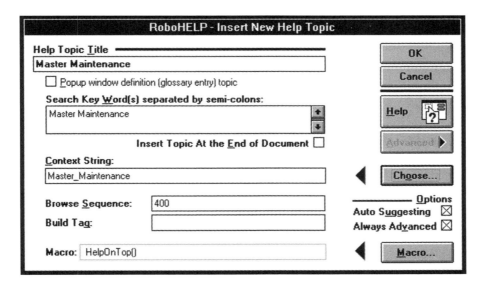

It also generates the source code required for context-sensitive jumps, cross references, indexes, topics, defined terms, pop-up definitions, graphics, bitmap hot spot links and so on.

> *RoboHelp supports the US and the major European versions of Word 6.0 in the same product and also provides special localized versions for Kanji and Chinese versions of Word.*

Two Way Conversion

RoboHelp also offers two-way conversion, automatically converting existing documents into Help systems or vice versa and it will also import any existing Help source code.

Simulation Mode and Custom Controls

The simulation mode allows you to test your design without the need to compile each version and the package includes VBX and custom control Help buttons so that you can add context-sensitive help to your application without the need for programming.

Screen Capture

If you have ever used PaintBrush to capture screenshots, you will understand the complexities that this software is trying to solve, including zooming in and out, copy and pasting the required shots and cropping to the correct size.

RoboHelp includes a special utility called 'Screen Capture' for capturing screen shots for use in printed documentation and in Help systems. Whenever you press *Print Screen*, it is automatically activated. You can edit the picture by invoking PaintBrush from this utility, as well as being able to define hotspots, zoom to selected areas of the picture any number of times and save the zoomed version of the picture.

This utility allows you to define multiple hotspot areas, browse your help project and choose the associated help topics visually, rather than having to remember complex Context IDs.

The Image Painter

The environment includes another powerful utility called the **PaintIt Image Painter** that can be used to edit existing icon, cursor and bitmap images or even to create your own original images. This utility is capable of creating images for VGA, EGA, Monochrome and CGA display systems and allows you to choose not only the type of image (icon, cursor, bitmap), but also to design that image for your specific system.

Sound and Video

You can easily integrate videos and sound into your Windows Help system using RoboHelp. An additional package is available from BlueSky software called the **RoboHelp WinHelp Video Kit** for this exact purpose. This package includes everything you need to create live video demonstrations of your

Windows applications and to integrate them (and other video and sound files) into your Help system.

This system allows you to record videos that explain complex procedures, in order to both teach applications and to demonstrate product features. In this case, the word 'video' doesn't imply the need for a video camera. You can see exactly this technique being used on the Infobase CD-ROM, where all the features of PowerBuilder v4 are demonstrated using full multimedia capabilities.

Suppose you want to explain how to use one of your applications. All you need to do is invoke this tool, start the application and run through the ins and outs of the software, exactly as if you were demonstrating it to a colleague. The video kit automatically records everything that appears on the screen including the mouse pointer and can even record your voice as you explain what you are doing.

The video kit also provides automatic incremental file naming. That is, every time you stop capturing and then start again, it automatically increases the file name by one. This allows you to create a collection of small video files rather than one large one or if you don't want capture all of the steps, you can simply take the shots you want to, and mix them together at a later date:

Overview: RoboHelp

By using this type of interactive multimedia help system, you can drastically reduce the cost of training in the use of your application. With the CD-ROM drive now becoming a standard feature rather than a gaming add-on, providing help with multimedia effects will soon become the standard that normal Windows Help systems have already become today.

The RoboHelp WinHelp Video Kit includes:

▲ **Software Video Camera**:   Allows you to record full-motion screen action and sound.

▲ **Video Tester**:   Allows testing of video and sound files after you create them.

▲ **Video Wizard**:   Automatically configures your help system to support video and sound functionality.

▲ **WinHelp Video/Sound Player**:   Plays the video and sound from within a windows help file.

▲ **Video for Windows**:   Plays the video at run-time.

You can reach this company at:

Blue Sky Software Corporation
7486 La Jolla Blvd, Suite 3,
La Jolla, CA 92037-9583, USA
Phone: 1-800-677-4Win, 1-619-459-6365
Fax: 1-619-459-6366

The Testing Tool: SQA TeamTest

Testing GUI applications is one of today's major issues. As organizations apply Client/Server technology to their mission-critical applications at an ever increasing pace, fast and effective testing is becoming more and more crucial.

There are two main components in SQA TeamTest:

- SQA Manager
- SQA Robot

SQA Manager

SQA Manager is the part of the testing package that allows you to define the test requirements, a task that it allows you to perform even before it has seen the code and therefore the variable declarations. TeamTest isn't designed to automate running tests the first time - no test tools do that. Rather, it assumes that testers will perform each test and generate a test script. Developing and running tests for the first time will be as difficult and time-consuming as it would be without an automated testing tool:

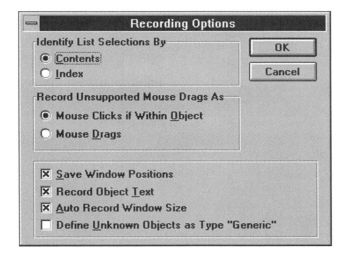

Once you develop the testing scripts, you can play back the scenario in either attended or unattended mode. Typically, the unattended mode is tailor-made for running complete regression testing of an application. The results of this test procedure are stored in a test repository and comprise a baseline against which future executions of the test are compared.

SQA Robot

SQA Robot is the tool that actually records and plays back results. All you need to do is click on the play-back button on the SQA Robot toolbar and select the procedure to be replayed. When the test procedure completes, the test log viewer informs you if the test passed. The test log viewer also lists each of the individual test events and their results, as well as a pass or fail indicator for the test as a whole.

SQA Robot is object-oriented in that it sends messages to Windows objects instead of simply replaying keystrokes and mouse movements. This approach enables SQA Robot to disregard cosmetic changes such as relocated controls, menu rearrangements and so on. Consequently, the need to perform regular maintenance to keep the text procedures in sync with minor application changes is no longer necessary.

While playing back the script, unexpected windows such as notification of an e-mail message or a Netware 'volume out of space' error message sometimes appear during testing activities. SQA Robot gives you several options on how unexpected windows should be processed:

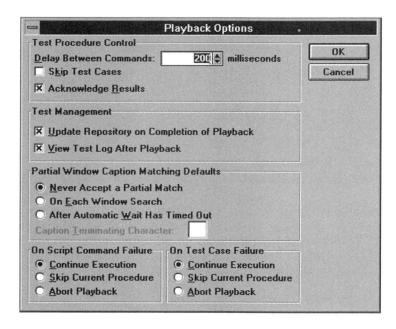

Playback testing can continue or terminate when it encounters an unexpected window or a screenshot of the unexpected window can be captured and stored in the test repository.

Several options are available that will determine SQA Robot's response to the window, including:

▲ Closing the window by sending a **WM_CLOSE** message to the active window.

▲ Selecting the default button on the window.

▲ Executing the keystroke

Test Scripts

SQA Robot generates test scripts in Microsoft's Visual Basic scripting language. SQA Robot uses Visual Basic to compile test procedures into an executable program, so you need to have Visual Basic 3.0:

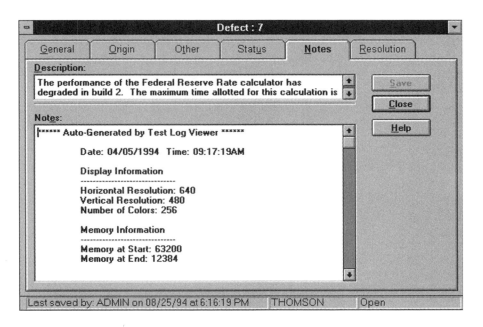

If you know Visual Basic script, you can extend or modify these scripts.

You can review the tests to determine whether they passed or failed. If a test fails, you can use one of several tools to compare the defective result with the base case:

▲ The **Object Comparator** compares objects such as CheckBoxes, RadioButtons, ListBoxes and so on.

▲ **SQA Text Comparator** compares alphanumeric data captured from a list, menu or clipboard.

▲ **SQA Image Comparator** lets you compare an image captured during playback with the same window or image captured during the baseline recording.

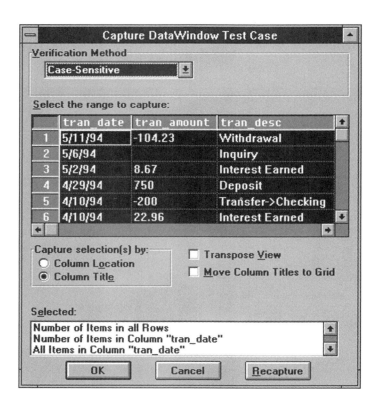

Overview: TeamTest and PowerBuilder

TeamTest offers specialized support for PowerBuilder's object-oriented development environment. The PowerBuilder support allows users of automated test procedures written in SQA TeamTest to directly 'see' into PowerBuilder objects such as DataWindows. The contents of these objects are typically invisible to other Windows products.

SQA TeamTest is one of the PowerSoft's CODE (Client/Server Open Development Environment) partners and by using the PowerBuilder API, SQA TeamTest determines the contents of those windows and can then run tests against user-defined criteria to determine if the content is correct. By building test cases into shell scripts, an entire application can be tested unattended. This is especially useful when you change something in the top-most ancestor window and want to check the effect of those changes in the entire application.

No automated test tool, even one as complete as SQA TeamTest, can tell you what to test, how much tweaking you need to do, or when all the defects have been eliminated from your software. However, tools such as TeamTest can help you to organize your testing, repeatedly executing the tests without deviation from the predefined steps and to monitor the occurrences of defects.

You can reach this company at:

SQA Inc.,
10 State St.,
Woburn, MA 01801.
Ph: 1-800-228-9922,
1-617-932-0110
Fax: 1-617-932-3280.

Watcom Interactive SQL and Advanced PowerBuilder Developers Kit

Watcom SQL is a shrink-wrapped database. By issuing this statement, we really mean that even though it is a complete stand-alone product, its inclusion as part of the PowerBuilder suite of applications makes it into the first choice for PowerBuilder developers testing out any of their applications on a Client/Server level.

In fact, this statement can lead you even further if you consider it in terms of a PowerBuilder application. As long as you are using Watcom SQL as your test bed database, you will never have to worry about any of those connection details as PowerBuilder and Watcom work seamlessly together.

In fact, all of the commands and other subsidiary information that you require to communicate with a Watcom SQL database are handled by the ODBC setup and your database profile. For example, the sample database that ships with the software suite, the Powersoft Demo DB, comes already configured.

Whenever you invoke the Database Painter, PowerBuilder automatically detects whether the specified database is running and connects your application to the Watcom SQL engine, if required.

> To further reinforce our statement, think about the work required to set up a Watcom database through the Database Painter. When you create the database, the painter automatically creates the necessary profile for you. Could life be simpler?

Focusing on the Watcom SQL Engine

However, the close links between PowerBuilder and the Watcom SQL engine are only any good to you as a database developer when you are using this particular database front-end development tool. If you need to work with the engine outside of the PowerBuilder environment, such as when your application is installed in the field, you need another way in which to interact with the database.

Fortunately, Powersoft have provided a tool, specially designed for this task as part of the PowerBuilder suite of applications. The current version now ships with the Interactive SQL utility, and allows you to gain direct access to the Watcom SQL engine, providing you with the necessary tools to perform any routine maintenance that is required.

In this section of the appendix, we take a look at this utility, investigating how it works, what it can do and what information it can provide on any of your Watcom SQL databases.

Invoke Watcom ISQL

To invoke this utility, double-click on the Interactive SQL icon, placed into your Powersoft Program Group during the installation of PowerBuilder. The interface is composed of four main windows, each of which can be selected from the Window menu. Each of these windows is indicated below:

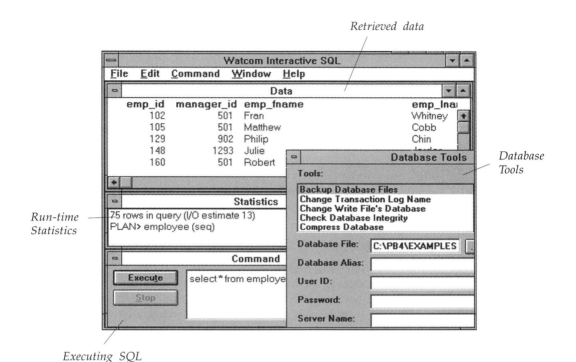

Retrieved data

Database Tools

Run-time Statistics

Executing SQL

To begin with, you must inform ISQL which database you are interested in. Select the Database Tools window and supply the full path and filename of the database you wish to connect to in Database File: and select the Connect... button.

> *Note that by filling in more information into this window, you will be able to automate the connection process. You should also be aware that if you attempt to execute a SQL statement when you are not connected, ISQL will prompt you for the database you want to interrogate.*

When you have successfully connected to the required database, you can now begin to make use of the facilities that ISQL has to offer. By entering SQL statements into the Command window, you can maintain the contents of the database just as if you were using the same SQL statements in PowerBuilder.

767

> ISQL requires one connection for each database that it is used to interrogate. This is over and above the connections used by any other software running together with the Watcom SQL database engine.

Any SQL statements that cause the database to return information will affect the content of the Data window, while the Statistics window is used to record the overall performance of the database engine.

However, if you are interested in some of the other tasks that you might perform whilst maintaining your database, you need to review the rest of the tasks offered by the Database Tools window.

ISQL Maintenance Tools

For the rest of this section, we will review each of the tools that ISQL has to offer to the database administrator who is interested in non-data related maintenance. Each of these tools can be run as a DOS command or via the ISQL interface. We will cover both of these methods of execution for each tool.

> *Note that the command line version is supplied as a legacy from the Watcom SQL Engine v3.0. If you are using this version of the engine, you won't have access to the Database Tools window, so you must use the command line method. V4.0 users can run these commands from File Manager by using File/Run....*

DBSTARTW

This command is used to create a connection to an existing database.

The syntax for the command line version is:

```
DBSTARTW  [switches]  <full  path  database  name>
```

> Note that if you use any of the switches described below, you must also include the -n switch to denote that the next entry is the name of the database.

The following command line would start up a connection to the database called **PSDEMODE.DB** located in the **C:\PB4** directory:

DBSTARTW c:\pb4\psdemodb.db

Some of the important command line options are as follows:

Switch	Description
-i	Disable triggers
-d	Disable fast I/O
-gp <Size>	Maximum page size in bytes- either 512, 1024, 2012 or 4096
-c <Size>	Maximum cache size
-b	Runs in bulk copy mode
-gr <Num>	Maximum recovery time in number of minutes

We have already seen how to use this tool through the Database Tools window, by filling in the required information and clicking on the Connect... button.

The command for run-time version is RTSTARTW. If you want to start in 32-bit mode, you should use DB32W and RT32T respectively.

DBINITW

This command is used to create a new database.

The syntax for this command is as follows:

```
DBINITW [switches] <new filename>
```

If you don't specify an extension for the database name, ISQL will automatically add the default extension of `.DB`. ISQL also creates the database with one standard User ID, 'DBA' with the normal default Password, 'SQL'.

The following command line would create a new database, place it in `C:\WROX` and give it the default User ID and Password, 'DBA' and 'SQL'. Note that the `-c` flag means that both of these entries are in capitals - remember that the Watcom SQL login is case sensitive.

DBINITW -c c:\wrox\testrun.db

Some of the important command line options are as follows:

Switches	Description
-c	Case sensitivity. All names (table, columns, and so on) and values are case sensitive in a Watcom SQL database. The default is case insensitive.
-e	Encrypt the database
-t <transaction log>	Change the name of the default transaction log file. By default, the transaction log file name is the same as database file name with a **.LOG** file extension
-n	Don't use a transaction log
z <col-seq>	Definition of the collation sequence or the file that contains the collation sequence. The collation sequence is used for all string comparisons in the database

You have access to this command through Database Tools via the Create Database option. When you select this option, ISQL provides this dialog:

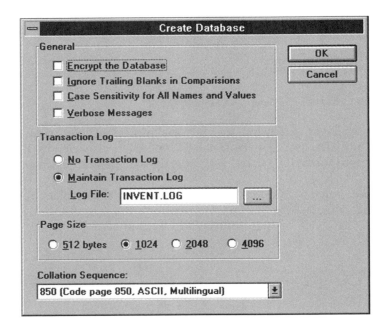

This provides you with all the usual options for the creation of your new database. Note that before you can use this tool, you must provide a new database name in Database File: on the main Database Tools window.

DBLOGW

One of the interesting features of Watcom SQL is the database administrator's ability to control the transaction log. The database engine will log all of its actions to any pre-defined file, or not at all, if you so wish. The command line syntax for this tool is as follows:

```
DBLOGW [switches] <name of the log file>
```

Some of the important command line options are as follows:

Switches	Description
-n	Stop using the specified transaction log.
-t	Change the transaction log to the specified file. While changing the transaction log, the database shouldn't be running.

The option to run this command line through the Database Tools window is called Change Transaction Log Name. If you select this after supplying the name of the database in question, ISQL displays this dialog:

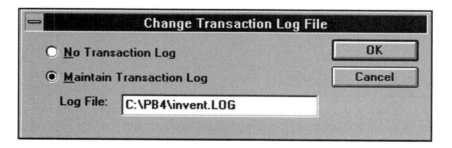

771

DBINFOW

Via this command, the Watcom SQL engine allows you to get summary information on the settings under which the current database is running. The syntax for this command line tool is as follows:

`DBINFOW [switches] database file name`

Some of the important command line options are as follows:

Switches	Description
-c 'keyword=value; keyword=...'	Specify the database connection information
-u	Output the page statistics

The Database Tools option for this command is called Database Information. When you select this option, after specifying the database name as usual, ISQL displays the following screen of information:

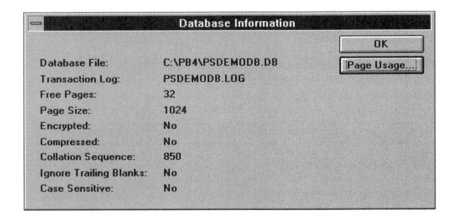

By clicking on the Page Usage... button, you can get more specific information on the database tables' memory usage. This information can be particularly useful for calculating bottlenecks in information flow around your network during peak periods of activity:

DBSHRINW & DBEXPANW

ISQL offers you the ability to compress any currently unused databases whenever disk space is limited. Using this technique, a database will usually be compressed to 40-60% of its original size.

The compressed form of the database will be written to a new file with a default file extension of `.CDB`. The original `.DB` version of the database will be left untouched, so if space is at a premium, you should now delete this file. The command line syntax for both of these commands is as follows:

```
DBSHRINW [switches] <database file name> [compressed file name]
DBEXPANW [switches] [compressed file name] <database file name>
```

The only important switch for this command is:

Switch	Description
-y	This option erases any previous output files without alerting the user.

> You should note that the Watcom SQL engine can't write to a compressed file.

The Database Tools option for this command is called Compress Database and Uncompress Database respectively. Once you have specified the database or compressed file to affect, ISQL will ask you where the output file should be created.

> ISQL demands that you enter a valid User ID and Password if you are compressing an existing database.

If ISQL successfully compresses a database, it will return a page of summary statistics related to the compression of the file:

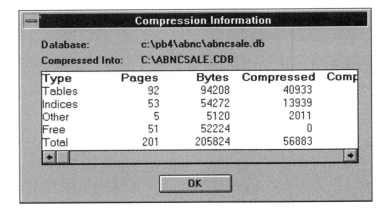

Type	Pages	Bytes	Compressed	Comp
Tables	92	94208	40933	
Indices	53	54272	13939	
Other	5	5120	2011	
Free	51	52224	0	
Total	201	205824	56883	

Database: c:\pb4\abnc\abncsale.db
Compressed Into: C:\ABNCSALE.CDB

OK

DBCOLLW

Watcom SQL has offered support for a customizable sorting and comparison order, otherwise known as a collation sequence, since v3.2. The built-in collation sequences support many single-byte character sets for various country, language and code page combinations.

> All the supported collation sequences are available in **SYS.SYSCOLLATION** table.

ISQL allows you to extract the details of a collation sequence into a file with this command. You can use this file with the DBINITW command while creating a new database to replicate a collation sequence automatically. This option can be very useful if you have designed your own custom collation sequences.

The syntax for this command is as follows:

DBCOLLW [switches] <output file>

Some of the important command line options are as follows:

Switches	Description
-e	Include empty mappings
-x	Use Hexadecimal for extended characters (7F-FF)
-z <label>	Collating sequence label
-y	Replace existing collation file without confirmation

The Database Tools option for this command is called Extract Collation from Database. When you have specified the appropriate Database File, User ID and Password, ISQL will display the following dialog:

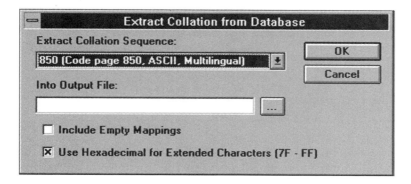

775

DBWRITEW

Another interesting feature provided by Watcom SQL is the ability to write all the changes to another temporary file, leaving the original database unchanged. This file, called a **write file**, is attached to one particular database and can be useful for field testing a database. This allows you to run tests against a database, even tests that might alter the structure or content of the database, without disrupting the database from a users point of view.

The syntax for this command is as follows:

```
DBWRITEW [switches] <database name> [write file name] [log name]
```

Some of the important command line options are as follows:

Switches	Description
-c	Create a new write file, replacing any existing files.
-d	Make the existing write file point to a different database.

The Database Tools option for this command is called Create Write File. When you have specified the Database File, User ID and Password, ISQL provides this dialog:

When you have specified the file name, ISQL creates the write file and, from that point on, any interaction you have with the database is stored in the write file, rather than executed against it.

DBBACKW

With this command, ISQL allows you to back up your database and transaction log, even when it is running. This allows you to back up the database without having to take it off-line for any period of time.

The syntax for this command is as follows:

`DBBACKW [switches] target directory`

Some of the important command line options are as follows:

Switches	Description
-x	Specify database connection information
-d	Name of the backup database file
-t	Name of the backup transaction log
-w	Name of the backup write file
-r	Rename and restart the transaction log
-x	Delete and restart the transaction log
-y	Create the target directory or replace existing files without confirmation

The Database Tools option for this command is called Backup Database Files. After you have provided all the usual information, ISQL displays the following dialog:

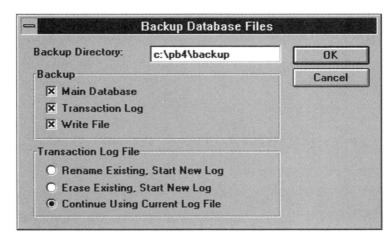

DBVALIDW

Before performing a full database backup, it is always a good idea to verify that the database file isn't corrupt. ISQL provides this command for this task, allowing you to scan every record in the database, including those in the system tables, checking that each has a correct index entry.

The syntax for this command is as follows:

DBVALIDW [flags] [table name]

The only important switch for this command is:

Switches	Description
-c 'keyword=value; keyword=...'	Specify the database connection information

The Database Tools option for this command is called Check Database Integrity. ISQL displays the following dialog for the current database:

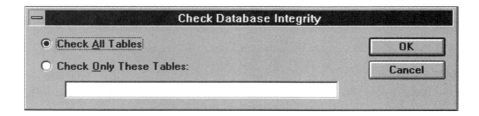

DBTRANW

One of the most useful commands that ISQL has to offer allows you to translate the transaction log file into the corresponding SQL statements.

The syntax for this command is as follows:

DBTRANW [switches] <input file> [output file]

Some of the important command line options are as follows:

Switches	Description
-a	Include Rollback transaction in the output.
-f	Output from the most recent checkpoint.
-r	Remove Rollback transactions (default).
-s	Output ANSI standard SQL transactions.
-t	Include trigger generated transactions in output file.
-z	Include trigger generated transactions in output file as comments.
-u <user1>,...	Only include the transactions from listed users.
-x <user1>,...	Exclude the transactions from listed users
-y	Replace existing translated transaction file without confirmation

The Database Tools option for this command is called Translate Transaction Log to SQL. Before ISQL allows you to run this tool, you must have specified the name of a transaction log for conversion. ISQL then displays this dialog:

779

DBUNLOAW

If you start to experience problems with your database, ISQL offers you the ability to download all of your data into an ASCII comma delimited file format. This allows you to recreate the database structure from scratch and return the unmolested data to its new home. This command also creates a file called **RELOAD.SQL** that contains the SQL statements required to automatically transfer the data back into your database.

> Note that each table's data is allocated to a separate ASCII file. The **RELOAD.SQL** file tracks these repositories, acting like an index for the structure.

The syntax for this command is as follows:

```
DBUNLOAW  [switches]  directory  name
```

Some of the important command line options are as follows:

Switches	Description
-d	Only unload the data.
-n	Only unload the data structure.
-r <sql file name>	File name to store the generated SQL statements.
-u	Unload the data in any order. Ordering is the default action.
-c	Specify the database connection information. Allowed keywords are **USERID**, **DATABASE** and **PASSWORD**.

An example of a typical set of SQL statements generated by this command is given below:

```
SQL Option Statements for user PUBLIC
%
% This command file reloads a database that was unloaded using "unload".
%
%
```

```
SET OPTION Statistics = 3;
SET OPTION Date_order = 'YMD';

%%%%%%%%%%%%%%%%%%%%%%%%%%%%%%%%%%%%%%%%%%%%%%%%%%%%%%%%%%
%     Create userids and grant user permissions
%%%%%%%%%%%%%%%%%%%%%%%%%%%%%%%%%%%%%%%%%%%%%%%%%%%%%%%%%%

GRANT CONNECT TO "DBA" IDENTIFIED BY "SQL";
GRANT RESOURCE, DBA, SCHEDULE TO "DBA";
GRANT CONNECT TO "Inventory" IDENTIFIED BY "Inventory";
```

The Database Tools option for this command is called Unload Database. After specifying all the usual information, ISQL offers you the following dialog:

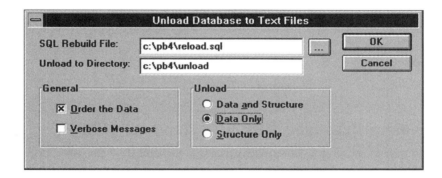

DBERASEW

All Watcom SQL databases, write files and log files are marked as 'read-only' to prevent accidental damage or deletion of the database files. You can delete these files from the operating system level, but the best way to remove these file is with this command.

The syntax for this command is as follows:

DBERASE   [flags]   <database   name>

The only important switch for this command is:

Switch	Description
-y	This option erases the database without alerting the user.

The Database Tools option for this command is called Erase Database or Write File. This tool also allows you to remove write files as you would expect.

Advanced Development Kit

PowerBuilder also ships some extra utilities as part of the Enterprise edition of the software. If you have purchased the desk-top edition, you can still get hold of these utilities by purchasing the Advanced Developers Kit.

This kit includes the following five utilities:

- ▲ PowerBuilder Extended Attribute Reporter (PEAR)
- ▲ DataWindow Extended Attribute Synchronizer (DWEAS)
- ▲ Stored Procedure Updates for DataWindows
- ▲ Cross Reference Report (Xref)
- ▲ DataWindow SQL Verifier (DwCheck)

PowerBuilder Extended Attribute Reporter (PEAR)

This utility retrieves all the extended attribute information for each column of the selected table in the database:

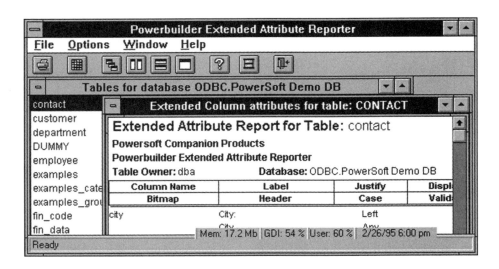

You can use this tool as a database documentor, creating table definitions for review purposes.

DataWindow Extended Attribute Synchronizer (DWEAS)

While creating a DataWindow in an application, PowerBuilder applies the extended attributes specified in the Database Painter to the DataWindow columns. After creating the DataWindow, any changes to the extended attributes will not affect existing DataWindows; in other words, the link isn't dynamic, but rather a one-time hit. Retrieving and matching extended attributes with the DataWindow column attributes can be a very complex and involved task.

To help you with this problem, Powersoft have included a utility called DWEAS that can re-synchronize the attributes. This utility creates DataWindows dynamically by applying extended attributes from the PowerBuilder system tables and retrieves column attributes for the selected DataWindow. Then it displays both the results and lets you change the attributes selectively, updating the PowerBuilder library automatically:

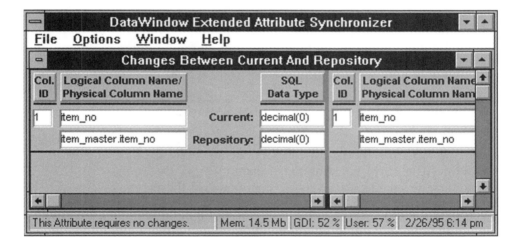

Stored Procedure Updates for DataWindows

One of the advantages of PowerBuilder's DataWindow objects is that they automatically create the necessary SQL **INSERT**, **UPDATE** and **DELETE** statements when you call the **Update()** function.

783

Another of its advantages is that it supports Stored Procedure as the data source. However, you should be aware that when you specify Stored Procedure as the data source for the DataWindow, PowerBuilder always generates the necessary SQL statements dynamically, only using the actual Stored Procedure for the retrieval of information from the database.

This utility retrieves all the column information from a specified DataWindow and lists all the stored procedures from the database. It lets you map stored procedure parameters to the DataWindow columns and specify the transaction object that you wish to use.

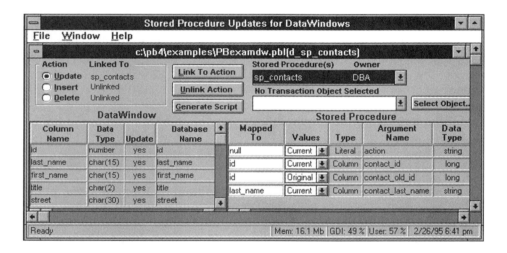

It then creates a script for using the Stored Procedures and saves it in the specified file. This file should be copied into the **sqlpreview** event of the DataWindow. The script contains the declarations for the Stored Procedures with mapping to all the DataWindow columns and the necessary code to execute the Stored Procedures. The last command calls **SetActionCode(2)**, which informs the DataWindow not to send the normal SQL statements to the database. By using this strategy, you can use Stored Procedures to update the information in your database, rather than being restricted to retrieval.

Cross Reference Report (Xref)

As we have seen, the Library Painter offers you the ability to browse through the titles of your objects looking for a specific string. Unfortunately, this facility is quite limited in that it will not list any object information, such as parent or descendant object, and if you want to search for all the object references in the entire application, you will need to search for each one separately.

To improve on this utility, Powersoft have provided Xref. Even though it is possible to write some of the other tools provided in the ADK using PowerScript, Xref is another matter - even if you could write it, it definitely wouldn't be as fast as Xref:

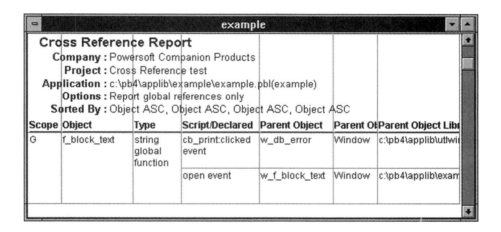

This utility retrieves cross reference information from your Library Painter and displays it in a DataWindow. It also displays information about parent object and objects that aren't currently involved in the application.

DataWindow SQL Verifier (DwCheck)

The final tool provided in the ADK is called DwCheck. This tool solves one of the other major problems which you may come across - that of a DataWindow SQL mismatch with database tables.

After creating the DataWindow, the database administrator might change the table definition or you might migrate the application from one database to another. Whatever the reason, the configuration change and the SQL statements generated for the DataWindow to access the original tables may now not be correct.

If the application is small enough, you can open each DataWindow and execute it to see if any problems occur. However, if the application is larger, this could become quite time consuming.

To automate this task, simply run the DwCheck against the database:

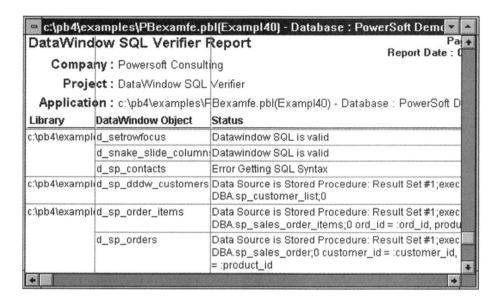

It runs through all the DataWindows in your application, displaying the results of the test in a report.

Upsizing from Watcom

There are countless reasons why you might develop your applications for use with a Watcom back-end database, such as:

▲ PowerBuilder ships with Watcom included in the box.

▲ Your company doesn't need the processing power of SQL Server.

▲ Your company doesn't have the revenue to support the outlay of capital for SQL Server.

▲ You are using it as a basic back-end database during application development.

▲ You are required to develop away from the production back-end database.

This appendix concentrates on how to move your Watcom databases over to SQL Server. This choice of target database is motivated by press releases made at the time of the Sybase/Powersoft merger. The figures included in these releases indicated that over 50% of all the PowerBuilder installations were using SQL Server as their production database back-end.

Introduction

Watcom SQL 3.2 was launched with the specific intention of keeping this database server in the same league as other server databases, adding huge performance boosts and sweet tools to previous versions. By teaming up with Powersoft, Watcom were suddenly a developmental force to be reckoned with.

With the latest release of v4.0 of their database engine, Watcom have continued this trend, especially now that they have entered into the 32-bit arena.

> *Note that Watcom SQL v4.0 is available in two versions, 16-bit and 32-bit.*

With v4.0, Watcom also introduced concepts such as stored procedures, triggers, referential integrity constraints and multiple table referencing statements. All of these improvements have reduced the gap between Watcom and SQL Server even further, but there are still some differences in implementation.

> *We will be concentrating on porting from Watcom SQL v4.0 to Microsoft SQL Server v4.2. The behavioral differences between Microsoft's and Sybase's SQL Server are only slight, so this appendix should apply to both versions, especially as we will highlight any important differences, as they appear.*

However, there will come a time when you need to upgrade from Watcom to a more powerful database, such as SQL Server.

> **This is not a design fault, but rather a matter of the right tool for the job. Watcom was recently recorded as providing the best response time for single user ad-hoc queries compared to any other database.**

The challenge of porting your Watcom database to another platform can be broken down into two distinct phases:

1 Making sure that the Watcom version of the database works properly.

2 Porting to the new platform, allowing you to take advantage of all the new features now available.

In this appendix, we are going to assume that your Watcom database is working correctly, and just concentrate on the differences between the Watcom and SQL Server platforms, so that the translation can be made as smoothly and painlessly as possible.

Data Types

This section explains a little about the Watcom data types and their SQL Server equivalents. If an equivalent doesn't exist, we will suggest a suitable SQL Server replacement:

Watcom data type	Explanation
Date	SQL Server doesn't support an equivalent data type. You should consider using **SmallDateTime** which occupies 4 bytes. This data also stores a time with the date, accurate to the minute. If you are using this column in **WHERE** clause or any expressions, use **CONVERT()** to translate it back to a date.
Binary(n)	This data type is available in SQL Server, but it has a maximum value of 255. There is another data type called **VarBinary(n)**, but this also has a maximum value of 255.
Char(n)and VarChar(n)	These data types are available, but the maximum value is 255, compared to 32,767 in Watcom.
Int/Integer	This data type is available. If you want to store a value below 255, you can use **TinyInt** in SQL Server.
Long Binary	Use **Image**
Long VarChar	Use **Text**
Time	This data type is not available - see **Date**

Continued

Watcom data type	Explanation
TimeStamp:	Unlike Watcom, SQL Server doesn't allow you any access to this data type through SQL - the software automatically updates the values for you.
Numeric/Decimal	This data type is not available.
Float/Real	These data types are available. The precision for **Float** is 15 digits, 7 digits for **Real**

GROUP BY

You must have noticed the limitations when using the **GROUP BY** clause in Watcom SQL. Remember that you must include all the columns in the **SELECT** list, except those columns in the functions.

For example, this SQL statement

```
SELECT transaction_date, transaction_type, quantity
FROM transaction_table
GROUP BY transaction_date, transaction_type
```

will result in an error that indicates that **quantity** can't be used unless it is in **GROUP BY** list.

However, the following **SELECT** statement, with an aggregate function that doesn't appear in the **GROUP BY** list, won't produce an error:

```
SELECT transaction_date, transaction_type, sum(quantity)
FROM transaction_table
GROUP BY transaction_date, transaction_type
```

Due to these limitations, you may not be able to take advantage of the **GROUP BY** clause in as many situations as you would like, forcing you to select either the Group presentation style or to create groups in the DataWindow Painter, both of which increases the load on your front-end and increases maintenance.

In the case of SQL Server, you should not encounter any of these limitations, as the Transact-SQL extensions allow you to use the **GROUP BY** clause as it was originally designed:

▲ When the **GROUP BY** clause is used, Transact-SQL allows you to include columns in the **SELECT** list that are not aggregated and that don't appear in the **GROUP BY** list.

▲ A **GROUP BY** clause can include columns or expressions that are not in the list of columns.

Both the SQL statements mentioned above work on a SQL Server and produce the results you would expect.

Cursors

If you want to use scrollable cursors, you need to use **Release** and **CursorLock** options in the **DbParm** parameter while connecting to SQL Server. For example:

```
Release='4.2', CursorScroll='Dynamic', CursorLock='OptVal'
```

There are four options available for **CursorLock** parameter:

▲ ReadOnly

▲ Lock

▲ Opt

▲ OptVal

Both **Opt** and **OptVal** options don't exclusively lock tables, but they do allow other users to read and update those tables. This is called **Optimistic Concurrency Control**, which means that other users can update the information, and any conflicts that occur when the original user returns this version of the data are resolved at that point.

In the case of **Opt**, it compares TimeStamps and if they are not available, it uses the selected values. In the case of **OptVal**, it always compares the selected values, whether the TimeStamps are available or not.

CursorScroll allows one of the following values, but is **Dynamic** by default:

▲ **Forward**: Cursors can only scroll forward, and no one can change the result set, the order or the membership while the cursor is open.

▲ **KeySet**: PowerBuilder saves and uses keys for a specified number of rows. You can specify the number of rows as follows:

```
Release='4.2', CursorScroll=80
```

In this type, while values in the result set can be changed by anyone, the order and membership are fixed when the cursor is opened. Rows can be accessed by either their relative or absolute position. You can also use the **ORDER BY** clause as part of **SELECT** statement.

▲ **Dynamic**: In this type of cursor, all three components - the result set, the membership and the order - can be changed. Rows can't be accessed by an absolute position and you are not allowed to use the **ORDER BY** clause as part of **SELECT** statement.

If you are using Sybase SQL Server, only the forward scrolling cursor (**FETCH NEXT**) is available.

DISTINCT

When the **DISTINCT** keyword is included in **SELECT** statement in Watcom SQL, the result set is automatically sorted, whether the table has a unique index or not. When you are using SQL Server, unless it has a clustered index, the result may not be sorted. To force a sort, you must include the **ORDER BY** clause in the **SELECT** statement.

> If there are any queries that assumes the result set is in a sorted order, you need to include **ORDER BY** clause while connected to SQL Server.

COMPUTE Clause

If you have a lot of processing power based at the server end of the equation, you can put this to use using the **COMPUTE** clause in the **SELECT** statement, one of the most powerful extensions to ANSI SQL.

By using this, you can eliminate most of the computed fields in the DataWindow. It generates summary values in a **SELECT** statement using row aggregate functions. The summary values appear as additional rows in the query results, unlike aggregate functions' results, which appear as new columns. This allows you to see both the detail and summary rows, in one set of results.

You can calculate summary values for subgroups, and you can calculate more than one aggregate function for the same group:

```
SELECT transaction_date, transaction_type, transaction_no, item_no, quantity
FROM transaction_table
ORDER BY transaction_type
COMPUTE sum( quantity ) by transaction_type
```

As DataWindows don't support rows returned by the **COMPUTE** clause, you can only use them in Embedded SQL.

Stored Procedures

Watcom SQL v4.0 also saw the appearance of support for stored procedures of a type. Unfortunately, they are still a long way from their SQL Server cousins. When you are using stored procedures as the source for your DataWindows, you will have problems converting to SQL Server, because although this database engine can detect the source, it can't automatically detect the result set as it does for Watcom SQL - you always need to manually define the result set.

Other than this difficulty, there are four major differences:

- Parameter Declaration
- Result Set Declaration
- Multiple **SELECT**s
- Return Status

Parameter Declaration

The syntax for the declaration of parameters for Watcom SQL is:

```
Parm type, Parm Name, Parm Data Type
```

795

An example of this declaration is given below:

```
CREATE PROCEDURE sp_list_item_balance(IN pBalance integer)
```

In SQL Server, the syntax is slightly different:

@parameter_name   datatype   =   [default]   [output]

For example:

```
CREATE PROCEDURE sp_list_item_balance @balance int =0
```

You only need to mention **output** when you need the value of the parameter back, whereas you must declare **IN**, **OUT** or **INOUT** depending on the requirements of your statement.

Result Set Declaration

In Watcom, you must declare the result set as the first statement in the stored procedure. For example, take the following **SELECT** statement:

```
SELECT item_no, description, balance from item_master ORDER BY item_no
```

For the above statement, you need to declare the following result set after the **CREATE** statement:

```
RESULT(item_no integer, description char(32), balance integer)
```

In the case of SQL Server, they are no longer required to declare the result set.

Multiple SELECTs

You can't have multiple SELECT statements in the same stored procedures without conditional statements, and you must also make sure that the result set always has the same structure, effectively limiting the capability of stored procedures.

There are no restrictions like this in SQL Server. You have the freedom to give as many SQL statements as you want, there is no need to declare the result set, and each result set may have a distinct structure.

Return Status

In SQL Server, you can also return the status of the stored procedure.

Triggers

Let's first look at Watcom SQL triggers. Triggers are special stored procedures which automatically execute whenever a specific event on a table occurs. These events are limited to inserting a new, deleting an old or updating a current row in a table.

Triggers are mainly used whenever declarative referential integrity and other declarative constraints are not enough. You can also log all the activities performed on a specific table, and even on a specific column, through a trigger.

```
CREATE TRIGGER InsertTrigger AFTER INSERT ON transaction_table
REFERENCING NEW AS NewTran
FOR EACH ROW
BEGIN
IF "NewTran"."transaction_type" = 'R' THEN
UPDATE "item_master"
SET "balance" = "item_master"."balance" +
"NewTran"."quantity","last_receipt_date" =
"NewTran"."transaction_date","current_price" =
"NewTran"."price"
WHERE "item_no" = "NewTran"."item_no"
ELSEIF "NewTran"."transaction_type" = 'T' THEN
UPDATE "item_master"
SET "balance" = "item_master"."balance" +
"NewTran"."quantity",
WHERE "item_no" = "NewTran"."item_no"
ELSEIF "NewTran"."transaction_type" = 'I' THEN
UPDATE "item_master"
SET "balance" = "item_master"."balance" -
"NewTran"."quantity","last_issue_date" =
"NewTran"."transaction_date",
WHERE "item_no" = "NewTran"."item_no"
END IF
END
;
```

You can design the trigger so that it executes either before or after the event - for example, before or after a row is inserted into a table. In the example code above, you can see that we've created a trigger that fires after a new row is added to the transaction_table.

If you want to check some column values in the newly inserted row, you can use the **REFERENCING** clause, as shown in the second statement. The **OLD** keyword can be used to refer to deleted rows.

> If you are using an **UPDATE** trigger, you can refer to both **NEW** and **OLD** in the same trigger.

To execute a stored procedure from a trigger, the syntax is:

```
CALL procedure_name( parm1, parm2,...)
```

SQL Server Triggers

On the other hand, SQL Server does the same thing a little differently. Triggers can only refer to two tables, called inserted and deleted. Whenever new rows are added or old rows deleted, SQL Server automatically adds them to the appropriate table and to one of these system level tables.

To execute a stored procedure from a trigger, you must use the **EXECUTE** command and the parentheses are not required:

```
EXECUTE procedure_name parm1_value, parm2_value  ...
```
or
```
EXECUTE procedure_name @parm_name = value, @parm_name = ...
```

When using Watcom SQL, because you can't declare default values to the parameters while creating stored procedures, you must specify values for each parameter declared in the stored procedure. Conversely, SQL Server does allow you to specify default values.

A trigger can be nested down to 16 levels. If a trigger changes a table on which there is another trigger, the second trigger activates, which calls a third, all the way down to 16. You can turn off the nested triggers as follows:

```
sp_configure 'nested triggers', 0
```

The above statement takes effect throughout the server - you can't specify this command against a single transaction or user level.

In v4.2, a trigger doesn't call itself in response to a second update to the same table. For example, if an update trigger on one column of a table results in an update to another column, the update trigger only activates once.

System Tables for User Details

In a Watcom SQL database, the user details are stored in the sysuserperm table and the group details are stored in sysgroup table. The owner of these tables is, by default, sys. There are three views - sysuserlist, sysgroups and sysuserperms - defined on these tables by sys.

These tables will be automatically created by the DBMS. If a user needs access to two different databases, he needs an entry in this set of tables for each database, although they can be the same User ID and Password.

While creating a group, the group name should be declared as a User ID. This means that a user is a group and that a group can be a member of another group - confusing setup!

For an SQL Server database, the setup is slightly different. All the user details are stored in the syslogins table in the master database - note that this database is created when you install SQL Server.

Typically, this database contains all the system details for the server and any databases that are stored upon it, up to a maximum of 32,567. Each of these databases has its own sysusers table that stores the names of all the users who can access it. Password checking is only performed once at the server level.

> *If you are listed in this table for 10 databases, once you log on to the server and pass that security check, you can access any of your 10 databases without any more security hassle.*

You need to use **sp_adduser** to add a user to the database, which basically adds a row in the sysusers table. In this case, the user name in the database and the login name are the same. If you want to have different names for each of these levels, you can use an alias. Your second name has to be associated to another name by calling the **sp_addalias** system stored procedure. This basically adds a row to the sp_alternates table in the specified database.

In SQL Server, a group name doesn't have to be a user ID, and the group can't be member of another group.

> **In both systems, Watcom SQL and SQL Server, passwords are not stored in an encrypted format on the database.**

Referential Integrity

Declaration referential integrity and domain checks are not available in SQL Server v4.2. You need to implement this functionality using the tools you have available, in other words, defaults, rules and triggers.

A default specifies a value to insert in a column, if a value is not explicitly supplied when the data is prepared for insertion. For example, let us create a default to item_description:

```
CREATE DEFAULT df_description as "Unknown"
```

After a default is created, you need to assign it to the appropriate column:

```
sp_bindefault df_description, "item_master.item_description"
```

In the same way, let us create a rule and assign the rule for measuring_unit:

```
CREATE RULE rl_measuring_unit as @unit in ( 'M', 'U', 'L', 'K' )
sp_bindrule rl_measuring_unit, "item_master.measuring_unit"
```

> *The variable name that is prefixed with '@' in the* **CREATE RULE** *command refers to the value in the* **UPDATE** *and* **INSERT** *statements.*

Locks

Row level locking is not available in SQL Server. Instead, SQL Server offers two types of lock: page level and table level. First, SQL Server tries to satisfy the client request with a page lock.

If the number of page locks applied by a process grows to more than 256, it will be escalated to table lock, but only if no other process has applied a lock on the same table. When a **SELECT** statement is issued, SQL Server immediately releases the lock on the page after it completes the read.

> It would be better to have a TimeStamp column for each table in the SQL Server table, especially when using PowerBuilder as the client. If the table contains a TimeStamp column, while updating and deleting, PowerBuilder automatically matches the TimeStamp value.

Copying Data to SQL Server Tables

If the amount of date is small enough, you should use the Data Pipeline Painter to automate the transfer of information from one database to another. As you will see, the Data Pipeline Painter can handle not only the transfer of data, but also the construction of new tables and extended attributes on the target system.

Using the Data Pipeline Painter

The Data Pipeline Painter allows you to transfer both definitions and information from one database to another. For example, if you wanted to move your Watcom database to SQL Server, the easiest way to do this is by using the Data Pipeline. You don't even have to move full tables between databases - you can choose to retrieve just the data you are interested in.

There is no restriction on the types and locations of the source and destination tables. They can be in the same database, different databases or even databases running on different DBMSs. By calling specific commands to execute saved Pipelines, you can also make use of the Data Pipeline, or even change the Pipeline definition, at run time.

Creating a Data Pipeline Object

In this section, we'll show you how to create a Data Pipeline Object that will copy data from the item_master table in **INVENT.DB** to an item_master table in **HISTORY.DB**. The setup for this simply requires you to create a new database in the Database Painter:

Create Local Database		
Database Name:	history	OK
User ID:	DBA	Cancel
Password:	***	Browse...
Start command:	db32w -d	Help
☐ Prompt for Password during Connect		More>>

Now go to the Data Pipeline Painter, click on the New button and select the source and destination connections:

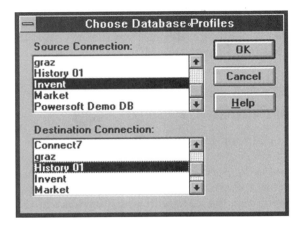

When you have made your selections, PowerBuilder opens up the standard table select dialog box allowing you to select the tables you want to copy. Select the item_master table and then build the SQL statement to retrieve the data from the source database:

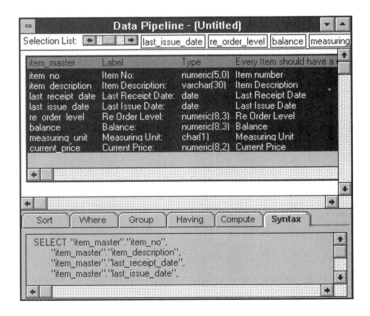

We want to select all the fields, so highlight them all and click on the Design icon on the PainterBar to specify attributes for the Pipeline:

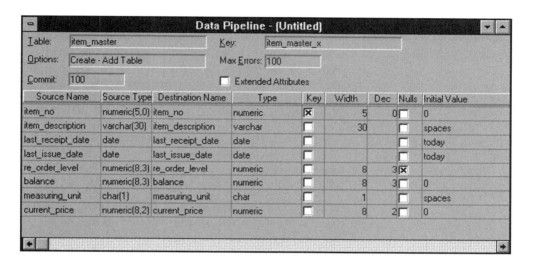

By default, PowerBuilder displays the source table name in the Table prompt. You can change this to specify a different destination table name if you wish. The value you specify for the Commit prompt is the frequency at which you want to commit the changes to the database.

If you specify 0, the changes will be committed only after the entire operation is complete. The Max Errors option specifies the maximum number of errors to allow during execution. PowerBuilder will stop executing the Data Pipeline when this figure is exceeded.

Extended Attributes

If you want to copy the extended attributes of the source table, you can check the Extended Attributes option, and if you are creating a new table or replacing an existing one, you can also specify a key. Depending on the destination database support, PowerBuilder creates either a primary key or an index on the key column.

The Options box allows you to select exactly what you want the Pipeline to do. You have the following options:

Option	Description
Create - Add Table	Creates a new table with the specified column names and inserts the necessary rows. This option also allows you to define all the additional information that the destination database can accept.
Replace - Drop/Add table	Drops the existing table and creates a new one. You can specify entire table schema, as for the above option.
Refresh - Delete/Insert Rows	If the row exists in the destination table, this option deletes it and inserts a new version with the values from the source table. You can only update key information, and you are not allowed to change any other table specifications. The destination table should already exist.
Append - Insert Rows	Insert rows into the specified table. You cannot change any table schema of the destination table.
Update - Update/Insert Rows	If the row exists in the destination table, PowerBuilder updates the row or inserts a new row into the destination table. The same restrictions apply that are applicable to the Refresh - Delete/Insert Rows option.

We want to create a new table in **HISTORY.DB**, so you can select the Create - Add Table option. When you click on the Execute icon, PowerBuilder will run the Data Pipeline Object and create the new table.

You can save this pipeline object and then use it whenever it is needed to create a backup of your data.

Points to Note

Don't create your triggers on the SQL Server tables before you pass the data into them, because if you uploaded data into a table with, for example, an update trigger, the associated code would be executed every time a new row was added.

Every row that you insert into a table in an SQL Server database is logged. If the data is large enough, consider exporting data into an ASCII file and use BCP (bulk copy) to import the data into the SQL Server tables.

BCP is a utility used for the bulk transfer of data, running in one of two versions: one is a fast version and the other is slow. If the target table has indexes or triggers designed against it, BCP automatically runs in the slower version. With this version of BCP, none of the triggers on the destination table are performed, while the data transfer will be slower and each insert has to be recorded into a log.

Other Interesting Concerns

Some of the other interesting concerns that you should be aware of when porting to a SQL Server platform include:

▲ Using CASE Tools

▲ Connections

▲ TransactionObjects

▲ Double Quotes

Using ErWin

While migrating to SQL Server, it would be better to use a CASE tool, such as ErWin, which has an interface with PowerBuilder. With just a few clicks, it generates all the required DDL statements and automatically adjusts the data types for SQL Server. In most cases, this will be good enough to transfer the database, but it is always worth testing the generated script before you run it as a whole.

Connections

Between the declaration of a procedure in PowerScript and its execution, don't use the same connection until the procedure has been successfully closed down.

Note that this restriction only applies to procedures that return data, because if they don't, the CLOSE statement is not required and the connection is immediately available for another process.

TransactionObject Parameters

SQL Servers don't use the UserID parameter in the TransactionObject. Therefore, whenever you refer to UserID and DBPass, you should use LogId and LogPass respectively.

> *Note that you should also always supply the name of the server in the TransactionObject's* **ServerName** *parameter.*

Double Quotations

SQL Server doesn't support column and table names on the right hand side of equalities. For example, **"transaction_table"."item_no"** in the **WHERE** clause will result in an error:

```
SELECT "item_master"."item_no",
"item_master"."item_description",
"transaction_table"."transaction_type",
"transaction_table"."quantity"
FROM "item_master",
"transaction_table"
WHERE ( "item_master"."item_no" = "transaction_table"."item_no" ) and
( ( "transaction_table"."transaction_type" = 'R' ) )
```

PowerBuilder Objects/Controls and their Events

PowerBuilder uses three objects and a whole plethora of Window controls to respond to the various events that occur while an application is running. Although you can create new events to which these objects can respond, the basic events that PowerBuilder supports are quite comprehensive and can be very useful for a fast system design.

In this appendix, we look at each of these objects and each of their PowerBuilder defined events, examining some of the pros and cons to their use, together with some of the unknown restrictions that you must take into account.

Application Object

An Application object has four events defined by PowerBuilder:

Event	Description
open	Triggered when an application is started.
close	Triggered when an application is closed. Typically the event is fired when a **Halt Close** command is issued, when you close the last window with **Close** command or immediately after the last command of an application script is executed.
idle	Triggered when the application is idle (no interaction with the application is registered, whether it is the movement of the mouse pointer or a key press) for the time specified by the **Idle()** function. One point to note is that an application is considered to be idle even though it is processing something. The idle event is strictly related to user interaction with the application.
systemerror	Triggered whenever an error occurs in the application. If the error occurs while retrieving data from or manipulating the internal of a database, the **itemerror** event associated with a DataWindow is triggered, rather than **systemerror**.

Menu Object

A Menu object has two events defined by PowerBuilder:

Event	Description
clicked	Triggered when you press *Enter* on the menu item or select that menu item by clicking on it.
selected	Triggered when you move the focus onto the appropriate menu item from another. Note that this event doesn't occur when you click on the menu item, even though the menu item has acquired the focus - the `clicked` event overrules this action.

> **You can't declare user defined events for menu items**

Window Object

A Window object has 23 events defined by PowerBuilder:

Event	Description
activate	Triggered when the window becomes active. It can also be triggered when an open event occurs. It isn't advisable to use the `MessageBox()` function in this event, as you will enter into an infinite loop. As you cancel the dialog, you activate the window and produce another dialog...

Continued

Event	Description
clicked	Triggered when the user clicks on the window - not on a control on the window, but the window itself. This event isn't triggered by the user clicking on the window title bar or any of the menu items associated with the window.
close	Triggered when the window is closed. This event occurs after the **closequery** event.
closequery	Triggered while closing the window, generated by either the **Close** command or from the system control menu. This event fires before the **close** event occurs. The **close** event isn't triggered if an error is generated in the **closequery** event script. Refer to Chapter 9 on PowerScript for some example code for this event.
deactivate	Triggered when the current window is deactivated. Writing commands like **MessageBox()** in this event may prevent you switching to other applications, because this event occurs even when you try to switch over. It may also cause your computer to hang if you use *Ctrl + Esc*.
doubleclicked	Triggered when you double-click in the window area, as opposed to any of the control in the window.
hide	Triggered when the window is hidden, typically when you call the **HIDE()** function or you use the **visible** property: **Window_name.Visible = False**
hotlinkalarm	Triggered whenever a DDE Server application sends or a DDE Client application receives data. Refer to Chapter 15 on DDE and OLE for more details.

Continued

Event	Description
key	Triggered whenever a user presses a key and the focus isn't in an editable area, such as a SingleLineEdit, a MultiLineEdit and so on.
mousemove	Triggered when the mouse moves over the window. This doesn't include moving the mouse pointer over any control in the window or the menu area which includes the toolbar and the title bar.
mousedown	Similar to **mousemove**, except that this event is fired when you press the left mouse button.
mouseup	Similar to **mousedown**, except that this event is fired when you release the left mouse button.
open	Triggered when the window is first opened. This event fires after the **resize** event, but before the **activate** event.
remoteexec	Triggered when a DDE client application sends a command. Refer to Chapter 15 on DDE and OLE for more details.
remotesend	Triggered when a DDE Client application sends data. Refer to Chapter 15 on DDE and OLE for more details.
remoterequest	Triggered when a DDE client application request for data. Refer to Chapter 15 on DDE and OLE for more details.
remotehotlinkstart	Triggered when a DDE Client application starts hotlink. Refer to Chapter 15 on DDE and OLE for more details.
remotehotlinkstop	Triggered when a DDE Client application ends hotlink. Refer to Chapter 15 on DDE and OLE for more details.
resize	Triggered when the window is resized. This event fires before the **open** event occurs.

Continued

Event	Description
show	Triggered when the window is hidden or returned to view, a task that typically occurs when a **Show()** command is issued or the **visible** property is used: **Window_Name.Visible = True** This event also occurs after the **active** event is triggered.
systemkey	Similar to **key** event, except that this event is fired when used in combination with the *Alt* key.
timer	Triggered after every 'n' seconds specified in the relevant **Timer()** function call in some part of that window's script. If the **Timer()** function isn't used, this event doesn't occur.
toolbarmoved	Triggered when the associated toolbar is moved.

Window Controls

The following controls are not defined with respect to the DragObject and so they don't have any events associated with them:

- Line
- Oval
- Rectangle
- RoundRectangle
- GroupBox

> **User defined events also can't be declared for these objects.**

All of the following events are available for every window control mentioned below:

Event	Description
constructor	Triggered when the control is first constructed. You should note that none of the window controls have an **open** event, whereas a Window has an **open** event, but it doesn't have the **constructor** or **destructor** events. These two events do exist for the Window objects, but they aren't made available to the programmer. You can prove this by running through a log that has recorded a Window being created. See Chapter 14 on Debugging for more details.
destructor	Triggered when the control is scrapped, but before the Window **close** event occurs.
getfocus	Triggered when the control gets the focus. Avoid using **MessageBox()** in this event. A control gets the focus when you select it by pressing *Tab* or click with mouse button.
loosefocus	Triggered when the control loses the focus.
dragdrop	Triggered when another object or control is dropped onto this one.
dragenter	Triggered when a control or object enters in this control's area.
dragleave	Triggered when the dragged control leaves this control area without dropping onto it.
dragwithin	When you move the dragged object or control in this control area without dropping it.
other	Any action other than the defined events for the control or object will trigger this event. Avoid using MessageBox() here. Make sure that you check the **Message.WordParm** before doing anything else in this script.
rbuttondown	Triggered when you click with right mouse button on this control or object.

Events Specific to Certain Controls

In this section, we look at the events that are particular to one particular type of control. Each of the controls has access to the events stated in their section as well as to all of the events listed in the common events table above.

CommandButton, PictureButton

Both the CommandButton and the PictureButton share the same additional event:

Event	Description
clicked	Triggered whenever you click on this type of control with the left mouse button. This is the event most often used when considering these types of control.

StaticText

StaticText controls have one extra event:

Event	Description
doubleclicked	Triggered when the user double-clicks with left mouse button. This event is very rarely used.

SingleLineEdit, MultiLineEdit

Both the SingleLineEdit and MultiLineEdit controls share one extra event:

Event	Description
modified	Triggered whenever the text inside the control changes. You can use this event to validate the user's entry on a character by character basis. If you want to validate the entire entry in one go, you should consider using the `loosefocus` event.

EditMask

This type of control has one specialized event:

Event	Description
modified	Same as SingleLineEdit/MultLineEdit control above. Since you can use the internal character validation for any entries from the user, you will probably not use this event very often.

ListBox

The ListBox control has two additional events:

Event	Description
doubleclicked	Triggered when the user double-clicks with left mouse button.
selectionchanged	Triggered whenever a different item is selected.

DropDown ListBox

The DropDownListBox control has three additional events associated with it:

Event	Description
doubleclicked	Same as ListBox
modified	This event is similar to SingleLineEdit control's event. It only makes sense when the DropDown ListBox is editable.
selectionchanged	Same as ListBox

CheckBox

The CheckBox control only has one additional event:

Event	Description
clicked	Triggered when the control is clicked with the left mouse button. Note that the control toggles between checked and unchecked, but if the **automatic** property isn't set, you will need to take care of marking the control as appropriate through programmatic means.

RadioButton

The RadioButton control only has one additional event associated with it:

Event	Description
clicked	Similar to CheckBox. When the **automatic** attribute isn't set, the RadioButton will not display its change in state even if you click on the control. You will need to take care of this task manually.

Picture

The Picture control has two additional events associated with it:

Event	Description
clicked	Same as CommandButton.
doubleclicked	Triggered whenever the user double-clicks with left mouse button.

Graph

The Graph control has two additional events associated with it:

Event	Description
clicked	Same as Picture control.
doubleclicked	Same as Picture control.

OLE 2.0

The OLE 2.0 control has 6 additional events associated with it:

Event	Description
clicked	Triggered when the user clicks on the control with left mouse button.
doubleclicked	Triggered when the user double-clicks with left mouse button.
datachange	Triggered whenever the OLE server notifies your control about a data change.
rename	Triggered whenever the server notifies the OLE control about the object's name changing.
save	Triggered whenever the OLE server notifies the control that the data has been saved.
viewchanged	Triggered whenever the server notifies the control about a change in the currently displayed data view.

Vertical Scrollbar

The Vertical Scrollbar control has 5 additional events associated with it:

Event	Description
linedown	Triggered whenever the user clicks on the down arrow with the left mouse button.
lineup	Triggered whenever the user clicks on the up arrow with the left mouse button.
pagedown	Triggered whenever the user clicks between the position indicator and the down arrow with the left mouse button.
pageup	Triggered whenever the user clicks between the position indicator and the up arrow with the left mouse button.
moved	Triggered when the user moves the position indicator by clicking and dragging.

Horizontal Scrollbar

The Horizontal Scrollbar control has 5 additional events associated with it:

Event	Description
moved	Same as Vertical Scrollbar control.
lineright	Triggered whenever the user click on the right arrow with left mouse button.
lineleft	Triggered whenever the user click on the left arrow with left mouse button.
pageright	Triggered whenever the user clicks between the position indicator and the right arrow with the left mouse button.
pageleft	Triggered whenever the user clicks between the position indicator and the left arrow with the left mouse button.

DataWindow

The DataWindow control has the largest number of additional events, 19 in all:

Event	Description
dberror	Triggered when an error, related to database, occurs in the DataWindow control.
doubleclicked	Triggered whenever the user double-clicks anywhere in the DataWindow control with left mouse button.
editchanged	This event is similar to SingleLineEdit control's **modified** event. It is triggered whenever the content of the edit control changes.
itemchanged	Triggered whenever there has been a change in the edit control and the user presses *Tab* or click on another field in the DataWindow control.
	This event isn't triggered when there is change in data and the DataWindow control as a whole loses the focus, say by the user clicking on a control other than the current DataWindow.
itemerror	Triggered whenever the data types don't match, violating the data validation rules associated with that field. If this occurs, the **itemchanged** event doesn't. This situation can be controlled with the **SetActionCode()** function.
itemfocus changed	Triggered once the **itemchanged** script is successfully executed.
printstart	Triggered before printing starts.
printpage	Triggered before each page is posted to the printer.
printend	Triggered once printing is complete.
resize	Triggered when the DataWindow control is resized.
retrievestart	Triggered before the DataWindow starts to retrieve rows from the database. This event is fired after the **sqlpreview** event.

Continued

Event	Description
retrieverow	Triggered for each row that is retrieved.
retrieveend	Triggered once data retrieval is complete.
rowfocuschanged	Triggered when the focus changes from one row to another. This will also be triggered while retrieving data.
scrollhorizontal	Triggered whenever the horizontal scrollbar is used.
scrolllvertical	Triggered whenever the vertical scrollbar is used.
sqlpreview	Triggered before a SQL statement is sent to the datasource. For data manipulation statements, this event is triggered once for every statement that it sends. While retrieving data (due to a **SELECT** statement or a Stored Procedure), this event is only fired once. This event isn't triggered for child DataWindows.
updatestart	Triggered before a DataWindow update begins.
updateend	Triggered once a DataWindow update is completed.

UserObjects

All standard UserObjects will have the same events that their parent control could use. Custom UserObjects only have two events: Constructor and Destructor. If the UserObject is external, all the events that are defined for that object are available.

INDEX

G

REVOLUTIONARY DELPHI PROGRAMMING

This book is aimed at software developers who have leapt upon Delphi as *the* language for Windows development, but have encountered the lack of developer level reading material. The book covers the advanced areas of the language, the 32-bit interests and the language's innate database connectivity. It provides the information that developers are crying out for, such as an in-depth look at Object Pascal, the InterBase engine and a look at Delphi working with OWL/Paradox/Windows API. The accompanying CD-ROM comes complete with a hypertext version of the book, a compendium of source code and over 100 MB's of tools, tips and demos.

AUTHOR: Various   ISBN: 1-874416-67-2   PRICE: $44.95 C$62.95 £41.99

THE REVOLUTIONARY GUIDE TO ACCESS - PROFESSIONAL DEVELOPER'S EDITION

Microsoft Access isn't restricted to a single user system. According to the market, Client/Server is the place to be, and Access has many powerful assets to lever you into the new database age. Written for developers, the book covers all the advanced features and explains the more interesting features that other books gloss over. By the end, the reader will be able to use Access to develop applications which integrate seamlessly with other office packages. Written by a leading commercial developer of Access based solutions, this book comes complete with a CD-ROM containing all source code, shareware tools and a hypertext version of the book.

AUTHOR: Stephen Wynkoop ISBN: 1-874416-39-7 PRICE: $44.95 C$62.95 £41.99

INSTANT SQL PRORAMMING

This book is the definitive guide to programming the 32 bit editions of Windows with Visual C++ 2.1. Comprehensive coverage of the MFC 3.1 provides the programmer with all the tools required to take advantage of the 32 bit architectures of Win 32s, Windows NT 3.51 and the forthcoming Windows '95 (aka Chicago). Written by one of the leading members of Microsoft's Visual C++ team, it is a must for Visual C++ developers. The book assumes that the reader is familiar with the concepts of object-oriented programming and comes complete with a CD-ROM containing all source code, a full hypertext version of the book and various third party tools and samples.

AUTHOR: Mike Blaszczak   ISBN: 1-874416-47-8   PRICE: $44.95 C$62.95 £41.99